Introduction: The American Crisis. v

CHAPTER 1: Why Our Founding Fathers Fought
Our Mother Country 1
CHAPTER 2: The War Young Washington Started. 11
CHAPTER 3: The Rich, the Poor, and the "Middling Sort" 25
CHAPTER 4: Patriots, Loyalists, Native Americans, and Slaves 35
CHAPTER 5: America Praying, America Thinking. 45
CHAPTER 6: King and Parliament 54
CHAPTER 7: From Massacre to Tea Party 63
CHAPTER 8: Tipping Point .72
CHAPTER 9: Heard round the World 82
CHAPTER 10: Of Green Mountains and Continental Ambitions . . .93
CHAPTER 11: Defeat and Triumph in Boston 109
CHAPTER 12: A Time of Decision. 121
CHAPTER 13: The Long Retreat 132
CHAPTER 14: Counterattack. 150
CHAPTER 15: Gentleman Johnny's Plan. 161
CHAPTER 16: The Capital Falls Yet the War Continues. 173
CHAPTER 17: Saratoga Glory and an Ally Earned 185
CHAPTER 18: Hope Dims, Winter Calls 198
CHAPTER 19: Springtime 209
CHAPTER 20: Out of Uniform. 222
CHAPTER 21: The Southern Strategy 235
CHAPTER 22: A Trial of Souls 248
CHAPTER 23: A Hero's Life 264
CHAPTER 24: The Backcountry War. 273
CHAPTER 25: Upside Down 289
CHAPTER 26: Never a Good War or a Bad Peace 307

INDEX 321

IN THE TIME
OF THE REVOLUTION
Living the War of American Independence

ALAN AXELROD

Guilford, Connecticut

An imprint of Globe Pequot, the trade division of
The Rowman & Littlefield Publishing Group, Inc.
4501 Forbes Blvd., Ste. 200
Lanham, MD 20706
www.rowman.com

Distributed by NATIONAL BOOK NETWORK

British Library Cataloguing in Publication Information available

Library of Congress Control Number: 2019954036

ISBN 978-1-4930-6639-1 (paperback)
ISBN 978-1-4930-3863-3 (hardcover)
ISBN 978-1-4930-3864-0 (e-book)

INTRODUCTION

The American Crisis

THE AMERICAN REVOLUTION WAS MORE THAN A WAR AND MORE, EVEN, than a war for independence. It was what the American philosopher Thomas Kuhn would call a paradigm shift. As he defined the phrase in his highly influential 1962 *The Structure of Scientific Revolutions*, a paradigm shift is not a change merely within known or accepted frameworks (paradigms) but a change that renders the accepted paradigms obsolete. Shattering them, it creates a new frame of reference.

The American Revolution transformed government but, more important, transformed an entire population from subjects of King George III to citizens of the United States, which was the first nation founded on a set of ideas, authorized by a body of men "in Congress assembled," and willed into existence by the blood and sacrifice of aspiring Americans. Before the United States, nations were based on tribes, race, territorial association, conquest, the hereditary—often "God-given"—right of monarchs, or, typically, some combination of these things. The United States, in contrast, was based on a philosophy of human rights, natural rights, and the defense thereof. It was formed, essentially, on a set of social contracts, the three most important of which we call the Declaration of Independence, the Articles of Confederation, and the Constitution.

But it is not the legal force of any agreement that created the nation and that continues to sustain it. Although Americans often seem to be among the most cynical people on the planet, we really do believe in such things as the right to life, liberty, and the pursuit of happiness, in justice and fair play, and in the sanctity of basic human rights. When the occasional demagogue rises to challenge these, his or her reign is typically short-lived. These were all values at the heart of the American Revolution, and they remain our values today.

But back to the cynicism. We Americans feel compelled to debunk so-called idealistic or great causes. Did the Civil War really have anything to do with ending slavery? You don't have to look very far to find more than a few people eager to tell you that it really was "all about economics" (as if economics had nothing to do with slavery). Similarly, many knowingly sneer at the American Revolution. Its *real* cause? They will patiently explain that a clique of wealthy colonial merchants and plantation owners were sick and tired of sharing their profits with British tax collectors.

With respect to both the Civil War and the American Revolution, the cynical view is not so much false as it is a half-truth—in other words, wholly inadequate to explain the events. If you want a simple, but still more complete, answer to what drove the American Revolution, it is this. A sufficient number of people either believed or were persuaded to believe that they were not living as fully, justly, and even as naturally as they could and should. Instead of justice, their lot was tyranny. Things were out of balance, and they burned to set that balance right.

Without doubt, tyranny existed in eighteenth-century North America. It was a land in which nearly three-quarters of a million persons, all black, were enslaved by the end of the revolution. But was the free white majority also the victim of tyranny?

Consider two of history's most famous revolutions, both of which came after the American Revolution.

The French Revolution (1787–1799) had many, often complex causes, but the main ones were these: The people of France were hungry, and the government failed to feed them. The government, an absolute monarchy, was remarkably indifferent to the condition of the people except when it came to meting out oppression to keep them in line. Technology and commerce created an expanding middle class, which was intolerably excluded from political power, and a class of French political thinkers, known as the *philosophes*, laid a compelling intellectual basis for radical reform.

Like the French Revolution, the Russian Revolutions of 1917 resulted most directly from the desperate want of the people. At the most basic level, the people of Russia were hungry, and the nation failed to feed them. Two classes of people, the peasantry (agricultural laborers) and the proletariat (the urban working population), who had both been excluded from all power for centuries, were fed up and ready to bring about change. As for the absolute monarchy of Russia, as in pre-revolutionary France, it was indifferent to the condition of the people and often harshly oppressive. In this environment, political leaders such as Lenin, Stalin, and Trotsky gave the cause of revolution political and intellectual direction.

At bottom, both the French Revolution and the Russian Revolutions were driven by a popular instinct for survival. Conditions had become so desperate, so intolerable, that change, by any means necessary, seemed the only viable option. Make no mistake, the history of these two great revolutions is rich and complex, but at the root of both was a single starkly simple quality: *desperation*.

This was not true of the American Revolution. Doubtless, the economics of life in the vast North American frontier regions was harsh, yet few Americans went hungry, let alone starved. Moreover, while many of the policies of the British monarchy were perceived as unjust, King George III was not a tyrant—though some American revolutionaries described him as such. He was a constitutional monarch, not an absolute monarch, his powers strictly limited by a parliamentary government. Although, as we will see, there was a fundamental injustice in British colonial government, King George III was, by the standards of his day, an enlightened monarch who may have treated the colonies with contempt but lacked the power to oppress the Americans with anything like the brute force Louis XVI used against his French subjects or Czar Nicholas II exercised against the Russians. In fact, most Americans retained ties of loyalty and affection to the British monarch and did not hate him. For that matter, the British government showed a willingness, albeit often a grudging willingness, to compromise and even yield on many colonial concerns. While it is easy to see the makings of a violent revolt in France and Russia, one has to squint very, very hard to detect anything comparable in eighteenth-century North America.

The American Crisis is the title of a series of pamphlets Thomas Paine wrote and published during virtually the entirety of the revolution, from 1776 to 1783. Paine, whose great pamphlet *Common Sense* (January 10, 1776) was instrumental in persuading the Continental Congress and the American people to declare independence from Britain, sought in *The American Crisis* to make the case for why the American people should support and sustain the revolution.

So, what *was* the "American Crisis" that justified the loss of some sixty-eight hundred Americans killed in action, sixty-one hundred wounded, and twenty thousand taken prisoner (of whom perhaps twelve thousand succumbed in captivity to disease)? What was the crisis that made it worth inflicting some twenty-four thousand casualties (killed, wounded, or captured) on British regular forces and twelve hundred killed among the so-called Hessian mercenaries in the British service?

In part, the justification was neither more nor less than the fact of geography. America is very far from England, separated from it by a vast ocean. Communication and travel between colony and mother country were difficult, expensive, hazardous, and slow. Conducting government across such distances was all but impossible, at least in terms of understanding and responding to the needs of the governed. The burden of distance made it increasingly difficult for the colonists to identify with the people and government of the mother country and for those in that distant land to identify with a subject population in North America. In the fullness of time, the colonies and the mother country simply developed separate and unique identities.

For a time, the British government was content to let the colonies pretty much govern themselves, but, as we will see, a series of North American wars culminating in the French and Indian War (1754–1763) increased the Crown's feeling of possessiveness toward the colonies. King George III wanted a tighter grasp on the people and the territory his country had fought to defend. Many in Britain felt that the Americans owed them a debt of unquestioning allegiance.

Whatever the nature of that debt, Parliament began levying heavy taxes and duties on the colonies. These were burdensome, but the real issue they raised was the fundamental injustice of being compelled to pay to support a government in which the colonies had no parliamentary representation. Ever since the Magna Carta of 1215, English men and women had enjoyed a degree of representation in the government they supported with their loyalty and their treasure. In fact, no British subject paid a single shilling to the king or the queen. Taxation was a power of Parliament, which represented the people, the will of the people, and the consent of the people.

The first demand of the "rebellious" American colonists was not for independence but for representation in Parliament. That is, they wanted the rights of English men and women. In a sense, the colonists considered these common English rights to be "natural," since, they argued, "God made us Englishmen." By the time the colonists finally went to war with the mother country, those rights were called the "rights of man," natural rights, God-given.

Such was the American crisis: a combination of mistreatment and injustice that was partly the result of shortsighted, uncomprehending, and wholly inadequate governance from Britain and partly a result of geography. The phrase "taxation without representation is tyranny" became a popular call to war among the colonists. Strictly speaking, tyranny is government by an absolute ruler who is unrestrained by law. This was not the case with the British monarch. However, from the point of view of colonists who had no representation—and therefore no voice—in government, the situation was one of functional tyranny.

Perhaps that was "crisis" enough on which to base a war. But there was more. Geography—distance, the great Atlantic Ocean—made true parliamentary representation a practical impossibility. Even if the British government had been willing to grant more of the colonists' demands, no power on earth could change geography, time, and distance. For this reason, the American crisis was especially resistant to any solution other than independence.

The crisis, then, was political, psychological, moral, and physical. Added to what we might call these negative pressures was a set of positive ideological drivers born of what cultural historians call "the Enlightenment," an era in which a remarkable array of European philosophers and scientists, from the late seventeenth century through the era of the American and French revolutions, rethought and revised virtually every area of human enterprise. The negative pressures set many Americans on a course toward revolution, but the positive pressures caused them to run that course with both hope and joy in anticipation not merely of righting some particular wrongs but of creating in the process a newer and greater world.

Chapter 1

Why Our Founding Fathers Fought Our Mother Country

WHEN A MARRIED COUPLE GETS A DIVORCE AND CANNOT AGREE AMICA-
bly on the terms, they plead their case in court before a judge. The law
provides a menu of reasons—"grounds"—such as adultery, desertion, or
domestic violence. Sometimes something or some things on this menu
adequately describe the grounds. Usually, though, the reasons are more
complicated than what can be captured in a word or two. The legal decision rarely reflects such human complexity. But it's a necessary place to
start. Chapters 2 through 7 will go deeper behind America's divorce from
Crown and Parliament, but let us begin with the simplest, most direct
publicly stated reasons for the breakup.

A TYRANT KING—REALLY?
In 1776, the Continental Congress tasked Thomas Jefferson with writing a brief document, the Declaration of Independence, for the purpose
of pleading the colonial case for independence. As Jefferson himself
acknowledged, "a decent respect to the opinions of mankind requires
[declaring] the causes which impel . . . the separation."

The fact is that few revolutions begin with a declaration. Most start
with despair and desperation. They begin as an emotional revolt against
urgent need, wrong, or oppression. Consider the French Revolution of
1789–1799. The vast majority of the French were hungry, and the nation
under Louis XVI could not or would not feed them. Although there was

a middle class rapidly rising in France, they were mostly excluded from political power. Time for change. Or take the Russian Revolutions of 1917. The vast majority of Russians were hungry, and the nation under Czar Nicholas II could not or would not feed them. The rural agricultural working class (the peasants) and the urban industrial working class (the proletariat) were excluded from political power. Time for a change.

Of course, both the French and the Russian revolutions were far more complicated than this, but the raw fuel for both was the same. People were suffering. People were dying and therefore urgently desperate. They resolved to fight for survival. An automobile built around a traditional internal combustion engine is far more complex than the gasoline that drives it, but without the gasoline, the car gets nowhere. In late-eighteenth-century France and early-twentieth-century Russia, the gasoline of revolution was despair and desperation.

And what of colonial America in the run-up to 1776?

There were economic problems. As we will see in Chapter 7, the Boston Massacre started out as a labor riot during an economic depression. On the colonial frontier, life was pretty rough. Yet for many desperate European immigrants, *colonial* America figured as a kind of promised land, a New World where life looked to be better than in the Old. The historical record suggests that hunger, much less starvation, was not a critical social problem in eighteenth-century colonial America. So, we have to probe elsewhere for a cause to rebel.

We know that King George III, his ministers, and the conservative faction in Parliament were politically tone deaf and often unfair when it came to the American colonies. They were often stubborn, unresponsive, and just plain thick-headed.

Now, there would come a time, as we will see, in which the word *tyranny* was bandied about, and Jefferson, in the 1776 Declaration, accused King George III of committing "repeated injuries and usurpations, all having in direct object the establishment of an absolute tyranny over these states"—that is, America. Was this accusation justified? As the word is usually understood, a "tyrant" is a cruel, oppressive, and evil ruler. Does this describe George III? Was he (take your pick) a Nero, a Caligula, an Ivan the Terrible, a Vlad the Impaler, a Hitler, a Mugabe, a Mao Zedong, an Idi Amin, a Pol Pot, a Saddam Hussein—or even a Louis XVI or Nicholas II?

Compare George III to the monarchs ruling other major colonial powers of the time, Spain and France. Unlike Spain's Charles III (1716–1788) or France's Louis XVI (1754–1793), George III was substantially constrained by a strong national "constitution" (a body of laws and traditions rather than a single document) founded on the Magna Carta of 1215. Add to this a powerful liberal tradition of common law deeply ingrained in the English culture.

The American Revolution began with the Battles of Lexington and Concord on April 19, 1775. Yet it was not until July of 1776 that the decision for independence was made. For more than a year, the British colonies were in violent armed revolt while most Americans continued

This 1859 painting by Johannes Adam Simon Oertel depicts the Sons of Liberty pulling down a statue of King George III in New York City on July 9, 1776, after Washington read the Declaration of Independence to locals. The statue was pulled down, but the work was performed by slaves at the direction of their owners. Eyewitnesses recall only soldiers and the "rougher sort" of civilians gathered to watch. There were no Native Americans present. WIKIMEDIA COMMONS

to feel toward George III a degree of loyalty and perhaps even affection. At least, they did not hate him. Even after the Continental Congress approved the Declaration of Independence and, on July 4, 1776, the colonies ratified it, many Americans did not agree with the long list of sins Jefferson tallied against the British monarch. Whence, then, the decision to embark on a bitter and violent divorce?

ABSENCE

To begin, there was the fact of the Atlantic Ocean, which separated Britain from its American colonies. A one-way trip in 1776 took a minimum of six weeks and could take as long as three months—if you survived the perils of the sea and dangers posed by infectious diseases in the close quarters of a small vessel. Not only was the crossing time-consuming and hazardous, it was also costly, well beyond the means of most travelers. If people and goods moved between London and the colonial American capitals slowly and expensively, so did letters and documents. The immutable fact of geography made remotely governing colonies difficult. From the perspective of the colonial subject, government was chronically unresponsive, representation was nonexistent, and beneficent authority seemed, in a word, *absent*. Crown and Parliament were absentee landlords.

Doubtless, the British government looked on the American colonies as the tail of the British bulldog. But, over the years, as Americans born in America came to outnumber those who had immigrated from Britain, the tail began to wag the dog. It is natural to feel affinity for your place of birth, especially if you have never even seen the place of your ancestors' birth.

So, geography alone—the intractable physical realities of space and time—provided a source of fuel for revolution. Yet, for a long time, Crown and Parliament were content to be *undemanding* absentee landlords. They reaped the rewards of possession of the American colonies, sources of raw materials to import and a market for manufactured goods to export, without interfering in colonial affairs. British colonial policy was what historians have labeled "salutary neglect." Profits were made, taxes were collected, and the colonists were left alone to govern themselves.

As we will see in the next chapter, salutary neglect began to change in a series of wars fought from the late seventeenth century through the middle of the eighteenth in North America, mainly between Europe's longtime rivals, Britain and France. These included King William's War (1689–1697), Queen Anne's War (1702–1713), and King George's War (1744–1748). Each was the North American theater of a European-based conflict: the War of the League of Augsburg (or Nine Years' War, 1688–1697), the War of the Spanish Succession (1701–1714), and the War of the Austrian Succession (1740–1748), respectively. In Europe, these conflicts culminated in the Seven Years' War (1756–1763), the North American theater of which was called the French and Indian War (1754–1763).

The 1754–1763 conflict was tremendously destructive to the colonies, and Crown and Parliament could no longer practice salutary neglect, especially since the colonists looked to the mother country for protection. Britain's costly military contribution to the war made the imperial government feel increasingly possessive of the colonies. Moreover, the expense of fighting a major war across an ocean created a massive debt, which, George, his ministers, and Parliament believed the colonies should help to defray.

On the colonial side, the French and Indian War stirred English patriotism and pride among many. But the increasingly heavy hand the London government took, intervening in colonial affairs, strictly regulating trade, and—soon—enforcing existing taxes and levying new ones, began to unknot the bonds of loyalty already thinly stretched across the broad Atlantic. There was also a feeling that Britain's military contribution to the French and Indian War had been both inept and indifferent. Many colonists, young George Washington among them, served in colonial militia units during the war and had reason to be critical of the quality of some officers and to be resentful of the disrespectful and belittling treatment colonial troops often received from them.

Historians continue to debate whether the French and Indian War tended to strengthen bonds between the colonies and Britain or weaken them. What does seem apparent is that the colonists who fought in the war were hardly awed by the performance of the British military. On balance, it may well be that British intervention in the conflict saved British North America from the French only to begin losing it to the colonists themselves. Moreover, while British victory ended the conflict with the French, fighting on the frontier did not end. Continued war between Native Americans and colonists strained British and colonial resources. In an effort to reduce tension between the colonists and the Indians, George III issued a proclamation on October 7, 1763 setting the Appalachian Mountains as the limit to western colonial settlement.

In the beginning, the Proclamation of 1763 appeared to work wonders, quickly ending Pontiac's Rebellion, a bloody conflict fought in the aftermath of the French and Indian War. In it, the Ottawa, Delaware, and Iroquois, loosely led by the Ottawa chief Pontiac, fought to reclaim lands they had lost in the war just ended. But as the "Proclamation Line" pacified Native Americans, it enflamed many settlers, who defiantly crossed it, provoking Indian raids throughout the trans-Appalachian frontier. When settlers who had defied the Proclamation Line called for help from royal authorities, they were rebuffed as the lawbreakers they were.

The Proclamation of 1763 deepened a growing division between the southeastern coastal region of the continent, the so-called Tidewater, home to the longest-established and wealthiest portion of the colonial population, and the western frontier, or Piedmont, region, whose people were on the economic margins. One would expect that the disaffected Piedmont would be stirred to revolution, whereas the wealthy and established Tidewater would embrace the status quo. In fact, because Tidewater people were more directly connected to Europe than the Piedmont, they were also more conversant with and receptive to the latest in ideas in philosophy, science, and government. This awareness and attitude introduced into the Tidewater a strong current of liberal thought, to which the more remote inland Piedmont was not exposed. As a result, the Piedmont tended toward both religious and political conservatism. As more and more frontier people defied the Proclamation Line, however, and violence with the Indians became widespread, the hitherto conservative Piedmont, increasingly resentful of being neglected by both the mother country and the Tidewater, was radicalized. Soon, ideological liberalism in the Tidewater made that population question colonial ties to the Crown and Parliament, while a rawer form of radical rebellion took hold in the Piedmont. The two regions were still divided from one another on many cultural issues, but they grew increasingly united not so much in a common desire for independence as in an evolving conception of tyranny. As for the coastal cities, Boston quickly coalesced around rebellion, but New York and Philadelphia tended to prize trade relations highly. The merchant classes in these cities favored maintaining the status quo with the British crown while the laboring classes drifted toward independence.

TYRANNY

Regardless of where eighteenth-century colonists lived—north, south, Tidewater, Piedmont, city or farm—chances are that they thought of themselves not as Americans but as English men and women who happened to live in America. The idea of breaking away from the mother country formed only after an awareness grew among more and more colonists that, while they were expected to be loyal English men and women, they were being denied the full rights and privileges of British subjects. Since King John had signed the Magna Carta in 1215, subjects of the Crown were entitled to representation in the government. The British monarch did not possess absolute power but was subject (in varying degree) to the will of Parliament, whose House of Commons, in turn, represented the will of the people.

What is crucial to bear in mind is that the monarch had no power of taxation. Parliament and Parliament alone had the power of the purse—and that was crucial to the rights of English men and women. They accepted taxation because the taxing authority was not the person who inherited the throne but the Parliament who represented not the king or queen but the people. What was becoming increasingly clear to many colonists was the truth that *they*—English men and women who happened to live across an ocean—were taxed and yet not represented by Parliament, the authority that taxed them. As we will see in Chapter 4, this realization would crystallize into a definition of tyranny. When it did, "tyranny" would no longer be some vague, subjective, highly emotional concept. It would be as objective as an equation: *Taxation without representation is tyranny.*

Taxation

The long era of so-called salutary neglect ended with the royal imposition of the Proclamation Line, which was the first step in a transformation from salutary neglect to what we might term malignant interference. The new approach came in a torrent of taxes—some new and others long-established taxes that simply had never been enforced before. The taxes were established by a series of revenue laws, many of which also regulated and restricted colonial free enterprise by forcing colonists to export their goods exclusively *to* England and to import other goods exclusively *from* England. This was felt as an even more oppressive burden than the taxes.

The cascade of taxes, duties, and regulations hit the colonial economy hard, which was already suffering from the depressive effects of the French and Indian War. To this injury was added the insult of what the colonists perceived as royal indifference and arrogance. Financially afflicted, the colonists were also made to feel abused. In 1765, a Quartering Act required colonial governments to furnish barracks and provisions for royal troops, the very personnel charged with enforcing the hated taxes and regulations. Already inclined to see taxation without representation as tyranny, the American colonists now saw themselves as also occupied by a "foreign" army. This made tyranny feel like much more than an equation. It was an invasion.

A tone-deaf London government turned the screw even tighter with acts designed to enhance the enforcement of the revenue acts. All violations of these acts were henceforth to be tried not in colonial courts, but in vice-admiralty courts, which answered to the Crown rather than to the people of America. Moreover, admiralty courts had no juries, which meant that one of the most sacred rights guaranteed to all English men and women by the Magna Carta—the right to be tried by a jury of one's peers—was denied to colonists accused of failing to pay taxes levied by a Parliament in which they had no voice.

Taxation without Representation

We need to return to the concept of taxation without representation. Even in the mid-1760s, the majority of colonists were not ready to argue, let alone agree, that George III and Parliament were on the attack against their *human* rights, the rights Jefferson, in 1776, would call "self-evident" and "unalienable." What a growing number of them *were* arguing was that they were being denied the rights long enjoyed by all British subjects.

On February 24, 1761, a prominent Boston lawyer, James Otis, made a speech that galvanized the popular sense of unjust discrimination by Crown and Parliament. The speech concerned "writs of assistance," which were legal orders compelling colonial officials to cooperate with royal officers in curbing and prosecuting customs and duties violations. One line from this speech rang out very loudly. Otis declared: "Taxation without representation is tyranny."

Another local attorney, John Adams, heard the speech and immediately wrote to his wife, the brilliant Abigail Adams, that Otis, impassioned, "burned with a fire of flame." That flame spread, and "No taxation without representation" became a battle cry. Everybody grumbles about taxes and onerous regulations. Those who heard Otis's speech or read it or heard about it experienced an epiphany. They realized that taxes and trade regulations were not the principal issues. No. It was all about the imposition of these taxes and other laws by a government that gave the governed no voice in the matter. The function of government and taxes and laws is to benefit the people. Fulfilling this function requires a government that embodies the will of the governed. Absent this, there is only tyranny. What is more, it is a tyranny that had been abolished among the English long ago, in 1215, by the Magna Carta. Thus, no subject of the king could be expected to tolerate it now—whether that subject lived in London, England, or Boston, Massachusetts. Parliament, in which the English people were represented, levied taxes. Not a penny of tax could be levied by an English monarch. And not a penny could rightfully be extorted from English men and women who lacked parliamentary representation. English men and women would never subjugate themselves to a tyrant.

So, a diagnosis of colonial discontent was born in 1761: *Taxation without representation is tyranny.* Now, what was the cure?

Some colonial leaders proposed to do nothing more than appeal to Parliament for representation. In reply to the appeal, Parliament claimed that, although its members were indeed elected from geographical districts, they really did not represent the districts that elected them. The political theory now proposed held that each member of Parliament represented *all* English subjects, including the colonists, even though they had no vote.

It was a lame argument, a non-starter. Worse, it provoked some colonial leaders to argue that even if Crown and Parliament *did* someday agree to some formula whereby the colonies would be directly represented in Parliament—and no one believed that Crown and Parliament ever would agree to this—proportional parliamentary representation for the colonies was manifestly a practical impossibility.

There were three reasons for this. First, the barrier of time and distance presented by the Atlantic Ocean was an insuperable obstacle to efficient, effective representation. Second, colonial interests were often very different from those of the mother country—especially where trade was concerned. Third, Parliament would never—and, really, *could* never—grant to the rapidly growing colonies anything like proportional representation. At some point in the not-too-distant future, it was clear, colonial population would exceed British population in Europe. Proportional representation that would be fair to the colonists as well as to the people of England just was not possible.

Here was the kernel of the independence movement. Taxation without representation is tyranny. Representation for the colonies is ultimately impossible. English men and women, wherever they happened to live, would never bow to tyranny. Therefore, the only option was independence from Britain.

But if Crown and Parliament refused—as they most certainly would—to accept this formulation of truth? The only course remaining would be revolution.

CHAPTER 2

The War Young Washington Started

THE FOUR-YEAR-LONG KING GEORGE'S WAR, THE THIRD OF THREE
wars involving the French, the British, and the Indian allies of each in
North America, ended in 1748, when the parallel War of the Austrian
Succession ended in Europe. This brought to the American frontier a
most fleeting peace, which began falling apart on March 16, 1749, when
King George II granted vast western tracts to the Ohio Company, a powerful syndicate of British traders and speculators. The grant came with
strings attached. Within seven years, the company had to plant a settlement of one hundred families and build a fort for their protection—or
forfeit the land. Both the French and Indians saw this as the start of an
English invasion into their territories.

ALLIES AND ENEMIES
In response to the English influx, the Marquis de La Jonquière, governor of New France, built Fort Rouillé (at the location of present-day
Toronto) to cut off trade between the northern Great Lakes and Oswego,
a British stronghold on the south shore of Lake Ontario in New York.
Jonquière also added fortifications at French-held Detroit and launched
a punitive raid against the English-allied Shawnee, which proved coun-
terproductive, driving that tribe deeper into the English fold. British
colonial authorities supported the aggressiveness of English traders and
purchased more western land from the Indians. In 1752, the British
negotiated a treaty at Logstown (Ambridge, Pennsylvania) between the
Iroquois Six Nations, Delaware, Shawnee, and Wyandot on the one side

and Virginia and the Ohio Company on the other. The treaty secured for Virginia a quitclaim to the entire Ohio country.

The British were in the process of gaining valuable Indian allies when the Miami (or Twightwee) Indian village at Pickawillany (present-day Piqua, Ohio) was raided by French-led Native American forces on June 21, 1752. In response, the Senecas, westernmost of the Iroquois tribes, asked the Virginia government to build a defensive fort at the forks of the Ohio, the site of present-day Pittsburgh. The Virginians responded with no response, a rebuff that sent the Miamis into the French camp—a move that instantly undid the Logstown Treaty and, as a result, began to drive English trade out of the Ohio Valley.

The new governor of New France, the Marquis Duquesne, was quick to pounce on the rupture in British relations with the Native Americans. He built a string of new forts extending from Montreal down to New Orleans. This intimidated the Iroquois and other English-allied tribes throughout the Ohio. By 1753, Britain's few dwindling Indian alliances were dissolving. Yet, at precisely this point, in far-off London, Lord Halifax, a principal booster of Britain's North American empire, prodded the Cabinet toward a declaration of war against France. He argued that the French, by trading throughout the Ohio Valley, had invaded Virginia. Cabinet and Crown ordered Virginia lieutenant governor Robert Dinwiddie to take military measures to evict the French from territory under his jurisdiction. Dinwiddie accordingly commissioned twenty-one-year-old Virginia planter and militia officer George Washington to carry an ultimatum to Captain Jacques Legardeur de Saint-Pierre, commandant of Fort LeBoeuf (present-day Waterford, Pennsylvania): France must vacate the Ohio country or face forcible eviction.

Washington set out from Williamsburg on October 31, 1753, with a small delegation. He reached Fort LeBoeuf on December 12, 1753, where Captain Legardeur politely rejected the ultimatum. Washington reported this to Dinwiddie, who ordered Captain William Trent to build at the forks of the Ohio the fort that Britain's erstwhile Indian allies had requested. On April 17, 1754, Captain Claude-Pierre Pécaudy de Contrecoeur, the new French commandant of Fort LeBoeuf, attacked the nearly completed British fort. Its commander and garrison surrendered to superior French forces without a fight. Contrecoeur renamed the structure Fort Duquesne.

In the meantime, on the very day the Ohio fort fell, Dinwiddie, unaware of the surrender, dispatched Washington with 150 militiamen to reinforce the fort Virginia no longer held. On May 28, Washington led forty of his provincials and a dozen Indian warriors in a surprise assault on a thirty-three-man French reconnaissance party. In the ensuing combat that followed, ten of the Frenchmen were killed, and the remaining twenty-three surrendered. Washington thus claimed the first victory of his military career in an encounter of which the English writer Horace Walpole would later write: "The volley fired by a young Virginian in the backwoods of America set the world on fire."

FIRE IN THE WILDERNESS

Washington had started the French and Indian War, which would soon become the North American theater of the Seven Years' War, an epic conflagration many historians consider the first "world" war, since it engulfed North America, Europe, and other French and British colonies, including in India.

But George Washington was not worried about the world. He understood he had more immediate problems. The French, he knew, would certainly retaliate against him—in strength. He scrambled to recruit more Delaware warriors but could muster no more than forty men. Recognizing that he and his small command were doomed, Washington organized a retreat. With the French closing in fast, he paused at Great Meadows, in northwestern Pennsylvania, not far from Fort Duquesne, and ordered the building of a makeshift stockade. He called it Fort Necessity, and, from it, he proposed to make whatever stand he could.

On July 3, 1754, some nine hundred French soldiers and Indian warriors under Major Coulon de Villiers attacked Fort Necessity. Vastly outnumbered, inadequately fortified, and fighting in driving rains that dissolved the hasty entrenchments, Washington surrendered Fort Necessity on July 4, after losing half his command. He and the survivors were permitted to march back to Virginia.

Washington had now had his baptism of fire, his first sweet taste of victory, and his first deep bitter draft of defeat. The idea of an American Revolution was not merely far off; it did not yet exist. If young George Washington was unaware that he had just started a world war, he could not have had the slightest inkling that the experience would prepare him to lead, some twenty-one years hence, an epoch-making war for American independence.

Dark Days of the British Colonies

All through the first four years of the French and Indian War, the British government and most of the English colonists showed a stubborn, racist, and remarkably stupid contempt for Native American alliances. The leadership of the British regular army was, if anything, even more contemptuous of what they called the "provincials," colonial militia officers and soldiers. Friction developed between the mother country and the colonies, both over military matters and trade. Some colonies resisted aiding the war effort. Powerful mercantile interests in New York valued a profitable trade with Montreal and boldly continued a major smuggling operation in defiance of an official ban. Beginning with the loss of the fort at the forks of the Ohio and the defeat of Washington, the English, not the French, were expelled from the Ohio country.

In contrast to the British disdain for Native Americans, the French embraced them and even intermarried among them. Having secured numerous Indian allies, they used the vast Ohio country as a staging area for raids into the East—into Pennsylvania, Maryland, and Virginia. At last, in December 1754, Parliament authorized Massachusetts governor William Shirley to reactivate for service two colonial regiments, about two thousand men. These regiments were to be joined by two of the British army's least reputable regiments, which set out for America in January 1755 from Cork, Ireland, under Major General Edward Braddock, a courageous but unimaginative commander. When the French responded the next month by dispatching to Canada seventy-eight companies of the king's regulars, the British expanded Braddock's command to seven regiments, for a total of ten thousand men.

As the European theater of the war—what would become the Seven Years' War—heated up, France saw that its future as a world power was at stake and escalated the North American conflict by funding widespread Indian attacks against British frontier settlements in early February 1755. A few days later, on February 23, Braddock arrived in Williamsburg, Virginia, and on April 14, in Alexandria, laid out his plan of attack. It was as ambitious as it was unrealistic. He assigned Brigadier General Robert Monckton to campaign against Nova Scotia, while he himself planned to lead a campaign to take Forts Duquesne and Niagara. The "provincials," under Governor Shirley, were relegated to reinforcing Fort Oswego and then advancing to Fort Niagara—just in case Braddock, having captured Fort Duquesne, had not yet taken Niagara as well. Braddock was confident that Shirley would find his regulars already comfortably ensconced in that objective. Another colonial commander, William Johnson—who, in contrast to most of the English, enjoyed a strong alliance with Native American warriors (the superb Mohawks)—was tasked with capturing Fort Saint Frédéric at Crown Point, New York.

By the end of 1755, two thousand Massachusetts provincials under John Winslow, together with a handful of British regulars commanded by General Monckton, had almost completely accomplished their mission. They wrested from the French control of Nova Scotia except for Louisbourg, the ideally positioned French naval base at Cape Breton, which guarded the Saint Lawrence River. But even after some ten months of preparation, the self-confident, blustering Braddock still struggled to get his expedition to Fort Duquesne under way. He faced two major problems. First, his battle plan called for recruiting Indian allies. Understandably, there were few takers. Second, Braddock was contemptuous of "provincials" and failed to consult the colonial governors on his plan of attack. In a preview of the no-taxation-without-representation political movement to come, the colonies resisted war levies and even refused to render the most rudimentary cooperation. The exception was Pennsylvania, which, at the urging of its postmaster general, Benjamin Franklin, supplied wagons for Braddock's army and built him a road into the western wilderness.

At long last, Braddock began leading two regiments of British regulars and a provincial detachment (under George Washington) out of Fort Cumberland, Maryland. An unwieldy force of twenty-five hundred men laden with heavy equipment made a slow, painful slog through the wilderness. Along the way, French-allied Indians raided English settlements and sniped at the advancing army. After weeks of this, Washington advised Braddock to detach a lightly equipped "flying column" of fifteen hundred men to make the initial attack on Fort Duquesne. Since the British general believed the fort was defended by no more than eight hundred French and Indians, he agreed.

By July 7, the flying column was encamped just ten miles from its objective. Fort Duquesne's commandant, Claude-Pierre Pécaudy de Contrecoeur, contemplated surrendering to Braddock's superior numbers but was talked out of it by a fiery subordinate, Captain Liénard de Beaujeu, who convinced Contrecoeur to put him at the head of just seventy-two regulars of the French Marine, 146 Canadian militiamen, and 637 assorted Indians in a preemptive attack on Braddock's camp.

On the morning of July 9, Beaujeu's forces attacked—from ambush—Braddock's line of march. At first, Braddock's men reacted professionally and effectively, efficiently returning French fire. Indeed, one British round found its mark in Beaujeu himself, killing that valiant officer instantly. His second-in-command, Jean-Daniel Dumas, stepped into the breach to rally the French and Indian forces, ordering the men to regroup *in the woods*. Instead of an open battle, Dumas set up another ambush. Braddock and his men assumed that the French had withdrawn. When, however, they were again attacked, the result was utter confusion in the British ranks. Trained to fight on open, formal European fields of battle, the regulars were now helpless against an invisible enemy they had thought vanquished. The redcoats fired wildly, often hitting one another in an orgy of friendly fire.

For his part, Braddock conducted himself with a degree of calm courage that profoundly impressed young Washington. But it was all to no avail. Braddock had five horses shot from under him as he tried to rally his troops. Washington, in the meantime, held his Virginia contingent together not by forming European-style ranks but by fighting like the

Indians—from cover and concealment. He and his militiamen persisted even as the regulars were mowed down. At last, Braddock himself was mortally wounded and had to be carried away by two provincial soldiers. Of 1,459 British regulars and colonials engaged, just 462 returned from the Battle of the Wilderness. Washington had had two horses shot from under him, and his coat was pierced by no fewer than four bullets. Yet he emerged unhurt. The French and Indians? Casualties were no more than sixty men.

Hearing of the battle, many Native American leaders, hitherto neutral or even inclined to side with the English, took up instead with the French and attacked English settlements along the length of the frontier. Moreover, the British regulars had flung away a fortune in arms and ammunition, abandoned their artillery, left behind Braddock's well-stocked money chest, and, worst of all, his personal papers, which detailed his plan of war, including the forthcoming campaigns against Forts Niagara and Saint Frédéric. The new French governor, the Marquis de Vaudreuil, reinforced those forts, using the cannon the English had left behind.

The Pennsylvania, Maryland, and Virginia frontiers were convulsed by Indian raids in the aftermath of the Battle of the Wilderness. William Johnson purposely deviated from Braddock's plan. Instead of advancing to Fort Saint Frédéric, he fought and defeated the French and Indians at the Battle of Lake George on September 8, 1755, and then built Fort William Henry on the south end of the lake. By installing a garrison here, Johnson proposed to consolidate the British gains in this area. George Washington, returned from the debacle at the Battle of the Wilderness, welcomed Johnson's strategy, and he persuaded Virginia authorities to build even more forts between the Potomac and James and Roanoke Rivers, all the way down into South Carolina. Partly on young Washington's advice, the British in general adopted a broad defensive strategy, hoping to prevent the French from pushing them any farther east. But the French governor, Vaudreuil, resolved on new strategy to nibble away at the British defenses. He made extensive use of Indians in a guerrilla campaign that avoided the forts and instead targeted the English frontier settlers.

By early 1756, having failed to take Forts Frontenac and Niagara as prescribed in Braddock's original war plan, Massachusetts Governor Shirley retreated to Albany, from which, on March 17, he dispatched

Lieutenant Colonel John Bradstreet to reinforce Fort Oswego, on the southeast shore of Lake Ontario. It was, after all, one of the most important of the English bases—and no one realized this more urgently than the French. They were already well on their way to severing the supply line to Oswego. Nevertheless, Bradstreet broke through the French positions and delivered much-needed food and supplies to Oswego. He even defeated a French and Indian attack on July 3.

Such English colonial triumphs were rare during the first three years of the war. By June 1756, English settlers in Virginia had withdrawn 150 miles from their prewar frontier, and George Washington moaned to Lieutenant Governor Dinwiddie that "the Bleu-Ridge is now our Frontier."

MORE BRITISH DISASTERS AND THE ASCENT OF PITT

On May 11, 1756, Louis Joseph, Marquis de Montcalm, arrived in Canada to take charge of French and provincial forces. Less than a week later, on May 17, England officially declared war on France in the start of Europe's Seven Years' War. After successfully supplying Oswego, Bradstreet, on July 12, warned his superiors that the vital fort was in grave danger. But Governor Shirley, who respected Bradstreet, had been relieved of command of the provincial forces by Major General James Abercromby, a British regular. Abercromby excluded Bradstreet from a July 16 council of war, in which he ordered Major General Daniel Webb, another regular, to prepare for departure to Oswego. It was a good idea, but Webb so dragged his feet that he and his command failed to reach Oswego by August 14, when the vital British fort fell to Montcalm. With the fort's fall, control of Lake Ontario was yielded to the French. It was a blow to the English position even harder than the defeat of Braddock had been.

The obvious lesson of Oswego was to value Indian allies and provincial troops. British command blithely continued to ignore such lessons. But, in December 1756, William Pitt the Elder became British secretary of state for the Southern Department, which put him in direct charge of American colonial affairs. Talented and imaginative, Pitt was a breath of fresh air among George II's ministers. Within three weeks of taking office, he ordered two thousand additional troops to Halifax, Nova

Scotia, intending to bring the war into Canada, through the Saint Lawrence Valley, and against Quebec.

But Pitt still had thick-headed regulars like Webb with whom to contend. Pitt wanted to take the French naval base at Louisbourg, but Webb once again moved too slowly. When he learned that Fort William Henry was menaced by Montcalm, Webb failed to act. Montcalm began his advance against Fort William Henry on July 29, 1757. Panic-stricken, Webb withdrew from the fort on August 4, leaving its defense to Lieutenant Colonel George Monro and 2,372 men—of whom all but eleven hundred were down with disease or injury. Opposing him, Montcalm commanded 7,626 men, including sixteen hundred Indian allies. Webb advised Monro to surrender quickly. Instead, the lieutenant colonel and his small band fought valiantly, holding out until August 9, 1757. Montcalm promised Munro safe conduct for his garrison only to allow his Native American auxiliaries to massacre some fifteen hundred soldiers, women, and children as they left Fort William Henry.

The loss of Fort William Henry meant the loss of control over Lake George, which William Johnson had won in hard battle. It was the low point of British fortunes in the French and Indian War—a historical moment the American novelist James Fenimore Cooper would dramatize in his *Last of the Mohicans* (1826). But Pitt's military reform policies were just beginning to take hold, and the tide of war began slowly to turn.

Pitt decreed a policy of cooperation with the colonists. In particular, he gave colonial assemblies a voice in managing the funds used to prosecute the war. Massachusetts immediately responded by raising a large and effective army. Pitt now made it a policy to seek rather than shun Indian allies. He also began to handpick the best—or least objectionable—regular officers to command major assaults. Among these was Brigadier General John Forbes, whom he assigned to campaign—yet again—against Fort Duquesne.

In contrast to Braddock, Forbes worked closely with the Pennsylvania governor and colonial assembly to obtain the supplies and recruit the men he needed for the campaign. He also enjoyed some success in recruiting Native American allies. Still, moving an army of five thousand provincials, fourteen hundred elite Scottish Highlanders, and dwindling numbers of

Indian warriors was not easy. On September 11, 1758, Colonel Henry Bouquet, commanding Forbes's Highlanders, impatiently sent eight hundred of them to reconnoiter Fort Duquesne. On September 15, that force was overwhelmed by a sortie of French and Indians who poured out from the fort. More than 250 Highlanders were killed in a matter of minutes. Yet the attack came at a high price to the French as well. Losses among their Indian auxiliaries were heavy, prompting many Native Americans to desert Fort Duquesne. Moreover, the English concluded the Treaty of Easton in October 1758, returning to the Iroquois western lands they had earlier ceded to Pennsylvania. For the English, this was the single most important diplomatic move of the French and Indian War.

Reversal of Fortune

Yet even as French alliances with Native Americans began to fracture, the British failed to retake Fort Ticonderoga (which the French had renamed Fort Carillon) from the French, thanks to an able defense by Montcalm. But Montcalm's victory at Ticonderoga would prove to be the last major French triumph of the war.

On July 26, 1758, Major General James Wolfe and Brigadier General Jeffrey Amherst, two of Pitt's ablest commanders, at last succeeded in capturing Louisbourg, Nova Scotia, thereby depriving France of its principal North American naval base. At the end of August, Fort Frontenac fell to Bradstreet's "provincials." With its loss, the French lifeline to Forts Niagara and Duquesne was severed, and France relinquished control of Lake Ontario to the British.

Fort Duquesne, to which General Forbes was slowly drawing closer, was now without a source of artillery or supplies. François-Marie Le Marchand de Lignery, the fort's commandant, launched a desperate raid against Forbes's position at Loyalhanna, Pennsylvania, on October 12, 1758. Repulsed, Lignery retreated to the fort, his few remaining Native American allies badly shaken. In November, he launched another raid. Forbes defeated it as well and captured three prisoners in the process. They revealed just how weakly Fort Duquesne was now held. Encouraged, on November 24, Forbes was about to advance against the fort from Loyalhanna. As they were setting out, he and his men heard a

distant explosion. Lignery had blown up the fort and fled to Fort Mach-
ault (present-day Franklin, Pennsylvania) to plan a counterattack. When
Forbes's army at last marched into Fort Duquesne, they found it both
gutted and deserted. The heads of Highlanders captured earlier had been
skewered atop stakes, the soldiers' kilts tied below.

Even in ruins, Fort Duquesne was a great prize. The power that
controlled the "forks of Ohio," the confluence of the Ohio, Allegheny,
and Monongahela Rivers, held the gateway to the Ohio country—the
western frontier. Forbes renamed Fort Duquesne Fort Pitt.

1759: The Year of French Disaster

If 1758 saw the tide of war turn decisively against France in the French
and Indian War, 1759 proved to be what historians of the war call "The
Year of French Disaster." Pitt drew up a three-pronged campaign against
the French, which included, first, the capture of Fort Niagara and the
reinforcement of Fort Oswego to sever the west from the Saint Lawrence
River. Second was a strike through the Lake Champlain waterway into
the Saint Lawrence Valley. Third was an amphibious assault on Quebec.

In February, William Johnson proposed an expedition against Fort
Niagara via the country of the Iroquois Six Nations. While Johnson
gathered large numbers of Indian allies for the assault, General Wolfe
prepared to take Quebec. On May 28, 1759, Rear Admiral Philip Durrell
landed a detachment on the Ile-aux-Coudres, in the St. Lawrence River,
northeast of Quebec. These troops advanced downriver to Ile d'Orleans,
nearer to Quebec, to await the main amphibious force under Wolfe
and Vice Admiral Charles Saunders, which landed on June 27. By July,
Wolfe's army of nine thousand men was in possession of the north shore
of the Saint Lawrence above Quebec. Montcalm attempted to burn the
British fleet at anchor by chaining rafts together, setting them ablaze, and
sending them downriver, but British seamen in small boats managed to
repel these assaults.

For the next two and a half months, Wolfe probed Quebec's defenses
without success. Failing to penetrate, he terrorized the city's civilian population, bombarding it day and night with his artillery. After weeks of
siege and bombardment, the citizens of Quebec pleaded with Montcalm

to surrender. The French general responded by threatening to turn his Native American warriors loose upon them. The people of Quebec were thus held hostage between the opposing armies.

As the siege of Quebec ground on, Fort Niagara fell to the British on July 23. On July 26, the French, outnumbered by the forces of British general Jeffrey Amherst, abandoned and blew up Fort Ticonderoga. Amherst moved against Fort Saint Frédéric next, taking it on July 31. French forces withdrew down the Richelieu River.

The city of Quebec, however, was not yet breached. Throughout the summer of 1759, Wolfe made several unsuccessful and costly attempts to storm Quebec. At last, on September 12, he made a systematic and stealthy approach to the Plains of Abraham, the high ground above the city. Montcalm had failed to anticipate an attack from that direction and had not fortified it. At daybreak on September 14, he, his troops, and the citizens of Quebec were astonished to see an enemy army forming battle lines on the Plains of Abraham. Up to this point in the war, Montcalm had performed brilliantly. Now, he blundered—and badly. He might have attacked while Wolfe was still mustering his forces. Instead, Montcalm waited until he had brought up all his men from nearby Beaumont to fully cover the approach from the Plains of Abraham—yet he did not wait for additional reinforcements from more distant Cap Rouge. In consequence, Montcalm ordered a charge against the advancing British that was both too late and yet premature. Wolfe had his men hold their fire until the last possible moment. Then they delivered it into the poorly organized French ranks with devastating effect.

After months of failed assaults, the climactic battle was over in a quarter of an hour, leaving two hundred French troops dead and another twelve hundred wounded. British losses were sixty dead and another six hundred wounded. Among the fatalities on both sides were the two commanders, Montcalm and Wolfe.

THE WAR ENDS, THE FIGHTING CONTINUES

The fall of Quebec decided the war, but the fighting did not end, as the French regulars and French colonials continued to resist. Yet the British continued to gain ground. Spain belatedly joined the Seven Years' War in Europe on the side of France, and England declared war on the new combatant on January 2, 1762. British sea power rapidly prevailed against Spain, and on November 3, France concluded with Spain the secret Treaty of San Ildefonso, by which it ceded to Spain all of its territory west of the Mississippi as well as the Isle of Orleans in Louisiana. It was all intended as compensation for the loss of its ally's Caribbean possessions in this late phase of the Seven Years' War.

By the Treaty of Paris, concluded on February 10, 1763, France publicly ceded all of Louisiana to Spain and the rest of its North American holdings to Great Britain. The treaty at last ended both the American and European phases of the Seven Years' War, but discontent among the Indians of the frontier regions ensured that, while the French and Indian War was over, warfare would continue sporadically and chronically.

The most serious conflict in the wake of the French and Indian War was Pontiac's Rebellion of 1763–1766. The Ottawa tribe, led by Chief Pontiac, together with leaders from other tribes, most notably the Delaware, Iroquois (principally the Seneca), and the Shawnee, attacked the western outposts the French had officially relinquished to the English. The source of the conflict can be traced to the fall of Detroit to the British on November 29, 1760, and General Amherst's decision to abolish the custom of giving "gifts" to the Indians, especially ammunition. Amherst's ill-advised edict prompted Pontiac to call a grand council on April 27, 1763, urging the Potawatomi and Huron to join his Ottawa in a joint attack upon Fort Detroit. Failing to breach the fort, Pontiac began raiding the settlers in its vicinity. Soon, much of the western frontier had been overrun.

When a group of Delaware demanded the surrender of Fort Pitt on June 24, 1763, Simon Ecuyer, commanding in the absence of Colonel Henry Bouquet, refused. General Amherst ordered Bouquet to commit one of history's first documented instances of biological warfare. Bouquet ordered Ecuyer to summon Delaware chiefs to the fort for a conference. There Ecuyer presented them with three "gifts": a handkerchief and two blankets. All were from the fort's smallpox-ridden hospital. In short order, smallpox was epidemic among the Delaware tribe.

The siege of Detroit was lifted in September, and on October 3, 1763, Pontiac at last agreed to peace in return for a pledge that English settlement would stop at the Appalachian Mountains. Although sporadic fighting continued into 1766, King George II's Proclamation of 1763 (October 7) brought the participation of Pontiac and his followers to an end. "We . . . declare it to be our Royal Will and Pleasure that no Governor or Commander in Chief in any of our Colonies of Quebec, East Florida or West Florida, do presume, upon any Pretence whatever, to grant Warrants of Survey, or pass any Patents for Lands beyond the Bounds of their respective Governments as described in their Commissions," the proclamation decreed, adding "that no Governor or Commander in Chief in any of our other Colonies or Plantations in America do presume . . . to grant Warrants of Survey, or pass Patents for any Lands beyond the Heads or Sources of any of the Rivers which fall into the Atlantic Ocean from the West and North West, or upon any Lands whatever, which, not having been ceded to or purchased by Us as aforesaid, are reserved to the said Indians. . . ."

AMBIVALENT VICTORY

The Proclamation of 1763 decreed the Appalachian Mountains as the legal limit of western expansion of the English colonies. This "Proclamation Line," drawn by royal edict and without consulting the colonies themselves, struck many colonists as unjust and even tyrannical. It weakened bonds of loyalty to King George III. It added to the growing list of doubts a growing number of colonists had about their connection to Britain. True, the menace of France had been defeated in the lower thirteen colonies. True, this was a source of much English pride among the English colonists. Yet so much of the war had been an exhibition of British military ineptitude and arrogance. Most especially, it left many in the colonies feeling that their mother country felt little affection and even less respect for them. Among those who entertained such feelings was no less a fateful figure than George Washington himself.

CHAPTER 3

The Rich, the Poor, and the "Middling Sort"

PEOPLE IMMIGRATED TO PRE-REVOLUTIONARY AMERICA FOR MANY reasons, giving the colonies a surprisingly diverse population. The Plymouth Plantation, the Massachusetts Bay Colony, Rhode Island, Maryland, and Pennsylvania were all founded on religious principles, but those principles were diverse. Even within the predominantly "Puritan" colonies—Plymouth and Massachusetts Bay, for instance—there was a wide spectrum of theology as well as economic status. If anything united the early immigrants of the original colonies, it was hope. All who voyaged to America did so with some variation on a hope and desire for a better life than they had known across the ocean.

The founding of one colony, however, was driven by an overt determination to give humankind a chance at a fresh start. James Edward Oglethorpe (1696–1785) combined the diverse personal qualities of military discipline—he was a general—with a selfless passion for philanthropy. In 1732, he organized a group of nineteen wealthy and high-minded individuals into a corporation that secured a royal charter to colonize a large portion of the lower south. He named the new colony Georgia, after Britain's then-reigning king, George II. It would be the last and southernmost of Britain's original thirteen North American colonies.

With his corporate partners, Oglethorpe conceived a bold plan to create in Georgia a haven for various Protestant sects. Even more important, he specifically wanted to provide a place of productive settlement for the vast and growing class of insolvent debtors who languished in British debtors' prisons. He was also looking to establish an alternative to incarceration for those convicted of certain relatively minor criminal offenses. Oglethorpe believed that Georgia would give the debtors a fresh start and reform as well as rehabilitate the criminals. He and his cofounders pledged to function as trustees of the colony, forgoing personal profits from the enterprise for a period of twenty-one years.

Oglethorpe set out to create an environment that would do even more than protect the persecuted, give debtors a new start, and reform minor criminals. He intended to fashion a legal and moral context that would give society itself a new start by eliminating as many of the causes of social stratification as possible. Difference in wealth and social station, he believed, was the source of most discord, strife, and crime in civilization as it generally existed. He therefore prohibited the sale of rum—both to encourage temperance and to remove Georgia from the infamous "triangle trade," by which slaves were imported into southern North America to work on plantations that produced (among other commodities) sugar, which was sold to New England, which turned it into rum, which was exported back to Africa, where it was traded for slaves. Not only did Oglethorpe want to take Georgia out of the slave-sugar-rum triangle, he outlawed slavery itself throughout the colony.

Perhaps Oglethorpe's most radical innovation was setting regulations to limit the size of individual land holdings. His objective was to create economic homogeneity, which he believed was essential to creating equality. The first colonists who arrived with Oglethorpe himself in 1733 were placed on fifty-five-acre farms, which they were forbidden to sell or transfer. They were allowed to acquire no more than a total of five hundred acres of property each.

Colonial Life Was Nothing Special

Oglethorpe's utopian project never got very far. That the great experiment in equality began was in itself an achievement, but the utopian aspect of Georgia ended very quickly. For one thing, few of the original one hundred Georgia colonists were debtors, victims of religious persecution, or criminals craving rehabilitation. They were land speculators looking to get rich, and they soon conspired to devise ways of getting around the five-hundred-acre limit. Once this obstacle was breached, vast plantations were rapidly established. To work these huge tracts most profitably, slaves were required, and so the ban on slavery was simply ignored. With that, Georgia became a place with very much land owned by very few. That few became the wealthy planter class, the gentry, and Georgia became just another American colony—with slaves, and in which inequality was the norm. Oglethorpe returned to Britain in disgust.

Typical of any other English colony in America, Georgia became home to seven broad social categories of resident.

At the very bottom were *enslaved field hands*. Although African slavery existed in all thirteen British American colonies and was legal in them all at the time of the Declaration of Independence in 1776, the greatest number of enslaved field hands were in the South. Climate and topography in the region were conducive to growing large quantities of cash crops, including cotton, rice, and indigo, on very large farms called plantations. The climate and topography of the northern colonies, in contrast, made large-scale agricultural enterprises less practical. Farms up north were mostly family enterprises, the produce of which was consumed for the most part by the family, with surplus, if any, sold on a more-or-less casual basis. The demand for agricultural slave labor was far lower in the North than in the South.

It is true that abolitionism—organized antislavery movements—flourished in the North far more than in the South. Many northerners were opposed to slavery on moral or religious grounds, but it is also a fact that, morality and religion aside, people in the North had little economic incentive to own slaves. Wealthy southerners, however, who owned and operated large plantations, had compelling economic motives for slave ownership. In any event, the northern colonies did not rush to outlaw slavery. Vermont became the first state to ban slavery by law, in 1777, during the revolution. The first antislavery society—the Pennsylvania Society for Promoting the Abolition of Slavery—was founded in 1775, the same year as the American Revolution began, and Pennsylvania's state legislature legally abolished slavery in 1780, as the end of the revolution slowly approached.

Enslaved house servants lived in every colony during the revolutionary era. They worked as cooks, laundresses, maids, manservants, blacksmiths, coopers (barrel makers), and as skilled laborers of various sorts. Socially, they were deemed to be considerably "above" the agricultural slaves. Doubtless, in some cases, their owners even treated them as something akin to "family," and they were, in fact, often addressed as "Uncle" or "Auntie." But they were still owned and enslaved. Like the enslaved field hands, they were either the children of slaves and therefore born enslaved or they were forcibly imported from West Africa and sold in slave markets in the Caribbean or "retailed" in slave markets operated throughout the colonies.

Slaves totaled nearly a quarter of the colonial population in 1760 and, by the end of the revolution, just a bit less. Four-fifths of America's slaves lived in the South, largely near the coast. In part, the coastal concentration occurred because the seaboard topography favored large plantations, whereas the inland regions were mountainous and heavily forested, conditions adverse to sprawling, industrial-scale agriculture. Another reason for the coastal concentration of southern slaves was that those wealthy enough to own them lived in the Tidewater. Those who occupied the Piedmont generally could not afford to buy, let alone maintain, more than one or two slaves at most—if any at all.

All American slaves were black, the first slave "cargo" arriving in Virginia in 1619. Slavery was therefore very long established by the time the Constitution was ratified in 1788, but that document never mentioned the word *slave* or *slavery*. Nevertheless, it both acknowledged and protected the institution until ratification of the Thirteenth Amendment on December 6, 1865. In its unamended form, the Constitution protected the slave trade—that is, the importation of slaves from abroad—for twenty years only, stipulating in Article 1, Section 9, that, starting on January 1, 1808, Congress was free to enact legislation abolishing the international slave trade (although individual states could abolish it at any time before that). This means that the international slave trade generally flourished during the revolution and for many years thereafter.

There was another social category of forced labor or quasi-slavery in colonial and revolutionary society. Those who fell into this category were called *indentured servants*. About a half-million European immigrants came to the thirteen colonies before 1775. Of this number, fifty-five thousand were prisoners—felons or debtors "transported" to America in lieu of being imprisoned in Europe. So, approximately four hundred fifty thousand European immigrants had arrived voluntarily between the seventeenth century and the eve of the revolution. The eminent American labor historian Christopher Tomlins has estimated that nearly half—48 percent—were indentured servants and three-quarters of these were under the age of twenty-five. (During the late eighteenth century, adulthood was generally considered to begin at age twenty-four.) Thus, indentured servitude was quite common in British North America. It was the means by which many poor Europeans funded their passage to the colonies. Their "indenture" was a contract by which the cost of the voyage was underwritten by an employer (or a ship's master, who sold the indenture to an employer on arrival in the colonies) in return for a period of service that was typically four to seven years—although three-year contracts were not uncommon. Once the period of the indenture expired, the person was no longer bound to the original employer and was free to seek employment elsewhere, remain with the original employer on a wage basis (if this was agreeable to both parties), or even set up in business on his or her own. While the indenture was in effect, however, its terms were enforced by law—although not uniformly throughout all colonial courts or the courts of the revolutionary period.

Because indentured servants were, virtually by definition, poor, they occupied a relatively low rung on the ladder of colonial society. But, at its best, indentured servitude was a start on a new life, and little stigma was attached to *having been* indentured. Although most indentured servants were farm laborers or domestic servants, some served their indentures as apprentices to skilled workers and artisans. These individuals received valuable training and experience from their masters and might well become prosperous tradespeople themselves.

While, at any given time, nearly half the European immigrants to the thirteen colonies were indentured servants, they were, by the outbreak of the revolution in 1775, outnumbered by free workers—a category that included those who had never been indentured and those whose indentures had expired. Thus, during the American Revolution, most white wage labor was free.

In strictly economic terms, black slaves made up the mass of the poorest class in colonial society, nearly 25 percent. White indentured servants were certainly poor, but, in contrast to the African-American slaves, their poverty was temporary. After serving their four-to-seven-year indenture, they more often than not went on to become property owners—farmers, merchants, skilled laborers, or artisans. Perhaps only 5 percent of former indentured servants remained truly poor.

Free blacks were not a numerous population group in revolutionary society, but neither were they rare. Generally, neither law nor custom accorded them the same rights as white citizens, but they could own property, and they were free to work a wide range of occupations, both skilled and unskilled.

Farmers were the most numerous social class in colonial and revolutionary America. Their farms were small, and they were operated with family labor—unless the family was too small to supply all the necessary workforce, in which case indentured servants, hired free help, or slaves were employed. In the case of slave labor, small farmers who owned slaves rarely owned more than two. Contrast this with the large planters, who typically owned a hundred or more slaves.

The middling sort was a common phrase in the eighteenth century used to describe the middle class, which was only beginning to emerge as a major social force during the American Revolution. Those of the middling sort included prosperous farmers (below the level of the large plantation but above the level of subsistence), tradespeople, and professionals. Paul Revere, a master silversmith, and Benjamin Franklin, a printer, were of the middling sort, and John Adams, a farmer, was also a lawyer. His farm was not a major source of income for him, but his profession put him firmly among the middling sort. Blacksmiths, coopers, wheelwrights, physicians, and store owners were all in this social category. They were small property owners, typically self-employed, and they lived in a degree of comfort.

At the top of American society during the revolutionary period was the *gentry*. In the context of a nation in the throes of a revolution launched by a declaration that enumerates, among other things, the "self-evident" truths that "all men are created equal" and are "endowed by their creator with certain unalienable rights," the word and concept of a "gentry" sounds a discordant note. Yet revolutionary-era society featured large landowners—George Washington among them—and very prosperous merchants, among whom was John Hancock. People at this station in life assumed that they were rightfully the ruling class. They led the American Revolution itself, and we can assume that their idea of a democratic government was less democratic than our own modern conception. Wealth earned the right to govern, and, in most states for some years after the revolution had ended, wealth earned the right to vote. Most states set a certain level of real property ownership as prerequisite for the franchise.

We should refine the self-conception among the gentry that they were rightfully the ruling class. In fact, they looked upon leadership as a duty, a solemn responsibility, one clearly set out in Luke 12:48: "For unto whomsoever much is given, of him shall much be required." Apart from the kind of service Washington rendered in the American Revolution, members of the gentry routinely served in local political and administrative office, in legal capacities such as magistrate, and in the church as vestrymen.

What Most Revolutionary People Did for a Living

Although most revolutionary-era Americans were either full- or part-time farmers, which generally put them at the lower end of the middling sort, the most dynamic segment of that middle class—and of revolutionary society—was made up of free workers. Whether they were part-time farmers, former indentured servants, apprentices, or established tradespeople, artisans, and professionals, the free workers had, to borrow the phrase Charles Dickens would make famous in the nineteenth century, great expectations. To be sure, many were poor (though not impoverished) and many were destined to fall short of their aspirations. Of the small farmers, some worked productive land productively, while others owned and worked property of low value with low productive potential and therefore barely managed subsistence. Many farmers did not even own the land they worked but were tenants. Among this group, doubtless, a fair number earned too little to support their families adequately.

Of the artisans, the social historian Jackson Turner Main estimated that about a third were poor and remained poor lifelong. This was especially the case among those working in crowded common trades. For example, the demand for woven cloth was plentiful, but so was the supply of weavers. The same was true of tailors, carpenters—a skill many men possessed in sufficient degree to undertake most do-it-yourself repairs—and coopers. Cobblers, who repaired shoes, were always in high demand, but cordwainers, who made new shoes out of new leather, worked in a more competitive and limited market. Most revolutionary Americans believed in repairing their shoes up to the point of disintegration. Nevertheless, many tradespeople saw their incomes rise and grasped opportunities for advancement.

While acknowledging that a significant number of free workers failed to overcome poverty or (more often) semi-poverty, let's focus on the segment of the middling sort who did at least well enough to support themselves and their families and even amass a modest estate. English speakers in both the mother country and revolutionary America would say of such members of the middling sort that they "had a competence." Since at least the early seventeenth century and well into the nineteenth, that phrase meant (according to the *Oxford English Dictionary*) possessing "a sufficiency of means for living comfortably." The once-popular eighteenth-century English poet Edward Young published between 1742 and 1745 the nine parts of a once-popular long poem titled *Night-Thoughts*. In one of its many thousands of lines is this sage observation: "A competence is vital to content." The equation between *a competence* (meaning enough money to live comfortably) and *content* tells us a great deal about life in the eighteenth century, including in revolutionary America. As a noun, *content* denotes a state of *satisfaction*. As an adjective, it more specifically describes a state of peaceful happiness.

Happiness? Now, where else have we seen that word used in connection with the American Revolution?

In 1825, many years after he drafted the Declaration of Independence, Thomas Jefferson explained in a letter to his friend Henry Lee what his aim had been when he wrote the document. He said that he had not been trying to "find out new principles, or new arguments, never before thought of," but, rather, aimed to present "an expression of the American mind, and to give to that expression the proper tone and spirit called for by the occasion. All [the Declaration's] authority rests on the harmonizing sentiments of the day, whether expressed in conversation, in letters, printed essays, or in the elementary books of public right, as Aristotle, Cicero, Locke, Sidney, etc."

Jefferson borrowed heavily from the great English philosopher John Locke, who wrote in his 1689 *Two Treatises of Government* that three "natural" human rights were essential for any just government to uphold: life, liberty, and property. In drawing on this for his list of "unalienable" rights, Jefferson lifted both life and liberty, but he substituted for Locke's "property" the "pursuit of happiness." Ever since, historians and cultural commentators, citing Jefferson's explanation that he was attempting to express "the American mind," have pointed out that (as Jefferson saw it) the "American mind" was bound up in thoughts of happiness, the pursuit of which was therefore very much an aspect of the American psyche or the "American dream."

And so it is.

But words matter, and we need to recognize what the word *happiness* meant in the era of the revolution. For most of us today, *happiness* is merely the state of being happy, and to be happy is to feel pleasure—to be cheerful, merry, jovial, joking, gleeful, carefree, and the like. In Jefferson's era, *happiness* included these meanings, but it more especially connoted the "content" that comes with "having a competence." Happiness was about possessing sufficient means to live comfortably. The word also described what the *Oxford English Dictionary* defined as the "state of pleasurable content of mind, which results from success or the attainment of what is considered good." The Scottish moral philosopher Francis Hutcheson (1694–1746) used "happiness" in this sense in his 1726 *An Inquiry into the Original of Our Ideas of Beauty and Virtue*, writing "that Action is best, which procures the greatest Happiness for the greatest Numbers." This formulation is also found in Joseph Priestley's 1768 *Essay on the First Principles of Government*, a book familiar to Jefferson and, to be sure, most of the other Founding Fathers. It also occurs in *On Crimes and Punishments*, published (in Italian) four years earlier, in 1764, by the great criminologist, jurist, and prison reformer Cesare Beccaria. During the early nineteenth century, the English legal and social reformer Jeremy Bentham (1748–1832) paraphrased it frequently as the basis of his moral utilitarianism, declaring that "the greatest happiness of the greatest number is the foundation of morals and legislation."

That phrase, "the pursuit of happiness," has intrigued almost everyone who has read it since 1776. Many have recognized it as an important clue not only to the American character or the "American mind," but to the nature of the American Revolution—its motives and its objectives. Surely, Jefferson chose the phrase carefully and deliberately. He understood the word *happiness* in its full eighteenth-century sense. He was also careful not to enumerate *happiness* itself as one of the three unalienable rights. Instead, he stipulated only the right to *pursue* happiness. Just as there was no guarantee that a free American worker would achieve "a competence" and enter the solid ranks of the "middling sort," there was nothing more than the right to the opportunity to pursue happiness.

Can it be that Jefferson had uppermost in mind the middling sort when he wrote the Declaration of Independence as an "expression of the American mind"? Certainly, the middling sort was the most fluid and malleable class of revolutionary society. It was the social station most capable of upward progress. In this, it most fully represented the great social promise of an America independent from an Old World, in which social class was very largely a function of birth and therefore all but immutable.

The American middle class had much to gain from independence, which would widen for them the scope of economic and political opportunity. At the same time, they had less to lose from the possible failure of the revolution than those at the very top of American society, the gentry. It was men from this social stratum who occupied the Congress that commissioned Jefferson to draft the Declaration of Independence, and it was these members of the gentry who solemnly subscribed to the oath that concludes the document: "And for the support of this declaration, with a firm reliance on the protection of Divine Providence, we mutually pledge to each other our lives, our fortunes and our sacred honor." They, perhaps more than anyone else in America, appreciated all that was at stake.

Chapter 4

Patriots, Loyalists, Native Americans, and Slaves

IN 1782, A YEAR BEFORE THE REVOLUTION ENDED, CONGRESS ADOPTED *E pluribus unum* as a motto for the United States. Consisting of thirteen letters, it was intended to express the nature of what was then a confederation of thirteen United States: "Out of many, one." It has also been widely interpreted as an expression of the unity of the diverse American people, citizens of a nation that elevated the rights of the individual. As such, the motto was always more an expression of aspiration than of achieved fact. As we saw in Chapter 3, American society was never homogeneous in terms of races, ethnicities, national origin, and socioeconomic station. In this chapter, we will see that, during the period of the revolution, America was also divided in another way, especially with respect to the war.

If revolutionary America was segmented into at least seven broad social categories, it was even more deeply divided into five categories that bore directly on attitudes toward the fight for independence. There were:

1. *Patriots*. Those who favored the revolution. Before July 4, 1776 and the Declaration of Independence, some Patriots supported the revolution for the purpose of gaining from Crown and Parliament a greater degree of colonial liberty and self-determination but drew the line at outright independence as a war aim. Other Patriots championed independence and were willing to fight a revolution to achieve it.

35

2. *Loyalists.* Those who remained loyal to George III, wanted the colonies to remain colonies, and therefore opposed both the revolution and independence.

3. *Neutrals or Undecideds.* Those who, for reasons ranging from indecision to business interests to divided loyalties (often because of family connections), remained on the fence or tried to be neutral in the struggle.

These are three of the categories. Let's pause for some calculations. In 1815, John Adams remarked in a letter to a friend that, during the revolution, he personally estimated that the population was divided roughly in thirds. A third were Patriots (they favored the revolution), a third were Loyalists (who opposed the revolution and wanted to remain attached to Britain), and a third were indifferent. More recent historians have considerably revised Adams's estimate. They calculate that between 20 and 40 percent of Americans were Patriots, passionate about the revolution, and that 15 to 20 percent were Loyalists, who wanted to remain loyal to England and King George III. Most surprisingly, current historians put the majority of revolutionary-era Americans firmly on the fence, figuring that they probably accounted for nearly half the population. These individuals were undecided about both the revolution and its goal of independence. The numbers of Neutrals or Undecideds were almost certainly greatest in the run-up to the war and during its first year, before the Declaration of Independence, but it is likely that their numbers did not decline regularly during the war but ebbed and flowed with the fluid fortunes of the struggle.

The final two categories of the revolutionary era are:

1. *Native Americans.* As in the French and Indian War (1754–1763), some Native American tribes took sides with the French or with the English, while others remained (or tried to remain) neutral. Traditional Euro-American historians tend to portray Indian combatants in both the French and Indian War and the American Revolution as victims or pawns or opportunists. In fact, they were typically quite strategic in the choices they made, siding with the faction that

seemed likely either to cause them the least harm or give them the greater advantage. Throughout much of the French and Indian War, the English denigrated the very idea of Native American alliances and thereby alienated the Indians. This did not necessarily carry over into the American Revolution. Both the British and the Continental Congress set up an "Indian Department" to court alliances. Although the Americans found stolid allies in the Oneida, Mahican (also called Mohican or "Stockbridge Indians"), and Tuscarora, the British forged many more alliances, the most important of which was with the Mohawk tribe, whose warriors were the most respected and feared on the Eastern Seaboard. We also need to note that Native Americans fought one another during the revolution.

2. *Slaves.* Emancipation was a powerful motive for black slaves to join either the American or British armies—both of which also accepted the enlistment of free blacks and even conscripted some of them. Both American and British commanders sometimes recruited slaves not just to build up their armies but to economically weaken masters who supported the opposing side. Patriot commanders recruited slaves of Loyalist masters, while British commanders recruited those belonging to Patriots. In either case, the reward was the promise of freedom—a promise not always kept.

Current research suggests that about nine thousand black soldiers (some free, some enslaved) served in American forces, including state militias, the Continental Army, the Continental Navy, and as privateers (sailors serving aboard vessels operating as state-sanctioned pirates or raiders). About five thousand black troops served in combat roles. The rest served in military support roles, as wagon drivers for the Continental Army, as laborers, or as servants to officers. Some volunteered as spies. If the nine thousand figure is accurate, this means that about 4 percent of the personnel of the Patriot forces in the revolution were black; however, their man-hour presence was greater than their numbers suggest. Black soldiers served an average of 4.5 years, with many serving for the eight-year duration of the revolution. This was about eight times longer than the average service of white troops.

Many more blacks, including over twenty thousand escaped slaves, fought for the British army. They enlisted in response to promises of freedom. Dunmore's Proclamation, issued on November 7, 1775, by John Murray, 4th Earl of Dunmore, royal governor of Virginia, proclaimed martial law and promised freedom to slaves—of Patriot masters only!—who joined the British military. The proclamation prompted eighty thousand to one hundred thousand slaves to flee their masters. Of these, fewer than two thousand joined Dunmore's forces, but the loss of so many slaves nevertheless caused militarily significant material damage to Patriot planters.

The Philipsburg Proclamation, issued by Sir Henry Clinton on June 30, 1779, was a kind of emancipation proclamation, which declared free all slaves in the "United States" who belonged to Patriot owners, whether or not they joined the British forces. Clinton's objective was to weaken the largest possible number of Patriot plantation owners. (In fact, Clinton eventually ordered the return of slaves to their masters; however, after the war ended, some three thousand former slaves were settled by British colonial authorities in Nova Scotia, where they were called Black Loyalists. Some eventually sailed to Sierra Leone, where they founded Freetown, today the capital of that African country.)

Who Were the Patriots?

Native American and African-American motives for siding either with the Patriots or the British were fairly clear-cut. Native American tribes made choices based on which side they believed was more likely to deliver to them the greatest benefit or cause them the least harm. In many cases, they favored the British because they calculated that Britain would prevail in the war and would, after defeating the Patriots, limit white American incursions into Indian lands. Slaves had an even simpler and more urgent motive. They joined whichever side promised them freedom.

More complex than the choices made by Native Americans and African Americans were the decisions made by white colonists. The choice was profoundly consequential: renounce king and country or remain loyal. Renunciation could be seen as striking a blow for liberty or as neither more nor less than an act of treason. Loyalty could be interpreted as British patriotism or acquiescence in tyranny. Moreover, both Patriots and Loyalists risked retribution from their neighbors.

What drove a Patriot's decision?

First, as we will see in Chapter 7, a revolutionary movement was well under way before 1775. Especially in Massachusetts, groups collectively referred to as the Sons of Liberty were active by the mid-1760s, battling the Stamp Act, which we will discuss in Chapter 6. Most of the so-called Founding Fathers of the United States were members of these organizations. For such "original" or "hardcore" Patriots, the decision to separate from the mother country came early and was based on ideological fervor, often fed by reading Enlightenment and contemporary political philosophers. Prior to the outbreak of the revolution, the proportion of those who supported the evolving Patriot cause may have topped 40 percent of the white population—whereas support for the Loyalists hovered around 15 to 20 percent, with the balance undecided or deliberately choosing neutrality.

The Yale historian Leonard Woods Labaree analyzed a voluminous sample of writings from Patriots and Loyalists and concluded that eight personality characteristics figured in their decision to join one side or the other. Patriots tended to be younger men and generally less well established in life than Loyalists, who were older, more fully set-up, and unwilling to risk changing a way of life that was working well for them.

Patriots were strongly convinced that their stance was morally justified, that the rights they embraced were, in truth, both natural and self-evident. In contrast, Loyalists believed that king and Parliament constituted the legitimate government and that the correct moral choice was to support legitimate authority. Patriots believed that they were being denied the rights of Englishmen and, on this ground, justified the physical attacks they made on royal tax collectors, customs inspectors, and the like. Loyalists believed that physically assaulting an officer of the Crown was never justified.

While many Patriots were successful merchants—John Hancock is a good example—their businesses tended to be less dependent on direct financial attachment to the British government and the British Empire than merchants of the Loyalist faction. Patriots also tended to be eager for action. Sensing that the iron was hot, they wanted to strike. In contrast, some Loyalists were passive. They were not actively opposed to independence, but they objected to fighting for it because they believed that independence would, someday, inevitably come of its own accord and in its own good time.

Patriots were confident that a freer system of government would replace the overthrow of British colonial rule, whereas Loyalists believed that destroying the current order, imperfect though it might be, invited a reign of extremism—either anarchy or tyranny. But perhaps the greatest difference was strictly attitudinal. Patriots were the party of hope and optimism, whereas Loyalists pessimistically supported the status quo, embracing the devil they knew while spurning the devil as yet unknown.

WHO WERE THE LOYALISTS?

Let's pursue the contrast between Loyalists and Patriots further, but this time from the Loyalist perspective.

In modern political terms, Loyalists would be identified as conservatives in that they favored the status quo and the established order. It is, however, one of the paradoxes of the American Revolution that a good case can be made that the Patriots were, in fact, *more* conservative than the Loyalists. The Patriots were not so much proposing to fight for radical change as they were proposing to fight to *reclaim* their *ancient* rights as English men and women. In fighting the tyranny of taxation without representation, they were doing nothing more than demanding what the Magna Carta had given all subjects of English rule back in 1215—a voice in government. The Patriots, in effect, were arguing that, by levying taxes pursuant to laws to which the colonial taxpayers had not consented, King George III, his ministers, and Parliament were acting radically—and illegally, and tyrannically. The Patriots, in contrast, were acting conservatively to *restore* long-held rights.

Nevertheless, Loyalists perceived themselves as conservative. Loyalty to the king and the system that went along with the monarchy was the conservative option. This harmonized with the demographics of the Loyalists, who were older, American-born to parents who were American-born, and generally long-established in their towns and localities. They were adherents to principle rather than profound thinkers. Whether or not King George III was a good and just king, he was the king, by divine right and inheritance the embodiment of the legitimate government. That fact overrode all else. It was immoral to oppose the king. One proof of this immorality was the hooliganism of some of the Patriots, who harassed, terrorized, beat, tarred and feathered, and generally abused duly appointed royal officers, such as customs assessors and tax collectors.

Whereas Patriots tended to approach questions of government with cold rationality, for Loyalists a sentimental affinity for Britain was more compelling than any ideological argument. Loyalists had—or felt that they had—more links to the mother country than Patriots had or felt. In a more immediate sense, Loyalists were fearful of the mob rule they believed would inevitably follow hard upon the downfall of the royal colonial order. Where human behavior was concerned, Loyalists were pessimists who expected the worst. In contrast, most Patriots had an optimistic belief in the essential goodness of free people.

Many Loyalists feared the growing diversity of the colonial American population—an influx of people from the lower socio-economic strata during the years preceding the revolution. Feeling themselves under siege by the newcomers, they craved the support of the Crown and Parliament, distant though they were. Besides, a good many Loyalists were old enough to remember the Jacobite rebellion of 1745 in England, in which Bonnie Prince Charlie (Charles Edward Stuart) sought to regain the British throne for his father, James Francis Edward Stuart. The defeat of Jacobites (supporters of the Stuart restoration) by the supporters of the House of Hanover resulted in widespread land seizures, which cast numerous wealthy families into sudden poverty. Those who experienced the collapse of the 1745 rebellion—or who had family members who had experienced it—had little taste for revolution. Nor did they want their established business interests endangered by being cut loose from the British Empire and its network of international trade. In short, whereas the Patriots looked forward to gaining great things from rebellion, the Loyalists feared losing all they had.

Finally, many Loyalists were Loyalist only by default. Some saw Loyalism as the default position, the middle-of-the road orientation. They were not about to let upstart Patriots push them to the sides. Still others were fatalists. Far from opposing independence, they believed it was inevitable—in the fullness of time. They believed that independence would come, but they had no desire to hasten its arrival through violent rebellion.

TIPPING THE BALANCE

Clearly, there were compelling arguments on all three sides of the revolutionary issue: revolt, remain loyal, do nothing. As in all things, few people were without mixed motives and some ambivalence. The Patriots therefore needed a single driving issue to tip the balance in their favor. They found it in that speech Boston lawyer James Otis had delivered on February 24, 1761, in which he coined the phrase "Taxation without representation is tyranny."

For many, this was the catalyst to action. Otis's formula appealed both to the intellect and the emotions. To the question, *Why a revolution?* a Patriot could now answer simply and directly, *Because we must reject taxes imposed by a Parliament in which we the taxpayers are not represented. Taxation without representation is tyranny!* True, Loyalists might counter with the Tory party line that Parliament represented the interests of all subjects of the British Empire. On its face, however, that argument was convenient, weak, and quite unconvincing.

COMMON SENSE

While the Patriot argument prevailed to the extent of starting the revolution with the Battles of Lexington and Concord on April 19, 1775, even the Patriots themselves remained divided on whether to press the fight all the way to independence or seek satisfaction through some political settlement with Crown and Parliament. As we will see in Chapter 12, within the Second Continental Congress, which convened in Philadelphia on May 10, 1775, even as the revolution was already under way, debate raged over the issue of separation from the mother country versus reconciliation with it.

At last, in January 1776, Thomas Paine, a recent immigrant from England, the working-class son of a Norfolk corset maker, anonymously published in Philadelphia a pamphlet titled *Common Sense*. It was the first extended, published argument for American independence. A

brilliant and rousing piece of propaganda, *Common Sense* straightforwardly presented the reasons for breaking free of England. Paine left no
stone unturned. Keenly aware of the anti-Catholic sentiment prevalent
in the colonies, he compared the British monarch to the Pope. More
importantly, he reduced the idea of the hereditary succession of kings to
laughable absurdity, he took on and gutted every popular argument for
reconciliation with Britain, and he clearly laid out the economic benefits
of independence.

While Paine took a kitchen sink approach to his subject, inventory-
ing every conceivable motive for separation, he developed two overriding
points most compellingly. He eloquently argued the inherent superiority of republican government over hereditary monarchy, and he nobly
asserted the urgent justice of recognizing and upholding equality of
rights among all citizens.

But the decisive argument Paine presented was that the American
Revolution was a world event, an epoch-making act in the history of
humanity. It was a struggle in which all peoples everywhere had a stake.
Never before had this view been presented, and Thomas Jefferson would
seize upon it in the summer of 1776 when he drafted the Declaration of
Independence. *Common Sense* was an instant colonial best seller. No fewer
than one hundred twenty thousand copies sold out in three months. In
1805, John Adams wrote, "I know not whether any man in the world has
had more influence on its inhabitants or affairs for the last thirty years
than Tom Paine."

THE PERSISTENCE OF LOYALISM

Common Sense paved the way for the Declaration of Independence and
its ratification, but Loyalism nevertheless persisted throughout the
revolution. The proportion of Patriots to Loyalists remains a subject of
much debate among historians, but most agree that somewhere between
15 and 20 percent of the white male American population during the
revolution were Loyalists. Historians estimate that, even at the height of
the war, probably nearly half of Americans of European ancestry struggled simply to stay out of the conflict. If these estimates are correct, the
American Revolution was fully supported by perhaps 40 percent of the

Thomas Paine, author of *Common Sense* and *The American Crisis*, pictured in an 1876 engraving after a 1792 painting by George Romney.
NATIONAL PORTRAIT GALLERY, LONDON

white male population throughout the thirteen colonies. In raw numbers, a calculation made by historian Paul H. Smith in 1968 puts the Loyalist population at about four hundred thousand out of a total 1780 white population of 2.25 million.

Whatever their exact numbers, the Loyalists made a significant military impact on the revolution. Many were active and vocal in their recruitment efforts, and in some places, especially the backcountry of the Carolinas, Loyalist recruitment far exceeded that of Patriots. Nevertheless, by the time independence was declared on July 4, 1776, the Patriots had purged all royal officials from office throughout every colony. To openly proclaim loyalty to the Crown was now officially forbidden. Loyalists either fled to Canada or to regions within the colonies where Loyalist sentiment was known to be strong. Those who remained in majority-Patriot areas either worked quietly or went to ground until British victories—and there were many, as we will see—prompted them to reemerge. The most committed Loyalists aided the British regulars or joined officially sanctioned Loyalist regiments. Fighting between such regiments and the American forces was often very bitter. In rural and frontier areas, warfare was frequently marked by the kinds of terrorist brutality that characterizes the guerrilla campaigns of civil wars and revolutions.

CHAPTER 5

America Praying, America Thinking

RELIGION PLAYED A MAJOR ROLE IN THE EUROPEAN SETTLEMENT—some would say invasion—of the Americas. The Spanish explorers of the late fifteenth century through the seventeenth century came, as the saying goes, armed with both Bible and sword. Their mission in part was to claim the New World for Christianity and to engage with the Native Americans to save their souls by persuading them to embrace Christ. The French also brought their missionaries but were rather less insistent on Native American conversion than the Spanish. As for the English, the settlement of New England began with the Puritan "Pilgrims," who sought a New Jerusalem in which to establish the purest possible form of Christianity.

Today, the popular historical view is that the eighteenth century, both in America and Europe, brought with it an emphasis on humanism and "reason" that were more or less incompatible with religious faith and downright antithetical to piety based on the letter of the Scripture. At the very least, there is a belief that eighteenth-century Americans did not share the earlier settlers' consuming passion for religion. Certainly, it is true that Puritanism was receding in the eighteenth century, but the Puritans represented only one small vein of Christianity. Based on the rate at which new churches were being built throughout the colonies and on the swelling rolls of church congregations in the years leading up to the American Revolution, there is ample reason to conclude that the level of colonial religious energy was not just high in the eighteenth century, but—at least during that century's first half—on the upswing. Between 1700 and 1740, an estimated 75 to 80 percent of the population regularly worshiped in church. Contrast this with a 2018 Gallup poll, which reported that, in 2017, 38 percent of adults attended religious service weekly or almost weekly, which was down from the 42 percent reported in 2008. When Gallup asked a similar question about attendance in the 1950s, figures reached 49 percent. Contrast figures for church attendance in America's mother country, the UK, during the period 1980 to 2015, where attendance declined from 11.8 percent of the population to just 4.7 percent.

THE GREAT AWAKENING

As the eighteenth century neared its midpoint, a popular Christian revival movement stormed through the English-speaking world, including England's American colonies. It was called the Great Awakening, and it was sparked in 1730s by the rhetorically intense fire-and-brimstone sermons of American-born Congregational pastor Jonathan Edwards. He was the most brilliant of the charismatic evangelical preachers known as the "New Lights." While Edwards's sermons had a strong philosophical foundation, those of his contemporary New Light, George Whitefield, partook of outright theological demagoguery. But both Edwards and Whitfield believed their era was undergoing a "wonderful work" of God.

The wonder was manifested in behavior of congregations that one critic of the Great Awakening, the conservative Christian minister Charles Chauncy, characterized as *"swooning away* and *falling to the Ground* ... bitter *Shriekings* and *Screamings*; *Convulsion-like Tremblings* and *Agitations, Strugglings* and *Tremblings.*" When Edwards, in 1734, delivered to his Enfield, Massachusetts, congregation "Sinners in the Hands of an Angry God," by far the single most famous American sermon ever preached, the result was weeping, fits, and fainting. Congregants seemed to writhe in the agony of the very hellfire Edwards's words so effectively conjured.

It is no accident that such a populist religious revival emerged during the accelerating disintegration of the rigid and learned orthodoxy of the Puritan fathers. This retreat of Puritan domination of both spiritual and political life took place amid the increasing political tensions that foreshadowed the French and Indian War and, ultimately, the American Revolution. In a time of ferment and uncertainty, many people were increasingly receptive to religion—but they wanted something more emotionally satisfying than the Puritanism of their recent ancestors. To those persuaded by the Great Awakening movement, its strong emotion seemed nothing less than evidence of God's approving presence piercing through the clouds of political and moral uncertainty. Inspiration came to one individual after another—and that word, *individual*, took on special importance. Born in the decline of Puritan orthodoxy, in which the faithful had taken their theology from a learned pastor and swallowed it whole and without question, the Great Awakening replaced religious interpretation imposed by external authority with spiritual impulses originating within the soul of each *individual* man or woman of faith.

The movement grew out of—and fed into—the distinctly American belief that the individual is the ultimate arbiter of right and truth. It is the very sentiment Thomas Jefferson incorporated into the Declaration of Independence. In 1789, Jefferson would consult with Abbé Sieyès and the Marquis de Lafayette to create for France's revolutionary National Assembly "The Declaration of the Rights of Man and of the Citizen." But in 1776, he addressed neither "Man" nor "the Citizen," but the universal rights of the *individual*. In the Great Awakening some thirty-five years earlier, the idea was that any individual can have an intimate, direct, unmediated relationship with the Almighty. Indeed, this same basic principle would not only inform the Declaration of Independence but is to be found at the core of the thought of American philosophers considered most typically American—the likes of Ralph Waldo Emerson, Henry David Thoreau, William James, and John Dewey, as well as the nation's "most American" literary authors. Think of Nathaniel Hawthorne, Herman Melville, Walt Whitman, Emily Dickinson, Ernest Hemingway, William Carlos Williams, Norman Mailer, and Jack Kerouac, just to mention a few.

Like the prospect of revolution and independence, the Great Awakening had a dark side, which even such ardent revolutionaries as John Adams feared. They pointed to the danger of individualism leading either to anarchy or, at the opposite end of the spectrum to the antithesis of individualism: mass hysteria, mob rule, demagoguery, cultism, and the abandonment of reason in a kind of ultimate fanatic intolerance. But it was the Great Awakening as the embodiment of a belief that true religion was a new birth, inspired by ideas preached as the Word, that most resonated with the climate in which a revolution was taking shape. It was those who tended to support the evangelical tenor of the Great Awakening—Presbyterians, Baptists, and Methodists—who not only went on to became the majority denominations by the end of the eighteenth century but who also supported the American Revolution. The doubters, those who did not necessarily oppose but who questioned the wisdom of independence, especially Anglicans and Congregationalists, receded in number.

DEISM

In the music of the great German Protestant composer Johann Sebastian Bach, every melody spawns a melody in counterpoint to it. As the Great Awakening swept America, another religious movement found an important audience. Deism, the elite counterpoint to populist evangelicalism, put the emphasis on morality and downplayed, even suppressed, the orthodox Christian view of Christ's divinity. Born of the seventeenth-century Enlightenment and gaining popularity in the eighteenth-century "Age of Reason," Deism did not doubt the existence of God as the uncaused "First Cause." Without question, God was the Creator—but, having created the universe, he does not interfere in it—no more than the clockmaker, having fashioned the timepiece, intervenes in its workings from day to day.

Deism was never a major American religion in terms of numbers of adherents. Its membership was confined to the intellectual elite, which included such prominent founding fathers as Thomas Jefferson and John Adams. In his old age, Jefferson went so far as to cut and paste a standard New Testament into a hand-bound manuscript book he titled *The Life and Morals of Jesus of Nazareth* but that is popularly known as the *Jefferson Bible*. Essentially a condensation, Jefferson's version of the New Testament eliminates all miracles and all references to Christ's divinity. What remains is a moral philosopher suited to live in a Deist universe. And, more importantly, fit for life in a rational American democracy, founded on "unalienable rights" bequeathed to humankind by the "Creator," who, nevertheless, has stepped back from His creation to allow—or require— humanity to create its own destiny.

Religion in the Revolution

For the most part, American religion sanctioned the American Revolution, offering worshippers moral justification for breaking with Crown and Parliament by assuring them that God approved the action. Resistance became righteous. Two hundred eighteen ministers officially served in the Continental Army as chaplains, and many more volunteered to serve as writers for the committees of correspondence—those shadow governments the colonists organized as America verged on revolution. Clergy also featured prominently as members of state legislatures, delegates to constitutional conventions, and members of the Continental Congress. A few ordained ministers served actively, in combat, as Patriot military officers.

Religion also played a part in opposition to the revolution. Most famously, Joseph Galloway, former speaker of the Pennsylvania Assembly and a good friend of Founding Father Benjamin Franklin, so ardently opposed the revolution that he returned to England in 1778. There he wrote a pamphlet, *Historical and Political Reflections on the Rise and Progress of the American Rebellion* (1780), in which he argued that the revolution was mostly a religious dispute between Presbyterians and Congregationalists. While some American ministers preached a Christian duty to oppose tyranny—including the tyranny of King George III—others just as earnestly preached a Christian duty to obey the duly enthroned Christian sovereign no matter what. In the case of the Church of England—still very important in revolutionary-era America—ministers were bound by solemn oath to support the British sovereign, who was also head of the Church.

Yet other denominations, such as the Quakers, were split by the revolution. Although Quaker theology elevated the individual and the moral and religious guidance emanating from the individual soul's "inner light," the Friends' faith was also intensely pacifist. As Quakers saw it, independence was highly desirable and perhaps even a moral duty, but war was absolutely immoral, regardless of cause.

Annuit Coeptis

One of the mottos Congress adopted for the Great Seal of the United States in 1782 is the Latin phrase "Annuit coeptis," which is usually translated as "[God (or providence)] approves (or favors) our under-takings (or commencement)." The fight for independence reinforced in American theology a millennialist strain, the idea that the new nation was providentially destined to be the seat of Christ's kingdom on earth, the New Jerusalem, the platform of the Second Coming. At the very least, an independent America would be the shining "City upon a Hill" Jesus spoke of in his Sermon on the Mount (Matthew 5:14), a model of Christian charity and governance for all the world to see and emulate.

Doubtless, millennialism helped to buoy the revolutionary spirit during the vast stretches of the war when the British seemed poised to crush the Patriot cause. Even more, it added to the optimism that followed the victorious end of the war in 1783. Rarely has a revolution ended with such hopeful emotion.

INTELLECTUAL CURRENTS OF THE REVOLUTION

Colonists were remarkably quick to establish institutions of higher learn-ing in America. Harvard, the first American college, was established in 1636, just sixteen years after the *Mayflower* brought its 102 passengers to New England, where they established Plymouth Colony. The College of William & Mary was founded in Virginia in 1693; St. John's was established at Annapolis, Maryland (as King William's School) in 1696; and Yale, in New Haven, Connecticut, in 1701. Harvard and Yale were founded for the express purpose of ensuring a supply of highly educated Puritan or Congregationalist clergy, but all the early schools were prod-ucts of a drive to maintain in wilderness America a connection with the currents of European Enlightenment thought. This connection would prove a vital source of revolutionary thinking.

THE SCIENTIFIC REVOLUTION

Sir Isaac Newton lived and labored a century before the American Revolution, but his work on gravitation, motion, and light revolution-ized how people think about the universe. This led to questioning how people should relate to their government and their rulers. What Newton convincingly showed the world was that the universe—reality—was governed by natural laws that needed neither preachers, nor popes, nor scripture, nor secular princes to explain. Mathematics accounted for it all. If the natural laws govern such basic phenomena as gravitation, motion, and the behavior of light itself (the very first thing God created!), was it not possible that natural laws could be discovered to govern the morality, behavior, affairs, and government of people?

We know that John Locke, the single greatest influence on Thomas Jefferson as he drafted the Declaration of Independence, was a friend of Newton's and a frequent correspondent with him on matters of philosophy. Locke was chiefly a social and political philosopher, but he was by training a physician, and his work on epistemology (the study of the nature of knowledge itself) made him highly receptive to Newton's revolutionary outlook. Clearly, he saw a connection between natural physical laws and natural laws that endowed human beings with the right to life, liberty, and property. Moreover, Locke felt himself humbled by Newton's insights. He embraced the process of scientific inquiry founded on healthy doubt and skepticism. These two qualities, Locke was convinced, made it critically important to create governments that gave individuals as much freedom as possible—especially freedom of thought. No one authority possessed the secrets to creating a better society; therefore, people needed to be free to think about this and to discover for themselves the best ways of organizing nations and improving civilization.

To be sure, the likes of Benjamin Franklin, Thomas Jefferson, John Adams, James Madison, and Alexander Hamilton were well versed in the works of Isaac Newton directly, but they may have been even more profoundly influenced by Newton's revolution in thought via Locke and other social philosophers who adopted science-based methods of skeptical inquiry.

A REVOLUTION IN THE AMERICAN MIND
"The Revolution was in the minds of the people, and this was effected, from 1760 to 1775, in the course of fifteen years before a drop of blood was drawn at Lexington," John Adams recalled in a letter to Thomas Jefferson, written on August 24, 1815.

What went through those American minds?

The European Enlightenment began in the seventeenth century and was carried through the eighteenth. Generally speaking, it applied scientific reasoning—as exemplified in the work of Isaac Newton and others—not just to science (or "natural philosophy," as it was then called) but also to politics, government, and even religion. Thanks largely to the colleges established so early in America, knowledge of the European Enlightenment quickly came to the colonies, creating what the prominent modern American historian James MacGregor Burns (1918–2014) called the American Enlightenment, a movement that created the broader intellectual context of the American Revolution by encouraging not just philosophical contemplation but the application of rational philosophy to the reform of life and government in America.

Education in eighteenth-century America, which had been instrumental in importing the Enlightenment, transformed first and foremost ideas of education itself. Religion was still important in college, but so was the inculcation of religious tolerance. What we think of today as the curricula of a liberal education were introduced in the run-up to the revolution. Students were exposed to literature, art, and music as well as science and mathematics. Moreover, programs of study became increasingly nondenominational as "moral philosophy" replaced theology. Early leaders and advocates of the American Enlightenment were the presidents of the first colleges: Jonathan Edwards (College of New Jersey, which became Princeton), Thomas Clap (Yale), and Ezra Stiles (also Yale). Political thinkers—and doers—of the American Enlightenment included such Founding Fathers as John Adams, James Madison, Thomas Paine, George Mason, Ethan Allen, and Alexander Hamilton. Two prominent members of this august group, Benjamin Franklin and Thomas Jefferson, were also "natural philosophers"—scientists. Franklin was a pioneer in the field of electricity, and Jefferson was a skilled amateur naturalist as well as an avid reader of scientific works. He was also a great educator, who not only became principal founder of the University of Virginia, but, a remarkable architect, designed its buildings as well as its first curricula. Other American scientists were active during the revolutionary period. William Smith, an Episcopal priest as well as founder of Washington College (Chestertown, Maryland) and St. John's College (which developed out of King William's School in Annapolis) and first provost of the College of Philadelphia (predecessor to the University of Pennsylvania), made important astronomical observations. David Rittenhouse became even more famous as an astronomer and mathematician, as well as a maker of scientific instruments. Benjamin Rush, a prominent Son of Liberty and a signer of the Declaration of Independence, was an eminent physician, who pioneered important areas of theory and was America's first explorer of the field of psychiatry. During the revolution, he served as surgeon general of the Continental Army. The great American painter Charles Willson Peale not only fought in the revolution but was an early eminent practitioner of natural history in America, organizing the first US scientific expedition in 1801 and founding "Peale's American Museum," which featured a vast array of botanical, zoological, and archaeological specimens, many of which Peale himself had collected.

These were the makers of the American Revolution. They were not just soldiers. They were not just politicians, activists, and rabble-rousers. They were men of the Enlightenment. For them, the revolution began in the mind, and that revolution would have religious, philosophical, and scientific dimensions. The political and economic independence they envisioned was just the beginning. Independence would, as they saw it, both enable and require a much broader and deeper revolution of thought, society, and civilization. America was going to be a great moral, intellectual, and political power in the world.

CHAPTER 6

King and Parliament

"AN OLD, MAD, BLIND, DESPISED, AND DYING KING" IS HOW THE POET
Percy Bysshe Shelley described George III in 1819. It is true, by then he
was deep in the throes of porphyria, a genetic blood disorder in which
compounds called porphyrins build up in the system, causing symptoms
including skin ulcers, body aches, abdominal pain, brown or purple or blue
urine, and a host of neurological problems, such as acute anxiety, confusion,
hallucinations, and paranoia—madness, in short. Far earlier in life, well,
things had been better for George III—at least physically. But he showed
so little promise that the noted British historian J. H. Plumb remarked of
him, "Had he been born in different circumstances, it is unlikely that he
could have earned a living except as an unskilled laborer." His exasperated
mother, Princess Augusta of Saxe-Gotha-Altenburg, was forever scolding
him in her German-accented English: "George, be a king!"

And he became one in 1751, when his father, Frederick, the Prince
of Wales, heir apparent to the throne, was struck in the head by a badly
but powerfully served tennis ball. Two weeks later, Frederick was dead,
and son George suddenly found himself next in line behind his uncle,
the reigning George II. The uncle's death, on October 25, 1760, thrust
twenty-two-year-old George III onto the throne of the United Kingdom.

Understandably, perhaps, the insecure young king was anxious to prove
himself worthy of his office. Eager to raise money to cover the high cost of
the combined French and Indian War and Seven Years' War, he rushed to
revive the long-dormant Navigation Acts. They were mostly laws forcing
the colonies to trade exclusively with the mother country. In need of cash,

the new king now wanted the Navigation Acts fully enforced. This suddenly drew the curtain on the period in colonial history modern scholars have called the era of "salutary neglect," a time when mother country and colony both got along because neither bothered the other.

MAKING THE COLONIES PAY

To enforce the Navigation Acts, king and Parliament revived another law, passed in 1755 but as yet unused, authorizing royal customs officers to issue "writs of assistance" to local colonial authorities, compelling their cooperation in apprehending smugglers and others who evaded the Navigation Acts. This arrangement outraged colonists, especially since a writ of assistance enabled officials to search warehouses and even private homes at will and without a court order.

Given the menace of the ongoing French and Indian War, any thought of actively resisting the government's actions was suppressed, and young George III reveled in having found a source of revenue from the colonies. His quasi-official prime minister at the time, William Pitt the Elder, counseled the king that the Navigation Acts were too harsh and would stir disloyalty. George impatiently responded by engineering Pitt's replacement by the ultra-conservative Lord Bute, who pleased the king but alienated Parliament and was himself forced to resign in 1763.

By this time, the French and Indian War was near its end. Ending with it was the colonies' principal incentive to meekly accept the newly enforced laws. George III now found himself in a position from which he was obliged to *earn* colonial loyalty. But instead of rendering to his colonies benevolent leadership, he and his government brought them chaos. Bute was succeeded as acting prime minister by Lord Grenville, who was rapidly replaced by the Earl of Rockingham, who was quickly supplanted by the return of Pitt the Elder, who promptly descended into insanity, leaving Britain without a prime minister for most of 1766–1768, an interval during which simmering colonial discontent, unattended, began to reach a boil.

At last, in 1770, George III and parliamentary conservatives settled on Sir Frederick North, a politician compliant with the king's wishes but soon heartily despised by liberals in England and just about everyone in the American colonies. Lord North aided, abetted, and executed every one of the king's initiatives intended to make the colonies pay for their defense while sacrificing more and more of their self-determination. Moreover, as mentioned in Chapter 2, the forthcoming series of oppressions unfolded against the backdrop of the "Proclamation Line," created by the royal proclamation of October 7, 1763, which set the limit to western colonial settlement at the Appalachian Mountains. An effort to placate the Indians and thereby end Pontiac's War, which followed the conclusion of the French and Indian War, the Proclamation Line stirred rebellious disobedience among colonial settlers, many of whom defied the limit everywhere along the trans-Appalachian frontier. Those settlers who willfully crossed the line were often attacked by Indians. When that happened, they called on royal authorities for military aid—only to be rebuffed as violators of a royal proclamation. This even further alienated those who lived on the frontier, a region traditionally conservative and therefore customarily loyal to king and country.

The Grenville Acts

Before he left the government and while the Proclamation crisis boiled over, George Grenville, acting in his capacity as first lord of the treasury and chancellor of the exchequer proposed to his sovereign a series of colonial taxation acts. Unlike the Navigation Acts, which were existing laws resur-

As prime minister of Great Britain from 1770 to 1782, Frederick North, 2nd Earl of Guilford, better known as Lord North, implemented many of the colonial taxation policies that led to revolution. The portrait is by Nathaniel Dance-Holland. NATIONAL PORTRAIT GALLERY, LONDON

rected from dormancy, these so-called Grenville Acts, passed by Parliament in 1764, were brand new. They imposed substantial import and export duties and were piled onto both the Navigation Acts and onto another revived set of early eighteenth-century revenue laws, the Acts of Trade. The taxes these imposed came at an especially bad time for the colonies, which were suffering through a post–French and Indian War depression.

As discussed in Chapter 4, while the taxes were burdensome, the colonists did not object to taxation as much as they did to what Boston lawyer James Otis had called, in 1761, "taxation without representation." Although George III desperately wanted the taxes and desperately pushed the taxes, only Parliament had the power to actually tax the British subjects it represented. But the colonists, though certainly British subjects, had no voice in Parliament. This, Otis, declared, made taxation "tyranny." Now, back in 1761, when he first said "Taxation without representation is tyranny," there were relatively few colonial taxes. Four years later, after passage of the Grenville Acts, there were many. Otis's electrifying phrase took on new and more urgent meaning.

Just consider how overwhelming the taxes that had been reintroduced or newly introduced in 1764 were. The Acts of Trade alone encompassed the Wool Act (protecting the British domestic wool industry by prohibiting the export of wool products from the colonies), the Naval Stores Acts (reserving many colonial raw materials—such as timber—for the exclusive use of the Royal Navy), the Hat Act (barring intercolonial export of hats), the Molasses Act (high duties on sugar and molasses imported into the colonies from French and Dutch islands), and the Iron Acts (fixing Britain as the only legal market for colonial iron).

Added to these were the new Grenville Acts, which included the Sugar Act (raising duties on foreign refined sugar and other goods imported from countries other than Britain) and the Currency Act (among other things, creating a new vice-admiralty court, which gave royal officials, not locally elected colonials, legal jurisdiction over all matters of taxation and customs).

The first of the Grenville Acts prompted a Boston town meeting on May 24, 1764. It proposed that the colonies respond to the new laws with a Non-Importation Agreement, boycotting most English goods.

STAMPS AND QUARTERING

The Non-Importation boycott made a significant dent in British trade. That was serious enough, but what George and his ministers failed to heed was the ominous signal the boycott sent. It was not just the act of a rebellious colony, but of a group of colonies acting in union. Instead of taking heed, however, and concluding that the American colonies were evolving into a nation, Parliament passed on March 22, 1765, the most egregious of the Grenville Acts: the Stamp Act.

This legislation taxed virtually all colonial printed material—the very vehicles of legal, commercial, intellectual, and, above all, political communication in the colonies. The law required that a royal tax stamp be affixed to newspapers, legal documents, and even dice and playing cards. Adding outrage upon outrage, the Stamp Act had the specific purpose of defraying the cost of colonial military defense. This included maintaining a standing British army in the colonies. With the French and Indian War over, nobody in British America wanted "redcoats" in their midst. Their presence seemed the very embodiment of tyranny—all the more because they were being asked to pay for it.

The Stamp Act moved the colonies to organize more thoroughly than ever before. This prompted one liberal member of Parliament, Isaac Barré, to refer to the colonial activists as "these sons of liberty." The name stuck, as the organizers of resistance and rebellion adopted it to describe themselves. Samuel Adams, formerly a Boston brewer and now a bankrupt merchant and fiery political agitator, organized a group he proudly dubbed the Sons of Liberty. Its members set out to harass and, frankly, to terrorize the royal stamp agents, officials who had the unenviable job of selling tax stamps and enforcing their use.

Adams's Sons of Liberty went about their mission so enthusiastically that every single stamp agent they confronted resigned on the spot. Sam Adams's second cousin John Adams wrote up a Stamp Act protest document for his hometown of Braintree, Massachusetts, titled "Instructions to the Town of Braintree." It was circulated far beyond the small town and became the model other New England communities followed to protest the legislation.

Thanks to both Adamses, local protests quickly morphed into a well-coordinated movement throughout the colonies. Down in Virginia, Patrick Henry, delegate to the colony's House of Burgesses, introduced into that body in 1765 the seven "Virginia Resolves." Number seven, the most important, proclaimed that Virginia—by right—enjoyed total legislative autonomy and was not subordinate to Parliament. When some conservative delegates shouted in response to Henry's reading of the Resolves "Treason! Treason!" the fiery orator reportedly replied: "If this be treason, make the most of it." Passed on May 30, 1765, the Virginia Resolves were *a* declaration of independence before *the* Declaration of Independence.

In 1765, along with the Stamp Act, Parliament passed the Mutiny Act, which included a provision immediately infamous throughout the colonies: the quartering of British soldiers in private houses. When colonists dodged the provision by simply denying its application to Britain's *overseas* colonies, Parliament passed the Quartering Act. It did repeal the requirement that private householders billet troops, but it instead required colonial authorities to furnish barracks and supplies for British troops at the expense of the colonists. The next year, the act was amended to require that taverns and inns board troops—and then seek reimbursement from their local colonial governments. Colonial legislatures simply refused to allocate funds for the support of redcoats.

THE STAMP ACT CONGRESS CONVENES

Refusing to allocate funds for quartering was a significant act in defiance of British authority. For James Otis, however, it was not defiance enough. He proposed calling all colonies to a Stamp Act Congress, which convened from October 7 through October 25, 1765, and drew delegates from South Carolina, Rhode Island, Connecticut, Pennsylvania, Maryland, New Jersey, Delaware, and New York—Virginia, New Hampshire, North Carolina, and Georgia declining to attend. Meeting in New York City, they drafted a fourteen-point Declaration of Rights and Grievances, the most important of which were the assertions that Parliament had no right to tax the colonies and that the royal vice-admiralty courts had no jurisdiction in the colonies. The declaration was sent to George III and to Parliament.

William Pitt led a parliamentary movement to repeal the Stamp Act, even as every colony except Georgia simply refused to enforce the act.

With his customary uncomprehending bluster, Lord Grenville called for the deployment of regular troops to enforce the Stamp Act. Benjamin Franklin, who had served in the Pennsylvania Assembly and as colonial postmaster general for the Crown, was now living in London as a commercial agent for Pennsylvania. He persuaded the many British politicians and officials with whom he was on most friendly terms that the colonies should not be forced to pay the Stamp Tax. He further warned that military intervention would provoke outright rebellion. On March 18, 1766, Parliament repealed the Stamp Act.

Whatever celebration the repeal occasioned in America was short-lived. On the very day of the repeal, Parliament passed the Declaratory Act, which declared that Parliament's authority to make laws binding on the American colonies was absolute and beyond dispute.

THE TOWNSHEND ACTS

In 1766, Charles Townshend replaced Lord Grenville as chancellor of the exchequer. Moreover, when William Pitt suffered a total mental collapse late in the year, Townshend also assumed control of the Cabinet. Where Pitt had been liberal, Townshend was conservative, and he quickly ushered through Parliament the three so-called Townshend Acts.

The Revenue Act levied duties on lead, glass, paint, tea, and paper imported into the colonies, stipulating that the revenues would be used to defray military expenses in the colonies and pay the salaries of royal colonial officials. This meant that colonial legislatures were powerless to cut off funding for Crown officials, who were, in effect, rendered independent of the will of the local population.

The second of the Townshend Acts created a small army of new royal customs commissioners empowered to seize merchant vessels and goods they judged noncompliant with customs regulations. The commissioners levied huge punitive fines, a third of which went to the royal treasury, a third to the royal governor of the colony, and a third to the commissioner who had made the seizure. Tyranny had turned to corruption. The third

Townshend Act was an order suspending the New York Assembly when it refused to comply with the Quartering Act.

Townshend's legislation revived the colonial anti-British boycott and occasioned the "Massachusetts Circular Letter." Drafted by James Otis and Sam Adams, the letter was circulated in February 1768 to the twelve other colonies. It contained three explosive propositions: First, the Townshend Acts were "taxation without representation"; second, all governors and judges *must* be answerable to colonial legislatures, not Parliament or the Crown; and, third, American colonists not only lacked parliamentary representation, they could *never* be properly represented in Parliament.

That third proposition was the most revolutionary of the three. If taxation without representation was tyranny *and* representation was a practical impossibility, then there was no alternative for the colonies but independence. With this, the "Circular Letter" ended by calling on Americans to draw up plans for coordinated resistance. To this, the royal governor of Massachusetts responded by summarily dissolving, for sedition, the colony's General Court. No matter. The letter had been sent, and New Hampshire, New Jersey, Connecticut, and Virginia announced their endorsement of it while the Massachusetts House of Representatives voted overwhelmingly against rescinding a single word of it.

A POWERFUL PERSONAL APPEAL

During the revolutionary period, American religion and thought, we observed in Chapter 5, focused most intensely on the individual. As powerful as the "Massachusetts Circular Letter" was, perhaps even more compelling was the work of Pennsylvania political thinker John Dickinson. His *Letters from a Farmer in Pennsylvania to Inhabitants of the British Colonies* was published serially during 1767 and 1768 in the *Pennsylvania Chronicle*, a popular colonial periodical. Moreover, the letters were copied and widely republished, both in America and in Great Britain.

Dickinson wrote in the first person, as a farmer speaking to other simple folk. He argued straightforwardly that Parliament had no right to tax the colonies solely for revenue. He argued that suspending the New York Assembly had been a tyrannical blow against liberty. And when it came to taxation without representation, Dickinson made an especially compelling argument. It was not only wrong, he wrote, it was actually against *British* law. Thus, Dickinson, in a form that everyone could understand, made clear that Parliament's revenue laws were not just an affront to colonial rights, they were an attack on the rights of all English people, wherever they lived.

Dickinson's *Letters* galvanized an independence movement throughout the colonies, but, even more important, the publication generated widespread support, both among the British public and liberal-leaning politicians, for a substantially liberalized colonial policy. Indeed, so widely did the *Letters* circulate that they prefigured what Jefferson would set out to do in the 1776 Declaration of Independence. They presented the American colonial situation to the entire world.

Driven by popular opinion—and especially intense political pressure from London merchants suffering under the effects of the colonial boycott—Parliament repealed all of the Townshend Acts on April 12, 1770.

Well, not quite all.

King George III stood firm in his insistence that there must always be at least *one* tax, if only to maintain the principle that the Parliament had the right to tax the colonies. In this case, that one tax was on tea, the iconic beverage of all Britons, whether they lived in London, England, or Boston, Massachusetts.

CHAPTER 7

From Massacre to Tea Party

ARGUABLY, THE PEOPLE OF THE FRONTIER HAD GREATER REASON TO rise up against the mother country than those in the more settled parts of colonial America. Yet, despite the Proclamation Line, most frontier folk, angry as they might be with George III and Parliament, felt a greater sense of alienation from the *colonial* governors and *colonial* legislators. The colonial ruling class were sons of the seaboard, well-established, and prosperous. It seemed that they cared very little about the uncouth people of the frontier. So, instead of protesting the lack of parliamentary representation in London, Herman Husbands, a western North Carolinian, decided to take militant steps to protest the lack of representation in the colony's own assembly. In 1768 or thereabouts, Husbands organized a combination protest and vigilante band he called the Regulators.

It seemed to Husbands and his followers that colonial officials did not care about the frontier until people in those parts failed to pay their colonial taxes. When western North Carolinians were harassed by tax agents, the Regulators protested. When the assembly paid no attention, Husbands led seventy Regulators on April 8, 1768, into Hillsboro, North Carolina, and reclaimed a horse seized for nonpayment of taxes. Eager to make clear, both to the people and the powers that be, just who committed this act of rough justice, the Regulators shot up the home of the local tax collector, Edmund Fanning. Although the man was collecting taxes for the benefit of the colony, he was, as it so happened, a Crown official. In effect, therefore, the Regulators and the emerging Patriots appeared to be on the same side. When some seven hundred—not just seventy—

Regulators subsequently liberated their leaders from arrest, William Tryon, the colony's royal governor, responded in September 1768 by personally leading fourteen hundred colonial troops (loyal to the Crown) against what had now swelled to an army of some thirty-seven hundred Regulators. This could well have exploded into a genuine battle, but the Regulators, while they outnumbered Tryon and his men, recognized that they were badly outgunned and withdrew. They continued committing acts of general rowdyism until 1771, when they waylaid and assaulted Fanning. After horsewhipping him, the Regulators ran him out of town and burned his house to the ground. In response, the North Carolina Assembly authorized action against the Regulators, whom they accused of treason. The result was the Battle of Alamance, fought near Great Alamance Creek in modern Alamance County, North Carolina, on May 16, 1771. Governor Tryon's force of one thousand members of the North Carolina Provincial Militia were outnumbered two-to-one. Nevertheless, it was the Regulators who backed down after a brief but deadly skirmish. The militia lost between nine and twenty-seven killed, with sixty-one wounded; the Regulators lost nine killed in combat and an unknown number of wounded. Several Regulator leaders were arrested, and seven were tried and subsequently hanged. Most of the rest of the Regulators rode west and settled on the far side of the Appalachians.

THE REVOLUTION DOWNTOWN

Doubtless, a betting man in 1771 would have found that the odds favored the outbreak of general uprising sooner rather than later. But he would have almost certainly put his money on the war's breaking out along the frontier. He should have looked back to the east instead.

It was a cold, bleak, snow-spitting early evening along the Boston wharf on March 5, 1770, when an off-duty British soldier dropped by Grey's ropewalk, a maker of ship's ropes, looking for a part-time job. Work was scarce in a town that could not seem to shake off the post–French and Indian War economic depression. Times were as gloomy as the weather, and when the small crowd milling about the ropewalk saw a "lobsterback"—that's what Bostonians scornfully called the British soldiers, whose backs were often marked by the angry red welts of the whips that were routinely used to discipline them—trying to cadge employment that, they felt, should go to a Boston workingman, the crowd taunted the soldier, threatened him with violence, and intimidated him into fleeing the waterfront.

Not content with their small victory, the mob began roaming the streets, apparently in search of more trouble. They found it at around nine o'clock. About sixty restless Boston men approached Hugh White, the redcoat sentry guarding the Customs House. Some in this crowd had just heard the story of how an apprentice named Edward Garrick had been sent to demand from a local British army officer payment for periwig the officer had ordered. When Garrick demanded that White take him to his commanding officer, the sentry replied by smashing him in the face with the butt of his musket. Another soldier chased the injured Garrick away at the point of a bayonet.

So, the mob, looming around White, started painfully pelting him and other troops with ice balls. Soon, British officers arrived, but could gain control over neither the angry mob nor their own men. At last royal army captain Thomas Preston organized a hasty detail of seven soldiers to rescue White. Paying the mob no heed, Preston ordered White to fall in with the seven-man detail he led. White obeyed, but the Bostonians refused to give up. The mob surged forward to block White's departure.

At this, Captain Preston ordered his troops to form a skirmish line where they stood. This ratcheted up the tension considerably. The Bostonians began hurling harder and harder ice balls at a redoubled tempo. They shouted taunts and curses, and they even dared the soldiers to open fire on them.

Preston summoned to his assistance Justice of the Peace James Murray, asking him to read the Riot Act to the colonial hooligans. The mob responded to the impromptu lecture with a veritable storm of fresh ice balls. Then someone in the crowd hurled the heavy wooden club he was carrying, aiming it straight at Murray. The justice of the peace proved agile. He ducked, and the club found its mark on Hugh Montgomery, a private in his majesty's army. The impact knocked him to the ground. But he recovered quickly, scrambled to his feet, cocked his musket, and fired off a round.

Whether by design or poor marksmanship, the shot went wild, hitting no one. But the mere fact of it moved one Richard Palmes, merchant, to swing the heavy billet of wood he held. Montgomery responded with a bayonet thrust, which sent Palmes running.

The germ of battle had been loosed.

Private Matthew Killroy leveled his musket against Edward Langford and Samuel Gray, the latter responding with a cross between a plea and a dare: "God damn you, don't fire!"

Killroy fired, and a musket ball tore into Samuel Gray's skull.

At nearly the same moment, another musket spoke. The jittery soldier must have accidentally loaded two balls at once because it was two rounds that smashed through the chest of Crispus Attucks, a forty-year-old fugitive slave from Framingham.

Attucks fell over and died instantly. Although hit before him, Gray did not die until later; so, we remember as the first man killed in the run-up to the American Revolution Crispus Attucks, of a race that would receive no tangible benefit from the coming fight for independence. His death was followed by three more, two killed instantly and a third mortally wounded before Preston barked out *"Don't fire!"* and rapidly walked before his men, knocking each of their muskets skyward.

Paul Revere's 1770 hand-colored engraving of the Boston Massacre of March 5, 1770. Samuel Adams commissioned the work as part of a propaganda campaign designed to ignite a revolution. SOTHEBY'S VIA WIKIMEDIA COMMONS

Bostonian Crispus Attucks, believed to have been a fugitive slave, was first among those killed in the Boston Massacre (March 5, 1770) and is therefore traditionally honored as the first casualty of the American struggle for independence. The signature is probably not authentic, and there is no certain evidence that the likeness is indeed that of Attucks. BRIDGEWATER STATE COLLEGE ARCHIVE, BRIDGEWATER, MASSACHUSETTS

COLONIAL JUSTICE

With six of his men, Captain Thomas Preston was indicted for murder by a Massachusetts colonial court. As Sam Adams gleefully stirred Boston's passion for vengeance, two local attorneys, John Adams and Josiah Quincy, volunteered to defend the accused. A colony demanding justice from king and Parliament, Adams believed, must itself offer justice to all accused. Adams and Quincy risked their reputations and their livelihoods to earn acquittal of Preston and four of his men on the grounds of self-defense. The Boston jury found two others guilty of the lesser crime of manslaughter, and they were sentenced to nothing more than discharge from military service with a punitive brand on the thumb.

TEA TIME

Sam Adams was not happy. His propaganda efforts aimed at turning the "Boston Massacre" (as Sam Adams labeled it) into a revolution were thoroughly diluted by the verdicts in the trials of the soldiers and their captain. Besides, in April 1770, the Townshend Acts were repealed. Would, then, the fires of revolution gutter out?

The repeal of the Townshend Acts did not include the tax on tea, to which George III and the conservative wing of Parliament desperately clung. The persistence of this tax might have caused little or no trouble. After all, as everyone knew, the tax could be avoided simply by buying tea smuggled from Dutch sources. As Lord North became aware of this

The Bostonians Paying the Excise-man, or Tarring and Feathering, a 1774 mezzotint attributed to Philip Dawe and published in London. Note the tea being forced into the tax collector's mouth. JOHN CARTER BROWN LIBRARY

dodge, he pushed through Parliament a new piece of legislation. The thing was, while the British East India Company had a monopoly on tea imports into the colonies, the enterprise was so poorly run that it kept losing money. The company deserved to go broke and get out of business. Doubtless it would have if Lord North had not been in bed with East India Company directors and investors. He wanted to help the ailing company. So, he devised a way to force the colonists to buy East India Company tea instead of the smuggled Dutch brand. North recognized that the East India Company paid *two* taxes on tea, one when the product landed in Britain, and another when it landed in America. His brainchild, the Tea Act of May 10, 1773, abolished the tax on importation into Britain but retained the duty due on tea landed in America. This would allow the British East India Company to lower its prices below those of the Dutch product. A cynical bean counter, North reasoned that the colonists would buy whichever tea was cheaper—namely the East India Company variety. He rejoiced in having found a way to stave off colonial rebellion while also extending a helping hand to the East India Company.

As it turned out, North badly misjudged and miscalculated. Under the new Tea Act, the East India Company did not wholesale its shipment to colonial merchants but sold exclusively to royally designated consignees in the ports of New York, Charleston, Philadelphia, and Boston. Ordinary American merchants were simply cut out of the trade.

Sam Adams and his Sons of Liberty saw a fresh opportunity. Their campaign of intimidation against the royal stamp agents had been instrumental in killing the Stamp Act. Now, the Committees of Correspondence—the activist organizations that coordinated antigovernment operations throughout the colonies—sent men to threaten the tea consignees. Like the stamp agents, these officials folded quickly under physical threat—at least in Philadelphia, New York, and Charleston. Add to this the refusal of American captains and harbor pilots to handle East India Company cargo, and tea ships were forced to turn back to London from Philadelphia and New York without unloading. In Charleston, tea *was* unloaded—but then immediately impounded in a warehouse, where it was stored until 1776, when the Continental Congress auctioned it off to raise money for the war.

Boston was a different story. When three ships landed at Boston Harbor, Committee of Correspondence men halted their unloading and demanded their immediate return to England. In response, the royal governor of Massachusetts, Thomas Hutchinson, refused to issue the permits necessary to release the ships from the harbor. They were thus caught betwixt and between, unable to unload but unable to leave Boston.

Sam Adams refused to take this as a defeat. He convened a Committee of Correspondence meeting on December 16, 1773, and drew up a plea to Governor Hutchinson for the issue of the exit permits. A crowd of more than seven thousand swarmed Boston's Old South Church, anxiously awaiting Hutchinson's reply. As Adams believed it would, word reached the church that the royal governor was refusing to yield.

At this, Samuel Adams ascended the pulpit of Old South.

"This meeting can do nothing more to save the country," he declared.

It was a dramatic pronouncement and a prearranged signal. No sooner was it uttered than what sounded like a Mohawk war cry arose from the crowd outside the church. As directed by the Committee of Correspondence, three "troops" of colonists, fifty men in each troop, their faces having been painted to look like those of Mohawk warriors, stalked off to Griffin's Wharf. Here they climbed into small boats and rowed swiftly out to the three tea ships riding at anchor in Boston Harbor.

Each troop boarded one ship. The crews onboard offered neither protest nor resistance. As they peacefully looked on, the faux Mohawks hurled into the harbor 342 tea chests valued at a total of £10,000 (almost $1.7 million today). This done, they climbed back into their boats and rowed to the Boston shore.

IMPACT

Very few nonviolent demonstrations in history can match the extraordinary effect of the Boston Tea Party. Thanks to the remarkably close coordination of the networks connecting Committee of Correspondence and Sons of Liberty chapters throughout the colonies, the event was quickly broadcast far beyond Boston Harbor. Revolution and independence suddenly became far more plausible considerations—and not just in American communities but in Parliament as well. There, liberal voices rose to move that all taxes and duties and trade restrictions be lifted from the American colonies.

But the conservative voices were even louder, led by George III himself, who warned, "We must master them or totally leave them to themselves and treat them as aliens." It was as if the king were declaring a war for independence. Certainly, his conservative cohorts in Parliament acted as if war was what they wanted.

INTOLERABLE ACTS OF COERCION

The Boston Tea Party provoked Parliament to pass a set of what the MPs themselves dubbed the "Coercive Acts." The colonists changed the adjective to "Intolerable." The new legislation, which came into effect in May and June of 1774, closed the port of Boston. That was just the first thing. The Intolerable Acts stifled representative government in Massachusetts by ordering that all members of the upper chamber of the Massachusetts Assembly would from now on be appointed by the Crown rather than elected by the colonists. In fact, most elected Massachusetts officials would henceforth be replaced by royal appointees, either chosen directly by the Crown or by the royal governor. Town meetings throughout the colony were to be restricted to just one yearly, and the administration of justice by colonial magistrates would be severely curtailed, with all capital cases to be tried in England or in another colony—anywhere but

Massachusetts. Adding tyranny upon tyranny, the old Quartering Act was revived and extended in preparation for the permanent quartering of British troops in the city of Boston.

After approving passage of the Coercive Acts, the king appointed French and Indian War veteran General Thomas Gage to serve both as royal governor of Massachusetts and as commander of all British forces in America. Not only, then, did the king install a new royal governor for Massachusetts, he made its royal government effectively a military government. It was a short step away from a declaration of martial law.

It is important that Crown and Parliament singled out Massachusetts and, in particular, Boston for punishment. Their intention was to make the colony and its capital city an example, a cautionary tale to keep the other colonies in line. Instead, the objects of the king's wrath, the people of Massachusetts and Boston, grew only stronger in their determination to fight.

When Gage arrived in Boston on May 13, 1774, he was greeted with worse than scorn. The city's churches tolled their bells for weeks on end as if marking an endless funeral. The people of Boston universally adopted black badges of mourning. Undaunted, Gage immediately acted to close Boston Harbor to all traffic, foreign and domestic. And then he ordered the colonial capital to be transferred from Boston to Salem. The General Assembly duly moved to that town, only to reconstitute itself as the "Provincial Congress."

Gage was having none of this. He ordered the "illegal" congress dissolved and sent a messenger to Salem to deliver the order. The delegates barred the doors against the courier while voting up a brand-new proposal. It was a resolution to convene a *Continental* Congress, made up of delegates from all of the colonies, and before any royal authority could stop them, the resolution was drafted, enacted, copied, and distributed to every colonial assembly in America.

"We must master them or totally leave them to themselves and treat them as aliens," George III had declared. And so, what had been up to now thirteen separate, disputatious, competitive colonies distributed along the length of the Eastern Seaboard rapidly rallied to the defense of Massachusetts and Boston and, in the process, lurched forward to solidarity and even union against their common oppressor.

Chapter 8

Tipping Point

The Boston Tea Party marked the height of the movement leading up to the revolution. The British response to the Tea Party, humiliating punishment for Boston, marked both the pre-revolutionary low point of relations between the colonies and the mother country and at the same time the first great high point of colonial unity.

Was there any hope for reconciliation between the Crown and its colonies?

Yes. Not only was war fever still curable, but the colonies, although most rallied around Boston, were not by any means unanimously sold on independence. If king and Parliament reached out to the colonies, relations could quite possibly have been patched up. But, with a genius for making a bad situation truly terrible, King George III signed the Quebec Act on May 20, 1774. Its impact on American colonists was deeply offensive and alienating.

Recall that the French and Indian War had delivered all of Canada from French into British hands. With the Quebec Act, the Canadian province was extended down into the Ohio Valley and the country of the Illinois River—essentially the Great Lakes region of what is today the United States. True, the people of Quebec were now legally British subjects, just like the people of the lower thirteen colonies. Yet they spoke French, and they followed the laws and traditions of France. Most important of all, they were not predominantly members of the Church of England or any other Protestant sect. They were Roman Catholics. To the people of the thirteen colonies, it seemed as if the king was forcing upon them, on their western frontier, an alien people, who spoke a foreign tongue, worshipped in a foreign church, and were until quite recently their sworn enemies. For his part, George III had hardly proved himself to be a tolerant monarch, but now he not only granted the French-Canadians freedom to worship as they wished but freedom to speak French as well.

The final insult? The Quebec Act bestowed upon the French-Canadians the very territory King George III had closed to the frontier people of New England by the Proclamation of 1763. True, the Quebec Act did not bar them from sharing the newly opened territory with the Canadians—so, in effect, it undid some of the damage of the Proclamation—but it did oblige these English men and women to share it on whatever terms the French-Canadian settlers demanded. That included agreeing to abide by French law—a violation of the Magna Carta, which, since 1215, guaranteed that subjects of the Crown would always be sheltered under the rights, liberties, and privileges of English law.

UNINTENDED CONSEQUENCES

George and Parliament intended the Quebec Act as a way of preempting rebellious rumblings from formerly French Canada. The unintended consequence of the act, however, was the further alienation of the thirteen colonies. Moreover, the Intolerable Acts passed in response to the Boston Tea Party moved the colonies to rally around Massachusetts and Boston in particular. The Port Act, which was the most oppressively punitive of the Intolerable Acts, was meant to cut Boston off from the rest of America. It was nothing more or less than a wartime blockade. But throughout the colonies, from New England clear down to South Carolina, food and other goods were transported to Massachusetts and to Boston overland, thereby evading the port blockade altogether. Most amazing of all were the shipments of wheat, which came from none other than Quebec!

As the colonies—Quebec included—threw Massachusetts a lifeline, Massachusetts sent out to them a call for political union in the form of what the Massachusetts Assembly called a "Continental Congress." The adjective was thoughtfully and brilliantly chosen. The word *Colonial* was rejected because it would have affirmed a subjugated status that was growing increasingly hateful. No one dared, however, label the proposed

Congress a *National,* because no nation yet existed. Instead, the Assembly chose the majestic-sounding term *Continental,* which was at once a statement of geographical fact yet, at the same time, implied that the future of the colonies lay westward, in the direction of the rest of the continent, rather than eastward, in the direction of the ocean, Britain, the Old World, and dependence upon it. It was an adjective that did not imply a nonexistent nation but did underscore that the identity of the colonies was now far more North American than British.

THE CONTINENTAL CONGRESS CONVENES

On September 5, 1774, fifty-six delegates from twelve colonies (Georgia abstained) gathered at Carpenters' Hall, home of the Carpenters' Company of the City and County of Philadelphia, a craft guild of master builders established in 1742. Philadelphia, the largest city in the colonies, was chosen for the first meeting of the Continental Congress because it was roughly midway between the New England colonies and those of the South, and Carpenters' Hall was one of the city's few buildings deemed appropriate in size and dignity to host the delegates. True, the State House, which is today known as Independence Hall, was no more than a block away, but the organizers of the Congress believed that the State House harbored far too many "Tories"—as those still strongly loyal to Crown and Parliament were called—who would not only spy on the delegates but generally inhibit the business of the meeting.

The Continental Congress was called to order on September 5, 1774, and its first substantial act was the endorsement, on September 17, of the "Suffolk Resolves" drafted days earlier in Massachusetts by Dr. Joseph Warren, disciple of Sam Adams. Warren's Resolves repudiated the Intolerable Acts, calling them violations of the British constitution, and urged Massachusetts to create an independent government and to refuse to pay taxes to Parliament until the acts were repealed. The Resolves advised all Massachusetts men to take up arms and to boycott all English goods. Approved by a convention in Massachusetts, the document was rushed to Philadelphia by a silversmith who volunteered as a Sons of Liberty courier, Paul Revere. By approving the Suffolk Resolves, the Continental Congress in effect endorsed the idea of independence for all the colonies.

Not that the Suffolk Resolves was the only document presented for debate. Joseph Galloway, a prominent Philadelphian, an attorney, former speaker of the Pennsylvania Assembly, vice president of the American Philosophical Society, and good friend of Benjamin Franklin, offered what came to be known as "Galloway's Plan of Union." It proposed a way to achieve a measure of political autonomy without leaving the embrace of the mother country. Galloway's idea was to persuade Crown and Parliament to grant the thirteen colonies the status of a semi-autonomous dominion within the British Empire. As such, it would be governed by a "grand council," the members of which would be elected by the people to three-year terms. They would be presided over by a president-general, who would be appointed by the king. This official's one power would be an absolute veto over the council. Singular though it was, it was an all-powerful, sovereign power.

As mentioned in Chapter 5, Galloway opposed independence, so strongly, in fact, that he returned to England in 1778, during the revolution. His 1774 plan united the colonies but ensured that their government would always be subject to the royal government. To a modern sensibility, this seems weak indeed, but the delegates gathered in Philadelphia were most attentive, and "Galloway's Plan of Union" was not only debated but put to a vote, falling short of adoption by just a single vote.

In addition to endorsing the Suffolk Resolves, the First Continental Congress separately reiterated its denunciation of the Intolerable Acts, the Quebec Act, and other coercive measures. A total of thirteen Parliamentary acts passed since the end of the French and Indian War were declared unconstitutional. As for the boycott, every delegate—even those who voted to approve Galloway's Plan of Union—pledged total support for the anti-British boycott until all thirteen acts were repealed.

On a positive note, the delegates drafted ten resolutions explicitly enumerating the rights of the English in America. Not only did this anticipate the Bill of Rights, which would not be adopted as part of the Constitution until 1791, it made clear that the role of a free republican government was to ensure individual rights—human rights. It was a radical notion in 1774.

In the run-up to the revolution, colonial boycotts on various English imports—especially tea—became increasingly common. This mocking caricature of "A Society of Patriotic Ladies, at Edenton in North Carolina" signing on to a boycott was published in London in March 1775. LIBRARY OF CONGRESS

On October 20, 1774, a week before adjournment, the congressional delegates signed a "Continental Association," effectively institutionalizing their colonies' pledges of adherence to a total boycott against trade with Britain. The "Association" foreshadowed a more far-reaching political and national union. This done, the delegates drafted a joint address to the American people and a jointly composed letter to King George III. After agreeing to meet again on May 10, 1775—assuming king and Parliament failed to adequately address their grievances—the First Continental Congress adjourned on October 26.

GAGE GETS MOVING AND REVERE TAKES ANOTHER RIDE

As the Continental Congress was preparing to meet in Philadelphia, General Thomas Gage, royal governor of Massachusetts and commander-in-chief of Crown forces in America, consolidated his troops in and around Boston. On September 1, he dispatched a detachment of regulars to Cambridge, across the Charles River from Boston, and ordered them to seize cannon and powder from colonial arsenals there. The impudently renamed "Provincial Congress" of Massachusetts, exiled to Salem, responded to the seizure by appropriating £15,627 to buy new arms and ammunition. The Salem group also appointed John Hancock to lead a central Committee of Safety. He was given the authority to call out the militia to resist further actions by Gage's redcoats. All of the colonies had a variety of militia units. In Massachusetts, a few regiments proudly revived a nickname that had been used in the colonies as early as 1756, during the French and Indian War. "Minutemen," they called themselves, in token of their common pledge to be continually on call so that they could assemble, armed and prepared to fight, on no more than a minute's notice.

Determined not to be outmaneuvered by Gage again, the Provincial Assembly, on December 14, 1774, sent Paul Revere, that silversmith horseman who had already delivered the Suffolk Resolves from Massachusetts to Philadelphia, riding to New Hampshire to alert John Sullivan, a major in that colony's militia and a delegate to the First Continental Congress, that Gage intended to send regulars to Fort William and Mary in New Hampshire's Portsmouth Harbor. Gage's purpose was to take possession of a large store of arms and ammunition held in the fort.

In response to Revere's timely alert, Sullivan selected Captain John Langdon as his second in command of men who volunteered to capture the fort from the small British force occupying it. They would collect the weapons, powder, and ammunition before Gage's men arrived at the fort in strength. Sullivan and Langdon turned out their volunteers in the best military style they could manage. The result was that the few British regulars manning Fort William and Mary were so awed by the sight of a highly disciplined and well-armed militia that they surrendered to Sullivan without firing a shot. The major and the captain hurriedly collected the cache of guns and powder and spirited them away. When Gage's troops arrived, they would find a vacant fort with an empty arsenal.

MOMENTUM

If the British garrison that surrendered Fort William and Mary was shocked by the military prowess displayed by the colonial militia, General Gage was downright befuddled. He simply could not believe how well organized, networked, and efficient the colonists were. The Massachusetts

Provincial Congress had purchased arms and assembled a militia almost instantly. Under Hancock, its Committee of Safety coordinated action throughout New England. Gage issued a proclamation calling everything that was happening treasonable, but by the time the document was published, the Provincial Congress had not only set itself up to fight a revolution, it had caused itself to disappear. Gage could find no band of traitors to clap into irons.

So, he turned to organizing his troops, to deploying and to arming them. At every turn, however, he was met by sabotage. Supply barges were sunk. Wagons, requisitioned from all over the countryside, essential for transporting a large army's multitudinous baggage, were vandalized, trashed. Stores of royal arms were looted. Gage had no choice but to face facts: Rebellion was under way. The outbreaks were too numerous and widespread to stop one by one, so he decided to deprive the rebels once and for all of arms and ammunition. Around midnight on February 25, 1775, he sent Colonel Alexander Leslie at the head of 240 men of the 64th Regiment of Foot out of Castle William, Boston Harbor, and en route to Salem, Massachusetts. His spies had told him that he would find there a large stash of purloined cannon and powder.

Leslie landed his soldiers at Marblehead, Massachusetts, from where he would advance to Salem. He had no idea that John Pedrick, courier for the Sons of Liberty, was way ahead of him and had already warned Salem of his approach. The town did have nineteen stolen cannon barrels, waiting to be joined to carriages. Heeding Pedrick's warning, however, the Salem militia transported the barrels into hiding places far outside of town. At the same time, militia colonel Timothy Pickering, with forty Minutemen, rode out to Salem's open drawbridge. He and his men raised the bridge and confronted Leslie and his 240 redcoats.

Outnumbering Pickering by two hundred men, Leslie imperiously demanded that the provincial commander lower the draw. When Pickering refused, the two sides prepared to open fire—whereupon a local clergyman intervened with the proposal of a compromise. Lower the draw, he advised Pickering, on condition that the British advance no more than "thirty rods" (495 feet) into the town. Once satisfied that

Salem had no hidden cannon, they were on their honor to withdraw from the town at once.

Unwilling to trigger an armed rebellion then and there, Leslie agreed, and Pickering, figuring that the preacher knew the cannon barrels had already been moved, pretended reluctance but then agreed as well. The result was a non-battle. The British colonel and his men moved thirty rods into Salem, looked around, saw nothing, and duly withdrew. Their march back to Boston took them through a village called Northfields. There, a woman named Sarah Tarrant opened her window and scolded the passing British troops: "Go home and tell your master he has sent you on a fool's errand and broken the peace of our Sabbath. What, do you think we were born in the woods, to be frightened by owls?"

It made for a nice anecdote. More important, Tarrant's taunt meant that she knew what was going on in Salem. And if *she* knew, it was clear that the colonies and the towns within them were talking to each other— all the time and about everything.

BACK IN THE SADDLE AGAIN

On Sunday, April 16, 1775, Joseph Warren sent the indefatigable Paul Revere galloping yet again in service of the growing rebellion. His mission was to warn John Hancock and Sam Adams that Gage had sent soldiers to arrest them.

Their offense?

On March 30, 1775, George III approved the New England Trade and Fisheries Act. More familiarly, it was known as the New England Restraining Act, its purpose being to restrict New England's trade to just two customers: Britain and the British West Indies. In response, Massachusetts reconvened the proscribed Provincial Congress, which called on Warren and his Committee of Safety to prepare the colony to fight a war. Even Gage was not blind to these goings-on and, on April 12, he proclaimed martial law, issued a blanket indictment against the entire colony, judging everyone to be "in treason." Yet, as if in a display of great magnanimity, Gage offered every subject a pardon—save Samuel Adams and John Hancock, whom he regarded as the instigators of everything.

Samuel Adams, engraved between 1810 and 1835 after a painting by John Singleton Copley. LIBRARY OF CONGRESS

IT'S LIBERTY OR DEATH

Massachusetts was the hotbed. Here, the majority favored a break with the mother country. In contrast, much of the South tended toward Toryism—but in Virginia, Patrick Henry, prominent attorney and member of Virginia's House of Burgesses since 1765, rose in speech on March 23, 1775. The venue was St. John's Church in Richmond, which served as an impromptu capitol, the colony's royal governor, Lord Dunmore, having dissolved the Burgesses on account of sedition.

"There is no retreat but in submission and slavery!" Henry declaimed. "Our chains are forged. Their clanking may be heard on the plains of Boston! The war is inevitable—and let it come! I repeat it, sir, let it come! It is in vain, sir, to extenuate the matter. Gentlemen may cry, 'Peace! Peace!'—but there is no peace. The war is actually begun! The next gale that sweeps down from the north will bring to our ears the clash of resounding arms! Our brethren are already in the field! Why stand we here idle? What is it that gentlemen wish? What would they have? Is life so dear, or peace so sweet, as to be purchased at the price of chains and slavery? Forbid it, Almighty God! I know not what course others may take, but as for me, give me liberty or give me death!"

"GIVE ME LIBERTY, OR GIVE ME DEATH !"

PATRICK HENRY delivering his great speech on the Rights of the Colonies, before the Virginia Assembly, convened at Richmond March 28ᵗʰ 1775. Concluding with the above sentiment, which became the war cry of the Revolution.

This nineteenth-century Currier & Ives lithograph is one of many that helped transform Patrick Henry's March 23, 1775, pro-independence speech to the Virginia Assembly into an icon of the American Revolution. LIBRARY OF CONGRESS

Patrick Henry's stirring speech made clear that those in Virginia with eyes to see and ears to hear well knew what was happening in New England. *The next gale that swept down from the north would bring to their ears the clash of resounding arms.* More eyes were opened, and more ears became attuned to detect the echo of musketry from those northern colonies.

CHAPTER 9

Heard round the World

As directed by Joseph Warren on April 16, 1775, Paul Revere rode off to Lexington to wake Sam Adams and John Hancock and keep them out of the clutches of General Thomas Gage. For all the riding he did, Revere was far more than an errand boy. He was, in fact, the revolution's first spymaster. In the run-up to the war and throughout the entire conflict, the Patriots created and maintained an elaborate and remarkably efficient espionage network. Nothing nearly as good was developed during the Civil War, whose spies were mostly poorly organized freelancers. In fact, the quality of espionage attained in the revolution was not matched until the emergence of the OSS (Office of Strategic Services) in World War II and the CIA that grew out of it after the war.

Revere coordinated a ring of Patriot spies operating out of Boston, who covertly observed Gage mustering his grenadiers, light infantry, and a flotilla of whaleboats. Revere reasoned that Gage was preparing to raid Concord, Massachusetts, where the Patriots had secreted a cache of arms and ammunition. He instructed his spies to monitor Gage's next moves closely to determine if he was moving his troops out of Boston overland or via the Back Bay in those whaleboats. If he chose the water route, Revere could be sure the British were headed to Concord. He therefore stationed a friend and spy, John Pulling, in the steeple of the Old North Church, on Salem Street in Boston's North End, instructing him to shine a single lantern from the steeple if he saw the regulars marching out of town on foot but two lanterns if he saw them embarking on the whaleboats.

THE CALL TO ARMS

On April 18, 1775, Gage sent cavalry officers out along the road to Concord to ensure that no "rebel" couriers were present to alert the countryside. Late that night, the British sergeants broke the sleep of between six and eight hundred light infantrymen and grenadiers. The best troops Gage had, they were quietly mustered on Boston Common under the command of Lieutenant Colonel Francis Smith, with the aid of Major John Pitcairn of the Royal Marines.

At about 10:30, they began to march. From his perch in the steeple, Pulling watched them head for the whaleboats. He duly slid open the slides on both of his lanterns and set them in the steep window. Revere and fellow courier William Dawes set out from Boston to alert everyone between that city and Concord that Gage's men were on the march. Dawes rode out on the longer overland route to Concord, while Revere rowed across the Charles to Charlestown, mounted his horse there, and galloped off around 11:00. All along the way, the riders sounded the alarm. It was not "The British are coming!"—as traditionally attributed to Revere—but "The regulars are out!" From every Patriot home, the Minutemen and other militia volunteers emerged.

By midnight, Revere was in Lexington, where he rode to the house of Parson Jonas Clark. Here, he knew, John Hancock (the parson's cousin) and Sam Adams were hiding out. Militiaman William Munroe, standing sentry outside the house, responded to Revere's shout of "Open the door!" with a request that he speak softly, explaining that the family had just retired "and doesn't want any noise about the house."

"Noise!" Revere exclaimed. "You'll have noise enough before long. The regulars are out!"

Chastened, Munroe sprang away to personally rouse Hancock and Adams—the latter emerging from the house and exclaiming, "What a glorious morning this is!" A sleepy Hancock glared at him. "I mean for America," Adams added.

William Dawes, a full hour behind Revere, met up with him in Lexington. They rode on together to Concord, picking up another courier, Dr. Samuel Prescott, along the way. All three continued riding, stirring the countryside from its slumber. But as Prescott and Dawes stopped to

The Midnight Ride of Paul Revere was imagined here by the twentieth-century American painter Grant Wood in a work from 1931. METROPOLITAN MUSEUM OF ART, NEW YORK

wake an important Sons of Liberty house, Revere galloped on—and ran right into a detachment of regulars. He was intercepted, and all three couriers summarily arrested. Prescott instantly broke free, and Dawes was able to make his escape a little later. Revere, however, was held. A British major named Mitchell cocked his pistol and pressed the muzzle against the silversmith's temple. Speaking in a low voice, he demanded to be told "everything."

In fact, this particular Son of Liberty was only too happy to do so. He informed the officer that every man in Middlesex was armed and ready to fight and that the regulars would find themselves in for a very hard time. With that, Major Mitchell ordered a subordinate to take Revere away. The courier was soon turned loose, however, after his captors realized that he had already alerted just about everyone between Boston and Concord and could do no further harm. Some historical sources say that Paul Revere returned to Lexington just in time to watch part of the brief "battle" on Lexington Green.

BEFORE THE DAWN
Well after midnight but hours before the dawn of April 19, 1775, Adams and Hancock began a long journey to Philadelphia. In the meantime, the bulk of Gage's men were still disembarking from their whaleboats at Lechmere Point on the shore of Cambridge. They looked ahead to a wearying sixteen-mile march to Concord. As it was, the predawn slog in the wet and chilly New England spring did not promise to be pleasant. That their landing, intended to have been made in deepest stealth, was greeted by loudly pealing church bells and musket fire erupting from invisible snipers told them that the march would also be extremely perilous.

The "welcome" with which the Patriots of Cambridge greeted his troops prompted Smith to send some men galloping back to Boston for reinforcements. Gone, obviously, was the advantage of surprise. What counted now was superior numbers. Not that Smith and Pitcairn intended to await reinforcements before beginning the march to Concord. They quickened the process of unloading their men from the whaleboats and hurriedly formed them into ranks, despite the sniper fire.

Without a spy network, the king's soldiers had no clear idea of what awaited them. Certainly, they did not know that, as they were preparing to set out from Cambridge, Patriot militia captain Jonas Parker was mustering his men on Lexington Green. The sixteen miles of road between Cambridge and Concord ran straight through Lexington, some ten miles northwest of Cambridge. Doubtless, the British would not have been terribly impressed even if they had known that the militia was assembling there. Parker had been able to muster no more than seventy or so volunteers, whose ragged ranks he set about "dressing" in as orderly a fashion as he could. They were not a disciplined group, they each brought their own muskets, and nobody had anything like a uniform. If they passed the predawn hours mocking the "lobsterbacks" they were about to confront, it is likely that the jokes ended as soon as they caught their first sight of the approaching vanguard, Major Pitcairn's marines, brilliant in the early morning sunlight. Criss-crossed over their bright scarlet uniforms were cartridge belts pipe-clayed spotless white. The look was sternly military. A very long "Brown Bess" musket rested on the shoulder of each man.

"So few of us. It is folly to stand here," one of Parker's men reportedly muttered in something like a loud stage whisper.

Reportedly, too, Parker bellowed in return: "The first man who offers to run shall be shot down." According to the almost certainly semi-legendary account that has drifted through history and down to us, Parker continued as the marines approached: "Stand your ground. Don't fire unless fired upon. But if they want to have a war, let it begin here!"

Stirring as the words, whatever they actually were, may have been, we do know that more than a few of the militiamen walked away, less in a fit of panic than in a desultory display of prudence. The desertions were apparently sufficient to prompt Pitcairn to exercise some restraint.

He brought his men onto the green and close up to militia. But he ordered them to halt, and instead of issuing the next logical orders—*Ready! Aim!*—he addressed those militiamen who had not deserted the green.

"Lay down your arms, you rebels, and disperse!" Pitcairn commanded.

Three courses of action were now open to Captain Jonas Parker. He could open fire, in which case his vastly outnumbered amateur soldiers would surely be cut down dead. He could abjectly surrender—relinquish weapons and melt away. Or he could issue a command of his own. With considerable presence of mind under the circumstances, he ordered his small company to fall out, explicitly adding that they were to take their weapons with them.

Presumably, Parker gambled that this would be enough to satisfy Pitcairn. It was not. The marine officer once again barked out his demand that the rebels lay their weapons on the green. Parker did not respond by repeating his own order. Nor did he come up with another. In the absence of any new command, someone fired. And then at least two more, probably even more, followed.

No one knows who fired these first shots of the American Revolution. No one even knows from which side the shots came. What is known is that they resulted in a minor leg wound inflicted on one of the marines, and two balls grazed Pitcairn's horse. In response, the marine commander ordered a volley, which, discharged, was instantly followed by an order to cease fire. Then Pitcairn called out: "Form and surround them!"

Pitcairn's men were very well-trained marines, which is why their commander was stunned when, instead of forming and surrounding as directly ordered, they let loose a second volley.

The first volley had put a number of militiamen to flight. The second prompted an undisciplined fire-at-will response from the militiamen. Apparently, this caused little or no injury to the marines, who, again without orders, their bayonets already fixed, charged the remaining militiamen who stood on the green.

It is one thing to stand firm in the face of musket fire but quite another to do so against a massed bayonet charge. Everyone except Jonas Parker took to their heels. He, in fact, had been wounded either in the first or second volley. Nevertheless, there he stood. Alone. He struggled to reload but was bayonetted before he could fire. He lay dead, one of eight militiamen killed in the first battle of the American Revolution. Another ten groaned under their wounds.

FROM LEXINGTON TO CONCORD

As battles go, Lexington was rather pathetic. Even Parker's stand can be interpreted as either remarkably heroic or foolishly futile. Yet the encounter served as a kind of tripwire, with news of it traveling much faster than the British columns could advance to Concord. From every nearby village and farm, militia volunteers converged on Concord. The influx was so great that no accurate count exists of Patriot militia forces involved in the Battle of Concord. Estimates range as high as twenty thousand men—a number that no modern historian credits. The most reliable consensus figure is 3,763, and that is a rough count of the total number of militiamen who fought during the battle. It is estimated not more than half this number was actively engaged at any one time. Instead, as one group of Patriots exhausted their ammunition or their stamina, others took their place. (The average militiaman went into combat with about forty rounds of ammunition.)

We know that when Lieutenant Colonel Smith arrived at Concord with the main part of the British column, he was initially unopposed, and the number of Patriot soldiers in town was about four hundred men under the command of local resident James Barrett. His troops were assembled not in town but on a ridge above it, overlooking the town and North Bridge across the Concord River. Smith, who accompanied his men as they entered Lexington, apparently took no notice that the high ground was occupied by Patriot militia. Instead, he and his staff officers seated their weary, thirsty selves at a local tavern and bought dinner and drinks. As they relaxed, the grenadiers followed orders to perform a house-to-house search for contraband munitions.

They had only very modest success. There were bullets in many houses, but no powder. Gun carriages were located, but no cannon barrels to mount on them. In response to an officer's demand for action, the carriages were set aflame—and it was the resulting flame and smoke that roused the militia to action.

"Will you let them burn the town down?" one of Barrett's impatient officers demanded.

No answer to the question is on record, but Barrett did order his men down from the ridge to march to the defense of their town. He admonished his soldiers to hold their fire unless they were fired upon.

A British light infantry captain was the first to see the militia's approach. Shocked, he formed up his company into two ranks. This was standard combat practice. The first rank, the front rank, when ordered, fired a volley in unison, peeled off to the left and right, and slipped behind what had been the second rank and was now the front rank. While this rank discharged its volley, the original first rank reloaded. Now the former second rank peeled off left and right and positioned itself behind what was again the first rank, which, having reloaded, was ready to fire.

This orderly swapping of ranks enabled a continuous sequence of volleys—provided that the necessary maneuvers had been thoroughly drilled and flawlessly executed. But *that*, apparently, was the rub. The first British company that engaged the Americans faltered in the execution of the fire-withdraw-reload-fire routine, and the volleys that resulted were ragged, clumsy, and ineffective. Troops bumbled and stumbled over each other as the front rank struggled to move behind the second. Moreover, the first volley was premature, fired from too great a distance, so that most of the shots fell well short of their intended targets. Two British rounds discharged in this initial engagement did find their marks, however. One killed militia captain Isaac Davis, the other Private Abner Hosmer—a twenty-one-year-old "drummer boy" who also handled a musket.

Militia soldiers truly were a band of brothers. Typically, they had grown up together in a small town or village. Often, they were related by blood or marriage. While this enhanced the cohesiveness of the military unit, it also deepened the sense of loss when a comrade fell. Yet, in contrast to the chaos that the initial casualties had created in Lexington, the militiamen gathered at Concord behaved very much like soldiers—like the warriors of a country determined to become free. As one popular account has it, the Americans returned fire not when an officer imperiously demanded it but in response to this appeal: "Fire, fellow soldier! For God sake, fire!"

Three British soldiers were killed, and nine more were wounded in the first exchange of musket fire. What is more, the British light infantry, which had anticipated encountering a disorganized mob, was stunned by the unanticipated efficiency and determination of the militiamen. The troops withdrew in great haste. This, however, also revealed the limits of the citizen-soldiers' professionalism. Barrett's men cheered wildly as the British fled. What they *should* have done, of course, what Barrett should have *ordered* them to do, was pursue the retreating light infantry. They should have pressed the pursuit in the knowledge that a force in retreat is at its most vulnerable. If you are running away from the enemy, you cannot shoot toward him. Trained commanders commanding trained soldiers never allow an enemy to fly away.

As it happened, only a single militiaman, carrying at the time not a musket but an axe, ran to the North Bridge, where the light infantry had abandoned its dead and wounded. One of the injured Britons was writhing prone on the bridge. Seeing this, the militiaman raised his axe and buried it in the stricken man's skull.

Even today, it looms as an act of gratuitous brutality. Clearly, it intimidated some of the grenadiers, who were just then coming back from the house-to-house search for hidden arms. They were seasoned veterans of European warfare, yet they were beyond appalled. How could colonists do such a thing to a fellow Englishman? Some believed that they had witnessed the militiaman not merely cleave the man's skull but scalp him. They concluded that they were being asked to fight white men who now embraced the combat tactics of the "red savage." The grenadiers who witnessed the incident on North Bridge were thoroughly dispirited, and the fight suddenly drained out of them.

RETURN TO LEXINGTON

Combat at Concord was finished by ten o'clock in the morning. Colonel Smith collected his wounded and began the return march to Boston. They were much too distant from the approaching reinforcements, some fourteen hundred in number (including 460 Royal Marines), marching out from Boston, to hear the cheerful sound of the fife-and-drum band that quickened their march. The tune it played had already become quite

Map of Boston and surrounding area, including Lexington and Concord at the time of the April 19, 1775, battles and the siege of Boston that followed. The map was created on July 29, 1775, for a member of Parliament.
LIBRARY OF CONGRESS

familiar to Bostonians, who even knew the lyrics, all about a fellow named Yankee Doodle who went to town "riding on a pony." For the regulars, it was meant to mock the bumpkin rebels. Later in the war, the Patriots adopted the tune as their own.

Led by thirty-three-year-old Lord Hugh Percy, the reinforcing contingent drew behind them two six-pound cannon. They were confident of making short work of the rebels—that is, if Smith and Pitcairn had not already done so. Yet Percy and his staff officers soon became uneasy. The streets through which they passed were preternaturally quiet. Where was everyone? While they did encounter one token of resistance—a saboteur had pried out the planks of the Charles River Bridge, which slowed the column's progress—the passage through Cambridge, whose citizens had been taunting and harassing British soldiers for months, was silent, unchallenged.

The situation changed radically once the troops were on the open road in the country. Suddenly, militiamen fired upon the advancing column from behind every rock and bush and tree and stone wall. Many fired from inside houses. In places, the road was a veritable gantlet—and the snipers were almost never located. It was more than mere harassment. Lord Percy's men were being hit and were falling in their tracks. In his later report to General Gage, Lord Percy wrote: "There was not a stonewall or house, though before in appearance evacuated, from whence the Rebels did not fire upon us."

Yet, a good soldier, he marched on, heedlessly determined to join forces with Smith and Pitcairn. He did not know that these two commanders were already in retreat and heading their way. Militiamen were pouring in from all directions on both the advancing British column and the retreating one. True, the militia was disorganized. Smith's light infantry even managed to stage several deadly counterattacks against isolated knots of Patriot citizen-soldiers. The regulars fought them with growing rage. In one place, they fell upon militia troops lying in wait in several houses. The British gave no quarter but killed the militiamen and then put to the torch the houses from which they fired

These scattered counteroffensives did not discourage the militia. The rolling "battle" had taken on a life of its own. Militia units continued to arrive. The Patriots continued to take up sniper positions, just waiting for both the retreating and the advancing columns to pass by so that they could pick off soldiers one after the other. As the day progressed, the Patriots became ever more adept at their work, setting up tactically effective fields of crossfire from both sides of the road.

Some of the older militiamen had seen action in the French and Indian War. They may have recalled how the British regulars were easily stymied, confused, and downright terrified by "irregular" tactics, such as fighting from cover and ambush. To his credit, Smith recognized what was happening to his men. At Lexington, he ordered a pause so that he personally could re-form his columns and instill the renewed discipline necessary to get his men safely back to Boston. While he set about this work, he sent Pitcairn with a detachment of marines to chase off any rebels who might decide to take potshots at the halted troops.

Smith acted reasonably but miscalculated nevertheless. When the militia descended on his halted soldiers at Lexington, they first targeted Pitcairn's patrol. With surprising discipline, they surrounded and engulfed the patrol, driving the marines back upon Smith's idled troops. Stunned, Smith did not order his men to fight back but to continue the retreat, this time on the double-quick.

By the time Smith had called that ill-fated halt at Lexington on the return to Boston, he and his men had been marching, fighting, or running away for some twenty hours. They were exhausted, acting the role of persecuted refugees rather than soldiers of the Crown. Imagine their relief when they were met, as they were leaving Lexington, by Lord Percy's arriving reinforcements.

Not that Percy's men were fresh and keen for combat. They, too, had been marching through relentless sniper fire. Percy decided that his men and Smith's should take a stand inside Lexington, keeping the militiamen at bay with the pair of six-pounders he had with him.

It was a desperate idea. The two cannon were hardly sufficient to stop the flood of incoming militiamen. But they did manage to hold them off for a time. The militia had numbers and spirit but lacked unified leadership. Under even marginally competent command with minimal coordination, the Americans could have dealt the professional British military a truly devastating blow. It is quite possible that most of Smith and Percy's combined force of eighteen hundred men could have been wiped out, pinned down in Lexington, and finished off or at least forced into the most humiliating of surrenders.

As it happened, however, the two British commanders were able to lead their men out of Lexington at about three in the afternoon and resume their long, dreary, punishing retreat. Every yard of their march was contested by snipers all the way back to Charlestown. There, the defeated expedition found protection under cover from the cannon of the British three-masted men-of-war riding at anchor in Boston Harbor.

REBELLION BECOMES REVOLUTION

The Battle of Concord, including the long retreat, cost the lives of seventy-three regulars with another twenty-six reported as missing and presumed dead. An additional 174 were wounded. Among the Patriot militias, forty-nine men were killed, five went missing, and forty-one were wounded.

Much encouraged by Concord, the Continental Congress authorized the mobilization of 13,600 troops in a "Continental Army." In the meantime, militia companies from all over New England converged on Cambridge. The day after their humiliation at Concord, the surviving soldiers of Smith and Percy hunkered down in their Boston barracks. In Cambridge, the Patriots planned how they would lay siege to the British army in Boston.

CHAPTER 10

Of Green Mountains and Continental Ambitions

FREDERICK NORTH, 2ND EARL OF GUILFORD—THE INFAMOUS LORD North whose high-handed taxation policies pushed the colonies toward revolution—suddenly went to the House of Lords, on February 20, 1775, bearing a plan for patching everything up. The Lords swiftly approved, as did the House of Commons, and the plan reached Boston the day after the Battles of Lexington and Concord. North offered to let the colonies tax themselves for the support of ordinary civil government, the colonial judiciary, and the common defense. Parliament, however, would retain all regulatory taxing authority.

The Second Continental Congress debated the proposal and, on July 31, 1775, rejected it. The sore point was not taxation, but the fact that Parliament was authorized to deal individually with the colonies, not with any form of colonial union. Whatever Lord North was willing to concede, he drew the line at appearing to create a new nation. Congress rejected the proposal on this basis, and that was extraordinarily significant. It meant that the people of the colonies—or, at least, their congressional representatives—no longer thought of themselves as British residents of New York or Massachusetts or Virginia. They thought of themselves as Americans. "The Revolution was in the Minds and Hearts of the People," Adams wrote many years later, in an 1818 letter. In fact, the revolution began when English men and women in America thought and felt themselves to be Americans.

It was no wonder that minds and hearts were changing. People throughout the colonies were remarkably well informed. John Hancock had seen to that, sending Committee of Safety couriers far and wide to carry the news of Lexington and Concord—even as the battle was still being fought. Within hours of the first casualties, the news had spread to New York and Philadelphia. Within days, the whole southeast had heard, Virginia included.

SELF-STARTERS

The news was an inspiration—not in some general sense, but very specifically. Connecticut responded to Lexington and Concord by tapping a prosperous New Haven merchant who doubled as a militia captain, Benedict Arnold by name, asking him to gallop to Massachusetts to plead the case for commissioning him a colonel and assigning him to lead the capture of Fort Ticonderoga.

"Fort Ti," as locals called it, was built during the French and Indian War at the junction of Lake George with Lake Champlain in northeastern New York. It dominated the principal route connecting Canada with the upper Hudson Valley. In addition, it was an arsenal, the stronghold in which the British stored their cannons. Arnold showed up, presented his proposal, and eyes lit up in Massachusetts. He galloped back to Connecticut, puffed up with the good news—only to discover that, in his absence, the Connecticut Assembly had approved very nearly the same plan and commissioned Ethan Allen, a popular Litchfield farmer and entrepreneur, to execute the mission. Not to be cut out, Arnold reported uninvited to the muster of the Connecticut militia ready to set out for the fort. He presented his Massachusetts commission, which failed to impress the Connecticut men. They told Arnold that they were Ethan Allen's soldiers and would "march home rather than serve under any other leader."

It was at this moment that Benedict Arnold confronted a quality he simply did not possess. Call it charisma. Call it command presence. It was the essence within certain leaders that makes people follow them, as if by unconquerable instinct. Like George Washington, Ethan Allen was physically imposing. In an era when few men even came close to six feet in stature, Allen was six-four. Born and bred in the village of Litchfield, Connecticut, he served in the French and Indian War, but saw no combat before taking up the muscular trade of iron monger. He sold his business in 1765 and relocated to Northampton, Massachusetts, where he indulged in what he openly confessed was a long spasm of "riotous living." That was bad enough for some of the locals, but he took special delight in telling indecent jokes about Northampton's men of the cloth, and in July 1767, by vote of the town's selectmen, he was banished from the place and told to take his wife and child with him.

Seeking to restore his fortune, he left his family with his brother in Salisbury, Connecticut, and secured a grant of acreage in what was then called the New Hampshire Grants, the area that later became Vermont. He set up in Bennington, at the time no more than a wilderness mountain outpost, and summoned his family in 1769. It was, to be sure, a rough place in need of taming, but Allen earned the admiration and respect of the rough men around him.

In 1770, Ethan Allen was elected colonel of a self-styled militia that was really no more than a band of vigilantes. They called themselves the Green Mountain Boys, and their founding purpose was to beat off a sheriff's posse dispatched by the government of New York to evict everyone who had received New Hampshire grants. Citing a charter awarded in 1664 to the Duke of York, the colony laid claim to the region and wanted everyone else out. The posse came—but never stood a chance. After he and the Green Mountain Boys evicted the New Yorkers who had come to evict them, Allen became one of the founders of what was briefly known as the Republic of Vermont. In January 1777, Allen and other settlers of the New Hampshire Grants region proclaimed their territory not only independent of Crown and Parliament, but of the thirteen American colonies as well.

The new republic raised its own army, which joined in resisting the British invasion from Canada. After sending General Burgoyne packing, however, the Republic of Vermont became essentially neutral in the American Revolution. It adopted its own constitution, which, unlike that which the United States later ratified, banned slavery. The Vermont Republic did not agree to become the fourteenth US state until 1791, eight years after the Treaty of Paris ended revolution.

This, then, was the time and place from which Ethan Allen and his Green Mountain Boys emerged. Independence? No one could tell them anything about that subject. Never mind that Allen had left his native Connecticut for Vermont, he and his Boys were willing to do what Connecticut wanted of them, and his men wanted nothing more than his leadership. Yet Allen himself heard out Benedict Arnold. Allen may have been rowdy, independent, and impulsive, but he was not an egomaniac. He saw in Arnold the makings of a military commander, and he eagerly invited him to share joint command.

THE TICONDEROGA CAMPAIGN

No central authority ordered the taking of Fort Ticonderoga. What drove Benedict Arnold and Ethan Allen was the sheer momentum of Lexington and Concord. It was what people before and since have called the "spirit" of liberty, and before sunup on May 10, 1775, something like two hundred to three hundred volunteers, the Green Mountain Boys among them, awaited the arrival of the boats that were supposed to take them within a half-mile's march of Fort Ti.

By daybreak, the boats had yet to arrive. At full daylight, just two materialized. The co-commanders, Allen and Arnold, believed they had but one significant advantage in the coming fight. It was surprise. They agreed that the longer they waited, the greater the chances that the regulars would discover them. So, they packed into the two small boats as many men as they possibly could. The number topped out at eighty-three, plus themselves. In the meantime, a storm blew up. If it didn't drown them, it would only enhance the surprise of their operation. After all, nobody would be foolish enough to launch an attack in a squall. They ventured the two miles over a choppy Lake Champlain.

The oarsmen among them were spurred less by the commands of the commanders than by the rising level of water in their leaky, storm-tossed boats. They made the crossing in what was doubtless record time. Though they were not drowned, they were far from dry as they advanced against the fort. As soon as they were within running distance of the stockade, they charged. A sentry materialized, leveled his musket, and fired. The Patriots clearly saw the powder flash but heard no shot. It was a misfire—a flash in the pan. The Americans now stormed the fort, and when another sentry managed to lightly wound one of Ethan Allen's officers with his fixed bayonet, Allen raised the sword he was using to lead the charge and brought down on the hapless sentry the flat of its blade. It knocked the regular out of the way, leaving him humiliated but unbloodied.

With that, Fort Ticonderoga was breached, and Allen strode into the stockade, Arnold close behind him. The two ran up a crude set of stairs, at the top of which was a lieutenant of regulars known to history only as Feltham. The ruckus of the assault had roused him from his bed, and, with one hand, he held up his hastily donned breeches.

"By what authority," he demanded, "do you presume to trespass on His Majesty's property?"

"In the name of the Great Jehovah and the Continental Congress!" Ethan Allen responded. It was the kind of declaration Benedict Arnold, for all his own audacity, could never have found it within himself to make.

Allen brandished his sword, demanding possession of the fort and everything in it. Nonplussed, Lieutenant Feltham called out to his commanding officer, a Captain Delaplace. Conscious that he lacked the manpower to resist, Delaplace surrendered Fort Ticonderoga and, with his few men, marched away unmolested.

The "conquest" of Fort Ti was a victory over authority that, once challenged, proved remarkably hollow. It was of a piece with Ethan Allen's early experience against the New York posse, and it revealed a great advantage the Patriots, despite their limited resources, would enjoy throughout the long war yet to unfold. Britain was a powerful nation, but

Ethan Allen captures Fort Ticonderoga "in the name of Jehovah and the Continental Congress" on May 10, 1775. The nineteenth-century engraving is by Alonzo Chappel.
NATIONAL ARCHIVES AND
RECORDS ADMINISTRATION

it lacked both the will and the practical means to bring the full force of its power across the broad Atlantic to fight the rebels into final submission.

After taking Fort Ti, Allen sent a small force to nearby Crown Point, to capture the fort there. Lightly held by a skeleton garrison, it also surrendered without a fight, and the two captured forts added seventy-eight cannon, six mortars, three howitzers, and ammunition to the small but waxing Patriot arsenal.

THE CONTINENTAL VISION

While Allen and Arnold took the two British forts, twelve colonies—Georgia again absented itself—met as the Second Continental Congress. As before, the site was Philadelphia, but, this time, the meeting took place not in Carpenters' Hall but at the State House. The change of venue was significant. The first Congress avoided the State House for fear of too many Loyalists haunting its halls. Throughout the revolution, Philadelphia would, in fact, continue to be home to many "Tories," but their presence in the congressional meeting place was clearly no longer a source of concern.

Presided over by a new president, John Hancock, the Second Continental Congress, on June 14, passed a resolution creating the Continental Army and, upon nomination by Massachusetts delegate John Adams, made George Washington its commander. A veteran of the

French and Indian War, Washington was nevertheless far from the most experienced military figure in the colonies, but his character—distinguished by dignity, modesty, and courage—was already legendary, and he was approved unanimously.

So, the *Continental* Congress, having created a *Continental* Army, turned its attention to the biggest geopolitical entity on the continent—Canada. A majority of the congressional delegates assumed that plenty of Canadians were surely thinking in the same continental

The official presidential portrait of John Adams, by John Trumbull, about 1792. THE WHITE HOUSE

terms as the Patriots of the lower thirteen colonies. It was not a mere delusion of grandeur. Canada was just as distant from the mother country as the lower colonies, and, because it was still predominantly French, it had precious little cultural connection to Britain. Why *wouldn't* it make common cause with the southern colonies?

On June 1, 1775, the Second Continental Congress authorized a commission to invite Canada to join the fight for independence. The stunning reply from up north? Thanks, but no thanks. As inflammatory as the Quebec Act had been in the lower thirteen colonies, it clearly won the loyalty of the vast majority of Canadians.

The Second Continental Congress refused to take no for answer. Having asked Canada politely, it passed, on June 27, a resolution to invade that country. Not only did both Ethan Allen and Benedict Arnold enthusiastically approve of the measure, Arnold acted preemptively, even before the invitation had been sent. On May 17, a week after the capture of Fort Ti, he led a raid on St. John's, some twenty miles southeast of Montreal, and there captured a sixteen-gun British sloop-of-war for the Continental Navy. This deed earned him command of Patriot forces on Lake Champlain. As it turned out, however, the appointment was short-lived. After Arnold held his new office just two weeks, Congress ordered him to turn over command to a more senior officer. Instead of complying, Arnold threatened to lead a mutiny. He soon thought better of this and yielded. By then, however, Massachusetts had also accused him of embezzling military funds. On this charge, he was later exonerated, but the handwriting was on the wall. He was a man in a hurry, a man on the make. In fact, he burned to invade Canada, not so much to realize the continental ambitions of his emerging nation as to win glory for himself, to surpass Ethan Allen, and ultimately to earn some high office.

The Second Continental Congress was having none of it. On June 27, that body appointed neither Arnold nor his rival Allen to lead the Canadian invasion but chose instead Major General Philip Schuyler. He seemed a safe choice. He was a veteran of the French and Indian War—although, like Ethan Allen, he had seen no combat action. He did have an eye for military talent, however, and chose as his second-in-command

Richard Montgomery, Dublin-born, a British officer in the French and Indian War, and a man of considerable competence and dash.

Congress authorized Schuyler to get under way in June. Poor health caused him to delay into early fall. Learning that the British were making ready to retake Forts Ticonderoga and Crown Point, Montgomery wrote a note to Schuyler telling him that he was heading immediately for Canada to prevent the assault on the forts. He marched out at the head of some twelve hundred men, including the Green Mountain Boys. Ethan Allen was with them but no longer as their commander. The Boys had elected one Seth Warner as their new colonel. It is believed that Allen's Herculean drinking bouts and generally undisciplined behavior had finally proved too much for too many of the volunteers. However Allen felt about his rejection, what he wanted more than anything else was to fight, and so he acquiesced to the election of a new commander and volunteered to serve the Canadian expedition in the role of a lowly scout.

As for General Schuyler, instead of acting to countermand the insubordinate Montgomery, he got a move on—even as he learned that General Washington had just yielded to the pleas of Benedict Arnold and gave him leave to lead a parallel advance into Canada. While Schuyler (and Montgomery) targeted Montreal, Arnold was assigned to capture Quebec.

On September 4, 1775, Schuyler and his men caught up with Montgomery. Together, they attacked St. John's, the place Arnold had earlier raided. Now garrisoned by two hundred or so regulars and a contingent of Indian auxiliaries, it was a very formidable objective. Whereas Fort Ti had been a pushover, the assault on St. John's became a siege. After two weeks of fighting, Schuyler's health broke down, and he was invalided to the rear, leaving his command to Montgomery. Under wilderness conditions, siege warfare was equally hard on both those laying siege and those who were besieged. As fall gave way to an early winter, half of Montgomery's army was down with fever. By this time, St. John's had received reinforcements and was now garrisoned by seven hundred men, and Montgomery sent Ethan Allen, together with militia officer John Brown, on a mission to find and recruit local Canadians willing to join the cause of independence.

While Brown set off for La Prairie, Allen roamed the Richelieu River in search of recruits and found, to his surprise, a number willing to fight. This gave Allen a unique inspiration. He would lead his recruits in the capture of Montreal. Before he could mount an assault, however, the men he had gathered began to melt away as quickly as they had joined. Reduced to a strength of just 110 men, Allen marched back in the direction of St. John's and rendezvoused with Brown—who had amassed some two hundred recruits. Allen's intention had been to continue all the way to St. John's, where he would reunite with Montgomery. Instead, he now decided that a total of 310 men was sufficient to capture Montreal, and, so, he drew up a hasty plan with Brown. He would cross the St. Lawrence River with his 110 men just below Montreal while Brown crossed above the town. They would then attack from below and above, in pincer-fashion, and snap up the prize.

Allen crossed the St. Lawrence in the predawn hours of September 25, but Brown could not get his men across, thereby leaving Allen exposed. As a result, he was captured along with twenty of his command, clapped into irons, and shipped off to England, to stand trial for treason. In a rare interlude of moderation and rationality, his captors came to the conclusion that hanging Allen would serve only to give the American Revolution a martyr. So, in June 1776, they sent him back across the Atlantic to Halifax, from which he was paroled in October to New York City, which was under British control.

Ethan Allen had a lucky escape from his misguided attempt to take Montreal, but the operation did significant harm to the revolution in that it moved Canadian popular sentiment from indifference to the American Revolution to outright opposition. It also prompted many Native Americans on the border between Canada and the lower thirteen colonies to side with the British.

MONTGOMERY AND ARNOLD

Allen and Brown were out of the campaign, but Montgomery was making measurable progress. His forces captured a British fort at Chambly on October 18, appropriated the supplies they found there, and were thus sufficiently supplied to continue the siege against St. John's. Worn down at last, that outpost surrendered on November 2, 1775. Victory in this case meant that one semi-starving, ragged, half-frozen group of soldiers suddenly had custody of another.

It was impossible to tell the siege party from those to whom they had laid siege, and, having gained St. John's, what, really, had the Americans gained? Two miserable months had been exhausted without having gotten any closer to a conquest of Canada. Still, Montgomery did his best to rally his troops by promising that hot food and warm clothing waited for them—*in* Montreal. Remarkably, the promise pushed them to take the town, which was defended by fewer than 150 British regulars, on November 13. In the process, Montgomery also captured three substantial British warships and a few smaller craft. His mission accomplished, he could do nothing more but await word from Benedict Arnold in Quebec.

Arnold had left Cambridge, Massachusetts, on September 12 at the head of eleven hundred volunteers. Their first catastrophe befell them before they even crossed into Canada. The season was at early fall, but Maine was already in deep winter. The bateaux, flat-bottomed boats they had ordered as transportation up the Kennebec River to Canada from what is today Augusta, Maine, had been hammered together out of uncured, green wood. In consequence, the boats fell to pieces when immersed in the icy river, which left Arnold and his army no alternative but to wade for some 180 semi-frozen miles. Slowed down, they ran out of food and started eating their soap. After they exhausted that source of fat, they began boiling anything made of leather, their spare moccasins included.

Men began dying of hunger, exposure, and privation. Even more, weary and disgusted, just walked away. On November 9, when Arnold's command finally reached the south bank of the St. Lawrence River, it was reduced nearly by half, to just six hundred men. What should have been a twenty-day journey had taken forty-five. His exhausted troops now faced the prospect of capturing Quebec, reportedly garrisoned by a few Royal Marines, some regulars, and as many as four hundred Canadian militiamen. Arnold reasoned that if he attacked quickly, before his men grew any weaker, he stood a fair chance of victory. But a powerful storm prevented crossing the icebound St. Lawrence for two days and nights.

That gave the British more than enough time to augment the Quebec garrison to a total strength of twelve hundred.

Arnold's thirst for glory drove him despite the British reinforcements. In the predawn dark of November 14, he and his men crossed the river and set out over the Plains of Abraham. After sweeping aside the militia posted there, Arnold made a brave show of sending a detachment toward Quebec under a flag of truce. His intention was to demand the garrison's surrender. Instead, he and his much-reduced army were greeted with a cannonade that pinned them in place while a British frigate, HMS *Lizard*, sailed up the St. Lawrence, stationed itself behind Arnold's position, and severed his only route of retreat.

Garrisoned within the fortress town that was Quebec, eight hundred troops prepared to attack the invaders. Arnold understood that the *Lizard* was also waiting to bombard any retreat. But he decided he had no choice. Like thieves in the night, the cold, hungry would-be conquerors sneaked off. They managed to slip under the silent guns of the British ship and withdraw to Pointe-aux-Trembles. Here, on December 2, they tied in with Montgomery and his men.

Even combined, their forces barely numbered a thousand. But here they were, and they resolved to march back to Quebec and try once more to capture it. The two commanders and their command got close enough to see Quebec when it suddenly occurred to them both that, lacking cannon, a siege would take far more time than they could possibly afford, especially since the people inside Quebec were dry, warm, and reasonably well fed. Those within the city walls would survive longer and more comfortably than those outside them.

Nature's clock was relentless—but no more than the tick-tock of the militia law. The enlistments of all of Arnold's New Englanders would expire the day after year's end, which was coming on fast. Just when the militia would be legally permitted to dissolve, with the influx of British reinforcements steady, Quebec would be defended by at least eighteen hundred British regulars and Canadian militia. In the light of these daunting realizations, Arnold and Montgomery attacked on December 31, the day before the expiration of enlistments. As if circumstances could not be more dire, they advanced to their objective in the face of a blizzard, and they advanced against a force they knew to be at least twice their own number.

Heroic or futile? Take your pick.

Montgomery moved forward from the left, his men dragging siege ladders through the drifting snow. Arnold advanced from the right, his six hundred leaning into pounding snow, ice, and bullets. One of the latter hit Benedict Arnold in the leg. Unable to walk, he passed command to Daniel Morgan, who would prove, later in the war, a master of unconventional combat. Under Morgan, the Americans breached Quebec's "Lower Town" wall. They hunkered down beside it to await the arrival of Montgomery, whose troops were still hung up on barricades and other obstacles.

In the meantime, the British garrison watched and waited from inside Quebec. When Montgomery and many of his officers were at pointblank range, they let fly a musket volley and a round of grapeshot. The antipersonnel artillery ammunition of the day, grapeshot consisted of a loosely bound cluster of small iron balls that, fired from a cannon, sprayed out to create a lethal field of fire. Montgomery and his officers fell as wheat before the reaper. Simultaneously, British general Guy Carleton, commanding the Quebec garrison, sent men to reinforce the Lower Town. There, Morgan and his soldiers surrendered.

January 1776 saw the sudden collapse of the continental vision of the Continental Congress. Of Arnold's force, fewer than half remained in the field. Forty-eight were dead, thirty-four wounded, and 372 had become prisoners of war. The rest had deserted. Arnold nevertheless refused to

"The Death of General Montgomery in the Attack on Quebec, December 31, 1775," by John Trumbull (1786). The first Patriot general officer killed in the revolution, Richard Montgomery fell in the disastrous American invasion of Canada.
YALE UNIVERSITY ART GALLERY

depart Canada. Wounded as he was, he lurked with his survivors on the outskirts of Quebec until April, waiting in vain for reinforcements.

As Carleton's Quebec garrison had swelled to more than two thousand, General Washington struggled to persuade the Second Continental Congress to fund a relief force. At last, it was ready to march by early spring. Congress sent Arnold a message promoting him to brigadier general and ordering him to leave Quebec for Montreal to assume command of American forces there. Major General David Wooster would leave Montreal to take command outside of Quebec.

On May 1, Wooster was joined by Major General John Thomas. The combined forces numbered twenty-five hundred, but disease and expiring enlistments chopped this down to six hundred fit for duty. The two generals decided that storming Quebec with such a puny force was suicide. On May 2, as the ice began to thaw on the St. Lawrence, Thomas learned that ships were incoming to Quebec bearing Major General John Burgoyne with thirteen thousand fresh British troops (forty-three hundred were Hessian mercenaries in the British service). Thomas ordered a withdrawal, which was fired upon by Royal Marines. The retreat became a rout. The army, become a rabble, drifted away. Smallpox swept it. Among the dead was John Thomas.

The American invasion was in shambles. Brigadier General John Sullivan, sent to reinforce Wooster and Thomas, reported to the Continental Congress on June 1, 1776, that "Every thing is in the utmost confusion and almost every one frightened as they know not what." It was a strange, unprofessional communication from a general, but the reply of Congress was even stranger and less professional. It ordered Sullivan to press on with the assault against Quebec.

Sullivan tried. He sent Brigadier General William Thompson at the

General John Burgoyne, as painted by Joshua Reynolds about 1766. THE FRICK COLLECTION

head of two thousand Continental soldiers to Trois-Rivières on the north bank of the St. Lawrence, about midway between Montreal and Quebec. Sullivan believed that no more than eight hundred British occupied Trois-Rivières. Capture that place, and he would have a base from which he could attack Quebec with a rational hope of prevailing. Sullivan had no way of knowing that Burgoyne's regulars were advancing and that six thousand regulars, not eight hundred, were already at Trois-Rivières, under the command of Brigadier General Simon Fraser.

During the night of June 6, Thompson landed ten miles above Trois-Rivières. Leaving 250 men to guard his bateaux, he advanced in company with his four regimental commanders, Arthur St. Clair, William Irvine, William Maxwell, and Anthony Wayne, at the head of 1,750 men. Wayne caught sight of the regulars in a clearing and quietly rallied his bone-weary men. They made a surprise attack, routing the numerically superior enemy. Thompson now followed up, his troops pursuing the fleeing British.

Then his men quite literally stumbled upon the entrenchments of Simon Fraser's principal force. In the dark, Thompson had no idea of just how hopelessly outnumbered he was. He attacked the men before him and, overwhelmed, was quickly thrown back. Desperately, Thompson scrambled to form up his scattered troops for a second attack. Realizing this would never work, he ordered a retreat. Neither Carleton nor Simon Fraser, it turned out, were in any mood to feed a couple of thousand POWs. What they saw before them was not a ragged rabble in full retreat. The two British commanders decided to leave the fleeing Americans to the wilderness, the Canadian militia, and, cruelest of all, to the Indians. About June 11, some eleven hundred American soldiers began traipsing into the village of Sorel. They were all that was left of the two thousand. The British had lost eight killed, nine wounded.

COUNTER-INVASION

In human terms, the long blunder that was the American invasion of Canada added up to tragedy. In military terms, it was worse: a self-multiplying loss. It not only wasted the lives of good men, it persuaded the British that these American rebels could be destroyed. The failure in

Canada was so complete that the British commanders decided to mount a counter-invasion of the lower thirteen colonies.

The key to the operation was gaining control of Lake Champlain, the waterway astride the border. For all his failings of character, Benedict Arnold grasped the strategic situation instantly. He saw that the British intended retribution, and he was not content merely to flee the scene of his failure. Having lost Canada, he was determined to prevent the British from using it as a platform for what he correctly assumed would be a counter-invasion. So, he transformed himself from newbie general to newbie admiral. He set his battered men to felling trees and rudely cobbling the timber together into crude approximations of freshwater vessels he called "galleys." The four he managed to construct were christened *Washington, Congress, Trumbull,* and *Gates.* In addition, his men put together eight or nine smaller "gundalows," flat-bottomed open boats with pointy prows fore and aft. The vessels were little more than gun platforms. *Washington* was seventy-two feet in length with a twenty-foot beam. It carried eighty men, who rowed it and also tended two eighteen-pound guns, two twelve-pounders, two nine-pounders, four four-pounders, a single two-pounder, and eight small swivel guns. The more numerous gundalows carried forty-five men each, a single twelve-pounder in the bow and a pair of nine-pounders amidships.

The British partially dismantled a Royal Navy ship, HMS *Inflexible,* and modified this ocean vessel for service on the shallow waters of Lake Champlain. They similarly rebuilt two schooners and a large gundalow. To this flotilla, they added one purpose-built *radeau,* a ninety-two-foot scow clumsily equipped with sails. They called her HMS *Thunderer* and loaded three hundred men aboard, along with two massive howitzers—short-barreled cannon that fired projectiles in high trajectories—a half-dozen twenty-four-pounders, and another six twelve-pounders. An impressive platform, *Thunderer* proved completely impossible to maneuver and, so, never made it into battle. But the British also threw onto the lake a number of longboats and gunboats—anything, in fact, that could carry armed men and a cannon or two.

On August 24, 1776, "Admiral" Arnold rowed ten of his fleet out of Crown Point and anchored the vessels off Valcour Island to await the construction of additional craft. When the British met him here on

October 11, Arnold had fifteen improvised boats altogether. The enemy bore down on these with twenty gunboats, thirty longboats, and some larger craft. Arnold tried to flee but realized it was too late. The Battle of Valcour Island was on.

The jerry-built, jury-rigged gun platforms fired on one another. Simple numbers dictated that Arnold's flotilla would take the worse of the beating. The two sides exchanged fire throughout the 11th and 12th. By sunup of October 13, Benedict Arnold had only *Congress* and *Washington* still afloat. Into these, he loaded those of his men still alive and conducted a fighting withdrawal all the way to Buttonmould Bay on Champlain's Vermont shore. Beaching what was left of *Congress* and *Washington*, he set the hulks ablaze and marched his men back to Crown Point—only to realize that this position had become indefensible. He burned everything standing in Crown Point and pressed on to Fort Ticonderoga. It was the rallying point from which the Canadian invasion had jumped off two years earlier.

A Sort of Victory

The Battle of Valcour Island was beyond question a tactical defeat. Arnold entered battle with fifteen vessels and lost eleven. Seven hundred fifty men fought, of whom eighty were killed or wounded. Of the roughly twenty British gunboats committed to the battle, none were so much as damaged. The larger vessels, *Carleton* and *Inflexible*, did suffer injury but remained serviceable. As for British casualties, they were inconsequential.

Yet, from this dreary coda to a disastrous invasion, Benedict Arnold wrested a surprising strategic victory. Built from scratch, his Champlain Squadron managed to bleed the momentum from the British counter-invasion—to bleed it so thoroughly, in fact, that General Carleton aborted his plan of tying into General William Howe's British forces in the lower thirteen colonies. Had Carleton gone through with what he had intended, he and Howe might well have brought the American Revolution to a premature end in 1776. Benedict Arnold won no glory in Canada, but his desperate ingenuity in retreat very possibly saved the revolution—which he himself, of course, would live to betray.

Defeat and Triumph in Boston

MAY 10, 1775, WAS THE DAY THAT ETHAN ALLEN AND BENEDICT Arnold captured Fort Ticonderoga and also the day that John Adams, delegate to the Second Continental Congress meeting in Philadelphia, moved that Congress effectively nationalize the militia force then assembling outside of Boston in preparation for battle against the British army garrisoned in that city. The militia known as "the Boston army" Adams proposed renaming the Continental Army. Congress approved, with the stipulation that the new Continental Army should be made up of men drawn from *all* the colonies. These troops would be added to the former "Boston army."

While the Continental Army was coming into being, Adams, on June 14, rose to nominate George Washington to command the force. With becoming modesty, Washington responded: "I do not think myself equal to the command." Maybe this was sincere. Maybe it was pro forma. Or perhaps it was simply disingenuous, because George Washington must have known that no one else in the colonies was more "equal to" the assignment than he.

A surveyor by training and a planter by vocation, Washington was not a professional soldier. But, at twenty-two, he had served as a lieutenant colonel in the Virginia militia and, in that capacity, started the French and Indian War when he opened fire on a party of French soldiers at Great Meadows, Pennsylvania, on May 27, 1754. He survived the retaliatory attack that followed—about half his men did not—and then he led the Virginia militia in the Battle of the Wilderness (near present-day Pittsburgh) on July 9, 1755. His commanding officer in that catastrophic

General George Washington, as painted by Charles Willson Peale in 1776. THE WHITE HOUSE

engagement was Edward Braddock, major general of British regulars, who led his force into the worst defeat the English suffered in that war. So, Washington at least knew the harsh realities of combat. He knew something about fighting, a little bit about winning, quite a bit more about losing, and far more about surviving to fight another day.

In the end, he accepted the congressional commission and stood by as Congress appointed his chief lieutenants: Artemas Ward (who was already commanding the Boston army); Charles Lee, like Washington, a prominent Virginian; Philip Schuyler, a wealthy New Yorker; Israel Putnam, a middle-aged Connecticut veteran of the French and Indian War; and Horatio Gates, a former British officer and a combat veteran. The Continental Army was a serious force, adding up to 27,500 troops by the close of 1775. Moreover, these soldiers were augmented by a variable number of militia forces. Worldwide, the British regular army numbered about one hundred twenty thousand men, but its peak strength in America was thirty thousand, and that was not reached until 1777. On land, therefore, British strength was far from overwhelming. It was the Royal Navy to which the Crown looked to defend its hold on the colonies.

It was also true, however, that the population of Britain numbered some eight million in 1775, of whom perhaps 2,350,000 could be counted as eligible for military service. Contrast this with a total colonial population of about 2,256,000, excluding Native Americans but including 506,000 slaves, who certainly could not be depended on to fight. Besides, Tories (pro-British loyalists) accounted for at least a quarter of the American population. Add in those who were neutral or apathetic, and perhaps no more than 40 to 50 percent of Americans wanted a revolution.

Yet Britain was in no position to muster anything approaching its theoretical military manpower. Denying the American colonists their independence was not popular in Britain. Some three hundred thousand Englishmen had enlisted in the army during the French and Indian War (which, in Europe, was fought as the Seven Years' War), but only about 10 percent of that number could be raised at any one time to put down the rebellion begun in 1775. As for the quality of troops, certainly British regulars were better trained than Americans, who also lacked such important military specialists as engineers, artillerists, and cavalrymen. Yet many of the colonists who had fought alongside the regulars in the French and Indian War were unimpressed by the performance of British regulars in frontier battles. They were trained to fight formal battles between armies in open European battlefields. As was seen in the British retreat from Concord, the regulars were vulnerable to unconventional tactics, including sniping and ambush. Not that the typical Patriot soldier was handy with a gun. Most, in fact, had never fired a weapon before enlisting. But a significant minority were accomplished hunters and, accordingly, reasonably good marksmen. Whereas the British soldier was relentlessly drilled in the manual of arms—trained to load, fire, and reload rapidly, without exercising any great care in aiming—those Americans who had firearms experience valued marksmanship over speed of weapons handling. Moreover, many of them carried their own weapons into combat. These were typically long rifles rather than the already obsolescent "Brown Bess" musket of the British army. The rifle took longer to load, but it was far more accurate and capable of greater range.

No doubt, the Patriots had a lot stacked against them. But the contest was not nearly as one-sided going in as schoolbook history often suggests, and by late May 1775, some ten thousand colonial troops surrounded Boston, which was the main British garrison in the colonies. The redcoat army was bottled up—but, in the absence of an American navy, British water traffic was pretty well unimpeded.

On May 25, HMS *Cerberus* sailed into Boston Harbor with three major generals sent to aid Thomas Gage in crushing the rebels. They were William Howe, senior among them, who had fought in the War of the Austrian Succession but also in the French and Indian War.

Unlike most of his regular army colleagues, therefore, he knew a good deal about the differences between fighting in Europe and America. His juniors, John Burgoyne and Henry Clinton, were neither as skilled nor as prudent as Howe. Burgoyne had earned the sobriquet "Gentleman Johnny" because he was an amateur playwright, a wit, a notorious ladies' man, a Tory member of Parliament, and, only lastly, a soldier. Nevertheless, he had a reputation for gallantry under fire and earned a level of respect from the common soldier that was beyond rare in the British service. Clinton was different from Burgoyne in every respect. Humorless and ill-tempered, he was a thoroughly unimaginative officer, an unimpressive leader, yet a competent manager.

GOING FOR THE HIGH GROUND

Gage did not fret about the character or quality of the officers sent him. He was just happy to have the help. He tasked Howe with destroying the American army and doing it, mind you, in a single decisive battle. Howe proposed an amphibious landing at Dorchester Point, to the right of Cambridge, while Clinton landed at Willis Creek, on the left. The objective was to converge upon and to deny to the rebels the high ground at Charlestown, specifically Bunker Hill, which overlooked both Boston and Cambridge, the main encampment of the rebel army, which was laying siege to the British garrison. As Howe explained, the amphibious attack would be backed by the massed artillery fire of the Royal Navy warships in Boston Harbor. After Bunker Hill was taken, Howe and Clinton would converge on Cambridge itself and wipe out the rebel encampment, nipping the revolution in the bud.

What British commanders did not realize at this time was that they were up against a well-developed network of Patriot spies. Unknown to Howe and his colleagues, the local Committee of Safety quickly discovered their plan. General Ward decided that the best move was to defend the high ground preemptively by immediately occupying and fortifying Bunker Hill. He knew it would not be easy. The Patriots were short on gunpowder, and Bunker Hill was exposed to the guns of the Royal Navy fleet. Add to this that the only avenue of retreat from the hill was by way of Charlestown Neck, a narrow isthmus that flooded at high tide. If the operation failed, the defenders of Bunker Hill could be wiped out.

When Ward apprised him of these risks, Major General Israel Putnam replied, "Americans are not at all afraid of their heads, though very much afraid of their legs. If you cover these, they will fight forever." With that, he accepted the challenge. Unfortunately, however, he also let his second in command, Colonel William Prescott, persuade him that it was better to occupy Breed's Hill than Bunker Hill, since Breed's Hill was less exposed to naval fire. Yet it was also lower and less steep than Bunker Hill, which made it more vulnerable to overland attack. Putnam put a small force on Bunker Hill to cover a possible retreat, but he deployed most of his men, twelve hundred of them, on Breed's Hill, ordering them to dig in.

In the meantime, Gage and Howe prepared twenty-five hundred ship-borne regulars for the attack. In addition to the sixty-eight-gun ship-of-the-line *Somerset* as well as two floating artillery batteries, the frigate *Glasgow*, and an armed troop transport named *Symmetry*, there were the guns of two small gunboats and *Falcon* and *Lively*, sloops of war. Add to this firepower some ground-based artillery, and it was clear that the Americans would be in for a brutal time.

Gage and Howe can be forgiven if they were confident that it would all be over soon. But they had no idea how fiercely the Americans would defend the hills.

"An Exact View of the Late Battle of Charlestown," better known as the Battle of Bunker Hill, was engraved by Bernard Romans, a Dutch-born mapmaker, who fought for American independence and served as a military engineer during the revolution. JOHN CARTER BROWN LIBRARY

Best Laid Plans . . .

When a Royal Marine aboard HMS *Lively* saw the Americans working on Breed's Hill rather than Bunker Hill, the sloop's captain opened fire against Breed's Hill. Taking this as their signal, the rest of the harbor fleet followed suit—without coordinating with Gage, Clinton, and Howe, who were not fully prepared to begin the infantry assault. Now, having lost the element of surprise, they realized that immediate action was required.

Clinton had the uncharacteristically original idea of departing from the amphibious plan by attacking across Charlestown Neck to hit the rebel rear. Both Gage and Howe objected, however, and instead insisted on disembarking from the Mystic River side of the peninsula and *then* marching overland around to the American rear. This would get more soldiers into the initial assault, which was important, but it also required waiting for the tide. And that gave the Americans, even under fire, an additional six hours to continue digging defensive trenches.

Putnam, who directed the action not from Breed's but from Bunker Hill, demanded reinforcements from Artemas Ward, who released twelve hundred New Hampshiremen under the command of John Stark and James Reed. They marched at a stately tempo four miles through incoming artillery fire. When one of his officers urged him to order a quick-march cadence, Stark replied that "one fresh man in action [was] worth ten fatigued men." He did not vary the beat.

It was one in the afternoon when the first British regulars disembarked at Moulton's Point, on the tip of Charlestown Peninsula. Suddenly, Howe realized just how formidable his objective was. The delay had given the Americans a lot of time to dig in. Moreover, the slow march of Stark's reinforcements plainly revealed the presence of many sharpshooters in their ranks. Now it was Howe's turn to pause. He decided to await arrival of his own reinforcements. This provided yet more time for the Americans to improve their defenses.

As finally reinforced, Howe divided between himself and Brigadier General Sir Robert Pigot a total of twenty-five hundred British regulars. Pigot was to commence the assault by attacking the earthwork defenses at the top of Breed's Hill. Howe ordered his ground-based artillery

to open fire on the hill-
top in preparation. After
a few shots, however, the
guns fell silent. Howe was
stunned to discover that
his artillerists had supplied
his six-pounder guns with
twelve-pound cannonballs.
They would not fit. This
left Pigot's troops, positioned for their assault,
fully exposed to Patriot
rifle fire from houses in
Charlestown. Pigot sent a
runner to the fleet with
instructions for them to
direct their fire against
Charlestown.

Map of the action at Breed's Hill, the principal
battlefield of the Battle of Bunker Hill (June 17,
1775). BOSTON PUBLIC LIBRARY

The British naval gun-
ners understood precisely what to do. They prepared "hotshots," cannonballs heated red hot. They also prepared loads of "carcasses," hollowed-out
cannonballs stuffed with flammable pitch, set ablaze with a fuse, and then
fired—in full flame. The hollow ammunition shattered on impact, spew-
ing fire. The close-set wooden houses of Charlestown were soon ablaze,
imparting a hellish backdrop to what was already a fiendish battle.

Howe decided the time had come to exploit the developing chaos.
He detached 350 of his best light infantrymen and deployed them along
the Mystic River beach. He then sent them roaring against the American front line with bayonets fixed. British officers had learned from the
French and Indian War that American militiamen feared bayonet attack
more than anything. In this case, however, the Americans did not flinch.
The fire from Putnam's and Stark's troops remained careful, deliberate,
and devastating, Putnam having issued perhaps the single most-quoted
command in American military history: "Don't fire until you see the
whites of their eyes! Then, fire low."

Just three Patriot volleys killed ninety-six elite soldiers of the Royal Army—while also killing or wounding every officer on Howe's personal staff. Howe did not cower, but gallantly led from the front. He miraculously escaped without injury but found himself deeply shocked by the accumulation of dead British soldiers.

Howe's Pyrrhic Victory

To the Americans, it looked as if the British onslaught was collapsing. Even Prescott, a reasonably experienced officer, cheered. But he also had the presence of mind to tell his troops that the battle was far from ended. Not everyone got the word, however, and some militiamen began to depart the field. Alarmed at this, Putnam did his best to coax the reserves lodged on Bunker Hill to transfer to Breed's Hill. Perhaps this would prevent its fall when the British renewed attack.

Howe, shaking off his shock, was ready to send a second wave fifteen minutes after the repulse of the first. This time, he cast aside tactics and, instead of splitting his forces in a kind of pincer maneuver, he opted for a brute-force frontal assault on the fortified position atop Breed's Hill, reserving only a small secondary group to keep the Mystic flank busy.

The second wave of British regulars rolled forward. And, like the first, seemingly melted away. For the second time that day, Pigot and Howe issued the command to retreat. They were, however, consoled by one realization. It was clear to them that the Americans were beginning to break. The front line was getting thinner—and it was apparent to the British commanders that many of the Americans were simply cowering behind the shadow of Bunker Hill. Perhaps the British commanders assumed that the fight had finally been scared out of them. But the Americans' problem was not a shortage of courage. It was a rapidly dwindling supply of powder.

The Americans had plenty of shot, but little gunpowder. Officers now ordered their men to split their prepared cartridges, which were made of paper and contained a measured amount of powder. The divided powder would drive more balls and bullets but not nearly as far. When Howe ordered his third assault, consisting of four hundred Royal Marines and Royal Army regulars, the defenders would not be nearly as effective. The Americans returned fire, but, this time, the

John Trumbull's 1834 depiction of the "Death of General Warren" is a romanticized but vivid evocation of the close-up violence of the Battle of Bunker Hill. MUSEUM OF FINE ARTS BOSTON

British breached their lines, and combat became hand-to-hand. While the British had bayonets, most of the Americans did not. Prescott accordingly ordered his men to "club their muskets," so they swung their weapons by the barrel and used the stock as a bludgeon to knock the bayonet-tipped enemy muskets away. But there were just too many now, and Prescott ordered a retreat.

It was by no means an ignominious rout. The Patriots fought even as they drew back, all the way down Breed's Hill and across to Bunker Hill. They continued fighting and firing as they crossed Charlestown Neck and withdrew onto the mainland. The toll on the British regulars continued to mount, but, even in a fighting retreat, a withdrawing force is especially vulnerable. It was in their effort to save themselves that the Americans suffered their heaviest losses.

In the end, Howe scored a strategic victory, taking both Breed's Hill and Bunker Hill. But the cost was a heavy tactical defeat. Of the twenty-four hundred regulars and marines actually engaged in combat, 1,054 had been shot, of whom 226 were killed. The dry and dour Henry Clinton put it this way in his diary: "A dear-bought victory, another such would have ruined us." Forced to give up the real estate they defended, the Americans nevertheless *felt* like victors. They had badly bloodied the army of King George III.

THE BRITISH GIVE UP BOSTON

So heavy were his casualties that General Gage decided against mounting a counteroffensive from Bunker Hill. As a result, the American army was reinforced in Cambridge, and the British regular garrison remained under siege.

General Washington did not arrive in Cambridge until July 2, well after the somewhat misnamed Battle of Bunker Hill. He formally took over command of the army from Artemas Ward, and while he welcomed the continuing influx of militia regiments, Washington struggled to assert his supreme command on a heterogeneous assortment of men and units. He also confronted shortages of weapons, ammunition, and provisions and, something that would vex him throughout the revolution, the brevity of most militia enlistments. His manpower was in continual flux, almost invariably downward, and he was keenly aware that the besieged British garrison would soon be getting reinforcements by sea.

Washington summoned his subordinates to a council of war on January 16, 1776. He presented to them his case for breaking off the siege with a showdown attack on the British garrison *before* its reinforcements arrived. He issued a call for thirteen militia regiments to serve during February and March. But when word of the terrible collapse of the American invasion of Canada (Chapter 10) arrived on January 17, Congress diverted three of the thirteen regiments for service across the border. Eager to move nevertheless, Washington proposed a surprise attack against Boston across the frozen Charles River. His subordinates countered with a plan to occupy Dorchester Heights in the hope of drawing the British out into open battle.

Fate intervened in the heavy-set and bespectacled form of Henry Knox, a Continental Army colonel who had only recently transitioned into military life from being the longtime owner of a Boston bookstore. Ethan Allen and Benedict Arnold had captured Fort Ticonderoga on May 10, 1775 (Chapter 10), whereupon Knox persuaded General Washington to let him transport that fort's fine artillery more than three hundred miles back to Cambridge. It was a daunting backcountry journey. Knox arrived at Ticonderoga on December 5, 1775, and instructed his troops to build forty-two sledges and then heap them with as much artillery as they could carry. He hitched the crude vehicles to eighty yoke of oxen—that is, 160 oxen in all. The long, rough journey ended on January 24, 1776, when the artillery began arriving in Cambridge. In all, fifty-nine guns were delivered—fourteen mortars, two howitzers, and forty-three cannon.

Washington's preparations did not go unnoticed. Yet General Gage made no response to them. Had they received better cooperation from the Royal Navy, it is likely Gage and Howe could have broken the siege. But the two services, land and sea, could never seem to coordinate effectively. Crown and Parliament responded by replacing Gage with his current subordinate, William Howe, who was given overall command of all British land forces in America on October 10, 1775. On January 27, 1776, General Howe's brother, Admiral Richard Howe, replaced Admiral Samuel Graves as commander of the fleet in a move intended to compel the land and sea forces to work together.

So, British leadership had been upgraded, and the Boston garrison expanded to about eight thousand—which, however, was still only half the number of the American troops gathering in Cambridge and on Dorchester Heights. During the night of March 4, 1776, a twelve-hundred-man labor detail covered by eight hundred Continental Army troops slowly moved a train of 360 ox carts loaded with barricades and other components of fortification up to Dorchester Heights, where many of Knox's guns had been positioned. By three o'clock on the morning of March 5, the heights were completely fortified. "The rebels have done more in one night than my whole army could do in months," Howe mournfully remarked.

Washington now not only owned the high ground over Boston and the harbor, his fortifications were located above the range of both British ground and naval artillery. Howe calculated that he would have to use twenty-two hundred men to storm Dorchester Heights. A storm prompted him to abort the assault, however, and he was doubtless also chastened by the ordeal of Bunker and Breed's Hills. Ultimately, Howe concluded that attacking the fortified Heights would be a needless effusion of blood. On March 7, therefore, he ordered the withdrawal of British forces from Boston. By nine o'clock in the morning of March 17, eleven thousand British soldiers and sailors were aboard ships of the royal fleet. They set sail for Canada.

And, through it all, Washington ordered his cannon to hold fire. Unknown to the Continental Army he commanded, he himself had secretly negotiated the British withdrawal with a promise of safe conduct and their solemn promise to leave Boston and its citizens unharmed. The siege had lasted eight months. For Washington and his new national army, it was a victory. For the Howe brothers, it was an opportunity to wage war from a new angle and to do so not by trying to pick off insurgent rebels one by one but by mounting an overwhelming invasion from Canada, which was securely in British hands.

CHAPTER 12

A Time of Decision

ASK THE NEXT RANDOM NON-HISTORIAN YOU MEET TO NAME THE DATE on which the American Revolution began. Chances are that "July 4, 1776" will come back at you. That answer is wrong. Now, depending on how you define "revolution," it is wrong by more than a year or a little less than a month.

Most historians and teachers of history agree that the American Revolution began on April 19, 1775, with the Battles of Lexington and Concord. That is when colonial military forces and the British army began shooting at one another. But was this violence a revolution or just a rebellion? It is a valid question because Americans were significantly divided in 1775 over whether to break away from the mother country. Pollsters didn't exist in colonial America, so nobody is sure of the percentages. But most historians believe that when the shooting started, about 20 percent of Americans were absolutely opposed to independence; another, almost certainly larger, minority absolutely demanded independence; while the rest were either indifferent, deliberately neutral, or simply undecided. At least one historian, Robert M. Calhoon, an authority on the Loyalists in the American Revolution, calculated that 40 to 45 percent of white Americans favored independence, 15 to 20 percent remained loyal to king and Parliament, and the rest endeavored to sit on the fence and express no opinion one way or the other. Some of the most recent historians guess that more than half of white Americans favored independence by July 4, 1776, but that Loyalists and the uncommitted nevertheless continued to represent a large minority. Moreover, these

121

historians tend to assume that when the revolution went poorly for the Patriots, support for independence declined.

On March 17, 1776, Americans had pushed a British army out of Boston, and that army kept going until it reached Canada. Even then, however, there was no majority consensus on precisely what the war—rebellion, revolution, whatever—was all about. As for Congress, it did not approve the final text of a Declaration of Independence until July 4, 1776—which is not, strictly speaking, the date of that independence. Legally, it came on August 2, 1776, when the approved document was signed by the delegates.

THE MODERATE VIEW

Joseph Galloway of Philadelphia, whom we met in Chapter 5, presented to the First Continental Congress on September 28, 1774, a "Plan of Union" intended to obtain for the colonies a measure of home rule without making them totally independent from the Empire. Essentially, it proposed the creation of a Colonial Parliament that would act together with the British Parliament in London. The Colonial Parliament would have delegates appointed by each of the colonial assemblies but would be presided over by a president-general appointed by the Crown. The Colonial Parliament would have veto power over decisions of the British Parliament affecting the colonies, especially with regard to trade and taxation. The Plan of Union was surprisingly popular, failing passage by a single vote. Disgusted with this result, Galloway decided not to serve in the Second Continental Congress. Instead, he wrote what he hoped would be a persuasive anti-independence tract, "A Candid Examination of the Mutual Claims of Great Britain and the Colonies: With a Plan of Accommodation on Constitutional Principles," but hardly anyone paid attention. As mentioned in Chapter 5, he left the United States in 1778, during the height of the revolution, and two years later, while living in Britain, published *Historical and Political Reflections on the Rise and Progress of the American Rebellion* (1780), in which he attempted to dismiss the American Revolution, still ongoing at the time, as essentially a religious quarrel between Presbyterians and Congregationalists.

Without Galloway's participation, the Second Continental Congress convened in Philadelphia on May 10, 1775, and intensely debated independence versus reconciliation. Maryland-born John Dickinson, whose

Letters from a Farmer in Pennsylvania to Inhabitants of the British Colonies (1767–1768) was a compelling condemnation of the infamous taxes of the Townshend Acts, presented the new congress with the so-called "Olive Branch Petition," which he proposed the delegates sign and send to King George III. Drafted with the aid of Benjamin Franklin, future first Supreme Court chief justice John Jay, and future associate Supreme Court justices John Rutledge and Thomas Johnson, it presented—respectfully, not to say meekly—the colonial grievances against aspects of British rule in the colonies but asserted love and loyalty to the king. It earnestly asked his "Majesty . . . to procure us relief from our afflicting fears and jealousies."

Led by John Adams, the New England delegates protested the petition, but a majority of the Second Continental Congress nevertheless endorsed it—albeit as individuals rather than on behalf of the congress. No less a figure than Richard Penn, descendent of Pennsylvania founder and proud Englishman William Penn, set sail for London and attempted to deliver it to the king. George refused to receive him and instead, even as Penn silently awaited his possible change of heart, issued a royal proclamation on August 23, 1775. It judged "our Colonies and Plantations in North America, misled by dangerous and designing men," to be in a state of rebellion. Accordingly, it commanded "all our Officers . . . and all our obedient and loyal subjects, to use their utmost endeavours to withstand and suppress such rebellion."

Thus, little less than a year before the colonies declared their independence, King George III proclaimed them to be in rebellion. Arguably, therefore, it was the king who made the first move toward starting a full-fledged American Revolution. Yet his own prime minister, Lord North—he whose tone-deaf policies had in the first place pushed the colonies farther and farther away—ushered through Parliament his own proposal for reconciliation. What is more, he managed to secure its approval from both the Parliament and the king. While the North proposal provided no real parliamentary representation for the colonies, it did cede to the colonial legislatures a great deal of the power to levy taxes. This was well short of independence yet was nevertheless a major concession—which, on July 31, 1775, just two days before adjourning, the Second Continental Congress rejected.

The liberal British statesman and champion of American independence Edmund Burke brought before Parliament on November 16, 1775, a bill to "Compose American Troubles." Burke's bill asserted parliamentary supremacy over royal prerogative in all colonial matters. It was a bold effort to cut King George III out of the loop and assume for Parliament direct authority over the colonies—whose independence or, at least, commonwealth status, Burke intended to engineer. The bill was voted down.

Some of the colonies made further efforts at reconciliation. On November 4, 1775, the assembly of New Jersey—a colony with many Loyalists—passed a highly peculiar resolution that summarily—and quite falsely—dismissed as "groundless" all reports of Americans seeking independence. On November 9, which was, coincidentally, the same day Congress learned that the king had refused to receive both Penn and his Olive Branch Petition, the Pennsylvania Assembly sent instructions to its Continental Congress delegation to "dissent from and utterly reject any propositions . . . that may cause or lead to a separation from our mother country or a change of the form of this government."

As for the Second Continental Congress, although it had been spurned by George III, it responded to the rejection of the Olive Branch Petition on December 6 by simultaneously reaffirming allegiance to the king while denying authority to Parliament because the colonies were not represented in that body.

THE RADICAL VIEW

Congressional delegates of the more radical colonies grew increasingly restive. Some colonies, including Massachusetts, summarily drew up their own constitutions, each of which was effectively a declaration of independence. Massachusetts asked the Continental Congress to create a model constitution for it and like-minded colonies to emulate. Congress declined, but by early 1776, Massachusetts, New Hampshire, and South Carolina had each written a new constitution conspicuously without royal authority. None of them, however, explicitly declared independence. Others, though, soon did, and by the time the Declaration of Independence was approved on July 4, 1776, seven colonies had effectively transitioned to independent states—at least on paper.

A Potent Dose of Common Sense

As 1775 drew to a close, America was at war with its mother country, but the objective of the combat-in-progress was still an open question. Dr. Benjamin Rush of Philadelphia, the most eminent physician in the New World, a Continental Congress delegate, and a champion of independence, regarded the unanswered question of purpose the same way as he regarded a patient's undiagnosed pain. In both cases, finding the right answer was an urgent matter of life or death. He called on an acquaintance of his, a recent arrival to Philadelphia from England, Thomas Paine, who had already established a reputation as a rebel and a writer. He asked Paine to compose a pamphlet—for pamphleteering was a strong shaper of public opinion in the eighteenth century—to lay out, straightforwardly and persuasively, the case for independence.

Paine sank his teeth into the assignment, rapidly churned out a manuscript, and delivered it to Rush, who read it with great joy and satisfaction. Rush first praised its "common sense" and then appropriated those two words for its title. *Common Sense* made up forty-seven printed pages, was published on January 9, 1776, and sold for two shillings a copy. Within its compact compass, it advanced just about every imaginable argument for independence. That in itself was a valuable service. But Paine brought to his subject an eloquent passion, at once compellingly rational and yet propelled by a rhetorical energy that many found impossible to resist.

Paine broadcast three principal themes. First, he made the case that not only was King George III a bad king but that the whole notion of rule by inherited authority was inherently nonsensical. Second, he argued that a republican form of government was the only rational form of government. Third, he argued that only a republican government could truly express and uphold equality of rights, which was the natural and common birthright of all humanity. The measure of the worthiness of any government, he argued, was the degree to which it defended this birthright. The British government, having failed in such defense, had therefore to be spurned. To these broad ideological arguments, Paine added a recitation of the pragmatic economic benefits of independence.

It was a brilliant sales pitch for breaking with Britain, and he closed the sale by elevating the American situation to a stage at once global and eternal: "O ye that love mankind!" he appealed. "Ye that dare oppose, not only the tyranny, but the tyrant, stand forth! Every spot of the old world is overrun with oppression. Freedom hath been hunted round the globe. Asia, and Africa, have long expelled her. Europe regards her like a stranger, and England hath given her warning to depart. O! receive the fugitive, and prepare in time an asylum for mankind." Although Paine was himself an atheist, he concluded *Common Sense* with a vision of secular salvation, in which the hope of all humanity rested with America and the Americans, the new chosen people. He gave the world, he gave all humankind, a stake in America's fate.

Common Sense was a bestseller—selling one hundred twenty thousand copies in its first three months. In its wake, the Continental Congress suddenly awoke. On February 18, 1776, it commissioned privateers—merchant captains, crews, and ships given license to raid and capture British commercial vessels. While the Continental Congress had created a Continental Navy on October 13, 1775, most American seaborne operations during the revolution were carried out by the far more numerous privateers. On February 26, the Continental Congress passed an embargo on exports to Britain and the British West Indies, and the next month, on March 3, Congress dispatched Silas Deane to France to negotiate with Britain's perennial rival and adversary for military aid. Eleven days after this, the Congress issued an order to disarm all Loyalists throughout the colonies—"Loyalist" being defined as anyone who continues to proclaim their allegiance to King George III. On April 6, the Continental Congress issued a proclamation declaring all American ports open to the trade of all nations—save Great Britain.

Several colonies were also swept up by the wave that followed *Common Sense* and the series of congressional actions. Virginia voted up a resolution of independence on May 15, 1776, proclaiming not merely its own independence but unilaterally declaring "the United Colonies free and independent states, absolved from allegiance to, or dependence upon, the crown or parliament of Great Britain." On that same date, the Continental Congress issued a recommendation to colonies that had yet to create a "Government sufficient to the exigencies of their affairs" to do so forthwith, and, on June 7, Virginia delegate Richard Henry Lee moved that the Congress officially echo his state's declaration by passing a resolution proclaiming "That these United Colonies are, and of right ought to be, free and independent States . . . and that all political connection between them and the State of Great Britain is, and ought to be totally dissolved." Moreover, Lee's resolution stipulated that Congress take "the most effectual measures for forming foreign alliances" and should begin preparation of a formal "plan of confederation" among the colonies.

DEBATE AND DECLARATION

Congress took Lee's resolution very seriously. In fact, champions of independence felt that it was a make-or-break step in the march toward independence and, for that reason, they put off debating it for three weeks on the assumption that too many colonies were "not yet ripe for bidding adieu to the British connection." In short order, however, Delaware, Connecticut, New Hampshire, New Jersey, and Maryland instructed their congressional delegates to vote for independence. On July 1, 1776, the debate commenced—despite a predictable objection from Pennsylvania's John Dickinson, who wanted to continue the delay. Adams and Lee demanded immediate action, whereupon South Carolina joined Pennsylvania in voting against independence. As it turned out, despite instructions, the Delaware delegation remained divided. New York, which was restructuring its government, abstained. So, at the end of the July 1 session, the vote was nine to four in favor of independence.

It was encouraging, but the radical faction of the divided Delaware delegation insisted on stirring the pot until an overwhelming independence majority bubbled to the surface. They summoned an absent member of their delegation, Caesar Rodney, on an eighty-mile breakneck midnight ride from Dover to Philadelphia. He arrived just in time to swing the Delaware vote to independence. This pushed the delegations from both South Carolina and Pennsylvania to join the independence party. New York continued to abstain, but the pro-independence majority, as of July 2, was overwhelming.

Lee's resolution of independence had passed three weeks after its introduction. But it was an internal document. What was now needed was a public declaration. The delegates had used the interval between introduction and passage of the resolution to appoint a committee to draft a declaration of independence. They chose John Adams, Benjamin Franklin, Robert R. Livingston, Roger Sherman, and Thomas Jefferson.

As an early instigator of the revolution, Adams was deemed the senior member of the committee and was therefore expected to lead the writing. At seventy, Benjamin Franklin was the senior-most member in age and was the only member who could lay claim to worldwide fame. He was celebrated as a scientist, inventor, writer, publisher, politician, and all-around wit. Livingston was a prosperous and distinguished attorney, who represented the more conservative side of the independence movement. Born in Newton, Massachusetts, Sherman was destined for the cobbler's trade but established a lively law practice in Litchfield County, Connecticut. A self-educated polymath, he would earn considerable renown as both a legislator and an economic theorist. Like Franklin, Sherman was the author-publisher of popular almanacs—but his were based on his own quite competent astronomical calculations. Last among this group—and, at the time, some might also have said least among them—was Thomas Jefferson. Educated at Virginia's College of William and Mary, he was a competent attorney with a flair for writing but absolutely no presence as a speaker. That put him rather in the shade within Congress. In a letter of August 6, 1822, to Massachusetts politician Timothy Pickering, John Adams tells the story of how Thomas Jefferson came to draft the Declaration of Independence:

> *The Committee met, discussed the subject, and then appointed Mr. Jefferson & me to make the draught; I suppose, because we were the two highest on the list. The Sub-Committee met; Jefferson proposed to me to make the draught. I said I will not; You shall do it. Oh No! Why will you not? You ought to do it. I will not. Why? Reasons enough. What can be your reasons? Reason 1st. You are a Virginian, and Virginia ought to appear at the head of this business. Reason 2d. I am obnoxious, suspected and unpopular; You are very much otherwise. Reason 3d: You can write ten times better than I can. "Well," said Jefferson, "if you are decided I will do as well as I can."*

In 1825, long after he wrote that draft, Jefferson explained in a letter to Henry Lee IV, son of Revolutionary War hero "Light-Horse" Harry Lee and half-brother of Robert E. Lee, what he was trying to do in writing the document. He explained that he was by no means attempting to "find out new principles, or new arguments, never before thought of," but, rather meant only "to justify ourselves in the independent stand we are compelled to take" and, finally, to "appeal to the tribunal of the world . . . for our justification." In the spirit of Richard Henry Lee's resolution, Jefferson sought to rationalize American independence to the rest of the planet. Mindful that never before had a people decided to break with a king for the purpose of creating a republic founded on the elevation of equality under the law, he decided, he told Henry Lee, to write a declaration that would "be an expression of the American mind, and to give to that expression the proper tone and spirit called for by the occasion. All its authority rests on the harmonizing sentiments of the day, whether

This fanciful but magnificent 1819 painting by John Trumbull depicts the five-man drafting committee of the Declaration of Independence presenting their work to the Continental Congress on June 28, 1776. From left to right, we see John Adams, Roger Sherman, Robert Livingston, Thomas Jefferson, and Benjamin Franklin.
ARCHITECT OF THE UNITED STATES CAPITOL

expressed in conversation, in letters, printed essays, or in the elementary books of public right, as Aristotle, Cicero, Locke, Sidney, etc."

As discussed in Chapter 5, the works of the seventeenth-century British philosopher John Locke figured importantly in eighteenth-century American thought, and he was the source who loomed most prominently in Jefferson's draft. Locke enumerated three basic human rights—life, liberty, and property. Jefferson wrote, "We hold these truths to be self-evident, that all men are created equal, that they are endowed by their Creator with certain unalienable Rights, that among these are Life, Liberty and" . . . and this is where Jefferson diverged boldly from his model, substituting for "property" the phrase "the pursuit of happiness."

Jefferson's draft included a raw condemnation of King George III for having "waged cruel war against human nature itself, violating its most sacred rights of life & liberty in the persons of a distant people who never offended him, captivating & carrying them into slavery in another hemisphere, or to incur miserable death in their transportation thither." Arguably, this passage was beyond hypocritical since Thomas Jefferson owned two Virginia plantations and staffed them with a total of 135 slaves. It makes some difference that what he wrote in the Declaration of Independence had more to do with the slave trade—the abduction of Africans from Africa and their transportation for sale in America—than with the institution of slavery.

In the end, both the hypocrisy and the anti-slave-trade sentiment were moot. Jefferson's fellow southern slave-owning delegates struck the reference to slavery from the Declaration. Thus, the document purporting to justify the cause of independence as a precondition for creating a nation in which all men—created equal—might enjoy their unalienable rights free from an oppressive government was also the birth certificate of a nation whose population included a large enslaved minority.

THE BELLS "RANG ALL DAY AND ALMOST ALL NIGHT"

The day we Americans celebrate as Independence Day is, of course, July 4. That was the date on which Congress approved the edited draft of the Declaration of Independence, which was printed and published five days later, on July 9, 1776. The original "Fourth of July" celebration was actually on that July 9 date. As John Adams wrote to one of the signers of the document, Samuel Chase, the publication was accompanied by bells, which "rang all day and almost all night." Earlier, on July 3, Adams had written to his wife, Abigail, that the "Second Day of July 1776," on which Congress voted for independence, "will be the most memorable Epocha, in the history of America." He concluded:

> *I am apt to believe that it will be celebrated, by succeeding Generations, as the great anniversary Festival. It ought to be commemorated, as the Day of Deliverance by solemn Acts of Devotion to God Almighty. It ought to be solemnized with Pomp and Parade, with Shews, Games, Sports, Guns, Bells, Bonfires and Illuminations from one End of this Continent to the other from this Time forward forever more.*
>
> *You will think me transported with Enthusiasm but I am not.—I am well aware of the Toil and Blood and Treasure, that it will cost Us to maintain this Declaration, and support and defend these States.—Yet through all the Gloom I can see the Rays of ravishing Light and Glory. I can see that the End is more than worth all the Means. And that Posterity will tryumph in that Days Transaction, even altho We should rue it, which I trust in God We shall not.*

CHAPTER 13

The Long Retreat

ALTHOUGH SOME OF THE GREATEST THINKERS OF THE AMERICAN REVolution came from Virginia, it was Boston and environs that constituted the conflict's fountainhead. There was a certain common sense in the Crown's initial strategy to suppress the rebellion. Howe and the others were assigned to decapitate the radical snake, cut off the uprising at its head, target the source of all the trouble. When the cost of attempting that proved shockingly high at Concord and Bunker Hill, British high command took another tack. Instead of attacking the very fortress of the revolution, why not begin with the weak spots? And by weak, what the Howe brothers meant was weak for the Patriots and strong for the Loyalists. Two colonies among the lower thirteen were perceived as especially fertile ground for Loyalism: South Carolina and New York. In part, doubtless, because the large British garrison in Boston had evacuated north to Canada, New York was the first new major target, a target that the redcoat generals considered especially soft. Besides, if the Crown could gain control of New York, the settled eastern regions would be severed from the frontier fringe. Eighteenth-century professional military officers had all been raised on *Caesar's Commentaries* and were well versed in the strategic concept of "divide and conquer."

WHEN THE BIG APPLE WAS THE THIRD APPLE
At the time of the revolution, Philadelphia was to America what Paris was to France and London to England. It was the biggest city and the most prosperous—though hardly the most radical. Even though the

Continental Congress met there, it was a city with a substantial Loyalist minority. Boston, the social and political cutting edge of America, was far less supportive of the status quo. It instigated the revolution.

New York City? It was third in population behind Philadelphia and Boston, but there is no question that geography and political demography made it a strategically appealing prize. Its situation on New York Harbor positioned it as a principal avenue from Europe and straight into the interior of the continent. The mouth of the lordly Hudson River opened broadly into the harbor, which, in time of peace, made for prosperous trading and, in time of war, provided a generous and secure anchorage for a large naval fleet. Add to this that New York was a "Middle Atlantic" place, the portal between New England and the rest of the colonies. Take New York, control the Hudson, and you had a stranglehold on New England (and Boston) to the north and the frontier to the west. Take New York and the Hudson, and you would sever New England, source of revolution, from the rest of the continent.

It certainly seemed an objective ripe for the plucking—yet not quite so ripe as General William Howe counted on. He was quite right in calculating that Patriots were in the minority in New York City proper. But his mistake was thinking in binary terms. Just because New Yorkers were not rabid Sons of Liberty didn't make them worshipers of George III. New Yorkers were committed to trade above everything. For them, it was never a question of loyalty to the Crown versus independence. To them, it was more about remaining profitably neutral throughout whatever trouble was coming. The objective was to remain on cordial trading relations with the mother country and her loyalists as well as those who sought to break free.

Howe's war plan was to return to the lower thirteen colonies, advancing southward from Halifax, Nova Scotia, to which he had withdrawn from Boston with his forces. En route, he would pick up some reinforcements from Loyalist elements and, coordinating an assault by land and sea, capture and occupy New York City. *This* would become Britain's new military and general power base in America. While holding New York—and controlling its great harbor—Howe planned to move up the Hudson River, taking control of it all the way to Albany, which would effectively sever New England from the rest of the roiling continent. At Albany, he planned to rendezvous with the forces of General Guy Carleton. The two would coordinate sufficiently to crush the rebellion between them.

HUDSON RIVER PRIZE

Charles Lee was a native of Britain and the son of a military officer, whose regiment he joined as a fifteen-year-old ensign in 1747. He came to North America during the French and Indian War, serving with the doomed Brigadier General Edward Braddock. He not only survived the lethal Battle of the Wilderness (also called the Battle of the Monongahela) on July 9, 1755, he embraced Britain's often ill-treated Indian allies, allowing himself to be adopted into the Mohawk tribe. As if that weren't shocking enough, he "married" the daughter of a Seneca chief. When the French and Indian War ended, Lee did not return to the dull routine of service in His Majesty's Army but became a mercenary and fought for pay in the Polish army. In 1773, he immigrated to America, where he flew into

"Charles Lee, Esqr—Major General of the Continental Army in America," an engraving published between 1776 and 1790, includes verse in German and French, the languages of two American allies. LIBRARY OF CONGRESS

the arms of the radicals. He exhorted them to raise an army. More than likely, he assumed he would be given that army to command. It was a presumptuous assumption if for no other reason than, even as he turned traitor against king and Parliament, he continued to collect his half-pay British military pension. He would continue to do so well after the Continental Congress commissioned him a major general, with only Washington and Artemus Ward outranking him.

Lee was, in fact, hardly an exemplary officer. Not only was he in the pay of the enemy, he earned a reputation while on siege duty around Boston for what a contemporary described only as "dirty habits," leaving the details to the imagination. But since Charles Lee was the third-highest-ranking officer in the Continental Army and a more experienced commander than he himself, Washington removed him from the siege of Boston in January 1776 to set up the defense of New York, a city Washington knew would sooner or later become a target.

Lee took his sweet time arriving for his new assignment. He did not reach Manhattan until February 4, having been felled by an attack of gout, doubtless a symptom of some of his "dirty habits." Nor did his attitude toward his assignment inspire confidence. He wrote to General Washington on February 19, 1776: "What to do with the city puzzles me. It is so encircled with deep navigable waters that whoever commands the sea must command the town." Washington may well have accepted this can't-do attitude as a realistic appraisal. In any case, Lee did come up with a plan, which called for between four thousand and five thousand troops to be deployed on Long Island, with the greatest strength concentrated at a fortified position on Brooklyn Heights, overlooking Lower Manhattan across the East River. He also proposed to send a contingent uptown, to defend Kings Bridge, joining Manhattan to the Bronx. Lee was convinced that holding Manhattan against a naval attack was impossible, so he would not even attempt to do so. His idea was instead to let the British disembark from their ships and invade Manhattan, a place, he argued, that presented a favorable battleground. Lee reasoned that a truly determined British force would ultimately prevail, no matter what he did. He intended, however, to make the attempt so costly that not only would Howe withdraw from the island, Parliament itself would be forced to contemplate simply letting the colonies go their way.

Given the realities, it was not an irrational plan. Indeed, something very like it would constitute the strategy George Washington applied to prosecuting the entire war. If Britain were truly determined to crush the American Revolution, Washington realized, it could. But he had seen enough of the British in the French and Indian War to know that they calculated military costs parsimoniously. Make holding the colonies costly enough, and the Parliament would compel even King George III to let them go.

This map shows Manhattan, part of Long Island, Staten Island, and part of New Jersey in 1776. The lower right of the map shows the Battle of Brooklyn Heights (August 27, 1776). LIBRARY OF CONGRESS

Washington must have felt sufficiently confident in Lee to delay his own arrival in New York to April 13, 1776. What he saw horrified him. Lee had built—absolutely nothing. What is more, he had departed the city to plan the fortification of Charleston, South Carolina. Belatedly, then, Washington himself set his Continental Army to excavating earthworks. Never one to panic, he can nevertheless be forgiven for feeling he was starting too late. What he failed to count on was how slow the British would be in actually making their assault. As it turned out, the nineteen thousand Continental and militia troops assembled to make a stand in New York had five long months to build fortifications. The British did not attack until September.

William Howe landed his first three troopships on June 25, 1776, off Sandy Hook, a spit that projected into Raritan Bay from New Jersey, toward Staten Island. Four days later, no fewer than 127 more vessels arrived, carrying a total of ninety-three hundred regulars. On July 12, William's admiral brother, Lord Richard Howe, arrived with his command of some 150 more ships, some of which carried reinforcements from across the Atlantic. Following soon after these were ships carrying both additional British troops and the German mercenaries generically called the "Hessians," even though only a fraction came from the landgraviate of Hesse-Kassel, ruled at the time by Landgrave Frederick II.

Sir William Howe commanded British land forces in America from September 1775 to May 1778. His brother, Richard, commanded Royal Navy forces until September 1778. NEW YORK PUBLIC LIBRARY

Thus, by mid-July, a huge force was arrayed against New York City—yet it made no move to attack. July ended, and August began. On August 12, more ships carrying more soldiers arrived, veterans of the first—failed—British expedition against Charleston. By the end of that month, William Howe commanded at Sandy Hook 31,625 troops, by far the largest force the British would ever wield at any one time in the American Revolution. It was greater than anything king and Parliament had fielded during the French and Indian War.

LONG ODDS FOR WASHINGTON

Washington's great disadvantage was being both outnumbered and outgunned. He did, however, have a defender's advantage in occupying fortified high ground. Many of the sixty-five hundred soldiers he deployed on Long Island were assembled under the highly capable Israel Putnam on well-fortified Brooklyn Heights. In the woods and farmlands south and southeast of Brooklyn Heights (the modern Brooklyn neighborhoods of Sunset Park, Parkville, and Flatbush), New Jersey militia general William Alexander and Continental general John Sullivan commanded sixteen hundred and fifteen hundred troops, respectively. There was another contingent on Governor's Island in New York Harbor, off the lower tip of Manhattan. In and around New York City proper were units of the twenty-four-hundred-man brigade of Thomas Mifflin, a prominent Philadelphian, who made his headquarters at Fort Washington, overlooking the Hudson at about present-day 180th Street. Due east of Fort

Washington, on the Harlem River, were eighteen hundred soldiers under George Clinton, whose mission it was to defend Kings Bridge, a vital link to the mainland.

By the time Howe was ready to attack, Washington commanded some nineteen thousand troops in and around New York City. This was the greater part of the mobilized, equipped, and battle-ready American army. In deploying them, Washington exercised a catastrophic lack of strategic comprehension. By dividing his troops between Manhattan Island and Long Island, so that they were separated by the East River and Long Island Sound, he reduced rather than multiplied the effectiveness of his forces. It is almost always a mistake to put a natural barrier between soldiers of the same army because it makes it virtually impossible to quickly transfer troops where they are most needed. Compounding this strategic error was a tactical blunder. Washington put large portions of both of his divided forces in range of the cannon of the British fleet. Indeed, the ships could bombard Manhattan and Long Island anywhere along the East and Harlem Rivers, while also disembarking invaders along the way. To put it bluntly, the Continental Army lay in the jaws of a giant trap, having been placed there by its commander.

It is, of course, easy to condemn Washington from a distance of nearly 250 years and (for us Americans, at least) from the comfort of the liberty and national identity Washington was so instrumental in securing for us. The fact is that George Washington had been commissioned directly by the Continental Congress, and that body pressured him relentlessly to hold New York City. Politically, this was understandable, but, as intense as the pressure must have been, Congress did not make it an order. Presumably, the delegates understood that decisions about how to use the Continental Army with respect to New York City were first and foremost military, not political. General Washington could have acknowledged the will of Congress but countered it with an appeal to military necessity. Like Charles Lee before him, he must have recognized that defending New York was hardly the best strategic course. Had he asserted himself, with respect to Congress, as a *military* commander, he would almost surely have chosen the far more strategically valid option of withdrawing his forces north, onto the mainland, far from the water, and into the woodlands of Westchester County. Here, Howe would be totally deprived of the Royal Navy's cannon and ability to move and land troops swiftly. Here, Washington's men would be able to avail themselves of natural cover to snipe at, ambush, and otherwise interdict and harass the advancing British columns. Yes, Howe could certainly take and occupy New York City, but where would he go from here? Deployed more strategically, the Continental Army could have made any British attempt to move overland out of New York City very costly.

HOWE ATTACKS

During the night of August 26, the 17th Light Dragoons, the 33rd West Ridings, the 71st Highlanders, the Guards, and a dozen other regiments silently took up positions in a part of southeast Brooklyn that is still known as the Flatlands. The three field commanders present were thirsty for vengeance against the "rebels." Henry Clinton had never gotten over the bloody cost of Bunker Hill. Charles Cornwallis arrived in New York, having just suffered defeat in his attempt to take Charleston. And Lord Hugh Percy had personally experienced the utter humiliation of the long retreat from the battlegrounds of Lexington and Concord to Boston. It was high time to put an end to colonial pretensions.

With admirable stealth, the three field commanders used the cover of darkness to position some ten thousand men in a great arc to the northwest, opposite Continental general John Sullivan's left flank. What was brilliant about this is that it meant the British would strike from the northwest, precisely the opposite of where the attack was expected to originate, which was the southeast. As a result, the element of surprise was complete. As Clinton, Cornwallis, and Percy struck from the northwest, five thousand Hessians marched in due north from the Flatlands while seven thousand Highlanders bore in from the west. In all, twenty-two thousand of the enemy attacked the American positions from three sides, rapidly overwhelming the thirty-one hundred Continental troops who were deployed in front of the fortifications on Brooklyn Heights.

Washington had planned to use his riflemen, skilled shooters all, to pick off and thin out the anticipated British onslaught. With so many attackers converging from three directions, however, rifles could not be reloaded and fired fast enough to make so much as a dent in the assault.

Yet if Howe and his field commanders were expecting to deliver a rout, they were disappointed. The American troops and their officers performed far better than the British regulars and the Hessian mercenaries had ever imagined. In particular, the New Jersey troops of William Alexander, a Scots-American officer people called Lord Stirling on account of his inherited Scottish title, held off the Highlanders long enough that the attackers suffered serious casualties. Stirling conducted a fighting retreat, keeping his force intact. Nevertheless, by noon on August 27, all American forces were falling back on the Brooklyn Heights fortifications.

It was beyond question a victory for British arms. Meticulously planned and vigorously executed, the attack had succeeded quickly—and yet it achieved very little. The American soldiers who had been deployed on Long Island had retreated, bruised but intact, to Brooklyn Heights, a fortified position from which it would be no easy matter to evict them. To make matters worse for Howe, the winds were against the fleet, so that no attack could be mounted from the water. Howe had been slow to mount his assault, and now, perhaps with the terrible toll of Bunker Hill on his mind, he took his time digging in around Brooklyn Heights. His intention was to assault the fortified stronghold at close range, but from well-covered positions. It was a prudent approach, but it cost Howe much time and momentum, assets of tremendous value in an attack. It also gave Washington a precious gift: more time.

WASHINGTON REDEEMED

Entrusted with the Continental Army, General George Washington had come precariously close to losing it in a single encounter. Now, using the time Howe had surrendered to him, he contemplated his next move. It was to transfer some of his Manhattan forces across the East River to reinforce Brooklyn Heights. He gave the orders, and it was done—and then Washington realized he had made yet another mistake.

By August 28, with Brooklyn Heights reinforced at great risk by troops from Manhattan, he saw clearly that the fortification would never withstand the full weight of the British assault. He now had an army to save—with even more men in imminent peril than there had been before he ordered reinforcement of the Heights. Washington had to evacuate. But that brought its own grave danger. No army is weaker than when it is in retreat, its back toward the enemy. Moreover, Howe was taking his time preparing *now*, but as soon as he saw that Washington was evacuating, even the slow-moving Howe would surely launch an instantaneous assault.

Aware of his errors, Washington did not despair of them. Projecting as he always did serene confidence in the face of his officers and men, he began at nightfall the silent movement of thousands of troops down from Brooklyn Heights and to the East River bank. They quietly boarded boats and crossed over to Manhattan. The weather was with him. It was awful. The night of August 29 brought thick fog and intense rain. They helped to render his movements invisible. Before daybreak on August 30, every man had slipped out of the Brooklyn Heights fortress and into Manhattan.

That is *not* what Howe's commanders believed. A Hessian major reported that he was unaware of the evacuation "until four o'clock in the morning." He believed, as did the British, that the "entire American army has fled to New England, evacuating also New York." All were quite

General Washington leads the retreat from Long Island across the East River to Manhattan during the night of August 29–30, 1776. The engraving, by James Charles Armytage, is from a nineteenth-century painting by Michael Angelo Wageman. NATIONAL ARCHIVES AND RECORDS ADMINISTRATION

unaware that the Americans had done no more or less than steal across the river and into Manhattan, and even after Howe discovered the truth, he allowed August to become September before advancing his forces toward Manhattan, positioning troops in what are today Long Island City and Astoria, both in Queens.

As for the Royal Navy fleet in New York Harbor, there was even sufficient leisure for the Patriots to try a most novel weapon against it. David Bushnell, a recent graduate of Yale College, had cobbled together from oak and iron bands a pear-shaped vessel he called *Turtle*. Measuring about seven and a half feet long by six feet wide, *Turtle* had room for just one mariner, who controlled two hand-driven screws for propulsion in four directions. He could also submerge the tiny vessel by pulling a hand-spring valve, which flooded a compartment in the hull, submerging the craft. Bringing it back to the surface required evacuating the water with a foot-operated pump.

Bushnell affixed a boom on the forward-facing part of *Turtle* and attached to its end an explosive mine. The idea was for the stealthy craft, submerged just below the surface, to approach a stationary target vessel, attach the mine to its hull below the water line, then pull back. The explosive charge was timed to detonate after *Turtle* had sufficiently retreated.

On September 6, a Continental Army volunteer, Sergeant Ezra Lee, having been personally trained by Bushnell himself, sailed the submerged *Turtle* up to the HMS *Eagle*, a sixty-four-gun ship-of-the-line, which was moored off Bedloe's Island—today called Liberty Island and home to the Statue of Liberty. After Lee was unable to attach the mine, he withdrew before the explosive detonated—harmlessly—in the East River. *Turtle* was tried against a few more targets but never succeeded in sinking a ship.

PEACE AND A MATTER OF TIME

Neither General Howe nor his admiral brother were much concerned about a failed rebel submarine. They were more interested in their frequent dinners with their prisoner of war, General John Sullivan, captured at the Battle of Long Island on August 27. Learning from the Howes that Parliament had given them considerable latitude in negotiating a peaceful settlement to the revolution, Sullivan persuaded the brothers to parole him so that he could go to the Continental Congress with their peace feelers. (It is quite possible that the Howes deliberately manipulated Sullivan into volunteering himself as an emissary.)

Congress proved quite responsive. It organized a committee consisting of Benjamin Franklin, John Adams, and South Carolina congressman Edward Rutledge to speak with the Howes. The meeting was held on September 11, on Staten Island, just opposite Amboy, New Jersey. Whatever good feelings preceded the meeting, they were instantly dissipated when General Howe excused himself early in the encounter, leaving his brother to deal with the committee. In the face of this diminished authority and Admiral Howe's caveat that his own authority was not plenipotentiary—anything agreed had to receive the endorsement of London—the committee abruptly left.

There would be no negotiated peace, but the mere fact that Congress had been willing to talk testifies to diminished support for the war in the wake of Washington's defeat on Long Island. Moreover, the gift of time the slow-moving Howe brothers had given Washington was beginning to work against him. Although Washington was counting on the passing days to wear down the British resolve to long continue the war, that same delay was working against General Washington. Although the men of the Continental Army were enlisted for long terms, enlistments of those in the militia, vital to supporting the army, were typically just three months long. Washington continually confronted the expiration of militia enlistments. And there was worse. Storms had interfered with supplying the troops in Manhattan. As their strength ebbed under short rations, some fell prey to endemic diseases such as dysentery and smallpox. Typically at this point, at least a quarter of Washington's army was at any given time too sick to fight.

At the start of September, General Nathanael Greene advised General Washington to burn New York and abandon it. Far from rejecting the proposal, Washington referred it to Congress, which responded on September 3 by passing a resolution against burning of the city. Yet it stopped short of demanding that Washington continue to defend it. With considerable good sense, the delegates decided that, if the city were lost, it could someday be recaptured—provided it was still standing. Washington decided against abandoning the city without at least trying to defend it. On September 7, he began distributing his troops. He stationed Henry Knox and Israel Putnam downtown with a substantial contingent. He assigned some nine thousand troops to defend the ground between Harlem and Kings Bridge. Finally, Greene was given the assignment of repelling any landings along the East River.

While Washington covered the obvious positions, he thought nothing of spreading his troops thinly over sixteen miles of Manhattan. This left mid-Manhattan with the least amount of protection, a small force of militiamen, who were somehow expected to stand their ground against an invasion party consisting of seasoned British regulars and Hessian mercenaries known for their brutality. On September 12, Washington's own subordinate commanders pleaded with him to consolidate his strength. Washington agreed to evacuate everything south of Fort Washington and making a stand, when the time came, where his fortifications were strongest. It was a timely decision, but it was not enough.

Manhattan Invaded

The weather, which had long been against Admiral Howe and his fleet, turned favorable on September 15, 1776, and, with this turn of wind, he divided his fleet, sailing part of it up the Hudson River on Manhattan's West Side and part of it up the East River on the island's opposite side. Troop barges were stopped and anchored on the East River at Kip's Bay, where today 34th Street ends at the FDR Drive. At eleven in the morning, following a brief bombardment, troops landed in eighty-five flatboats. The militiamen Washington had assigned to repel the landings cut and ran and infected with their terror other units, including some of the Continental Army.

Hearing the opening barrage, General Washington personally galloped down from his Harlem headquarters. Seeing his front lines in chaos, he rode his horse into the moiling mob that was supposed to be an army. He waded into the men, lashing out at them with his riding crop. Some he managed to rally before an aide forcibly grabbed the bridle of his mount and led both horse and rider off, only steps in advance of the Hessians. Whatever his flaws as a general, cowardice could never be counted among them. He was not so much fearless as simply oblivious to danger.

While the contingents under Knox and Putnam stayed put in Lower Manhattan, the disordered militia at Kip's Bay followed Washington back uptown. The forces headquartered in Harlem advanced farther north to the high ground of Harlem Heights and Fort Washington. Unsurprisingly, Howe chose not to give chase but instead marched inland and fanned out uptown only as far as today's 42nd Street.

As the sun set on September 15, General Howe established forward positions from McGowan's Pass west-southwest to the Hudson River, at about the present location of 105th Street. His troops bedded down for the night. Those familiar with Manhattan as it is today know it as a flat island, at least until one gets well north of Harlem. The leveling of the lower four-fifths of the city was all the work of developers working throughout the nineteenth century. In the eighteenth century, Manhattan Island was quite hilly and some of it even downright rugged. Just before dawn on September 16, Lieutenant Colonel Thomas Knowlton led a hundred elite troops calling themselves the Connecticut Rangers down a steep defile known as the Hollow Way. It ran quite precipitously down from Harlem Heights (today's Manhattanville neighborhood) to the Hudson River. When Knowlton and his Rangers ran up against soldiers of the celebrated and much-feared Black Watch Highlanders, he engaged them, withdrawing, however, as more Highlanders approached. Observing, General Howe mistook Knowlton's withdrawal for the beginning of an American rout. Accordingly, he ordered a general attack.

In an act of inspiration combined with necessity, Washington used the very militiamen who, having panicked at Kip's Bay, followed him northward, to make a surprise attack against Howe's forces. It was their opportunity to redeem themselves—and, as Washington hoped they would, they seized it. Cowed though they had been earlier, they now behaved like tigers, charging through a buckwheat field that fronted the Hudson on the site of modern Barnard College. They ran full tilt into the Highlanders, who, stunned, turned tail. Beholding this, Howe, who had expected imminent victory, was dismayed beyond reason. The rebuff of the Highlanders was, after all, a minor encounter involving very few troops. Perhaps images of Bunker Hill again ran through his imagination. For whatever reason, he was paralyzed. He should have hit Washington and hit him hard. Instead, he stood still. For four days, William Howe and his immense invasion force did nothing.

MANHATTAN BURNS, A SPY HANGS

In the predawn hours of September 21, fire broke out in a house near Whitehall Slip, at the southern tip of Manhattan. The blaze quickly moved north and west, engulfing 493 houses before *British* troops got it under control. Howe blamed the Americans for starting it, while Washington blamed Howe. Whoever or whatever caused the conflagration, extinguishing it occupied Howe's troops and, with the defeat in the buckwheat field, lengthened the British delay in attacking Fort Washington and adjacent Harlem Heights.

In the meantime, on the very day of the fire, twenty-one-year-old Connecticut schoolmaster Nathan Hale was arrested or captured—accounts vary—as a Patriot spy. Except for his obvious courage, Hale was not well suited to espionage. He stood out in any crowd as both very tall and also quite plump with a head of flame-red hair. This conspicuous figure walked around Manhattan obviously and copiously taking notes on seemingly everything. Some say a British officer became sufficiently suspicious to stop and search him. His notes were found in his coat, and he made no attempt to lie about what he was: a spy for General Washington. Others believe he was apprehended by Robert Rogers, major of Loyalist Rangers. All we know for certain is what General William Howe wrote in his diary on September 22: "A spy from the enemy by his own full confession, apprehended last night, was executed [this] day at 11 o'clock in front of the Artillery Park."

Hale had been accorded no trial—spies almost never were—but he was allowed an opportunity to speak from the gallows. No one took notes, but John Montresor, a British soldier who had witnessed the hanging, later told an American officer, William Hull, that the young man had died with moving dignity, choosing as his departing words, "I only regret that I have but one life to lose for my country."

ON TO WHITE PLAINS

Howe remained strangely inert through the remainder of September and well into October. On the 16th of that month, Washington, reasoning that he was hardly in a position to mount a counterattack once Howe finally struck and concluding from the movement of troop barges that the long-delayed attack was likely coming soon, decided at last to abandon Manhattan. He left garrisons at Fort Washington and (directly across the Hudson in New Jersey) Fort Lee, and then marched out in a northerly direction to the village of White Plains in Westchester County. Howe conducted a sort of slow-motion pursuit, moving so slowly, in fact, that his column was more than once ambushed by hit-and-run raids by Washington's rear guard. These cost Howe significant casualties.

Reaching White Plains far in advance of Howe, Washington distributed his forces on three hills—only to commit yet another tactical error. He did not fortify Chatterton's Hill, the highest of the three, dominating not only the other two hills but all of the surrounding land. Somehow, the American general failed to see it for what it was: *the* key military objective in the whole area. He entrusted the defense of Chatterton's Hill to sixteen hundred militiamen under Alexander McDougall of New York.

For once, William Howe was not slow to take advantage of an opportunity. No sooner did he arrive in White Plains than he noted the lack of fortification on Chatterton's Hill. He launched an artillery barrage followed by a poorly executed infantry assault that was instantly redeemed by a splendid cavalry charge. Indeed, it was the first use of cavalry in the American Revolution, and it produced a withering effect on the American militiamen. They panicked as the Romans panicked at the onslaught of Hannibal's elephants. The more seasoned troops from Maryland and Delaware took the place of the militiamen, who had melted away. But even they were finally sent into retreat, and Howe claimed Chatterton's Hill.

That he had captured the great prize in White Plains seems not to have sunk in on General Howe. He took the hill, held the hill, and then did nothing further. From its commanding height, he could have suppressed all resistance as he sent units in pursuit of Washington's retreating army. Instead, the Continental Army slipped away to North Castle, where supplies, including fresh ammunition, were waiting. Although they had been chased from Long Island, Manhattan, and now from White Plains, Washington's men realized that they had inflicted heavier casualties on the enemy than they had themselves suffered. For their 150 killed and wounded, they had killed or wounded 214 among the British in addition to ninety-nine Hessians.

A Change of Direction

Early in November, Washington noted that William Howe had suddenly changed direction, turning back toward Manhattan. After meeting with his officers, Washington concluded that Howe intended to invade New Jersey.

It was a good guess but quite wrong.

Fort Washington, which its namesake had left garrisoned by two thousand men, had been newly reinforced with an additional thousand. On November 14-15, thirty flatboats landed a British assault force against Fort Washington. Suddenly, the reason for Howe's return to Manhattan became crystal clear. On the fifteenth, Howe's assault force demanded Fort Washington's surrender. When the garrison refused, the British attacked from three directions on November 16.

In the meantime, word of the operation reached Washington, who galloped to Fort Lee, New Jersey, directly across the Hudson from the beleaguered fort. In company with Generals Putnam, Greene, and Hugh Mercer, Washington risked his life crossing the Hudson to make a very stealthy reconnaissance. The conclusion was inescapable. Fort Washington was beyond rescue. Indeed, it surrendered at three that very afternoon. Still, it was another costly victory for the British. Although fifty-three Americans were killed in the Battle of Fort Washington, 458 British and Hessian troops were killed or wounded. Nevertheless, 2,818 American officers and enlisted soldiers became prisoners of war.

THE RETREAT BEGINS

Fort Lee surrendered four days after Fort Washington. These were strategic American citadels, and now they were in British hands, and all of Manhattan and much of the Jersey bank of the Hudson were under British control. While Howe had not destroyed Washington's army, he had split it up. Charles Lee was in command of forces in North Castle, Westchester County. William Heath had command of a sizable contingent at Peekskill, about fifty miles up the Hudson from Manhattan. As for Washington, he was left to save his army by marching a long and dreary march through the flat New Jersey landscape with nothing to look forward to but a frigid winter's encampment somewhere far from the city he had lost.

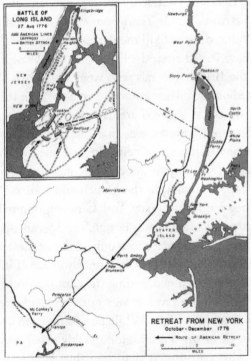

Washington's long retreat from Long Island to Manhattan to White Plains, Peekskill, and New Jersey during October–December 1776. UNITED STATES ARMY CENTER OF MILITARY HISTORY

CHAPTER 14

Counterattack

ONE HUNDRED TWELVE YEARS IN THE FUTURE, IN 1888, THE GERMAN philosopher Friedrich Nietzsche would publish under the heading "Maxims and Arrows" in his *Twilight of the Idols* one of his most quoted aphorisms: "What does not kill me makes me stronger."

It could have issued from the lips of George Washington in 1776.

Most of the British generals who went up against Washington were competent mediocrities. They knew the rules of war, including the most important of which: When you are defeated, you are beaten. What they failed to understand, however, was that the upstart Washington did not subscribe to many of the rules, including that one. Maybe it was because while Washington was not always competent, he was never a mediocrity. His early defeats, beginning in the French and Indian War and carrying through the long retreat from New York City, taught him never to concede defeat no matter how often he was beaten. This was an aspect of his character. It was an aspect of character seen only in the greatest and most controversial of generals. "You are not beaten until you admit it," World War II's George S. Patton Jr. often said, adding the admonition, "Hence DON'T."

For Washington, however, it was not only evidence of character, it was also a key strategic insight. While he was far from immune to tactical and even strategic errors, Washington quickly developed an unshakeable definition of what constituted victory in this American Revolution. He knew that no fledgling nation would ever destroy the military might of Britain. It would be foolish and fruitless to try. But in this revolution, Washington understood, the English were nevertheless vulnerable.

London was across the Atlantic. The thirteen American *states* were *here*—on this side of the ocean. Washington and his army were at home. Howe and his army were in a foreign land, far from home. They could and they would capture more than a few American cities and towns. Let them. It did not mean a British victory and an American defeat. It would not end the war. The end would come only when one side or the other stopped fighting.

Washington resolved not to be the first to stop. What he hoped, what he believed, was that the British lacked his resolve. Washington knew that there was significant opposition in Parliament to holding onto the colonies at any cost. This being the case, he reasoned that the British would indeed stop fighting *if* the fighting became sufficiently costly. To be sure, he felt the pain of defeat keenly. The loss of New York must have ached like a raw wound. To be in continual flight from the British must also have been an agony. No matter. Losing a battle, relinquishing a city, these were *bad things*, but fighting on was *everything*.

STAYING ALIVE

Nietzsche's "What does not kill me makes me stronger" assumes the possibility of being killed. Washington understood that to keep fighting, he had to keep his army alive—not only as a collection of individual human beings but as an army, an organized, disciplined force. The first step in survival was to avoid being destroyed by Howe. Washington did this by retreating first to the north and then to the west, into New Jersey.

The American landscape offered a great deal of room in which to retreat, but Howe was not his only enemy. Poorly funded, Congress squeezed every penny before relinquishing it to the Continental Army. Not only was Congress parsimonious, it was inefficient. From the very beginning, Washington fought for supplies—everything from shoes to rations to muskets and rifles and powder. Yet even if he managed to evade Howe and stave off starvation and nakedness, a third threat loomed: the relentless expiration of troop enlistments.

Washington's army was melting away before him. Prior to the three lost battles of Long Island, New York City, and White Plains, he commanded about nineteen thousand troops. Following these battles, he was left with 16,400. And *these* were ineffectively divided. Pausing at Newark, New Jersey, Washington had just forty-four hundred men directly under his command. Another thousand were with William Alexander ("Lord Stirling"), divided between the Jersey towns of New Brunswick and Rahway. General William Heath led four thousand at Peekskill, New York, and Charles Henry Lee had direct control of the greatest number, seven thousand, who were still in the White Plains area.

Washington struggled to deploy these separated forces effectively. He needed Lord Stirling's thousand-man contingent to hold their positions so that they would be available to oppose any attempt the British might make at amphibious operations intended to get ahead of Washington. He also decided that Heath should stay put to defend the Hudson River highlands against a British thrust designed to cut off the Mid-Atlantic region from New England.

This left Lee's large contingent. Washington urgently wanted to combine Lee's seven thousand troops—which included the most experienced regulars in the Continental Army—with his Newark-based troops. Accordingly, he ordered Lee to march to him. When Lee responded with delay, Washington turned up the pressure. Lee responded, via Washington's adjutant general, Joseph Reed, that it was impossible for him to cross the Hudson River at Dobbs Ferry in time to be of help. Washington therefore ordered Heath to send half his troops, two thousand men, to him via Kings Ferry.

Here, then, was a fourth threat to survival. For a long time, Charles Lee craved command of the Continental Army. He was convinced that he was demonstrably more qualified than Washington, and, to prove his point, he was willing to sacrifice the troops now directly under Washington's field command. By passively refusing to reinforce the commander-in-charge, he would topple him.

HOWE'S OPTIONS

Howe had multiple options for destroying the Continental Army. He could advance up the Hudson, dispose of Heath, and lay open an overland route from Canada by which more troops could augment the invasion. Or, if he chose, he could continue north himself, into New England.

Alternatively, he could capture the capital of the rebellious colonies, Philadelphia, while engaging portions of Washington's retreating army as he advanced on his objective.

But Howe was still in no hurry. The traditional fighting season was drawing to a close, so, instead of dealing the American Revolution one of these crushing blows, he went about setting up winter quarters in New Jersey—at Amboy, New Brunswick, and Princeton on his eastern front, and in Bordentown and Trenton on his western front, along the Delaware River. He assumed that Washington had at least as little appetite for a winter fight as he had; therefore, finishing off Washington and his army could wait for spring.

Howe ordered Henry Clinton to march out of New York with some six thousand men to occupy Newport, Rhode Island, which he intended to serve as his base for a New England campaign—again, come spring. To ensure an undisturbed winter's rest, Howe tasked Charles Cornwallis with chasing Washington off by pursuing him beyond New Brunswick, New Jersey.

As Lee was jealous of Washington, so Cornwallis believed himself a better soldier than Howe. He decided to exceed his orders by not merely shooing Washington away but destroying the fraction of the Continental Army he led. Cornwallis drove his army hard, and by November 29, it was bearing down on Newark. Washington and his command evacuated, marching at a quick pace toward New Brunswick, struggling to keep ahead of Cornwallis's advance guard, which consisted of Hessians. Ill-clothed and ill-equipped, Washington's contingent looked like a pitiful rabble, but their dearth of supplies meant that they were not burdened by the heavy loads their pursuers carried. They outran Cornwallis and reached Trenton on December 3.

Washington hoped that Charles Lee would be waiting for him there, but Lee had not moved with Washington's urgency, and on December 7, Washington crossed the Delaware into Pennsylvania. The British, then, had chased him out of New York, across all of New Jersey, and over the Delaware into Pennsylvania. Washington now fanned out his four thousand men over about twenty-five miles of Pennsylvania riverfront. This, he reasoned, would make it harder for Cornwallis to roll him up. To further impede his pursuers, he dispatched troops to find and wreck every boat capable of crossing the lower Delaware.

Cornwallis and his men were thoroughly fatigued. George Washington had not outfought him, of course, but he had outrun him. With Howe's permission, Cornwallis made camp on the Jersey side of the Delaware. He, too, decided to await spring.

LEE'S RECKONING COMES

It was November before Charles Lee arrived in New Jersey with his army in tow. He made the supremely arrogant error of "confessing" in a letter to Heath while on the march that he doubted Washington was capable of making competent use of his forces on the Delaware. His own preference, Lee wrote, was to "reconquer . . . the Jerseys." Accordingly, instead of marching double-quick to Washington on the Pennsylvania side of the Delaware, he halted just below Morristown, New Jersey, encamping his soldiers there while he rode off three miles to Basking Ridge, where a widow named Mrs. White kept a little tavern he knew, as it were, intimately.

On November 13, Lee started another letter, this one to General Horatio Gates, who, he was well aware, thought even less of Washington than he. "Entre nous," he began, "a certain great man is most damnably deficient." Before he could finish his missive, however, a squad of British dragoons broke through Widow White's door and claimed Lee as a prisoner of war.

Little did the dragoons know what a favor they did the cause of independence. Because Lee's army was three miles' distant from its commander, that force was now free to march unimpeded to Washington on the Delaware. The troops did so with alacrity, and Lee was lucky to escape trial as a deserter from the British army. He was instead held as a POW in New York, where, on March 29, 1777, he proffered to his captors a plan to "unhinge the organization of the American resistance" by regaining control of Maryland, Pennsylvania, and Virginia. Astonishingly, they saw no value in the plan and released Lee in April 1778 as part of a prisoner exchange. His attempt at treason was not uncovered for nearly seventy years, long after Lee's death, and the general was welcomed home by his brother American officers at Valley Forge. (In the course of the revolution, Lee went from bad to worse. His miserable performance at the Battle of Monmouth Courthouse [June 28, 1778] earned him a year's suspension, during which he picked a fight with Friedrich von Steuben, the German officer who served the Continental Army as its inspector general. That encounter nearly resulted in a duel, but a subsequent dispute with Lieutenant Colonel John Laurens did blow up into a duel, in which Laurens wounded Lee badly enough that he could not accept a *third* challenge, this from General "Mad Anthony" Wayne. All three breaches of civility occurred during Lee's yearlong suspension. Congress ultimately rescinded his commission on January 10, 1780, and he died in Philadelphia two years later.)

THE MARCH TO REDEMPTION

Thomas Paine was encamped with Washington's forces on the Pennsylvania bank of the Delaware. It was evening, and he pulled up a drumhead beside the campfire. It served him as an alfresco desk as he penned the first of the papers that would be collected years later, in 1783, as *The American Crisis*. This one, published individually on December 19, 1776, began: "These are the times that try men's souls. The summer soldier and sunshine patriot will, in this crisis, shrink from the service of his country; but he that stands it now, deserves the love and thanks of man and woman. Tyranny, like hell, is not easily conquered."

The stirring prose rivaled *Common Sense* itself and instantly rallied many of the discouraged and the doubtful—those "sunshine patriots"—back to the cause of independence. New recruits answered the call. Still, by Christmastime, Washington had no more than six thousand soldiers fit for duty. More would surely join, but if he waited for them, current enlistments, set to expire on New Year's Eve, would reduce his immediately available rolls to fourteen hundred. Moreover, if a hard freeze set in, the Delaware River would be transformed from an icy watercourse to a solid roadway. Right now, because Washington had grabbed up everything floatable, the British and Hessians were stuck on the New Jersey side of the river. Come the freeze, and they would surely march across the river and attack the American camp.

Not that they felt any urgency about it. With good reason, the British commanders believed that the American forces were shivering and hungry and doomed to dissolve themselves before winter was over and the fighting season arrived. It was, in fact, a reasonable assessment, and it seemed safe to assume that Washington himself must have known that his small army was in no condition to mount a counteroffensive. No competent general would try.

And yet Washington was convinced that, risky as a counterattack was, inaction meant certain defeat—and, what is worse, certain and shameful defeat. Besides, reports were reaching him daily of widespread popular resistance against the British occupation of New Jersey. Moreover, Pennsylvania militia, acting independently of Washington, were making one hit-and-run raid against British installations all along the river. Washington learned that these actions had drawn a great many Hessians away from Trenton and down south to Mount Holly, New Jersey, in an effort to suppress the raiders.

On December 22, Washington received a communique from his dashing aide-de-camp and adjutant-general of the Continental Army, Colonel Joseph Reed:

> We can either give [the Mount Holly militia] a strong reinforcement—or make a separate attack—the latter bids fairest for producing the greatest and best effects. We [officers] are all of the opinion my dear general that something must be attempted to revive our expiring credit, give our Cause some degree of reputation & prevent total depreciation of the Continental money which is coming very fast. . . . Even a Failure cannot be more fatal than to remain in our present situation. In short some enterprize must be undertaken in our present Circumstances or we must give up the cause.

Reed recommended an attack on Trenton, adding: "Delay is now equal to a total defeat."

He was preaching to the choir. With Reed's message in hand, General Washington called his officers to a council of war. He presented Reed's proposal for crossing the Delaware to attack Trenton, now occupied by Hessians. Not a single officer dissented. Turning to Colonel John Glover, in command of a regiment of salty Marblehead (Massachusetts) fishermen, Washington asked if he could get his troops across the river. Glover assured him that his "boys" would "manage it."

The Patriots had no love for the British regulars, but they loathed and dreaded the Hessians far more. Hired guns, they had a reputation for gratuitous cruelty against combatants and noncombatants alike, women and children included. Yet they were not the first enemy Washington had to defeat. The Delaware River was neither fully liquid nor fully frozen. Roiled by a swift current on Christmas night, its waves propelled miniature icebergs with a fierce momentum. In the dark, under a driving ice storm, Washington loaded twenty-four hundred soldiers and eighteen cannon into the Durham boats he had so assiduously hoarded. They were sturdy, and they had to be, with the icy sheets, shards, and boulders battering their hulls.

The crossing was made at McKonkey's Ferry—today called Washington's Crossing—nine miles above Trenton. While Washington embarked, some one thousand militiamen, led by General James Ewing, were preparing to cross at Trenton Ferry, their mission to block any attempted Hessian retreat. In addition, Colonel John Cadwalader was assigned to lead a diversionary crossing at Bordentown, New Jersey.

Thanks perhaps to the aid of Colonel Reed, it was a better tactical plan than any Washington had yet drawn up. As every veteran knows, however, plans tend to end precisely where the action begins. As it turned out, Ewing could not make it across the treacherous river in the night and storm. He had to turn back to the Pennsylvania riverbank. Cadwalader encountered one difficulty after another and was effectively kept out of the fight. Even Washington suffered a serious weather delay. Determined to disembark in New Jersey by midnight, which would give his men plenty of time to reach Trenton before daybreak, he did not complete the crossing until three on the morning of December 26. By the time his men were all disembarked on the Jersey side, formed up, and on the march, it was four. Any assault on Trenton would be made in the full light of day.

It was a sufficiently serious circumstance to prompt Washington to ponder aborting the mission. He later wrote: "As I was certain there was no making a Retreat without being discovered, and harassed on repassing the River, I determined to push on at all Events." It was damned if you do, doubly damned if you don't.

So, Washington's cold, wet soldiers trudged the nine miles from the Delaware's icy bank toward Trenton. Desperate to preserve what little of the element of surprise might still be his, Washington ordered total silence—no conversation—and he forbade the striking of flint or matches. So, there would be no comforting tobacco for a pipe, either. Adding to the soldiers' silent anxiety was the awareness that hours and miles of soaking snow and freezing rain made muskets and rifles unreliable. Who knew what would happen when the trigger was pulled? Washington therefore ordered his men to fix bayonets. If their weapons failed to discharge, they could still thrust.

BATTLE

The Hessian sentry was alert. "Der Feind! Heraus! Heraus!" ("The enemy! Get up! Get up!") was the cry that greeted the approach of Washington's assault force. The Hessian commander, Colonel Johann Gottlieb Rall, valiantly rallied his men, making himself instantly conspicuous in the process—and suffering the consequences accordingly. He slumped to the ground, mortally wounded, a musket ball having torn into his chest.

The early loss of their commander intensified the chaos created by the surprise attack on a force still sleeping off the boozy festivities of Christmas night. Some reports say the fight went on for two hours. Others put it at no more than a half-hour. Either way, at the end of it, 106 of the twelve hundred Hessians engaged lay dead or wounded. The rest were prisoners of war. Most historians believe that Washington suffered no more than four wounded, but some reports record two Americans killed in action and two frozen to death.

Washington was eager to press the counteroffensive further with immediate attacks on Princeton and New Brunswick. The failure of his other commanders to cross the river, however, forced him to re-cross the Delaware back to Pennsylvania. No matter. An army the enemy considered beaten had just defeated some of Europe's best soldiers. The revolution lived on.

General Washington inspects Hessian colors captured at the Battle of Trenton (December 26, 1776). The lithograph, published in 1914, is from a painting by Percy Moran. LIBRARY OF CONGRESS

PRINCETON

The Trenton triumph persuaded men whose enlistments were due to expire on New Year's Day to agree to six more weeks of service. Crossing his forces into New Jersey again, Washington deployed them in and around Trenton. Cornwallis marched out of Princeton at the head of nearly eight thousand fresh soldiers. They reached Trenton on January 2, by which time Washington's men had excavated defensive earthworks along the Assunpink Creek south of town.

Washington left just four hundred men in his entrenchments, ordering them to be as noisy as possible and to keep their fires lit at all times. The objective was to trick Cornwallis into believing he was about to do what he most wanted: bag his fox—capture the entirety of Washington's contingent.

As Cornwallis and his army bedded down for the night, planning to attack Trenton at daybreak, Washington, at one o'clock in the morning of January 3, began withdrawing the bulk of his force toward Princeton. Cornwallis had assigned twelve hundred troops under Lieutenant

Colonel Charles Mahwood as his rear guard. At first light, Mahwood marched to join Cornwallis at Trenton.

That is when he saw the glint of bayonets. Assuming these were Washington's troops retreating from a defeat at Trenton, Mahwood was stunned when Patriot general Hugh Mercer engaged his twelve hundred men at William Clark's orchard near a Quaker meetinghouse, thereby beginning the Battle of Princeton.

Initially, the American militia fumbled. Seeing this disaster-in-the-making from afar, Washington spurred his horse to the scene, riding through a storm of bullets. His presence put iron in the militiamen's spines. They rallied and held off Mahwood long enough for Henry Knox to rain down an artillery barrage upon them. This was followed quickly by the arrival of Daniel Hitchcock's brigade of Rhode Islanders and Massachusetts men, along with Pennsylvanians under Edward Hand. They reinforced Mercer's line, and Mahwood and his men were totally routed. It was a Patriot victory somewhat dimmed by the loss of the brave and skilled Hugh Mercer, who fell mortally wounded in the snowy orchard.

Instead of pursuing the fleeing attackers, who, he knew, were flying into the embrace of the main part of Cornwallis's force, Washington deflected to Princeton, quickly defeating the small number of British soldiers who were still there, and thereby "liberating" the town—at least for the time being. Washington could not afford to occupy and hold Princeton, however. For he was aware that Cornwallis would inevitably counterattack with far superior numbers. He therefore bowed to the tactical necessity of leaving town, but he positively fumed over the realization that he did not have sufficient numbers to follow through on his original plan to assault New Brunswick, where Cornwallis had stockpiled a massive cache of supplies, not to mention the Royal paymaster's war chest, holding some £70,000.

Washington led his men to Morristown, which would serve as their winter quarters. Here he could plan for the spring, having won two morale-lifting victories, which injected new life into the war for independence and drew fresh enlistments. As for Howe, Cornwallis, and Baron Wilhelm von Knyphausen, commander-in-charge of the Hessians, theirs would be a long winter of a discontent both unwelcome and unanticipated.

CHAPTER 15

Gentleman Johnny's Plan

THE EXHILARATION OF THE VICTORIES AT TRENTON AND PRINCETON did not last long in the frigid New Year of 1777. Washington's Morristown encampment suffered an outbreak of smallpox, a disease endemic in the eighteenth century and readily incubated in the close quarters of military life. Like many people of his generation and age, George Washington was immune because he had survived the disease in his youth. There was little he could do about the smallpox except to keep the stricken as separate from the others as possible. Another problem bearing on physical survival was a shortage of both food and clothing, about which Washington continually petitioned Congress. In the meantime, he ordered his noncommissioned officers to drill the men, and he also put them to work building a fort on a hillock overlooking Morristown. A task designed to take the minds of men off their cold and hunger, it served no tactical purpose and doubtless for that reason was called Fort Nonsense.

SPRING AND HOPE

Spring brought relief from the weather along with the welcome news that Benjamin Franklin and Silas Deane, both commissioned by Congress as emissaries to France, were progressing well toward persuading Louis XVI to ally his kingdom with America. At the moment, the king was reluctant to enter into a full alliance against the hated English, but he did permit private French companies to export muskets, clothing, and other supplies to the Patriots. In June, a different French export arrived on American shores. Despite his aristocratic title, the young Marie Joseph Paul Yves

The Marquis de Lafayette, painted by Joseph-Désiré Court on commission from the Historical Museum of Versailles, 1834. PALACE OF VERSAILLES

Roch Gilbert du Motier, Marquis de Lafayette, was an ardent democrat. He joined a party of other European zealots, including his military mentor, the German officer Johann de Kalb, in offering his services to the revolution. Washington was pleased with the spirit of arrivals from Europe, but he valued far more the solid military training they brought with them.

Spring also reawakened the somnolent martial spirit among the British. The flamboyant "Gentleman Johnny" Burgoyne had returned to London during the winter and occupied his leisure in reworking a plan General Guy Carleton had attempted (and failed) to carry out in 1776. It was an operation designed to divide New York along the Hudson, cutting off New England from the rest of the colonies. The idea, as always, was to decapitate the revolution by severing it from its political and intellectual origins. Burgoyne submitted his revision, which he titled "Thoughts for Conducting the War from the Side of Canada," to Lord Germain, secretary of state for the American colonies, on February 28, 1777. An impressive plan, it called for a three-pronged advance through New York, the largest portion of the army marching south along Lake Champlain and the upper Hudson while a smaller force raided throughout the New York backcountry, from Oswego through the Mohawk Valley. Finally, Howe was to dispatch an army up the Hudson to meet with Burgoyne's main force at Albany. This third force was a vital jaw of the pincer that would snip off New England's access to the rest of America.

Both King George III and Lord Germain approved the plan, doing so, however, without consulting Generals Guy Carleton or William Howe. Presumably hoping to preempt Howe's displeasure over violation of the chain of command, Germain also approved Howe's plan for attacking Philadelphia. He did not stop to consider that if Howe was devoting his forces to Philadelphia, he would have nothing left to send to Albany as his half of the pincers. In other words, Germain had heedlessly ordered two mutually exclusive missions. While Burgoyne was unaware of Germain's act of double-booking, he did later discover a letter Howe wrote to Carleton informing him that he was not about to march to Albany. Nevertheless, Burgoyne decided to go through with his plan. Perhaps he believed Howe could somehow be prevailed upon to march to Albany after all. Apparently, George Washington was not the only commander who lived in hope.

BURGOYNE ON THE MARCH

Burgoyne marched out of St. John's, Newfoundland, on June 17, 1777, leading seven thousand British regulars and Hessian mercenaries. In addition, he had 138 cannon and four hundred Native American auxiliaries. His objective was Lake Champlain and Fort Ticonderoga, which Ethan Allen had captured from the British back in May 1775. Tadeusz Kosciuszko, a Polish military engineer who had joined the revolutionary cause in August 1776, greatly improved Ticonderoga's fortifications, which prompted the Patriot press to dub it the "Gibraltar of America." What the fort still lacked, however, was manpower. Major General Arthur St. Clair, the Continental Army commander in charge of the Lake Champlain area, was undermanned and therefore supplied Fort Ti with nothing more than a skeleton garrison, perhaps 20 percent of the strength required to defend against a determined attack.

Burgoyne reached Lake Champlain on July 1, 1777, and divided his forces there, sending his British regulars down the west side of the lake and his Hessians, under Baron Friedrich von Riedesel, down the east. Riedesel was tasked with occupying Mount Independence, the high ground across the lake from Fort Ticonderoga. Attired for European marching, heavy packs and all, the Hessians found the wilderness slog painfully slow going, especially in the heat of high summer. The British contingent, in contrast, had a wide-open march and advanced far more quickly. Burgoyne ordered the forest cleared for his artillery. He intended to bombard the fort before assaulting it. One of his engineers, a Lieutenant Twiss, took note that Mount Defiance, rising some eight hundred feet southwest of the fort, had been left unoccupied by the Americans. Twiss pleaded with Burgoyne's artillery commander, Major General William Phillips, to give him some artillery to position atop the mountain. When Phillips objected that the uphill pull would be impossible, the engineer replied, "Where a goat can go a man can go and where a man can go he can drag a gun." With that, Phillips gave him some artillery, and Fort Ticonderoga soon found itself directly below the mouths of British cannon.

General Arthur St. Clair surely observed the arrival of the British, and this spectacle alone was sufficient to intimidate him into evacuating the fort. Thus, Fort Ti fell back to England without a shot having been fired.

St. Clair knew that Washington had a standing order governing withdrawal from Fort Ticonderoga, should doing so ever become necessary. The garrison was to retreat to Mount Independence—a position still unoccupied, since Riedesel's slow-moving Hessian column had yet to arrive. St. Clair led his men to the mountain but immediately decided to go against the standing order. He withdrew posthaste to Skenesboro, at the distant south end of Lake Champlain. Clearly, he would do just about anything to avoid combat with Burgoyne.

Bad enough that St. Clair turned tail. In his utter panic, he also failed to destroy the boat bridge that extended across Lake Champlain. This proved a gift to Burgoyne, giving his Advance Corps, under the Scots general Simon Fraser (father of the fur trader and explorer of the same name), a route of pursuit. Fraser first bumbled into a New Hampshire regiment on July 7. It quickly surrendered to him.

So far, the Americans under St. Clair were faring miserably against Burgoyne—until Colonel Seth Warner, who commanded the rear guard of St. Clair's main force, turned about and counterattacked Fraser. Warner's men fought with considerable ferocity. His riflemen were dead shots, and Fraser's lines were badly mauled. With his force melting away, Fraser was preparing to retreat when, at long last, Riedesel and his Hessians arrived to reinforce him.

It was a spectacle these deep woods had never before seen. The Hessians advanced as if on parade, accompanied by a full-dress regimental band. More important, they flanked Warner's men and closed in with a savagely disciplined bayonet attack. American troops were notoriously deficient in the use of the bayonet, and Warner's men began to give way before a weapon they greatly feared.

Hearing the sounds of battle, St. Clair dispatched a militia unit to reinforce Warner. The militiamen simply refused the order, however, and when Warner saw that no help was coming, he ordered his troops to scatter, instructing every man to save himself. Some four hundred of the one thousand Seth Warner commanded were killed, captured, or simply went missing. Six hundred lived to rejoin St. Clair's main column, which holed up in Fort Edward, a disused outpost along the Hudson.

TICONDEROGA AFTERMATH

When he received word that Fort Ticonderoga had been recaptured, King George III burst into his wife's dressing room and exuberantly announced: "I have beat them! I have beat all of the Americans!"

The king's joy was premature, as the victory was not nearly so consequential as he thought. Nevertheless, Washington and Congress were aghast at what they deemed St. Clair's cowardly incompetence. They summoned him to a court-martial, which acquitted him. It was not an unreasonable verdict since, even though he gave up the fort without offering any defense, he preserved most his army. Since destroying that army had been a key objective of Burgoyne's campaign, St. Clair deprived him of the full measure of victory; nevertheless, Burgoyne had to be feeling pretty good. He was now just twenty miles from Albany, where he hoped—yes, *hoped*—to tie in with troops under Generals Howe and General Barry St. Leger.

But Burgoyne had no rational reason to assume that Howe would break off his Philadelphia campaign. And yet he acted as if Howe would be there. Nor was it the only odd decision he made. Instead of completing the last twenty miles to Albany by transporting troops and equipment in boats via Lakes Champlain and George and then into the Hudson, as his very own plan specified, he put his soldiers to the hard, tedious, and time-consuming labor of hacking out a wilderness road. Burgoyne's expensive tastes were known to tempt him to various acts of remunerative corruption, and some believed he had made an illicit bargain with one

Philip Skene, prominent Loyalist of Skenesboro, to cut a road between his town and Albany.

Outrage

Burgoyne's reputation was about to suffer a more serious blow than an accusation of mere larceny. He had issued a public proclamation inviting Indians loyal to the Crown to attack any rebels who got in their way. At the same time, he issued "certificates of protection" to all Loyalists who asked for them, which, Burgoyne solemnly guaranteed, would make them immune to Indian attack. But on July 27, 1777, Jane McCrea, a young Loyalist woman who lived with her brother on the Hudson River between Saratoga and Fort Edward, was captured by one of "Burgoyne's Indians" while she was on her way to Fort Edwards to visit her fiancé, a Loyalist in Burgoyne's service. The Indians started back to Fort Ann, where Burgoyne was headquartered. A Mrs. McNeil (American cousin of General Simon Fraser) and Jane McCrea were with them—but on their arrival at the fort, they carried only Mrs. McNeil and what Jane McCrea's shocked and grief-stricken fiancé immediately identified as the scalp of his bride-to-be.

Word of the atrocity traveled like wildfire, and the American Loyalist community was outraged. Worse, when McCrea's killer was identified as a Wyandot named Panther, Burgoyne refrained from bringing him to justice. He dared not alienate his Native American allies. General Horatio Gates, commanding Patriot forces at Bennington, Vermont, wrote a fiery open letter to Burgoyne:

> That the famous Lieutenant General Burgoyne, in whom the fine Gentleman is united with the Soldier and Scholar, should hire the savage of America to scalp Europeans and the descendants of Europeans, nay more, that he should pay a price for each scalp so barbarously taken, is more than will be believed in Europe, until authenticated facts shall, in every Gazette, convince mankind of the truth of the horrid fate. . . . The miserable fate of Miss McCrea was particularly aggravated by her being dressed to receive her promised husband, but met her murderer employed by you.

Now men in and around Bennington trooped into Gates's headquarters, asking to join the militia against Gentleman Johnny Burgoyne.

On July 29, Burgoyne completed the Skenesboro road to Albany. It represented a month of labor, during which the local American forces regrouped and resupplied themselves. Alarmed, Burgoyne's subordinate officers urged their general to set off for Albany—*now*. Not to be goaded, Burgoyne chose instead to encamp his army outside of Fort Edward, there to await the arrival of all of his forces. He intended to march into Albany at the head of everything he had—all to impress General Howe. Yet, on August 3, a dispatch from Howe reached Burgoyne, congratulating him on the capture of Fort Ticonderoga but informing him that he was indeed headed "for Pennsylvania, where I expect to meet Washington." Howe did promise that if his quarry happened to go "northward," he would "soon be after him to relieve you."

Burgoyne's hope, delusional as it had always been, was finally dashed—though he took comfort in knowing that General Barry St. Leger would meet him. He could only hope that St. Leger would come with enough men to deal the rebels a decisive blow. In the meantime, he kept Howe's missive a secret, apparently for the sake of the morale of forces.

THE BATTLE OF ORISKANY

On June 18, 1777, some prisoners of war told Barry St. Leger, who was headed for Fort Stanwix, an American outpost at what is today Rome, New York, that the fort was very heavily garrisoned. St. Leger believed them and accordingly delayed his attack on the fort. In fact, Fort Stanwix was weakly held by Colonel Peter Gansevoort and no more than a 750-man garrison. During the delay, Gansevoort sent Ahnyero, a prominent pro-American Oneida warrior, from Fort Stanwix to infiltrate a pro-British Indian council set to convene at Oswego late in July. In this way, Ahnyero learned the details of St. Leger's stalled plan to attack Fort Stanwix. Shortly after this, however, a reconnaissance force St. Leger dispatched to reconnoiter the fort revealed that Stanwix was, in fact, ripe for the plucking.

On August 3, St. Leger at last advanced toward Fort Stanwix, making a display of much pomp and circumstance—banners flying and band playing. His hope was to intimidate the garrison into bloodless capitulation in the manner of Arthur St. Clair at Fort Ticonderoga. But when St. Leger, just out of artillery range, sent a surrender demand, Ganesvoort rebuffed him. On August 4, the British general commenced an artillery bombardment. Impressive as it was, the barrage killed just one of Gansevoort's garrison. St. Leger's Native American snipers, however, took a heavy toll on the fort's defenders.

On August 6, militia general Nicholas Herkimer, learning that Fort Stanwix was under siege, managed to get a message through the siege lines and into Gansevoort's hands. Herkimer's message informed Gansevoort that he was at the Indian town of Oriskany, ten miles southwest of Fort Stanwix, and had eight hundred militiamen. He asked Gansevoort to coordinate with him in attacking St. Leger. Gansevoort let fly three cannon shots as a signal that he had received Herkimer's message and would comply. He sent two hundred men under Lieutenant Colonel Marinus Willett to link up with Herkimer. Before reaching him, however, Willett's men surprised one of St. Leger's encampments, killing some twenty British but also alerting St. Leger to their presence. St. Leger blocked Willett's path to Herkimer.

Herkimer was determined to await a successful sortie from Fort Stanwix before launching his own attack, but his militiamen were not willing to wait. Believing he was facing a mutiny, Herkimer, against his own judgment, decided on an immediate attack.

St. Leger was ready for him. He assigned a Mohawk military and political leader named Thayendanegea, better known to his British allies as Joseph Brant, to lead four hundred Native American warriors in conjunction with four hundred Loyalist troops, the Tory Rangers (under John Butler), and the Royal Greens (commanded by John Johnson), to make a surprise attack on Herkimer's force. They fell upon the militia general six miles outside of Fort Stanwix. The Battle of Oriskany began at ten o'clock in the morning on August 6.

Within minutes, most of Herkimer's officers lay dead, and Herkimer suffered a severe leg wound, trying to command his men even as he bled to death. A full regiment ran away, but the rest of Herkimer's men rallied fiercely and engaged the enemy hand-to-hand. Brant and the white Loyalist troops were stunned as both sides suffered heavy losses until a severe thunderstorm brought a temporary halt to the mayhem.

After the storm passed, John Butler ordered his Rangers, whose uniforms were green, to turn their coats inside out, exposing a lining that looked from a distance like the American uniforms. They marched into the American lines, but the trick was soon discovered, and their infiltration beaten off. Seeing this, Brant's warriors deserted, and Butler and Johnson had no choice but to order a retreat. Herkimer was dying and did not order his men to pursue the withdrawing enemy. They were likely too diminished to have done so effectively in any case. Half of Herkimer's force had

Chromolithograph after George Romney's painting of Joseph Brant (Thayendanegea), a Mohawk leader of Native Americans allied with Loyalists.
WIKIMEDIA COMMONS

been killed, wounded, or captured. Thirty-three British were dead, and forty-one wounded. Among the British-allied Indians, perhaps one hundred were killed or wounded. Among these were no fewer than twenty-three war chiefs.

The Battle of Oriskany ended in a draw, a mutual drubbing, really. Yet St. Leger could claim a narrow edge, since he checkmated Herkimer's attempt to reinforce Fort Stanwix. Acting on this, St. Leger again demanded Gansevoort's surrender, warning him that "If the terms are rejected, the Indians, who are numerous and much exasperated and mortified from their losses in the action against General Herkimer, cannot be restrained from plundering property and probably destroying the lives of the greater part of the garrison." It was Willett who responded:

Tough American militia general Nicholas Herkimer, though fatally wounded, continued to give orders at the desperate Battle of Oriskany (August 6, 1777) in the wilderness of New York. WIKIMEDIA COMMONS

"Do I understand you, Sir, . . . that you come from a British colonel, to the commandant of this garrison, to tell him, that if he does not deliver up the garrison into the hands of your Colonel, he will send his Indians to murder our women and children[?]"

Once again, the Americans refused to surrender. General Philip Schuyler, fifty miles from Fort Stanwix, sent a Massachusetts brigade under Ebenezer Learned to relieve the fort. He then sent the First New York Regiment under Benedict Arnold to harass Loyalist forces in the region. Arnold captured Major Walter Butler (the brother of Tory Ranger commander John Butler) and Hon Yost Schuyler, another prominent Loyalist. He interrogated the prisoners, offering Hon Yost Schuyler a full pardon if he returned to St. Leger's camp and told the Indians there that Walter Butler, Joseph Brant's close friend and confidant, had been captured and would be hanged. Hon Yost Schuyler did as he was asked— and also wildly exaggerated his estimate of the strength of Arnold's force. The effect of this disinformation was extraordinary. Six hundred Native American warriors deserted St. Leger, who lifted the siege of Fort Stanwix on August 22. Believing that he was about to be overtaken by a very large force under Arnold, St. Leger abandoned a large store of equipment and artillery as he fled with his army.

THE BATTLE OF BENNINGTON

Thanks in no small measure to William Howe's refusal to coordinate with him, the supremely arrogant John Burgoyne saw the momentum drain from his campaign to boldly sever New England from the rest of revolutionary America. By the summer of 1777, he was also suffering an epidemic of desertion. He had the presence of mind to understand that his army was dissolving not so much from fear or discouragement but simply from hunger. Provisions were dwindling, and Burgoyne believed a quick raid on nearby Bennington, Vermont, which contained a generous cache of Continental Army supplies, would do wonders for both the physical and mental welfare of his army. Food would restore morale and thus stanch the outward flow of soldiers.

Burgoyne dispatched some of the very few Indians who remained in his service on a mission to steal horses, which were necessary for a hit-and-run raid. The Indians worked swiftly but, on their return, demanded a high price for the stolen ponies. When Burgoyne resisted, the Indians, unwilling to haggle, simply cut the horses' hamstrings, crippling them and rendering them worthless.

Without horses, the raid seemed doomed before it had begun. Nevertheless, Lieutenant Colonel Frederick Baum, the Hessian commander Burgoyne had assigned to lead the operation, was unconcerned. Even without an adequate number of mounts, he was confident he could defeat what he thought was a garrison consisting of a mere handful of militiamen. An initial skirmish at Cambridge, New York, on August 12, confirmed him in his confidence. His Hessians easily routed fifty Americans.

What Baum did not know was that General John Stark, veteran of Bunker Hill, had been reaping a recruitment bonanza fueled by the Jane McCrea atrocity. By the time he learned that Baum's Native American allies were looting the countryside, Stark had assembled a strong force. He sent two hundred militiamen to drive off the Indian raiders but encountered Baum's much larger main column of Hessians along the way. The militia deftly withdrew, grateful that a powerful thunderstorm on August 15 dissuaded Baum from a pursuit. The delay imposed by the bad weather gave Stark sufficient time to add four hundred more reinforcements, veteran Vermont militiamen led by none other than the gallant Seth Warner.

The intense rainfall having thwarted his ability to raid, Baum dug his men into defensive positions. On August 15, Stark and Warner surrounded Baum on the front, rear, and flanks. Their attack was incredibly well coordinated, closing on the Hessian position from every side. The Indians, Loyalists, and Canadians attached to Baum ran off, and Hessian and British regulars were left to resist the converging attack for two terrible hours. At last, it was the Hessians themselves who began to desert. Baum watched his army melt away. He rallied the remainder, ordering a saber charge into the American ranks. But there were too many of them now, and the charge was soon arrested. Baum suffered a fatal wound. With their commander out of action, the remaining Hessians surrendered.

In the meantime, Hessian reinforcements led by Lieutenant Colonel Heinrich von Breymann arrived on the outskirts of Bennington. Here, Stark's troops were no match for them—but more of Warner's Vermonters reached Bennington in time to allow Stark to regroup. In concert with the Vermont militia, he counterattacked Breymann—hard. By the time this phase of the Battle of Bennington ended, 207 Brits and Hessians lay dead. Another seven hundred became prisoners of war. American losses were thirty killed and some forty wounded.

For Gentleman Johnny Burgoyne, the news was all bad. Howe was never going to meet him in Albany, the Hessians had been crushed at Bennington, and Barry St. Leger had not taken Fort Stanwix. Nevertheless, he stubbornly decided to continue his march into Albany. As his troops crossed the Hudson on September 13, 1777, he called out to them: "Britons never retreat!" Then he ordered that the boat bridge they had just crossed be dismantled—to *ensure* that they could not retreat.

CHAPTER 16

The Capital Falls Yet the War Continues

BRITAIN WAS A STORIED EUROPEAN EMPIRE AT THE TIME OF THE American Revolution. America was a collection of colonies with dreams of nationhood. It is easy to assume that Washington and his colleagues had chosen a mission impossible. Yet while it is absolutely true that George Washington had on his hands a major war against a great global power but precious few resources with which to fight it, it is also true that Britain had neither the will nor, ultimately, the practical ability to bring to bear against the "rebels" anything approaching its full economic and military power. Just consider why General Burgoyne's master plan for invasion collapsed. It was attributable less to his limitations as a military commander—though he was indeed limited—than to a shortage of *available* resources. Instead of coordinating with Burgoyne to cut off New England, William Howe chose to capture Philadelphia. He did not believe he could do both. Like Washington, Howe and Burgoyne were not given all that they needed to fight a major war over a large area. Both were compelled to prioritize.

DID HOWE PRIORITIZE WISELY?
Philadelphia was the capital city of a would-be nation. It was the seat of what little central government the rebellious colonies had, the Continental Congress. On the face of it, therefore, it could be reasonably argued that Howe saw an opportunity for a decapitating blow against the revolution. Yet it was not as if Congress had some vast infrastructure established in Philadelphia or that the city had a long pedigree favoring

independence. In truth, Congress could be set up anywhere, and Philadelphia was certainly an important American city—the largest at the time—but it was hardly a hotbed of revolutionary thought and zeal. In fact, its population leaned more toward loyalty to Crown and Parliament than it did toward independence. On balance, the far more strategic course was the one Burgoyne pursued. He was not targeting politicians. He wanted to destroy, in the field, the principal army of the revolt and, in the process, sever the region most committed to independence, New England, from communication with the rest of America. Howe's target was more symbolic than operational. As it turned out, retaining possession of Philadelphia was not at all critical to the Patriots' war effort. The survival of Washington's army, however, was, and so was the freedom to maneuver from coastal New England through the western frontier.

A DOABLE OBJECTIVE

Yet there was something to be said for targeting Philadelphia. Strictly military strategy aside, the British needed a win. Washington's victories at Trenton and Princeton had injected new life into the revolution. They made the redcoats and their Hessian minions look weak. Philadelphia was a prestigious objective, if not an especially strategic one. Moreover, it was a very feasible objective—and, situated on the most "civilized" slice of the Eastern Seaboard, it presented the kind of battlespace that European troops were most familiar with. It was a field of battle advantageous to the British.

And William Howe very badly needed a feasible objective. He was a seasoned commander, a veteran of the French and Indian War who racked up in that conflict the most impressive—or least unimpressive—record of any British officer. He was also younger than most senior British commanders, having been promoted to major general in 1772, when he was only forty-three. Yet he was slow-moving and overly cautious. Well, he could afford to be when his objective was as straightforward as Philadelphia. Besides, while king and Parliament desperately needed a victory, Howe needed it even more. He had been brought in to replace the disappointing Thomas Gage. King, Cabinet, and Parliament had great expectations of Howe. So far, these had hardly been realized.

Should he have subordinated himself to Burgoyne and his plan? At some level of Howe's consciousness, there must have been the notion that Burgoyne's failure in the wilderness would make a splendid contrast with his own success in the heart of American civilization—the rebel capital, the desk at which the Declaration of Independence had been signed. One wonders, too, if Howe was actually well aware that Philadelphia was politically no Boston. There were plenty of Loyalists to woo in this fairly conservative city. Occupying it would likely not be the nightmare that it was in radical Boston. Any number of old, established families would welcome the British regulars with open arms, and there was reason to believe that the city, once under occupation, would be fertile ground for recruiting active Loyalist aid against the Continental Army.

Burgoyne did salve his conscience with the thought that, if the Loyalists rallied to his cause, Philadelphia would fall to him rather quickly, quite possibly in time for him to release a contingent of men to reinforce poor old Johnny Burgoyne. Moreover, he rationalized, attacking Philadelphia would inevitably draw Washington's forces away from Burgoyne. Surely, Washington would march to the defense of the capital of the revolution.

The truth is that General Howe had little respect for Washington's generalship. After all, despite Trenton and Princeton, he had revealed a certain talent for making military blunders. While Howe himself may be accused of having blundered by failing to coordinate with Burgoyne's northern campaign, he probably sincerely believed that menacing the revolution's capital city would lure Washington into making virtually the very same blunder. If Washington swallowed the bait, he would be transferring his precious resources to the defense of Philadelphia instead of joining forces with Horatio Gates against Burgoyne. In this, Howe was not mistaken.

George Washington snapped at the bait and sent everything he had to defend Philadelphia. It might have been a truly tragic decision—had Howe avoided making the very mistake so many British commanders committed so very often. He underestimated just how effective the Continental Army and even the militia forces had become. Howe, of all commanders, should have known better. Lexington, Bunker Hill, Trenton, they all showed that the American forces could be remarkably worthy adversaries.

A Case of the Slows

During the Civil War, President Abraham Lincoln was repeatedly frustrated by the excessive caution of the general he had chosen to command the Union's flagship Army of the Potomac. Exasperated by Major General George B. McClellan's failure to move decisively against the Confederate capital, Richmond, Lincoln complained that McClellan was afflicted by "a case of the slows." The very same could have been said of William Howe and his apparent incapacity simply to get a move on. Like almost every other operation he had led, Howe's advance against Philadelphia was carried out at a pace that was not so much methodical and deliberate as it was nearly somnolent.

By summer 1777, the Continental Army had left its Morristown encampment to take up a position on the banks of the Neshaminy Creek in Pennsylvania. It was not a strategic maneuver pursuant to some clear-cut plan. It was just a way of waiting to see what the British would do next.

The wait was extended through most of the season, because it was not until the end of August that British military intentions became clear. The Royal Navy fleet under William Howe's admiral brother, Richard, materialized at the head of Chesapeake Bay. Washington knew that the ships carried troops and the troops would land. Because they were clearly going to land on the Chesapeake shore, their objective must surely be Philadelphia.

The battle plan Howe submitted to Secretary of State Lord Germain specified an overland march to Philadelphia. Presumably, his decision to advance most of the way by boat instead was intended to speed up the operation. Under William Howe's leadership, however, the decision actually slowed operational progress. He had begun preparing the expedition to depart New York City in April, but it was July 23 before the fleet, loaded with fifteen thousand troops, finally embarked. And even after it was at last under way, Howe made a decision that added to the delay. Instead of taking the direct water route via the Delaware River, he decided to go around Cape Charles and then up the Chesapeake. Presumably, he feared that the Delaware presented navigation hazards or was well defended by the Patriots. A little judicious inquiry would have dispelled both misapprehensions.

To make matters worse, Howe did not put in at Delaware Bay, where he could have disembarked at the very well-established port of New Castle, Delaware, just thirty-three miles from Philadelphia. Instead, he sailed up Chesapeake Bay to Head of Elk, Maryland, nearly twice the distance from his objective. The journey required more than a month's sailing—July 23 to August 25. Fifteen thousand fully equipped troops were packed below decks in the heat of midsummer, and the overheated trip transformed lusty fighting men into fever-plagued invalids by the time they disembarked. Realizing that he needed to give his troops time to recover, Howe rested them at Head of Elk. Besides, he need the extra time to find cavalry mounts to replace the large number of horses that had died during the voyage.

Washington could only count his lucky stars. The multiplied delays gave him more time to both assemble and move his army. On August 24, he led some eleven thousand men in a grand parade through Philadelphia before marching south to do battle with Howe and his top lieutenants, Charles Cornwallis and Baron Wilhelm von Knyphausen, the new commander-in-chief of the Hessians.

Astoundingly, despite Howe's bumbling, Washington was somehow taken by surprise. Near the road to Kennett Square, Pennsylvania, on the Pennsylvania side of the line with Delaware, a group of girls at play were warned by a band of riders to go home, quickly. "The British regiments are coming up the road!" they warned.

The girls spread the news, considerably embroidering it, so that it seemed an eyewitness report of Howe's entire British army on the march. Washington believed it. Without further reconnoitering, he transferred most of his forces to intercept what he assumed was Howe's main force. This movement left most of the fords across Brandywine Creek in southeastern Pennsylvania totally undefended. Howe took advantage of this to cross that watercourse, which put him in position to pounce on Washington's columns from the right rear. As at the Battle of Long Island, the commander of the Continental Army found himself facing the enemy from exactly the opposite direction he had anticipated.

BATTLE OF BRANDYWINE

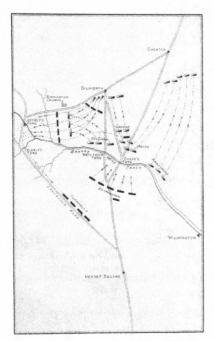

Battle of the Brandywine (September 11, 1777) from John Fiske, *The American Revolution* (Boston: Houghton, Mifflin & Co., 1891).

John Sullivan's New Hampshire militia took the first blows. Green troops led by a notoriously mediocre commander, they crumbled. That began the disintegration of Washington's diminished line all along the Brandywine. Knyphausen's Hessians hit the American center at Chadd's Ford, Pennsylvania, and Howe and Cornwallis crossed the Brandywine at two more undefended fords. Now the British were in position to flank most of Washington's army while Sullivan did what little he could to contain the damage he was suffering. He dispatched troops under General Adam Stephen and William "Lord Stirling" Alexander to attempt to check at least part of the British advance. Although well-intentioned, the maneuver opened a gap in Sullivan's already breached line. Seeing it, Howe pounced with a bayonet charge that reduced Sullivan's contingent even further. When Washington was apprised of the growing catastrophe on the Brandywine, he sent troops under General Nathanael Greene to plug the breach. By the time Greene arrived, however, the British bayonets had created maximum chaos.

The situation went from bad to worse as Knyphausen's Hessians stormed through the American center even as Howe and Cornwallis made an unopposed crossing of the Brandywine. The Continentals poured fire into the advancing Hessian ranks, who, thoroughly disciplined, seemed unfazed. They smashed through the blue-and-buff line and overran and captured the Continental artillery. Knyphausen now turned this artillery against the retreating Continentals. As Joseph Clark, a young New Jersey soldier, scrawled in his diary that night, "our army was something broke."

The Battle of Brandywine ended with nightfall. Washington's battered army withdrew to Chester, Pennsylvania, a position from which they could still oppose Howe's advance to Philadelphia. Of the approximately eleven thousand American troops who fought at Brandywine, thirteen hundred had been killed, wounded, or taken prisoner. Eleven precious cannon were captured. Howe lost 577 men, killed or wounded.

PERSEVERANCE AND A MASSACRE

Enoch Anderson, a Delaware militia captain, confided to his diary that the defeat and retreat produced "not a despairing look, nor . . . a despairing word. We had solacing words always ready for each other—'Come, boys, we shall do better another time.'" But if Washington's army still exhibited considerable morale, Congress was reeling back on its heels. No less a figure than Alexander Hamilton, a gallant officer, pleaded with the delegates to evacuate Philadelphia. He feared that the revolution might not survive the capture of the government. On September 18, Congress fled, pausing at Lancaster, Pennsylvania, before setting up an interim capital in the Pennsylvania village of York.

Washington, in the meantime, gave his army the night to rest at Chester before moving his men out the next morning. He began his withdrawal in the direction of Philadelphia just as Howe arrived in Chester and occupied it. On September 16, while Congress was still preparing to evacuate, Washington briefly engaged a portion of Howe's forces at the White Horse Tavern and at Malvern Hill, both west of Philadelphia. The Polish freedom fighter Casimir Pulaski, an experienced cavalry officer, had just begun assembling a modest mounted branch for the Continental Army. It was these troops who engaged the Hessians at Malvern Hill, managing to hold them at bay until Anthony Wayne arrived with a larger contingent of infantry. The Americans now outnumbered the Hessians here and could have scored a much-needed victory had not a sudden and severe thunderstorm put an unexpected end to the fighting. The Patriots' powder and cartridges, stored in shoddy boxes, quickly became waterlogged and useless. Anthony pulled his troops toward Reading Furnace (in Chester County), where a store of dry ammunition was kept.

On September 18, the Hessians turned their attention to the Continental Army encampment and depot at Valley Forge. Finding it unguarded, they raided its stores, taking a great quantity of flour and other vital supplies. Howe even set up a small outpost there. Seeking some way to score even a small win against Howe, Washington ordered Wayne to march out from Reading Furnace with fifteen hundred men and four cannon to Warren's Tavern, near Paoli, a Pennsylvania town named by its founder, innkeeper Joshua Evans, in honor of the Corsican freedom fighter Pasquale Paoli. Evans had no particular affiliation with Paoli but conferred the name after Irishmen, celebrating St. Patrick's Day at his inn, toasted the apostle of an independent Corsica some forty-five times.

Wayne's mission was to lead his troops in what American soldiers did so well—not a head-on, face-to-face, set-piece battle, but a swift surprise attack on the rear guard of a larger British contingent. Wayne was a fine general, one of the Patriots' very best, but, this time, he had committed the error of failing to recognize the consequences of operating in a part of Pennsylvania that was full of Loyalists. He should have assumed that his movements were being reported to Howe, as, in fact, they were. The British commander sent a contingent under Major General Charles Grey to raid Wayne's camp during the predawn hours of September 21.

Unlike Howe, Grey was not wedded to conventional tactics. He ordered his men not to load their Brown Bess muskets and instructed those who had already loaded theirs to remove the flints from their gunlocks, so that the weapons could not be fired. The surprise assault was to be carried out in stealthy silence, using only bayonets. For this tactic, the general would become infamous as "No-Flint" Grey.

The camp was asleep, and the slaughter was swift. By Grey's count five hundred of Wayne's men were killed in the "Paoli Massacre." Wayne's doubtlessly more accurate count was 150—and, because the American general remained calm in the face of terror, he not only retained all of his precious artillery, he evacuated most of his command to safety. As for Washington, a veteran though he was of the French and Indian War and of several bloody losses so far in the revolution, the Paoli Massacre shook him to his core. He regrouped his troops at Pott's Grove (modern Pottstown), Pennsylvania, which prompted Howe to alter the direction of his advance. The British general sent the main part of his army across the Schuylkill River. On September 26, his subordinate Cornwallis led four British and two Hessian regiments into Philadelphia. Washington remained at Pott's Grove, making no move to defend the capital.

GERMANTOWN

Germantown is today a Northwest Philadelphia neighborhood. In 1777, however, it was a separate village to the north of America's premier metropolis. Cornwallis chose it as his encampment. General Washington was facing harsh scrutiny. Several of his officers openly questioned his fitness for command, and it seemed only a matter of time before Congress would begin doing the same.

Cooler heads, however, prudently did the math. The loss of Philadelphia was a blow to morale, to be sure, but it had not materially changed the capacity of the Continental Army to conduct war. Moreover, Congress continued, without interruption, to govern the colonies from its exile in York, Pennsylvania. Add to this the cost to the British of taking Philadelphia. The prolonged campaign had kept Howe from reinforcing Burgoyne's grand invasion. Now it was not New England that had been cut off from the rest of America. It was Burgoyne and his army.

Yet Washington was often his own harshest critic, and he was hardly content to lick his wounds. Brandywine, Paoli, and Philadelphia forged a painful chain of defeat. Much as having

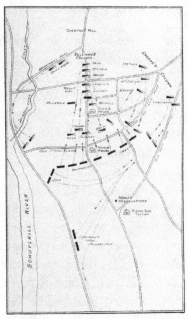

Map of the Battle of Germantown (October 4, 1777) from John Fiske, *The American Revolution* (Boston: Houghton, Mifflin & Co., 1891).

The British used the house of Benjamin Chew as a fortress during the Battle of Germantown (October 4, 1777), where it was the scene of much bloodshed. At the time a village outside of Philadelphia, Germantown is today a city neighborhood, and the house (also known as Cliveden) is at 6401 Germantown Avenue. MODERN PHOTO BY DJMASCHEK, POSTED ON WIKIMEDIA COMMONS

been chased out of New York and across New Jersey into Philadelphia had prompted the bold counterattacks at Trenton and Princeton, so Washington now plotted a bold move against British-occupied Philadelphia. He would hit Howe, and, this time, he would not aim for some rear guard. He would strike where the redcoats were strongest. Germantown was his chosen field of battle.

At daybreak, October 4, 1777, the army of George Washington, now consisting of eight thousand Continentals plus three thousand militiamen, engaged Howe's advance elements on the outskirts of Germantown, in which about nine thousand men under Lord Cornwallis were lodged. Washington's forces were superior in number to both the advance units and Cornwallis's encampment, and they moved against the 40th Regiment, which quickly withdrew into Germantown, taking a defensive position in and around the large house of Benjamin Chew. Built of local stone, it was a ready-made fortress. From it, men of the 40th fired on Continental Army troops led by General Sullivan.

It was a bitter fight. Despite Washington's numerical advantage, assaulting a strong defensive position was always a costly proposition. Wisely, Washington proposed skirting the Chew house and marching directly into Philadelphia proper. Henry Knox, the Boston bookseller who became commander of the Continental Army's artillery, had what he believed was a better idea. He prevailed upon Washington to take a stand, so that his cannon could bombard the Chew house.

There was merit in adopting a policy of never leaving an enemy at your rear, but Washington should have known that Patriot gunpowder was highly unreliable and that if his principal objective was to retake Philadelphia, he should simply move ahead to retake it. A fortress is only dangerous if it is assaulted. Pass it by, and it becomes irrelevant. As it turned out, Knox's cannonballs lacked the barrel velocity to do anything more than bounce off the Chew house walls. In the hour squandered on the bombardment, the Continentals suffered considerable and quite unnecessary casualties.

There was worse. While Knox's fire proved ineffective, it was loud, and one of Washington's subordinates, General Adam Stephen, hearing the cannonade, assumed that the Battle of Philadelphia was in full flower and that he was late to the fight. He double-timed his forces into what he thought was desperate combat, and he soon found himself shrouded in an early-morning fog. Vaguely glimpsing troops in the middle distance, he ordered his men to open fire. As it turned out, his target was the rear of Anthony Wayne's column, with which Stephen's advance elements soon collided. The result was a combination of tragic friendly fire casualties as well as panic and chaos. The operation to retake Philadelphia was badly blunted, and the confusion and delay soon backed up into General Nathanael Greene's advance, so slowing it that making a coordinated attack on Cornwallis's encampment became impossible. Washington reluctantly ordered a retreat.

And, so, the Battle of Germantown was added to the string of American reverses.

Washington lost 152 men killed and 521 wounded. At least four hundred Continentals and militiamen became prisoners of war. True, Howe also suffered heavy losses, 535 killed and wounded, but he still held Philadelphia.

Such was the short-term, tactical assessment of Germantown: unquestionably a defeat for George Washington. Yet, from a strategic perspective, the outcome of the battle appeared very different. Accompanying the Continental Army was a contingent of French military observers. They were untroubled by the defeat Washington had suffered but inordinately impressed by the American commander's aggressive audacity. The loss of Philadelphia would have discouraged most commanders from mounting so ambitious a counteroffensive. Certainly, no British commander would have done it. Washington, however, had eagerly seized the initiative. The French observers were persuaded that the Continental Army was now a credible force led by an inspiring and courageous commander. Their enthusiastic report to King Louis XVI drew France nearer to making a full and formal military alliance with the United States.

WHERE'S JOHNNY?

Far to the north, "Gentleman Johnny" Burgoyne was approaching the moment at which we left him in Chapter 15. He had discovered that Howe was not going to unite with him at Albany. He had learned of the heavy Hessian losses at Bennington. He had received word that Barry St. Leger had failed—quite miserably—to capture Fort Stanwix on Lake Champlain.

It was very clear. His grand plan for ending the American Revolution with one sweeping strategic operation was faltering, perhaps fatally. He pondered withdrawing to Fort Edward or Fort Ticonderoga. That was, in fact, the logical move. Insofar as it had the best chance of keeping his army intact, it was also the right move. But it went contrary to what he understood as the spirit of his orders from London, a place so very distant from the backwoods of New York. Neither his own plan nor his orders from the secretary of state contemplated falling back. Burgoyne therefore saw no option other than to "force a junction with Sir William Howe." Never mind that Howe was otherwise occupied about 250 miles to the south.

CHAPTER 17

Saratoga Glory and an Ally Earned

"BRITONS NEVER RETREAT!" WITH THAT, GENERAL JOHN BURGOYNE started his army on the way to Albany. It should have been a quick twenty-mile march, but Patriot insurgents had been busy dismantling the many small bridges spanning countless small streams. These watercourses were not difficult for infantry and cavalry to ford, but Burgoyne's force was extensively encumbered with supply wagons and artillery, which could not cross even shallow water without a bridge. At each ruined span, Burgoyne had to stop and set his men to work rebuilding or building anew. Progress, therefore, came at an excruciating mile a day—on a good day. Some days were without movement at all.

Sabotage bogged down progress, which was also impeded by the lack of Indian scouts. Burgoyne had started with many Native American auxiliaries, but the ignominious defeat of the Loyalists and Hessians at the Battle of Bennington and the loss of Fort Stanwix had convinced most of the Indians to abandon Burgoyne. So, on September 16, 1777, he failed to *see* the American forces were close by. How close were they? Close enough for Burgoyne to *hear* the roll of reveille drums off to the south. He dispatched a scouting party in that vague direction, but it returned with intelligence no more specific than a sighting of wagon tracks leading to Freeman's Farm. It was a deserted property, essentially nothing more than an unharvested field with stalks of untended wheat bending with the breeze.

Objectively speaking, Freeman's Farm was a melancholy sight. But to Gentleman Johnny Burgoyne, weary of ambush emerging from the forest, it was a gladdening vision. His army, like any other European army, had been trained to fight on a battle*field,* an open expanse conducive to maneuver. Now, if he could only lure the sources of those drums to the field of Freeman's Farm. In his anxiety to engage the enemy precisely where he wanted him, Burgoyne impatiently split his army in three, thereby violating the tactical maxim advising against "dividing your forces in the face of the enemy." On September 19, he ordered Simon Fraser to lead a contingent of twenty-two hundred down the path to Freeman Farm's western fields while he himself personally led eleven hundred men south and then west with the intention of rejoining Fraser on the farm. If either of the two columns encountered any Americans, they would effectively envelop them in a converging pincers movement, the one commander driving them back against the other. East of both Fraser and Burgoyne would be a third column, consisting of eleven hundred Hessians under Baron Friedrich Riedesel, which was sent marching southward down the river road. If everything worked according to Burgoyne's vision of the battle, the Americans would be totally enveloped on the abandoned field of Fraser's Farm by *three* converging columns.

It was a perfectly seductive plan spoiled only by the total absence of hard intelligence. Burgoyne had no way of knowing if the Americans would materialize where he wanted them to be and when he wanted them to be there. It was a hunch—or a wish—based on nothing more than the sound of a drum roll.

And there was another imponderable. The three columns would be totally out of sight of one another as they advanced. Burgoyne planned to coordinate their movements using small signal cannon. That might have worked if the three commanders had any knowledge of the ground through which they were marching. Unlike the smooth farm field, the terrain surrounding Freeman's Farm was rugged and broken. There was no way to reliably calculate, let alone coordinate, a rate of march over such challenging ground.

So, Burgoyne advanced to attack an enemy who was not yet where he wanted him to be and might never get there. Without scouts, he proposed to rely on sound—the firing of signal guns—but if this failed to be sufficient for coordination, he was leaving himself wide open to what commanders call "defeat in detail," attack on any of his three divided forces. The only way to prevent defeat in detail was to ensure that the divided forces would reunite before any of them met the full fury of the enemy.

Neither Burgoyne nor his two subordinates seems to have appreciated just how precarious their position was. For while they were effectively blind, the Americans were observing their every movement. If ever there was an opportunity for an ambush attack, this was it. Unfortunately, however, the commander-in-charge was Horatio Gates. Veteran of the British service in both the War of the Austrian Succession and the French and Indian War, Gates was both jealous and mistrustful of Washington and suffered from all the conservative tactical traits that afflicted British commanders, including William Howe.

He watched Burgoyne and watched him some more but did not move to exploit the Englishman's fatal tactical blunder. His second-in-command, the dashing and aggressive Benedict Arnold, begged him to pounce while Burgoyne was clearly isolated. By the time Gates finally yielded to Arnold's pleas, Riedesel was drawing near. But there was still time, and Gates assigned the attack to a unit of highly skilled riflemen under the brilliant frontier fighter Daniel Morgan along with a detachment of light infantry led by Henry Dearborn.

Of the three British columns, Burgoyne's own center column was the first to break through the rugged woods and into Freeman's field. At this moment, it was the British who were in the open, fully exposed and utterly vulnerable. From Morgan's men, who were concentrated in the thick woods on the south edge of the field, shots were immediately fired. The shooting was precisely targeted and deadly effective. In short order, every single British officer in the front line fell dead.

Without doubt, Morgan knew how to play to his strengths. He had a large contingent of sharpshooters who were skilled at firing from concealment. What he did not have, however, was an army of men trained to European standards of discipline. Giddy to behold the deadly results of their own marksmanship, they stormed out of the woods and poured willy-nilly into the field, rushing the bewildered men still standing in the British front line. That line broke and ran for the rear—but then Morgan's men suddenly found themselves in collision with Burgoyne's arriving main column. Now it was their turn to fall back in disarray as they sought cover in the woods.

Observing this, Morgan feared that he had suffered a devastating blow. Where soldiers in conventional armies responded to the call of the bugle, Morgan's frontiersmen answered to his distinctive turkey call. Its sound worked its magic, instantly snapping his men into something like orderly ranks. Morgan's men shook off their spasm of fear and confusion and were once again ready to fight. The British were slower to recover from the attack that had descended on them, killing most of their officers. They continued to run back toward the main body of Burgoyne's column. Unaccustomed to seeing British soldiers move in such a chaotic state of panic, many soldiers in the arriving column opened fire, mistaking their comrades-in-arms for undisciplined rebels. A large number of Burgoyne's troops fell victim to friendly fire.

The British commander, in shock, could do little but watch. When would Fraser fire his signal gun? *Where was he?*

At last, Burgoyne decided that something, anything, had to be done. Firing his own signal cannon, he led those of his men who had not yet been engaged onto Freeman's Farm, rapidly forming up his lines along the northern edge of the field. It is not entirely clear what happened on the American side. Most historians assume that Benedict Arnold essentially seized command from Gates and suddenly led seven American regiments down from Bemis Heights just south of the farm while Morgan and Dearborn took up positions along the southern edge of Freeman's field.

With this, the Battle of Freeman's Farm commenced in full earnest. Over some three or four hours, the firefight was intense. The Americans, most of them, fired from cover on the periphery of the field, cutting viciously through the ranks of three British regiments, which stood with perfect discipline shoulder to shoulder. But it was not all one-sided slaughter. Burgoyne trained his artillery on the Americans. Each time Morgan, Dearborn, or Arnold sent a sortie out of the woods, the British artillery would mow them down and drive them back.

The American commanders were extremely anxious to bring the battle to a decision. They needed to wipe out Burgoyne's army before the other two contingents—one under Riedesel, the other under Fraser—arrived.

For Burgoyne, the objective was precisely the opposite. He needed to prolong the exchange in anticipation of tying in with the rest of his forces.

Riedesel showed up first, breaking through the woods and onto the field at its eastern perimeter. Instantly, he opened up with his artillery. Wisely, Arnold had galloped back to Bemis Heights to rally more troops. He was not on the farm when the Hessians arrived, and, in his absence, the Americans struggled to hold their ground. At last, by nightfall, they fell back. Fortunately for them, Fraser did not reach Freeman's Farm until the fighting was all but over.

ARNOLD VERSUS GATES

As the sun set, General Burgoyne took count of his casualties. Six hundred of his men, most of them from the eleven hundred he had personally led, were killed, wounded, or captured. Three regiments, about eight hundred men in total, took the main force of the combat. Of this number alone, 350 had been killed, wounded, or captured. It was a devastating casualty rate of 44 percent. On the American side, losses were sixty-five killed, 208 wounded, and thirty-six missing.

Remarkably, Burgoyne refused to acknowledge defeat. Because he remained in possession of Freeman's—abandoned and barren—Farm, he claimed a strategic victory, despite his heavy tactical losses. Had Burgoyne been a shrewder and fiercer commander, he might well have turned his pyrrhic victory into a genuine triumph. Horatio Gates had failed to take any initiative in the conduct of the battle. Had Burgoyne taken advantage of Gates's inaction,

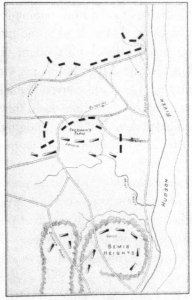

Battle of Freeman's Farm, first of the battles of Saratoga (September 19, 1777) from John Fiske, *The American Revolution* (Boston: Houghton, Mifflin & Co., 1891).

and now with his full army assembled, he could likely have scored a decisive victory. Instead, he struggled to recover from the shock of his losses.

On the American side, Gates had an opportunity of his own. Riedesel had left a garrison of nine hundred Hessians at Bemis Heights to guard all of Burgoyne's supplies. Gates's forces consisted of some four thousand soldiers, more than sufficient to wipe out the garrison and appropriate Burgoyne's supplies. From the Heights, he would also have been in position to hold those supplies, and Burgoyne would have been left to face a stark choice: surrender or starve.

Benedict Arnold saw, with brilliant clarity, this situation as well as the opportunity it presented. He argued savagely with Gates, pleading to be allowed to lead a raid on the Hessian garrison. Gates refused. Moreover, he deliberately left Arnold out of the report of the Battle of Freeman's Farm, which he sent to Congress—a battle Arnold had, for the most part, led. In response to this affront, Arnold asked Gates to issue him a pass to the Philadelphia front, where, he explained, "I propose to join General Washington, and may possibly have it in my power to serve my country, tho I am thought of no consequence to this Department." For his part, Gates summarily stripped Arnold of command and exiled him from his headquarters. Aghast, Gates's other officers begged Arnold not to leave. Simultaneously, they prevailed upon Gates to reinstate the offended Arnold. Gates grudgingly agreed to allow him to stay with his army, but he refused either to apologize or to formally reinstate him.

The name of Benedict Arnold would, in the fullness of time, become a synonym for *traitor*. But at Freeman's Farm, he was a Patriot hero—and he was about to prove even more valuable. For the engagement at Freeman's Farm was only the first phase of what has entered history as the Battle of Saratoga. In the second phase, at the fight at Bemis Heights, Benedict Arnold would prove gloriously, recklessly inspiring.

The Fall from Bemis Heights

For a general who claimed to have just won a battle, Burgoyne was morose. He had at last abandoned any hope of meeting up with Howe. Sir Henry Clinton, to whom Howe had entrusted command of the garrison holding New York City, promised to send three thousand troops to him, but that was far short of the seven thousand Burgoyne knew Clinton had available. Not only was Clinton miserly with his men, he refused to rush the parsimonious contingent into motion. It was October 3 before he even got them on the move. By this time, Burgoyne was essentially stranded. He had too few men to conduct any significant offensive, but he dared not risk descending from Bemis Heights to make a retreat.

It was a terrible predicament, which Clinton compounded by giving the reinforcements permission to capture three weakly held Patriot Hudson strongholds, Forts Montgomery, Clinton, and Constitution, en route to Saratoga. Exasperated by the prolonged delay, Burgoyne sent a message to Clinton asking

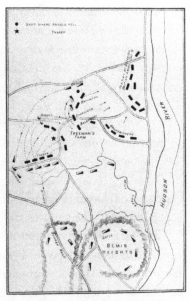

Battle of Bemis Heights, second of the battles of Saratoga (October 7, 1777) from John Fiske, *The American Revolution* (Boston: Houghton, Mifflin & Co., 1891).

whether he should continue his march to Albany or attempt a retreat. He explained that he could not remain where he was beyond October 12. Clinton's reply was about as unhelpful as any message ever sent from commander to subordinate: "In answer to your letter of the 28th of September by C.C. I shall only say, I cannot presume to order, or even advise, for reasons obvious. I heartily wish you success."

It is just as well, perhaps, that Burgoyne never received the letter. Continental Army surgeon Dr. James Thatcher recorded this in his diary on October 14, 1777:

> *We have been trembling alive to [the] menacing prospect [of the arrival of Clinton's forces in Albany], but our fears are in a measure allayed by the following singular incident. After the capture of Fort Montgomery, Sir Henry Clinton despatched a messenger by the name of Daniel Taylor*

*to Burgoyne with the intelligence [that he was not rushing to Albany];
fortunately [Taylor] was taken away as a spy, and finding himself in
danger, he was seen to turn aside and take something from his pocket
and swallow it. General George Clinton [the American commander
and no relation to Henry Clinton], into whose hands he had fallen,
ordered a severe dose of emetic tartar to be administered. This produced
the happiest effect as respects the prescriber, but it proved fatal to the
patient. He discharged a small silver bullet, which being unscrewed,
was found to enclose a letter from Sir Henry Clinton to Burgoyne.*

Thatcher concluded his diary entry: "'Out of thine own mouth thou shalt
be condemned.' The spy was tried, convicted and executed."

The fact was that Clinton's message not only never reached the
hapless Burgoyne and would not have helped him even if it had, it was
also irrelevant. Almost immediately after sending the message, Clinton
received an order from Howe asking for reinforcements. Since Howe
was both Clinton's and Burgoyne's commanding officer, there was no
question what Clinton would do. He ordered the commanding officer
of the three thousand men he had sent marching northward to have his
troops turn about-face, abandon all three of the forts they had captured,
and make their way south to Philadelphia.

Burgoyne, then, was left to twist slowly, slowly in the autumn wind.
Yet he was not completely idle. He put his men to work digging a system
of entrenchments and redoubts on Bemis Heights, determined to create
a mighty fortress against the anticipated assault by Gates.

While Burgoyne entrenched, Gates received reinforcements, troops
under the command of the very able General Benjamin Lincoln. No
sooner did Lincoln arrive than he used his men to execute the favorite
tactic of so many Continental generals. He made a series of hit-and-run
attacks against Burgoyne's rear positions. For his part, Burgoyne was worried—though mainly because he did not know how long he could endure
being nibbled away by General Lincoln. In truth, Burgoyne was in far
deeper trouble than he knew. Lincoln's arrival increased Gates's army to
eleven thousand men. That was more than twice the five thousand Burgoyne had with him on Bemis Heights.

On October 7, Burgoyne decided to act. He sent out a reconnaissance-in-force consisting of 1,650 men. His objective was to probe Gates's army in an effort to discover precisely what he now faced.

General Burgoyne was not left long in doubt. Gates ordered Morgan to attack the right flank of Burgoyne's reconnaissance sortie while another contingent, under General Enoch Poor, hit the left. Gates issued no orders to Benedict Arnold, who nevertheless decided on his own authority to attack a breastworks behind which some of Burgoyne's reconnaissance-in-force had taken cover. When this attack was completed, Arnold suddenly galloped, with great ostentation, across the line of British fire to meet an advancing column of Continental troops led by General Ebenezer Learned. They were headed toward the British right, and Arnold—with no authorization whatsoever—assumed command of them. He nudged these freshly arrived troops away from the right and led them instead in a brute-force frontal assault against a Hessian position known as "Breymann's redoubt." His objective was to neutralize the serious defensive threat presented by these troops, so that the other elements of attack would have free rein against Bemis Heights. In the course of this recklessly heroic gesture, Arnold's mount was shot out from under him and he himself was shot in the leg. Unable to continue leading the assault on Breymann's redoubt, Arnold was carried from the field. The Patriots cheered their heroic leader.

Saratoga Ending

Burgoyne's position on Bemis Heights had now become untenable. His officer corps was shredded, and one of the best of all the British commanders in America, Simon Fraser, had been killed. Although Breymann's redoubt remained active, the other elements of the American assault were relentless. Burgoyne lost some six hundred killed or wounded. Gates's command suffered fewer than 150 casualties.

Burgoyne did manage to break free and made a headlong retreat with his surviving troops to the town of Saratoga. Roused from his habitual torpor, Gates gave chase. On October 12, he easily outflanked Burgoyne's Saratoga position, cutting him off from the Hudson, which was his only hope of possible rescue.

In setting off for Albany—which he never reached—Burgoyne had sought to rally his men with the admonition "Britons never retreat." At this point, they could not have retreated even if Burgoyne would have ordered them to do so. On October 13, he sent a message to General Gates asking for surrender terms. When Gates offered no terms other than unconditional surrender, Burgoyne, incensed, refused.

Burgoyne was outnumbered more than two to one, and he was cut off from retreat, supply, or the possibility of reinforcement. Gates knew that the power was all his—and yet he compromised. On October 16, he met with Burgoyne and drew up the so-called Saratoga Convention. Burgoyne and his men would not be made prisoners of war. Instead, they would be paroled to England in exchange for their pledge of never again "serving in North America during the present contest."

It is not clear why Gates extended this courtesy to Burgoyne. Perhaps he did not want to burden himself, the Continental Army, or Congress with the care and feeding of prisoners. Perhaps, as a former British officer, he felt some fellow feeling for General Burgoyne—who did later explain to Lord Germain that the terms of the Saratoga Convention effectively saved five thousand men for the British army. The troops could be honorably used for European service, freeing up an equivalent number from that service for duty in North America. In any event, on October 17, Burgoyne and Gates dined together, Burgoyne gallantly offering a toast to General Washington and Gates to King George III. What this exchange of courtesies belied was that the significance of the defeat of an entire British army by a colonial force was not lost on Louis XVI. The combination of Washington's aggression at Germantown on October 4 and Burgoyne's surrender twelve days later set the stage for a full and formal alliance between the United States and France.

THE START OF SOMETHING

While Europe was almost thoroughly a continent of aristocracy, most of its nations looked upon the American Revolution as they had the French and Indian War. Both were remote theaters of a greater *world* conflict, a struggle of global empires, that had begun in the seventeenth century. The Continental Congress saw an opportunity in the long-running imperial

General Burgoyne surrenders at Saratoga (October 17, 1777). The 1821 painting is by John Trumbull. The central figure is the American General Horatio Gates. Other major figures are (from left to right, beginning with mounted officer), American Captain Seymour of Connecticut (mounted), American Colonel Scammel of New Hampshire (looking toward Seymour), British Major General William Phillips (the balding figure), British Lieutenant General John Burgoyne (offering his sword to Gates), and American Colonel Daniel Morgan (in white). ARCHITECT OF THE UNITED STATES CAPITOL

struggle between France and England to make a war-winning alliance. The French and Indian War had ended in French defeat. The new United States would offer France an opportunity to even the score.

Selling the French government on a full-scale alliance was no slam-dunk. Louis XVI and his ministers were not deaf to the rumblings of the revolution that would ultimately end the emperor's reign and life. Should the French help a distant nation to come to birth without a king? Besides, how much of a chance did the Americans have against a great power that had so recently defeated France itself?

Congress began by courting aid short of a military alliance, but it was France's own foreign minister, Charles Gravier, comte de Vergennes, who made the first move toward such an alliance when, in September 1775, he sent a secret agent, Achard de Bonvouloir, to America to report on the odds of a successful break with the mother country. Very quickly, in

November 1775, Congress created a five-man Committee of Correspondence, chaired by Benjamin Franklin, to reach out to "our friends abroad." "Secret" or not, Achard de Bonvouloir showed such interest in America that the Committee approached him directly. Based on Achard's enthusiasm, Congress, in April 1776, sent Silas Deane, delegate from Connecticut, to Paris to purchase, on credit, uniforms and equipment for twenty-five thousand men, along with artillery and other munitions. He was also instructed with feeling out an alliance.

Vergennes was interested but could not yet commit to an open alliance. He therefore approached Pierre Augustin Caron de Beaumarchais, famous as the playwright who created the wily barber/valet Figaro in his *Le Barbier de Séville* (1775). Vergennes commissioned Beaumarchais to invent a company, which was to function as a front for laundering money Louis XVI, together with another of England's enemies, Spain, would covertly send to America. Thus, Roderigue Hortalez & Cie. was born, a trading company that funneled cash to the American Revolution without the English taking note. Vergennes also asked Beaumarchais to recruit private investors in the phony firm.

Historians believe that funding through Hortalez bankrolled Washington's victories at Trenton and Princeton and furnished almost all of the weapons and ammunition used in the Saratoga victories. Millions of French *livres* were routed into the American Revolution long before Louis XVI made an official alliance.

While Vergennes and Beaumarchais pushed the growing alliance from the French side, Benjamin Franklin, almost seventy years old when the revolution began, promoted it from the American side. During 1767 and 1769, he had served in France as business agent for the colony of Pennsylvania. Based on this experience and his international reputation as a philosopher, inventor, scientist, and man of business, the Committee of Correspondence persuaded Congress to send Franklin to join Silas Deane and the prominent Virginian Arthur Lee in Paris to negotiate a treaty of alliance with France.

Franklin arrived on December 4, 1776 and immediately began work, building on the Hortalez scheme as well as the activism of some young and idealistic Frenchmen already eager to fight in what they saw as a great revolution for the entire world. Most prominent in this group was the Marquis de Lafayette. Orphaned at thirteen, his noble family left him a fortune, which helped him win, in 1774, the hand of the daughter of the powerful duc d'Ayen. This gave him access to the court of Louis XVI and a life of sumptuous leisure—had he wanted that. Instead, after hearing the Duke of Gloucester proclaim his sympathy for the cause of American liberty at a dinner on August 8, 1775, Lafayette decided to fight in the American cause. He took with him Johann Kalb (called Baron de Kalb, though the title was fictitious), a Bavarian-born Frenchman serving in the French army, and both obtained commissions as major generals in the Continental Army.

Lafayette was not presented to General George Washington until August 1, 1777. The older man formed an instant friendship with the gallant marquis, who was a thoroughly trained European military officer. Washington sent him into the Battle of Brandywine (September 11, 1777) under Nathanael Greene, in which the Frenchman performed heroically and sustained a severe thigh wound. He recovered sufficiently by November 25 to lead a victorious skirmish against Hessians at Gloucester, New Jersey, and on December 1, 1777, he was assigned command of a Virginia light infantry division.

That same month, spurred by the Saratoga victories and Washington's boldness at the Battle of Germantown (despite his defeat), French commissioners announced to Franklin on December 17, 1777, that Louis XVI had decided to publicly recognize the independence of the United States of America. France became the first nation to do so. On January 8, 1778, Vergennes told the American treaty commission that the French government was ready to conclude a formal alliance—two, actually. The Treaty of Amity and Commerce memorialized French recognition of American independence, and the Treaty of Alliance created the military partnership. Congress ratified both treaties on May 4, the French ambassador in London announced the treaties on May 13, and the British government recalled its ambassador from Paris. On June 20, Britain declared war on France. After many tactical false starts and stumbles, the alliance would prove war-winning for Washington and a political, military, and cultural disaster for the British Empire.

CHAPTER 18

Hope Dims, Winter Calls

HAVING RATHER EASILY TAKEN PHILADELPHIA, WILLIAM HOWE WAS now left to calculate the actual cost of that conquest. There was the failure of Burgoyne's invasion and the defeat of a British army, and there was the ongoing cost of holding Philadelphia. Not only had the city's acquisition failed to end the American Revolution, it barely put a dent in it. Now Philadelphia belonged to Howe, and he had to do whatever was necessary to avoid letting it become a liability, as occupied Boston had been.

The first step, Howe believed, was to neutralize two Patriot-held Delaware River forts, Fort Mifflin on the Pennsylvania bank and Fort Mercer on the Jersey side. Between the two, the Americans had stretched spiked barricades—called a *chevaux de frise*—to prevent the passage of ships to and from Philadelphia. For his part, Washington called on the Chevalier de Mauduit du Plessis, a French military engineer, to assist Colonel Christopher Greene, commanding Fort Mercer, to set up an effective defense. Washington had few men to devote to garrisoning the two river forts. He sent just four hundred Rhode Island troops to occupy Fort Mercer. Reasoning that this was too small a garrison to defend a large fort, Mauduit du Plessis ordered a new interior wall to be built, which effectively reduced the area in need of protection and thereby allowed for a denser defense with fewer men.

THE BATTLE OF FORT MERCER

Howe sent two thousand elite Hessian *jägers* ("hunters"—light infantry troops) under Colonel Carl Emil Kurt von Donop on October 21, 1777, to capture Fort Mercer. At 4:30 on the afternoon of October 22, Donop sent an emissary to Greene, imperiously demanding surrender. When Greene refused, Donop ostentatiously formed up his forces for the attack, creating a contemptuous display intended to intimidate the outnumbered Americans. Well after dark, at nine that evening, Donop commenced his attack in two separate columns.

With the battle cry "Vittoria!" the north column stormed over the breastworks—and the troops suddenly found themselves plopped into an empty compound, totally walled off from the fort proper. Unaware of this, Donop led the western column through the abatis, the fort's outer obstacles of felled trees, their ends sharpened to points aimed against attackers. Once past the abatis, they advanced across the trench surrounding the fort. So far, it was a textbook assault.

But then Donop's men confronted a tall berm, a ledge Mauduit du Plessis had mounded up between the trench and the parapet. Somehow, Donop had neglected to bring along scaling ladders. Now, like the north column, Donop's men were stymied, stalled midway in the process of assaulting a fort, transformed from troops on the offensive to so many human targets.

Greene ordered a volley of grapeshot, cluster ammunition fired from cannon and intended to spray out in a pattern to kill as many soldiers as quickly as possible. Added to this was a continuous barrage of musket fire trained on the jostling ranks of the now helpless Hessians. Almost mercifully, Donop was among the first to fall, disabled by a shot through the leg. The wound quickly proved mortal. The Hessians retreated, re-formed, and attacked the fort's south wall. It was a monumentally stupid idea because the south approach to the fort was swept not only by defenders within Fort Mercer but by troops stationed in rowing galleys out on the Delaware. Fire poured in on the Hessians from both the front and the rear. Of the twelve hundred soldiers sent to storm Fort Mercer, four hundred were killed or wounded, versus fourteen Americans killed and twenty-three wounded.

On the next day, October 23, the sixty-four-gun Royal Navy frigate *Augusta*, the forty-four-gun *Roebuck*, and the eighteen-gun *Merlin* approached the chevaux de frise. Stopping at this line, the vessels opened fire on the rowing galleys. Presumably, the naval commanders were counting on cannon fire simply overwhelming the galleys. Instead, the galleys coordinated their fire with the guns of Fort Mifflin and fought back fiercely. A fortunate shot—fortunate from the American perspective—caused HMS *Augusta* to explode shortly after noon. By 3:00 p.m., *Merlin* was forced aground, where it ignited and also exploded. Amid this chaos, HMS *Roebuck* prudently withdrew.

THE FALL OF FORT MIFFLIN AND THE BATTLE OF THE KEGS

An enraged Howe was now determined to capture Fort Mifflin. Garrisoned by just fifty more men than its companion across the river, it had not had the benefit of reengineering by Mauduit du Plessis, and its inland aspect was considerably more exposed than that of Fort Mercer. Howe's forces opened fire on November 10 from five floating batteries stationed in the river. Major André-Arsène de Rosset, Vicomte de Fleury, a French engineer hurriedly dispatched to lend a hand to Mifflin's commandant, Colonel Samuel Smith, focused on patching the damage created by the batteries. But the batteries kept up their fire for five days, easily outpacing all efforts to repair the walls. On November 14, Smith, badly wounded, was evacuated, and command fell to Major Simeon Thayer, who steadfastly refused to surrender.

In the end, it was not Thayer but Fort Mifflin itself that gave up. By nightfall on November 14, the fort was no more than a pile of rubble, and the remains of the garrison, two hundred men plus Thayer, evacuated to Fort Mercer on November 15. Howe began bombarding that structure during November 20–21, finally forcing its abandonment. This led to what Francis Hopkinson, a signer of the Declaration of Independence who was also a minor poet, dubbed "The Battle of the Kegs" in a bit of doggerel he penned.

In January 1778, David Bushnell, the inventor of the *Turtle* submarine (Chapter 13), lashed together bunches of kegs packed tightly with gunpowder and set them adrift down the Delaware with the current. They were rigged with contact triggers that exploded on contact with a ship's hull. "Infernals," the British sailors called them, and troops and Royal Marines aboard the Royal Navy vessels took to firing their muskets at anything floating on the river. This caused the expenditure of much ammunition and the fraying of many nerves, but it did render the infernals harmless—even as it made Howe's men the target of Hopkinson's mockery:

> These kegs must all be routed.
> Or surely we despised shall be,
> And British courage doubted. . . .
>
> From morn till night, these men of might
> Displayed amazing courage;
> And when the sun was fairly down,
> Retired to sup their porridge. . . .
>
> Such feats did they perform that day
> Against those wicked kegs, sir,
> That years to come, if they get home,
> They'll make their boasts and brags, sir.

ATTRITION

The loss of the river forts, like the loss of Philadelphia, was a hard blow to the Patriots. Yet Howe was not reveling in it. He had taken heavy casualties, had lost time, and had forsaken Burgoyne and five thousand British soldiers in the process. But as unhappy as Howe was, George Washington now found himself in a most precarious position—not at the hands of William Howe, but at those of his own comrades in arms. On the face of it, Washington was 0 for 4 against Howe (defeated by Howe at Brandywine, Germantown, and the two Delaware River forts) and 0 for 2 against Horatio Gates, his own jealous subordinate (two victories at Saratoga—never mind that Morgan and Arnold deserved the credit). Howe did not realize that his most valuable victory was having sown doubt about the competence of General George Washington.

In Congress, Samuel Adams, Richard Henry Lee, Thomas Mifflin, and Dr. Benjamin Rush saw the growing discontent over Washington's military leadership as an opportunity to shift control of the revolution back from Virginia and Virginians to New England and New Englanders. Instead of being grateful for the alliance with France, these hardliners feared that Benjamin Franklin and Silas Deane, whom they thought of as partisan members of Washington's inner circle, were selling out America's destiny to France. They began an insidious campaign to undermine Washington by questioning his fitness to continue leading the military effort toward independence.

In this climate of discontent, the so-called Conway Cabal took shape against the commander of the Continental Army. It was named after one Thomas Conway, an Irish Catholic who grew up in France and joined the French army in 1747. Early in 1777, he secured his commanders' permission to fight in America. When Conway arrived in Morristown on May 8, 1777, Washington asked Congress to commission him a brigadier general. Congress did just that, but it was not enough for the ambitious Conway, who wrote numerous letters to delegates seeking higher rank. One of the letters disparaged Washington, calling "his talents for the command of an Army . . . miserable indeed." He also shamelessly flattered Horatio Gates. "Heaven has been determined to save your country," he wrote to him after Saratoga, "or a weak General and bad Councilors would have ruined it."

Word of Conway's letter spread, eventually reaching Washington via the faithful General William Alexander ("Lord Stirling"). When Washington confronted Conway forthrightly, he resigned his commission on November 14, 1777. This should have been the best possible outcome, since the resignation was voluntary, but Thomas Mifflin, perhaps Washington's most outspoken critic and newly elevated to the presidency of the congressional Board of War, not only rejected Conway's resignation but summarily promoted him to major general and conferred on him the post of inspector general of the Continental Army. This did not put him above Washington, but, rather, parallel to him, giving him special authority to monitor the efficiency of the army and its officers.

Washington was outraged, less about the personal affront than over the effect that the promotion of Conway over twenty-three more senior brigadier generals would have on morale. Nevertheless, Washington went out of his way to avoid further friction by telling Conway that he would respect all decisions of Congress. Incredibly, Conway told Congress that this response was a deliberate attempt to undermine his authority as inspector general. Washington protested this accusation to Congress—which, unfortunately for Conway, was by this time receiving rumors of a "secret correspondence" between Conway and Horatio Gates. Panicking because he sensed that both congressional and public opinion were shifting against him, Gates told Washington that Alexander Hamilton—Washington's aide-de-camp, and an officer for whom he had deep respect and affection—had covertly copied some of his correspondence, including Conway's letters to him. In effect, Gates was accusing Hamilton of deliberately stirring discord.

Washington refused to take this bait. He calmly but firmly replied to Gates that his knowledge of the Conway letter had originated not from Hamilton but through Gates's own aide, James Wilkinson. Moreover, he issued this reply to Gates not in private but through the Continental Congress. In this way, George Washington dragged the Conway Cabal into the sunlight. Before Congress and the American people, Washington's critics suddenly appeared small-minded, ungrateful, and conniving. They were Lilliputians attacking a giant.

Unmasked, the critics fell silent, and Congress delivered George Washington a vote of confidence. What is more, the commander of the Continental Army took no action against Horatio Gates. He regarded him as no more than a journeyman general, but the Continental Army needed journeymen. For his part, Gates recognized the great favor Washington had done him, and the two men worked together, well and without rancor, for the rest of the war. As for Conway, he had the good sense to tender his resignation yet again. This time, Congress—Mifflin included—was quick to accept it.

Thus, Washington survived enemies both foreign and domestic in a season of war by cruel attrition. His most formidable adversary in this campaign of endurance then emerged in its full fury. Winter arrived, and the Continental Army faced it with little to wear, little to eat, and not much by way of decent shelter. Washington had selected Valley Forge, Pennsylvania, for his army's winter encampment. Located west of the Schuylkill River, it was between Philadelphia, which the enemy held, and York, where Congress had taken refuge. It was a good tactical position, readily defended, well drained, and sufficiently forested to supply timber for huts and fuel. At the same time, it was rather far from any substantial town and was wide open to the elements. Since the Philadelphia campaign had not ended until December 11, well into winter, troops were settling into winter quarters late, tired, and dangerously low on provisions.

They did the best they could, but for six months, from December 1777 to June 1778, ten thousand men lived in hurriedly constructed windswept, snow-whipped huts. Four out of ten soldiers had so little clothing that they almost never dared to venture outside of their shelters. The winter killed a quarter of the encampment, twenty-five hundred men. Throughout it all, Washington pleaded with Congress. "What then is to become of the Army this Winter?" he asked in a letter of December 23, 1777. "And if we are as often without Provisions now, as with it, what is to become of us in the Spring?"

Congress at this time had no power to levy taxes and was therefore chronically short of funds. Even worse, the system for supplying the army was poorly developed, inefficient, and riddled with corruption. This was compounded by the fact that most farmers in the vicinity of Valley Forge had Loyalist leanings and, in any event, preferred selling their produce to the British and Hessians, who paid promptly and in cash.

After the revolution the Valley Forge winter of 1777–1778 became the stuff of myth and legend. The horrors—the privation, the semi-starvation—were real enough, although the winter was actually no harsher than what was typical in the region, and the toll taken on the army was heavy but not far out of the ordinary for an army in winter during the eighteenth century, especially in a rural environment. Crowded encampments were subject to epidemic illness, especially dysentery, pneumonia, and, all too often, deadly typhus, and rations were typically spartan or downright nonexistent.

Yet, in one respect, Washington made the very most out of the time his army spent in Valley Forge. He rigorously trained and drilled his men, transforming a band of farmers and tradesmen into soldiers. At Valley Forge were Lafayette and Kalb, thoroughly trained European officers with a great deal to teach and a willingness to teach it. There was also a Prussian officer, Friedrich Wilhelm Augustus von Steuben, who had been born and raised in the Elbe River fortress at Magdeburg, Saxony-Anhalt,

Germany, where his father was a military engineer. Military life was in Steuben's blood. By seventeen, he was already an officer, and he saw action in the Seven Years' War and served on the staff of no less a military giant than Prussia's Frederick the Great. The job of a staff officer boils down to ensuring that the orders of headquarters are efficiently executed in the field. In most armies of the era, staff officers were few and far between. They were nearly nonexistent in the Continental Army, but Washington had enough knowledge of recent European history to know that efficient staff work was one

Baron Friedrich Wilhelm von Steuben, as depicted by the American painter Ralph Earle about 1786. WIKIMEDIA COMMONS

of the secrets of Frederick the Great's matchless record of victory. He believed that Steuben's staff experience could help to dramatically transform the American army, especially since even the British had only rudimentary staff echelons.

The reasons for Steuben having left the Prussian army in 1763 have never been fully explained, but through 1775, he had difficulty finding suitable employment, either in the German or French government or military. In France, he met a friend of Benjamin Franklin who recommended that he speak to Franklin about joining the Continental Army in America. Impressed with Steuben, Franklin wrote a letter of recommendation to Washington. Franklin even arranged for Hortalez & Cie. to pay Steuben's expenses to the United States, and he arrived in Portsmouth, New Hampshire, on December 1, 1777. Steuben reported to Washington at Valley Forge on February 23, 1778, and immediately set to work to create a comprehensive training program for the Continental Army. He also personally selected a cadre of one hundred standout soldiers to train personally. Each individual in this small group in turn chose one hundred men to train. These men each trained another one hundred, and so on. Before the winter was over, every soldier at Valley Forge had received intensive personal training by the most competent soldiers available. In effect, the Continental Army was being infused with legendary Prussian discipline through a kind of exponential progression. Valley Forge became truly a forge on which a superb army was hammered out.

A World War

Recall that Thomas Jefferson drafted the Declaration of Independence in part because, as he put it, "a decent respect to the opinions of mankind requires" that the reasons for independence be justified to the world. In the same spirit, Thomas Paine, in *Common Sense*, sought to define the American struggle for independence as an enterprise of importance to every man, woman, and child on the planet. So, the American Revolution attracted Lafayette and Steuben as well as Johann Kalb. Widely known as the Baron de Kalb, Kalb was, in fact, the child of Bavarian peasants who had managed to achieve the post of lieutenant in a German regiment of the French infantry in 1743. In 1768, the French government sent him on a covert mission to the North American colonies to assess the colonies' state of allegiance to Great Britain. He fell in love with America, and when the revolution was under way, he eagerly joined Lafayette in volunteering.

Kalb assisted Steuben in training the Continental Army at Valley Forge, but his first significant combat assignment did not come until April 1780, when he led a mission to relieve the siege of Charleston, South Carolina. The port city fell to the British before he arrived, but he went on to fight in the Battle of Camden, South Carolina (August 16, 1780), where he was fatally wounded.

Two additional European officers proved indispensable to the Continental Army. Tadeusz Kosciuszko was a Polish nobleman who had graduated from the military academy at Warsaw. He was sent to Paris to study military and civil architecture and, on his return to Poland in 1774, taught drawing and mathematics to the daughters of a general, Józef Sosnowski. Kosciuszko fell in love with one of his students, and the couple attempted to elope but were caught. Eager to evade the wrath of General Sosnowski, Kosciuszko fled back to France, where he was soon caught up in the growing passion there for the American Revolution, which he joined in 1776.

In August 1776, the Pennsylvania Committee of Defense in Philadelphia hired Kosciuszko to help design fortifications to defend the residence of the Continental Congress against the British. In spring 1777, he joined Horatio Gates as an engineer, directing the rapid construction of the fortifications that were instrumental in preventing General Burgoyne from retreating during the Battles of Saratoga. After Saratoga, Kosciuszko went to West Point, New York, to augment the fortifications there, and in March 1780, he was named chief of the Continental Army's engineering corps. He served in the war's southern theater under Major General Nathanael Greene.

Tadeusz Kosciuszko survived the American Revolution, and although a grateful Congress voted to grant him United States citizenship and commissioned him a brigadier general in the new US Army, he chose to return to Poland to fight for the independence of his homeland from Russia. He won several victories but, badly wounded in one engagement, was captured by the Russians in 1794 and held as a prisoner of war for two years.

He returned to America in 1797, where the people of Philadelphia greeted him warmly. Before leaving for France in 1798 to promote the cause of Polish freedom, Kosciuszko freed the slaves who had worked on his American property and even set aside a portion of his estate to be used to pay for their well-being and education. Kosciuszko was deeply disillusioned by Napoleon's reneging on his promise to support the establishment of an independent Poland. He withdrew from public life after the final defeat of Napoleon at Waterloo and endeavored to work with Czar Alexander I to create a new, independent Polish government. This effort came to nothing, but, as he had freed his slaves in America, Kosciuszko freed all of the serfs on his family's holdings in his native Poland.

The revolution's other celebrated Polish volunteer, Casimir Pulaski, was destined to give his life to the cause of American independence. Pulaski had fought to liberate Poland from domination by both Russia and Prussia. A relentless insurgent, he was a marked man in Poland and made his way to France via Saxony. He was living on a shoestring in Paris when he drifted into the densely populated orbit of Benjamin Franklin in December 1776. When Franklin discovered that Pulaski was a skilled cavalry officer, he knew that he could be of enormous use to Washington. The Continental Army did not have a separate cavalry branch, a fact that put it at great disadvantage. Franklin talked Pulaski into joining the American war effort and wrote his customary letter of recommendation to General Washington.

Pulaski proved to be an obstinate and haughty officer, a man many found difficult to get along with. Nevertheless, he was a superb cavalry tactician, and he created and trained the Pulaski Legion in 1778, the first dedicated cavalry unit in the Continental Army. In May 1779, he commanded the legion in the defense of Charleston. On October 9, 1779, he was mortally wounded when he led a daring cavalry charge during the Battle of Savannah.

Valley Forge marked the time and place in which these fine European officers passed on their knowledge to soldiers who were struggling to survive a harsh winter. The likes of Kalb, Lafayette, and Steuben, as well as Kosciuszko and Pulaski, fought in the American Revolution not to serve the agenda of Louis XVI—who wanted nothing more than to weaken Great Britain—but because they all had an irrepressible passion for liberty, for the "rights of man," and for human dignity. The independent nation that was destined to emerge from the American Revolution was a nation of immigrants, and some of the revolution's most conspicuous heroes were themselves either foreign nationals or newly arrived immigrants. The American Revolution was, in a profoundly meaningful sense, a world war. As Thomas Jefferson and Thomas Paine had hoped it would, the American Revolution evolved into a struggle fought not only to establish the political freedom of one nation but on behalf of all humankind.

Chapter 19

Springtime

Eighteenth-century armies emerged from winter quarters diminished by disease and idleness. That was part of military life—and death. The Continental Army was hard hit by the first but entirely escaped the second. Thanks to the European volunteers, experienced Old World military officers, they greeted the return of fighting season, spring 1778, as a far more efficient and disciplined army than they were at any time before. While their number was diminished, their fighting quality had been honed. They were razors.

Washington, his officers, and his men also looked forward to fighting alongside the formidable French. But in the Continental Congress, emotions were mixed. An important faction of that body conceded that France made for a formidable ally, but they worried that its war aims hardly coincided with those of the United States. Moreover, they feared that Ben Franklin and Silas Deane, in negotiating the alliance, had already ceded too much of America's future to yet another foreign monarchy, one with whom they had so much less in common than with the British.

The supporters of the alliance countered that, yes, we wanted to win independence, whereas the French wanted only to beat Britain. So what? The only way to win independence was to beat Britain—and the experience of the war thus far was proving that we could not do this alone.

The pro-alliance faction looked to the present and to the short-term future. Alliance with a foreign power was the only way to win this revolution, they argued. The skeptics, however, insisted on asking what would happen after victory. With Britain driven out, what would stop France from reestablishing its own North American empire? Rule by Louis XVI, surely, would be even more onerous than by George III. In February 1778, William Howe asked to be relieved as commander-in-chief of British forces in America. Clearly, the new Franco-American alliance was for him the proverbial last straw. Even more clearly, therefore, this was hardly the time for Congress to rebuff the French.

Early in March, Lord Germain tapped Henry Clinton to replace Howe, a promotion that Clinton did not welcome. No realistic British officer any longer believed that defeating the American "rebels" would be easy. They recognized that the revolution had become a quagmire, a contest of who could—or would—hold out longer, and Clinton's assessment was that the Americans had the advantage. They were fighting at home and for their homes. To make matters worse, on March 21, he received orders from Lord Germain directing him to send five thousand of his troops to the Caribbean island of St. Lucia and an additional three thousand to reinforce St. Augustine and Pensacola, Florida. Both places were under direct threat of French invasion. Suddenly, London was shifting the mission from suppressing American rebels to defending against French threats to a colony already slipping from England's grasp.

Clinton now had eight thousand fewer soldiers to hold New York and Philadelphia, and when he confronted Lord Germain with this fact, the response he received was stupefying. Lord Germain directed Clinton to pull the occupation force out of Philadelphia and use it to reinforce the defenses of New York City. In other words, the capital of the revolution, the possession of which cost British lives and treasure, not to mention the sacrifice of Burgoyne's entire army, was to be simply relinquished.

THE BATTLE OF MONMOUTH

Before daybreak on June 16, 1778, General Washington received intelligence that Henry Clinton was moving his artillery out of their redoubts (fortified positions) around Philadelphia. He, of course, did not know of Lord Germain's instruction to Clinton, and, without this knowledge, he would not have assumed that the British commander was preparing to give up Philadelphia. After all, why would he? So, he guessed that the new commander needed the artillery for some specific operation, most likely an offensive in New Jersey with the objective of eliminating militia resistance there. Based on this assumption, Washington convened a council of war on June 17. The upshot was that the American commander took the advice of Charles Lee, which was to keep his troops quartered at Valley Forge until Clinton's intentions became more apparent.

The Battle of Monmouth was fought on June 28, 1778, near the Monmouth Court House in New Jersey. NEW YORK PUBLIC LIBRARY

If Lee's advice was based on his experience against the somnolent William Howe, both he and Washington must have been surprised at the remarkable speed with which Clinton moved. Just one day after Washington's council of war, on June 18, Clinton was on the march with ten thousand regulars and three thousand local Tories, all moving out of Philadelphia. They were heading toward Haddonfield, New Jersey. Washington sounded the alarm and designated the Marquis de Lafayette to lead a strike force against Clinton's rapidly advancing column. General Lee objected, demanding the command for himself. Since Lee was second in command to Washington and considerably senior to Lafayette, Washington reluctantly gave in and put Lee at the head of the force.

It was a bad mistake. On June 28, the leading edge of a New Jersey militia unit skirmished with some of Clinton's best regiments. It was obvious that the militiamen needed help—*now!*—but Lee did nothing. When Washington directly ordered him to attack, Lee fumbled. Instead of consolidating his forces into one concentrated blow, he scattered his men and then watched, horrified, as Clinton defeated them in detail.

Fearing that he would lose his entire army, Lee ordered a retreat, which he managed no better than he had the attack. A unit under "Mad Anthony" Wayne was cut off, isolated, and surrounded. Unlike Lee, Wayne was a great tactical commander with nerves of steel. Acting

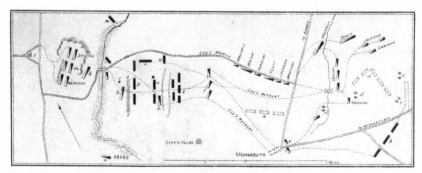

Map of the Battle of Monmouth (June 28, 1778) from John Fiske, *The American Revolution* (Boston: Houghton, Mifflin & Co., 1891).

boldly, he was able to extricate his forces from their desperate predicament while, in the meantime, George Washington, alone, galloped full-tilt into the midst of Charles Lee's retreating army. Lafayette watched as Washington summoned Lee, summarily relieved him, and assumed command himself. This, Lafayette later remarked, instantly "stopped the retreat." The panic was almost instantly dispelled by what Lafayette called the commander's "calm courage." Whatever shortcomings he had as a tactician and strategist, Washington was an extraordinarily effective leader of men, especially in a crisis.

Defeat was averted. But that is hardly the same as victory. Washington headed off a catastrophic rout, but he could not restore the aggressive momentum Lee had squandered. What should have been a stunning attack on Clinton's advancing column instead settled into a slugging match near Monmouth Court House on June 28, 1778, under a relentless high-summer sun. Among the casualties were thirty-seven Americans and sixty British regulars, all victims not of bullet and sword, but of sunstroke.

The battle ended in a draw brought on by mutual exhaustion. By the time both sides broke off, 356 American troops had been killed or wounded or were missing, with 358 British killed or wounded—though some authorities believe that British losses were quite a bit higher.

The First Test of the Franco-American Alliance
News of the Franco-American alliance sent a shockwave through the British command in North America, but the effectiveness of the alliance

had yet to be tested on the field. In the aftermath of the draw at Monmouth Court House, Washington saw an immediate opportunity to put the alliance to work. He pursued Clinton's withdrawing army, hoping not merely to catch up with but to envelop him. A pincer movement requires a pair of converging forces. Washington therefore ordered a Franco-American amphibious operation in the north, which would converge on Clinton as Washington continued his pursuit.

The French naval contingent of this operation was commanded by Admiral Charles Hector Théodot, comte d'Estaing—a commander apparently disdained even by his own superiors. Did delegating a major naval command to d'Estaing suggest that the French were less than thoroughly committed to the alliance? Hard to say, but, from the beginning, he performed miserably. He sailed out of Toulon on April 13, 1778, embarking on what should have been a thirty-day transatlantic voyage, which instead consumed nearly three times that span, eighty-seven days. This meant that he was too late to carry out the mission originally assigned him: to blockade the British fleet in Chesapeake Bay. Of more immediate consequence to Washington's pursuit of Clinton, d'Estaing was too late to land a sufficient number of the soldiers he was transporting to cut Clinton off from water routes of supply and transport. Combined with the converging movement against Clinton, this might have prompted the commencement of treaty negotiations between the British commander and Washington.

When d'Estaing missed his opportunity at Chesapeake Bay, he turned toward New York City to engage the British fleet there. It was not a bad idea, but he failed to obtain any advance information about navigating New York Bay. Only after he arrived on July 11 did he learn about Sandy Hook Bar, a natural obstruction lying across the bay and under the waves. He worried that his largest warships drew too much water to clear the bar. This drove him to spend the next eleven days indecisively pondering whether to attempt to cross the bar or not. Unable to make a decision, d'Estaing simply turned around and departed New York Bay on July 29, sailing north to Newport, Rhode Island, where he decided to land the four thousand troops he carried for the purpose of reinforcing some ten thousand Americans under John Sullivan and his subordinate commanders, Nathanael Greene and Lafayette.

By this time, Washington realized that his plan to envelop Clinton would come to nothing. He consoled himself with the thought that the French could at least be effective farther north. This time, however, it was the Americans who moved too slowly. By the time New England militia reinforcements tied in with Sullivan's army, Clinton had dispatched ample reinforcements to Major General Robert Pigot, commandant of the Newport defenses. This was discouraging to Sullivan, but he still had a chance to make a successful attack—if he could coordinate with d'Estaing.

As it turned out, he could do no such thing.

To begin with, the two allied commanders thought very little of one another—and not without some good reason. By the time d'Estaing landed near Newport and began disembarking his troops, the British fleet sailed into view. D'Estaing's best move would have been to disembark the troops on the double and then confront the approaching fleet. Astoundingly, however, against the anguished protests of General Sullivan, Admiral d'Estaing reloaded those troops he had managed to disembark and put back out to sea to meet the enemy. This had two effects, both of them bad. First, he wrecked the prospects of the land operation. Second, he quite uselessly exposed land troops to the dangers of a naval battle.

But, then, even *that* battle was never fought. A severe storm on the night of August 11 scattered the British and the French fleets, battering both relentlessly, so that neither was fit for a fight. Admiral Richard Howe slipped south to New York—*he* knew that big ships could clear Sandy Hook bar—and put in to repair the storm damage. After this, he sailed to the West Indies, to which his fleet had been ordered. D'Estaing, in the meantime, limped off to Boston to refit his fleet, carrying with him four thousand French soldiers to a place where they were not needed, even as General Sullivan stood, stranded and unreinforced, at Newport, confronted by the British, who *had* received reinforcements.

THE BATTLE OF RHODE ISLAND

African-American troops fought on both sides in the American Revolution, but because the British aggressively recruited the slaves of Patriot masters, more African-American troops fought for the British than for the Americans—about twenty thousand for Britain versus nine thousand in the American forces. When General Washington took command of the Continental Army, he permitted free blacks who had already fought to reenlist through 1776. The Continental Congress, however, and most states (Virginia was the exception during part of 1776) barred African-American recruitment, whether free or slave. During the Valley Forge winter of 1777–1778, when Continental Army numbers dipped, Congress approved a Rhode Island proposal to raise an African-American regiment. Other states began recruiting free blacks for their militias early in 1777. Both of the Carolinas and Georgia never accepted black troops, but, in all other states, African-American volunteers served in racially integrated militia units.

It was an African-American militia unit commanded by a white Rhode Island officer named Christopher Greene that rescued General Sullivan's Continental Army force at the Battle of Rhode Island, also known as the Battle of Newport, on August 29, 1778. Greene's men fought with such ferocity that Sullivan was able to extricate his siege force from Pigot's counterattack. That saved his army and was therefore a tactical victory. Strategically, however, it was an American defeat. The battle at Newport was supposed to deliver a decisive blow against the British. Instead—and thanks only to an African-American relief force— it was neither more nor less than a narrow escape.

THE BATTLE OF STONY POINT

Some five thousand militiamen, appalled by Sullivan's performance, refused to reenlist after their enlistments expired following the Battle of Rhode Island. It is true that General Washington had little reason to be happy with the French or with General John Sullivan after this battle, yet neither Washington nor the British was ready to count the French out yet. Their mere presence had ended any hope Henry Clinton may have entertained of organizing a new invasion from Canada, certainly not now that London had ordered so many of his own regulars to the West Indies. He now determined that his best alternative was to mount a relatively modest offensive from his remaining base in New York City.

On May 30, 1779, Henry Clinton transported some six thousand regulars in seventy Royal Navy ships and 150 flat-bottom boats up the Hudson

River. His objective was West Point, a fortress that controlled the lower Hudson. If he could capture this strongpoint, Clinton believed he would greatly reduce the flow of men and materiel to and from New England.

The first step was to take another fort, Stony Point. Clinton's soldiers captured the lightly defended outpost, on the Hudson's west bank, some thirty-five miles north of New York City. After they next also occupied Verplanck's Point, on the opposite bank, Clinton directed his engineers to fortify these positions, which he intended to use as platforms from which to assault his main objective, West Point.

Washington appreciated the urgency of preventing Clinton from gaining control of the Hudson River, chief waterway to and from the western frontier. Washington had devoted a good deal of time to overseeing the creation of a remarkably effective network of Patriot spies, and he now employed a militia captain, Allen McLane, to scout out the fortifications at Stony Point to identify approaches vulnerable to assault. On July 2, Allen disguised himself as a farmer and escorted a Mrs. Smith into the fortress to visit her sons, who were supposedly Loyalists serving with the British. The daring and dangerous ruse succeeded remarkably well. McLane got a good look at the fortification from the inside and duly reported to General Washington that the works were far from completed and therefore eminently vulnerable.

Less than two weeks later, on July 15, 1779, Washington dispatched "Mad Anthony" Wayne and 1,350 handpicked men to make a surprise attack. Wayne had not forgotten what "No-Flint" Grey (Chapter 16) had done to him at Paoli. Wayne gave his men the same instruction Grey had given his: attack with bayonets exclusively. He wanted an attack as devastating as it was stealthy. To enforce this gunpowder-free edict, he ordered all muskets, except for those of a single battalion, to remain unloaded.

The attack was made at midnight, and although the garrison was certainly taken by surprise, the well-disciplined British regulars quickly rallied, opening fire on Wayne and his men with their muskets as well as cannon. The American army of 1779 was very different from the army that fought prior to the Valley Forge winter. The men were thoroughly drilled and highly disciplined. On the advance, they did not stop to return a single shot. Instead, they refused to become standing targets and continued their forward march in the very teeth of British defensive fire. As Wayne had intended, they stormed the fort and captured it in a ferocious bayonet attack that killed sixty-three British regulars and wounded an additional seventy. The absolute determination of the assault convinced 543 regulars and their officers to surrender. They were made prisoners of war, and all their artillery and equipment were appropriated by General Wayne, who had lost fifteen killed and eighty wounded.

George Washington had once called Stony Point the "key to the continent." Now it was his—but he decided that he could not afford to garrison it, and he instructed Wayne to tear down the British works and withdraw. The strategic gain from the Battle of Stony Point was therefore limited to depriving the British of its possession and thereby protecting West Point and control of the Hudson, at least for now.

EMERGENCE OF A HERO

Ultimately, perhaps the most important result of the Battle of Stony Point was the tremendous boost the victory gave to flagging Patriot morale. Among those inspired by the fierce battle was one of Wayne's own and most capable officers, Major Henry "Light-Horse Harry" Lee. Exhilarated by the triumph, he volunteered to lead a raid on another British strongpoint, Paulus Hook, an outpost on the site of present-day Jersey City, New Jersey, occupying a strategic position directly across the Hudson River from lower Manhattan.

Henry Lee was no kin to the bumbling Charles Lee but instead belonged to another Lee family, one already famous in Virginia and, as it turned out, destined to produce a half-dozen notable soldiers, the most celebrated of whom was Henry Lee's son Robert E. Lee, who would lead the Army of Northern Virginia in the Civil War.

Henry Lee earned his celebrated nickname from his command of a unit of light dragoons, soldiers who rode into battle but then fought dismounted, as infantrymen. The light dragoons were elite troops, called the Light Horse, hence their major's sobriquet.

Light-Horse Harry had the services of another Stony Point veteran, the intrepid spy Allen McLane, who scouted Paulus Hook in advance of the attack, as he had scouted Stony Point. He reported back to Lee that

General Henry "Light-Horse Harry" Lee was one of the ablest commanders in the Continental Army and the father of Confederate general Robert E. Lee. NEW YORK PUBLIC LIBRARY

the British garrison there consisted of no more than two hundred men and that the position was therefore ripe for the taking.

On August 18, 1779, McLane guided Lee and four hundred of his Light Horse dragoons through the rugged approach to the fort. It was critically important that the approach be made and completed at low tide, because a moat protected the only route in or out. At high tide, the moat filled and, with the incoming current, became impassable. The plan, therefore, was to attack at half past midnight on August 19, when the chances of preserving the element of surprise were at their highest and the tide at its lowest.

Even with McLane's guidance, progress through the night was slow, and by the time Lee had formed up his dragoons at the edge of a salt marsh no more than five hundred yards from the fort, he discovered that about a hundred of his men were either lost or had deserted. With his force thus reduced to three hundred, Lee nevertheless decided against aborting the attack. He ordered his men not to prime their muskets, lest an accidental discharge give them away. As for the attack, it would emulate Stony Point: bayonets only.

The three hundred dragoons and their major quietly stormed the small fort, and the Battle of Paulus Hook was over and won in under a half-hour. Fifty British regulars were slain, and 158 became prisoners of war. Light-Horse Harry and his men suffered just two killed and three wounded. Hearing the sound of British alarm guns on the New York side of the Hudson, however, Lee quickly took his prisoners in hand and fled Paulus Hook as fast as he could.

THE SPRINGFIELD OPERATION

While the Continental Army was a much-improved force after Valley Forge, it was nevertheless chronically undermanned, and Washington rarely had the strength to mount anything more than hit-and-run raids. These were sufficient, however, to drain Clinton's own thinly spread resources. Each Patriot raid, each sortie was another wearing episode in this long war of attrition, and in June 1780, Baron Wilhelm von Knyphausen, commanding Hessian forces and assigned temporary command of the occupation of New York City while Henry Clinton campaigned in the South (see Chapter 21), decided that it was time for a decisive counterthrust.

Knyphausen's informants had reported that not only was the Continental Army on the verge of mutiny, but the civilian populace in and around Springfield, New Jersey (in present-day Union County) were so war-weary that they were talking about rallying to the side of the Loyalists. The Hessian commander's intelligence was not entirely unfounded, but it was misleading nonetheless. Mostly unpaid, very poorly fed, often nearly naked, the soldiers of the Continental Army constantly grumbled and did so loudly. Anyone listening to them could be forgiven for thinking that an insurrection was in the offing. As for the people of Springfield, as elsewhere in New Jersey, numerous Loyalists lived alongside Patriots. It would have been difficult to say which faction dominated at any particular time, but, clearly, Knyphausen saw and heard what he wanted to see and hear.

On June 7, 1780, he led six thousand troops from Staten Island to Elizabethtown (present-day Elizabeth), New Jersey. Forming them up here, he marched them to the tiny village of Connecticut Farms, the modern town of Union, about two and a half miles southeast of Springfield. Confident in what his informants had told him about the Loyalist leanings in the area, he set about trying to recruit "Tories" for an attack on Washington's major encampment at Morristown.

To the baron's dismay, he was not met by eager takers at Connecticut Farms. Instead, he was greeted by musket fire from New Jersey militiamen, and, before long, the militia troops were reinforced by Continentals. Enraged, Knyphausen paused in his hasty withdrawal from Connecticut Farms just long enough to burn a local church and a few other buildings, in the process killing the wife of Reverend James Caldwell, almost certainly by accident. The arson and the murder—or manslaughter—consolidated the will of the people against him and his Germans. Knyphausen took the hint and retreated in haste to Elizabethtown, where he regrouped.

On June 23, Knyphausen felt sufficiently restored to launch a new attack, this time against the larger town of Springfield. The local Continental commander, Nathanael Greene, had under him no more than one thousand troops against Knyphausen's six thousand. Unsurprisingly, the Hessians quickly captured Springfield—only to find themselves being fought to a standstill by Greene and a growing force of New Jersey militia, highly motivated by the outrage committed against Connecticut Farms and Mrs. Caldwell.

For his part, Knyphausen once again responded with a reprisal, putting to the torch all but four of Springfield's fifty-odd houses before withdrawing from New Jersey back to Staten Island. Presumably, he marched off feeling that he had taught the people of Springfield and vicinity a lesson. Instead, his terrorism swept away any popular disengagement from the revolution or discontent with General Washington. New Jersey militias came alive and organized resistance to the British and Hessians that, with the help of a small Continental Army force, drove them right out of the state.

Peace Feelers

The events of 1778–1780 in and around Philadelphia and throughout much of New Jersey, from Camden up to the towns facing New York City across the Hudson, eroded the British will to keep up the fight, especially with the French now threatening the profitable sugar and slave trade in the West Indies. Even George III and Tories in Parliament, the major supporters of the war against independence, were seriously pondering the wisdom of making a negotiated peace. The king, early in the spring of 1778, appointed Frederick Howard, 5th Earl of Carlisle, to head a peace commission, authorizing him to deal directly with the Continental Congress and, if he saw fit, to suspend any act of Parliament affecting the colonies that had been passed since 1763.

While the time might have seemed right to the Crown and Parliament, to the Continental Congress negotiation made little sense. By relinquishing Philadelphia, the British were looking weaker than they ever had before. Why, then, negotiate anything short of the mother country's recognition of American independence? On April 22, 1778, Congress resolved that any person or group that "pretended to come to terms" with this peace commission would be condemned as an enemy of the United States.

The Carlisle Commission members, unimpressed by the congressional threat, simply took a new approach—new in this war but tried and true in the history of war and geopolitics. They offered several congressional delegates handsome bribes to vote for a negotiated peace. To the credit of these men, none seems even to have been tempted. Not only did the bribery offer taint any legitimate purpose the commission may have had, it made the London government look all the weaker and more desperate.

Undaunted, the commissioners announced a new offer. The colonies would be granted a large degree of autonomy as a kind of commonwealth province or free state. To sweeten the offer, a blanket amnesty would also be granted, forgiving every rebel and rebel leader. Carlisle himself sought to make this offer more appealing by focusing on what he knew were fears among the less radical congressional delegates, that France would soon enough betray its American ally. This prompted the fiery Marquis de Lafayette to challenge Carlisle to a duel for having assailed the honor of France.

The head of the commission never responded to Lafayette. Instead, on November 27, 1778, he and his fellow commissioners folded their tents and decamped, thoroughly persuaded that the Americans were stepped too far into revolutionary sacrifice to accept anything other than a total break. So, the war continued, even as enthusiasm and commitment on both sides continued to wax and wane. The difference was that, in Britain, the liberal faction of the government became increasingly influential, as did its favoritism toward American independence while, in America, the zeal of the Loyalists, while still intense in some places, unmistakably ebbed. As for France, the alliance, thus far disappointing, was about to bear fruit.

CHAPTER 20

Out of Uniform

THE AMERICAN REVOLUTION HAD BECOME WHAT GEORGE WASHINGton believed it would be: a war of attrition. By definition, this meant a long war, some eight years, from 1775 to 1783. As wars go, however, it was fought mostly at a fairly low intensity. The Civil War of 1861–1865, half the length of the revolution, consisted of seventy-six incredibly intense and massive battles in addition to some 310 smaller battles and thousands of named skirmishes. The American Revolution had just sixteen major battles. These were Lexington and Concord, Bunker Hill, Ticonderoga, the Boston Siege, Valcour Island, Brandywine, Germantown, Long Island, Trenton, Princeton, Oriskany, Saratoga (Freeman's Farm and Bemis Heights), Monmouth Court House, Charleston, Cowpens, Camden, and Yorktown. Most of these were won or lost or drawn in a few hours or less. Only a few lasted a day or more.

So, where did all the time go?

The revolutionary battles we remember by name account for perhaps two or three months out of the war's eight years. These named engagements were the traditional battles, the contests fought between armies or portions of armies, usually more or less in the style of European combat. To some extent, the rest of the eight years were occupied in winter encampment and in movement from place to place, but, mostly, they were filled with violence on a smaller though no less terrible scale—a continuation of the frontier fighting between whites and Native Americans that had been a feature of life in the New World since 1492. These frontier and wilderness combats were typically fought by small numbers of men far from major towns. Modern military historians would label them "low-intensity" because, though numerous and widely distributed, each individual encounter was short, sharp, and produced relatively few casualties. It was low-intensity—if you did not happen to be involved in it.

We think of the American Revolution as a war between the Patriots and the redcoats. This was the case with most of the sixteen "major" battles, but most of the revolution as a whole was a backcountry conflict. It involved Patriot versus Loyalist militia groups and, often, each side's Native American allies. Some battles pitted Patriots against British-aligned Indians, and a smaller number set Patriot-allied Indians against Loyalist militia. Sometimes, Native Americans raided white frontier settlements. British-aligned Indians tended to target predominantly Patriot settlements, and those Indians allied with the Americans hit Loyalist villages and isolated outposts. Finally, quite often, Native Americans fought one another. In some cases, the opposing sides were aligned with opposing interests, Patriot versus Loyalist, but, more often, the Indians continued to act on existing enmities that had little or nothing to do with the ongoing war between the whites.

The character of combat in the wilderness war was a rhythm of raid and counterraid. Often, it was neither more nor less than ambush, murder, and reprisal in the wilderness.

WHOSE SIDE ARE YOU ON?

The British learned a hard lesson from their experience in the French and Indian War: It is better to have Native American allies than Native American enemies. The French were far more successful fighting alongside Indians than the British were. Accordingly, after that war, British colonial administrators set up an Indian Department dedicated to forging friendly relations and even military alliances with key tribes. For its part, the Continental Congress tried to follow the British example, creating an Indian Department of its own.

Both sides had the right idea, but, in the American Revolution, the British had a significant advantage. First, a great many Native American leaders attempted to steer a neutral course, often without success. Of those who took sides, most picked the British. They believed that Crown and Parliament could limit the spread of white settlement—white invasion—whereas, left to their own devices, the land-hungry Americans would grab all they could.

The most enduring and effective Anglo–Native American alliance had its origin before the start of the revolution. William Johnson was an Irishman who left his native land at the age of fifteen and settled in the Mohawk Valley northwest of Albany. He quickly established profitable trade with the Mohawks, and this was extended into close personal relationships as well. When his first wife, a white woman, died, Johnson married Degonwadonti, known to the English settlers as Molly Brant. She was the daughter of Johnson's friend Nichus Brant and Nichus's Mohawk wife, Owandah. Molly had a younger brother, Joseph Brant, whose Mohawk name was Thayendanegea. Johnson informally adopted him, and "father" and "son" fought side-by-side in the French and Indian War. Moreover, Brant rose within the Mohawk tribe while earning the respect of colonists.

William Johnson died in 1774. Joseph Brant, a much younger man, continued a friendship with Johnson's son Guy. This relationship was the seed of the English alliance with the Mohawks, which was especially strong during the early years of the American Revolution. And the Mohawks were formidable Allies to have. Not only were they fiercely skilled combatants, they were the richest and most important of the six tribes of the powerful Iroquois Confederacy. The Mohawks persuaded three other Iroquois tribes, the Senecas, Cayugas, and Onondagas, into making alliances with the British.

The other two Iroquois tribes, the Oneidas and the Tuscaroras, allied themselves with the Americans. This proved to be a valuable alliance, especially since the Oneidas brought along with them the Mahicans (also known as the Stockbridge Indians), who were bitter enemies of the Mohawks. The Oneidas were brought into the American fold in part by their respect and friendship for a teacher and Presbyterian minister named Samuel Kirkland. James Dean, who served as an agent for the Continental Congress's Indian Department, played the key role in persuading the Tuscaroras to rally to the American cause. Valuable though these alliances were, they were far less formidable than the British tribal connections, but, whether allied with the Americans or the British, the Indians ended up deriving little benefit.

The Iroquois Confederacy, a powerful force, was significantly diminished by being split between the two warring white factions.

AGENTS OF TERROR

White historians, especially during the nineteenth century, rarely gave Native American leaders much credit for statesmanship and military strategy. In fact, they often acted with even more deliberate strategic thought than either the British or the Americans. This notwithstanding, the Patriots as well as the British regulars and Loyalist militias often used their Indian allies as instruments of terror. William Tryon, the Loyalist governor of New York, urged British military commanders to "loose the savages against the miserable Rebels in order to impose a reign of terror on the frontiers." Britain's prime minister Lord Chatham feigned horror at such a policy, calling it "unconstitutional, inhuman, and unchristian," yet he did nothing to stop it.

Why would he? By September 1776, the frontier of Virginia, Pennsylvania, and New York had been driven to panic by Native American raiding. By the close of 1777, the Cherry and Mohawk Valleys of New York and the Wyoming Valley of Pennsylvania were continually raked by a cycle of raid and reprisal. In April 1778, Loyalists mustered a large force of Native American allies along the upper Susquehanna. Acting in concert, they hoped to strike a decisive blow that would end the cycle with a Loyalist victory. At the Native American town of Tioga, Pennsylvania, the Loyalist militia colonel John Butler put together a force of four hundred Tory Rangers and other militiamen and joined them to some nine hundred Senecas and Cayugas. Butler recognized that the typical Indian action was a hit-and-run raid. He was determined to do something very different, to make a deep and lasting impression to gain control of the Wyoming Valley of northern Pennsylvania.

With his Indian allies, Butler built boats for the trip down the Susquehanna while a Seneca chief, Gu-cinge, led four hundred warriors against settlements along the west branch of the river. Simultaneously, Joseph Brant assembled a mixed force of Native Americans and Tories, 450 in total, to strike against New York's Cherry Valley at the headwaters of the Susquehanna.

Cherry Valley was a soft target. It had been raided repeatedly since 1776, but its residents took few steps to defend themselves. The local militia colonel, Samuel Campbell, tried to make his force look bigger by outfitting twenty-six boys with pointy paper hats and giving them wooden rifles to hold. The thing is—this desperate ruse fooled Brant, at least temporarily, sending him off to attack nearby Cobleskill instead of Cherry Valley. Captain Christian Brown's twenty militiamen augmented by thirty-seven Continental soldiers from Colonel Ichabod Alden's 7th Massachusetts Regiment defended Cobleskill but were no match for Brant's 450 men. The village was burned, thirty-one Americans were killed, and six wounded.

In Pennsylvania, the Wyoming Valley looked to be in better shape, with a system of fortified dwellings that were designated as forts. These included Wintermoot's (or Wintermot's), Forty Fort, Jenkins' Fort, Wilkes-Barre Fort, and Pittston Fort. Under attack, however, they were quickly neutralized—and one fort, Wintermoot's, was held by Loyalists, who gave up without a fight. Jenkins' Fort succumbed to attack on July 2.

Forty Fort was another story. It was garrisoned by 450 Continental troops and militiamen under Continental Army colonel Zebulon Butler (no relation to John Butler) and militia colonel Nathan Denison. After the two refused to surrender, John Butler put Wintermoot's to the torch on July 3 to make the garrison at Forty Fort think they had withdrawn. Denison and his militiamen fell for it and set off in pursuit of what they assumed were John Butler's retreating forces. Zebulon Butler, more experienced, tried to stop Denison, warning him that it looked to be a trick. Denison mocked him and persuaded the entire 450-man garrison to sally out of Forty Fort. No sooner did they do this than they found themselves in a deadly ambush. Three hundred Americans were killed or wounded and Forty Fort razed.

Now the Wyoming Valley was defenseless. John Butler led a rampage of destruction while Joseph Brant turned his attention back to Cherry Valley. On July 18, he raided Andrustown, seven miles west of Cherry Valley, capturing fourteen settlers, killing eleven, then burning the town. After further raids throughout the valley, he attacked German Flats (present-day Herkimer, New York) on the Mohawk River on September

12. By then, however, the townspeople had fled, but that didn't stop Brant from burning down the empty buildings.

The raids were costly, yet instead of dispiriting the Patriot frontier, they stirred retaliation against Native American villages. Militiamen spared not one of them. Warriors were slain along with women, children, and old men. Brant withdrew but returned to Cherry Valley in November. By this time 250 Continental soldiers of the 7th Massachusetts Regiment under Lieutenant Colonel Ichabod Alden had arrived to defend the valley. They were far too small a force. On November 10, eight hundred Loyalists and Indian allies ravaged Cherry Valley, not merely killing the defenders, but scalping and mutilating them. Some warriors reportedly committed acts of cannibalism. Within a few hours. Cherry Valley ceased to exist.

GENERAL SULLIVAN'S EXPEDITION
Washington focused on the highest-profile battles, those between the Continental Army and the British army with its Hessian auxiliaries. His reasoning was that these engagements would make the biggest impact across the Atlantic, back in London. As for the frontier, he mostly relied on local militia under local leadership to do the best it could. But the Cherry Valley Massacre, as it was called, crossed a red line. It was slaughter, and Washington sent Major General John Sullivan on a punitive expedition, the preferred punishment being extermination. He wanted the Iroquois Confederacy broken up, annihilated.

The campaign was commissioned at the start of 1779, but Sullivan did not get under way until June 18. He led twenty-five hundred Continentals from Easton, Pennsylvania, to the Susquehanna with the intention of burning Iroquois settlements throughout the Susquehanna Valley as he and his men marched north to the southern border of New York. Another Continental commander, Major General James Clinton, at the head of fifteen hundred troops, was tasked with marching through the Mohawk Valley to Lake Otsego and then down toward the Susquehanna. Thus, the Indians would find themselves caught in the jaws of a pincers, Sullivan closing in from the south, Clinton from the north. In addition, Colonel Daniel Brodhead was to lead six hundred men from Fort Pitt (present-day Pittsburgh) up the Allegheny River, burning every Iroquois village and killing every Iroquois individual they encountered. The operation would culminate in a rendezvous between Sullivan and Clinton at Tioga. United, the two would march their combined forces north, meeting Brodhead at Genesee. The fully consolidated force would then advance due north to Niagara, continuing a campaign of extermination. George Washington had authorized a major Indian war.

Sullivan, as usual, was competent but dull, and the lugubrious pace of his progress was more than Clinton could bear. His patience exhausted, Clinton launched, on April 21, a six-day raid from his base of operations at Canajoharie on the Mohawk River. His men killed a dozen Onondagas, captured thirty-four, and burned down some fifty houses. Among these was the Iroquois longhouse, the headquarters in which leaders of the Iroquois Confederacy traditionally met. For the Iroquois, the longhouse was more than a building. It was a political and spiritual metaphor, the figurative embodiment of the Confederacy, which members pictured as a great "longhouse" spanning what is now upper New York State. Perhaps the greatest blow was that Clinton's Indian auxiliaries were Oneidas, members of one of the two Iroquois tribes that had allied with the Americans against the British and the three Iroquois tribes aligned with them. For the white population of America, the revolution meant independence. For the most powerful Native American alliance, it meant division and dissolution.

But neither Clinton nor Sullivan checked Joseph Brant before he stormed against Minisink in the Mohawk Valley, burning that settlement, and killing some 140 of 170 American militiamen who had rallied to the town's defense, and it was August 9 before Sullivan reached Newtychanning, an important Seneca village. Sullivan was chagrined to find it deserted. He set fire to its twenty-eight buildings and set off for Tioga, where he finally tied in with Clinton and then posted General Orders to the combined force. Essentially, it was a declaration of all-out war on the Iroquois, and during all of August and September 1779 Sullivan and Clinton leveled Indian villages throughout the region. They were almost all completely deserted, and while the destruction must have been devastating, it was hardly decisive. As a military force, the Iroquois were at large and active.

THE FARTHER FRONTIER

The frontier of Cherry Valley, the Mohawk Valley, and the Susquehanna was the "near frontier" in the late eighteenth century, a transitional region between the thickly settled seaboard and what came to be called the "Old Northwest," the vast region north of the Ohio River and east of the Mississippi. Along with Kentucky, this was eighteenth-century America's "far frontier." Its distance from the centers of the revolution—Tidewater Virginia, coastal New England, Philadelphia, and Charleston—did not remove it from the war.

On July 2, 1775, the leaders of the five Shawnee septs (bands) met at Chillicothe on the Little Miami River, in what is today the state of Ohio. They gathered to plan a common response to the influx of white settlers in Kentucky, which, from their perspective, was an invasion. The venerated Chief Cornstalk called for absolute neutrality in the fight among the whites. He advocated awaiting the resolution of this conflict before acting against the settlers. His counsel was rejected, and Shawnee warriors stormed through the new Kentucky settlements throughout the fall of 1775.

And yet the settlers kept pouring in. At the time, Virginia had governance over frontier Kentucky, and in June 1776, the senior Virginia militia officer there, George Rogers Clark, made the trek to Williamsburg, Virginia's capital, to ask authorities to send him troops. While Clark was on this errand, the Shawnee subchief Pluck-kemeh-notee, called by the English and Americans Pluggy, led a series of raids in Kentucky. When he was killed, the Shawnee chief Black Fish gathered some two hundred warriors and led them in a vengeance-driven campaign targeting every settler they encountered. On or about July 4, 1776, a great council was held among the Shawnees, Iroquois, Delawares, Ottawas, Cherokees, Wyandots, and Mingos. Amid this show of solidarity, Cornstalk himself renounced neutrality and pledged aid to the British. "It is better for the red men to die like warriors than to diminish away by inches," he proclaimed. "Now is the time to begin. If we fight like men, we may hope to enlarge our bounds."

By the end of January 1777, Black Fish had driven most settlers out of Kentucky. On April 24, he attacked Boonesboro, laying siege to it for four days. Although one settler was killed and seven others wounded—among them Daniel Boone, the town's founder—Boonesboro endured the siege. Black Fish withdrew, though he made hit-and-run raids on other settlements.

But he and Cornstalk had missed their window of greatest opportunity. Clark was given permission to raise a Kentucky militia. His plan was not to defend Kentucky directly. He believed it more important now to hit the enemy at his sources. He therefore decided to lead the army he would raise against British outposts at Kaskaskia, Cahokia, and Vincennes, all in modern Illinois and Indiana. This accomplished, he intended to take the most important British fort in the Old Northwest—Detroit. Clark had no formal military training, but he was a born strategist of great vision. He saw all of these British strongpoints as the sources of supply for the Shawnees and allied tribes who raided Kentucky. Neutralize these places, and the raids would stop, he thought, forever.

But in the midsummer of 1777, before Clark could raise and organize his forces, Shawnees in concert with Wyandots, Mingos, and Cherokees raided Wheeling (in present-day West Virginia). This was on the very fringe of the Virginia frontier, and it moved the Continental Congress to send Major General Edward Hand to recruit Pennsylvanians, Virginians, and Kentuckians to mount a major attack on a British-operated Native American supply depot on the Cuyahoga River, near present-day Cleveland, Ohio. Cornstalk, bearing a white flag, made the mistake of entering Fort Randolph, at the junction of the Ohio and the Kanawha Rivers, to deliver a warning to Hand. If he attacked, the Shawnee and allied tribes would retaliate. Not only did Captain Matthew Arbuckle, commanding Fort Randolph, dismiss the warning, he seized Cornstalk, his son Silverheels, and another warrior. He intended to hold them hostage to extort good behavior from the Shawnees. On November 10, 1777, however, a white hunting party, learning that the chief was being held under token guard, broke into the fort, killed all three Shawnees, and then mutilated their bodies. This roused the Shawnees to war, and Hand was unable to suppress them.

The killing went on week after week. On February 8, 1778, the Shawnee chief Blue Jacket, with 102 warriors, took captive a twenty-seven-man salt-making party at Blue Licks, Kentucky. Among those taken was Daniel Boone, the frontiersman who had opened Kentucky to settlement and founded Boonesboro. In captivity, he pretended to turn traitor and accepted adoption into the Shawnee tribe. He was taken to the British officer, Henry Hamilton, who served as the Crown's liaison with the Native Americans on the frontier. They called him "Hair Buyer" because he paid bounties for American scalps.

Hamilton the Hair Buyer believed Boone, who not only persuaded him to delay a planned attack on American-held Fort Pitt but also gathered intelligence about the renewed assault on Boonesboro. As soon as he had heard enough about the situation there, Boone made a stealthy escape and reached Boonesboro just in time to lead the resistance there and to get a word of warning to Fort Pitt. Boone's wily insurgency was crucial to saving the far frontier, but during much of 1778, Black Fish led Shawnees as well as Wyandots, Mingos, Delawares, Miamis, and Kickapoos in highly destructive raids throughout the region.

As late as the end of May 1778, George Rogers Clark had managed to raise an "army" of no more than 175 men. He decided to make do with this small force in attacking Kaskaskia and Cahokia, the first phase in his planned assault on British-held Detroit. He loaded his men onto flatboats on June 26, 1778 and reached the mouth of the Tennessee River four days later. From here, he hit Kaskaskia, taking its small garrison by surprise and seizing the outpost with a shot. Establishing his base of operations here, he moved on to Cahokia, which also surrendered to him without resistance.

Now he was ready for his next objective, Vincennes, Hamilton's headquarters. Clark knew Vincennes would not surrender without a fight—and that the garrison there was larger than his miniscule band. His only chance, Clark decided, was to use speed to substitute for numbers. In the dead of winter, on February 5, 1779, he set off on a brutal 150-mile march, reaching Vincennes on February 23. He managed to capture a few prisoners outside of town. They revealed that the fort here, Fort Sackville, was defended by just a few hundred men—more than 150, but not that much more. Still, a siege was not an option because Hair Buyer had merely to wait for a relief force. Clark decided, therefore, that his only viable option was deception. He sent one of his prisoners into the village of Vincennes with a letter proclaiming his intention to capture the village on behalf of Virginia and the United States. He explicitly warned all those loyal to King George III to repair to the fort because they would get to quarter from him. As a finishing touch, Clark appended to the letter the signatures of a great many officers. Their names were real enough, but they were nowhere near Vincennes.

While Hamilton and the elders of Vincennes contemplated the letter, Clark gave his men sticks on which he tied cloths painted to resemble regimental banners. He then had them move about, marching to and fro. After a time, believing—hoping—he had thoroughly intimidated the defenders of Vincennes and Fort Sackville, Clark attacked as loudly as possible. The Native Americans instantly deserted the British, and, what is more, a band of Kickapoo and Piankashaw Indians approached Clark to volunteer their services. Henry Hamilton promptly surrendered both Vincennes and Fort Sackville.

Clark was pleased with his victories, but he soon discovered that capturing the principal forts of the Old Northwest did not end the Kentucky raids. On the contrary, by 1780, raids became so frequent and widespread that Clark abandoned his plan to take Detroit. Instead, he acted against the local Shawnees and their Loyalist allies. It was more a matter of management than triumph, and warfare between white Americans and Native Americans would not end in the Old Northwest until 1795, twelve years after the Treaty of Paris that ended the Revolution. That was when "Mad Anthony" Wayne defeated Blue Jacket, Tecumseh, and Little Turtle in the conflict known as Little Turtle's War. Wayne's victory at the Battle of Fallen Timbers (August 20, 1795) resulted in the Treaty of Greenville, by which the Shawnees and their allies ceded the disputed territory.

BACK TO THE NEAR FRONTIER

Though he did not bring absolute victory, Clark achieved significant results in the Farther Frontier, whereas Sullivan accomplished little against the Native Americans of northwestern New York. Arguably, Sullivan's relentless vandalism increased the intensity of warfare here. On May 21, 1780, the Loyalist commander Sir John Johnson led a large raid by a mixed force of Native Americans and Loyalists against the Patriot forts of the Mohawk Valley. Some six hundred combatants, four hundred Loyalists and two hundred Indians, burned Johnstown, New York. On May 23, Indians led by Joseph Brant razed Caughnawaga and Canajoharie before advancing along the Ohio River into Pennsylvania. Here, they overwhelmed a one-hundred-man Pennsylvania militia unit under

Archibald Lochry, killing five officers and thirty-five enlisted soldiers. The rest were made prisoners.

Brant and his men returned to New York, where they tied in with Johnson's Loyalists and the Seneca chief Cornplanter, creating a force of eighteen hundred Loyalists and Indians. They descended upon the Scoharie Valley on October 15, then marched up the Mohawk River, putting to the torch all that they found, so that, in just five days, Johnson and Brant managed to destroy at least as much as Sullivan had in a whole month of marching. There was a cost. Brant was wounded and out of action until early 1781. He rapidly made up for the lost time, raiding the already hard-hit Mohawk and Cherry Valleys. Washington, who had precious few troops to spare, sent Colonel Marianus Willett with 130 Continentals and a handful of militiamen to do whatever they could. Under the very able Willett, this small force managed to suppress raiding for the rest of summer. When the raids resumed in October, Willett was ready. He responded aggressively and, in one encounter, killed Walter Butler, the most important Tory military leader in the entire region. This amounted to a decapitating blow, essentially scattering the raiders.

WAR WITHOUT END

The intermission in the frontier war did not last long. Joseph Brant took the place of Walter Butler. He held a meeting with Chief Abraham, leader of an Indian band known locally as the Moravians—Delawares who had been converted to Christianity by Moravian missionaries. Brant tried earnestly to recruit Abraham and his men to fight the Americans, but they refused. In response, British authorities ordered the Moravians to leave Pennsylvania and resettle in the Ohio country. Accordingly, Abraham and the Moravians set out for the banks of the Sandusky River, but were stopped in their tracks early in 1782 when a deep winter famine overtook them. With his people starving, Abraham sought and received permission to move back temporarily to the western Pennsylvania mission towns they occupied on the Tuscarawas River.

The refugees returned at a very bad time. Mohawks and Delawares—unconverted Delawares—had just finished an especially intense succession of raids. Colonel Brodhead, now assigned command of the Continental Army in the area, ordered Colonel David Williamson to lead troops in reprisal actions. Williamson found Abraham and his Moravians at the mission town of Gnadenhutten, in modern Ohio. He told Abraham and the forty-eight men, women, and boys with him that they would all find both shelter and protection at Fort Pitt, to which he would lead them. Williamson asked the chief to send messengers to Salem, another missionary town nearby, and fetch the Indians who lived there. They, too, would be welcomed at Fort Pitt.

No sooner did the men, women, and children arrive from Salem than Williamson set his troops among them to bind the wrists of each one—about ninety people in all. Thus bound, they passed the night. Come morning, Williamson announced that they would all be executed as just punishment for the Delaware raids. The commander waited until sunset to execute the members of the group, one after the other, by means of a single mallet blow to the back of the head.

Somehow, two boys escaped death. They lived to tell their tale, and they told it, eliciting stern condemnation from American officials—but not so much as a censure. It goes without saying that the atrocity provoked retaliation. It was massive and widespread, with Native American warriors raiding all the way into Kentucky, yet again forcing the abandonment of the Kentucky frontier. It was not until November 1782, with the main phase of the American Revolution over and done with, that George Rogers Clark managed to piece together a sufficiently large militia force to intervene. He chased off the raiders and burned Chillicothe, considered the Shawnee "capital," as well as many other Shawnee towns and villages. Far worse, Clark destroyed some ten thousand bushels of corn, the ration on which the Shawnees and their allies needed to survive the winter. *That* cruel blow at last brought an intermission in the chronic raiding even as, on November 30, 1782, the United States and Britain concluded preliminary articles of peace by which King George III agreed, among other things, to formally cede the entire Old Northwest to an independent United States.

But this did not end the warfare between white Americans and Native Americans in the Farther Frontier. What prevailed, briefly, was a pause in what felt like an endless frontier war, which would move progressively westward, ending late in the nineteenth century, well after the United States celebrated its first hundred years of independence.

CHAPTER 21

The Southern Strategy

SUFFERING HEAVY CASUALTIES IN CONCORD AND AT BUNKER HILL AND forced to evacuate from Boston, the British shifted their strategy from attacking the core of revolutionary zeal to its periphery. Commanders started looking for soft targets, places and regions in which Loyalist sentiment was strong. The lower South was just behind New York in concentration of Loyalists. It was a relatively new region, not long accustomed to anything like self-government, and its economy and culture were already based on large plantations, which meant that it had spawned an influential class of large landowners, baronial in attitude and staunchly resistant to change, let alone revolutionary change.

But the embrace of the status quo is hardly the same as a willingness to fight for Crown and Parliament. Loyalists abounded, but relatively few were willing to fight. It is believed that about thirty thousand colonial Loyalists served as combat troops under British officers—not at any one time, but over the course of eight years of revolution. In the lower South, much of Britain's fighting was done by Loyalist units and not regulars. Some were talented soldiers motivated by some of the very impulses that moved Patriot volunteers. They were defending their homes. But the great majority of deep-South Loyalists were untrained, and the regular British officers that commanded them considered the whole lot highly unreliable.

THE ORIGINS OF A SOUTHERN THEATER
The American Revolution, as a military struggle, began in New England, but there was early trouble in the South as well. Virginia—in the upper

South—was governed by John Murray, 4th Earl of Dunmore, and best known as Lord Dunmore. Although firebrands in his colony—the likes of Patrick Henry, George Washington, and others—were as zealous for independence as Sam Adams and John Adams up in New England, Dunmore was a royalist through and through. Late in 1775, the Virginia Council of Safety—a southern version of New England's Committees of Public Safety—recruited a thousand militiamen and posted them at Great Bridge, a causeway across a marshy stretch of the Elizabeth River about ten miles outside Norfolk, a hotspot of rebellion. Lord Dunmore personally led two hundred British regulars, a band of Loyalists, and a few Royal Marines, along with a small unit of runaway slaves calling itself the Loyal Ethiopians, to occupy Norfolk, put it under military control, and nip in the bud incipient rebellion there.

Far from intimidated, the Council of Safety militia attacked on December 9, killing sixty of Dunmore's troops at Great Bridge and putting to flight Lord Dunmore himself. The governor rushed as many of his Tory troops and British regulars as he could onto British warships anchored in the harbor. That accomplished, he prepared to weigh anchor and give up Norfolk to the Patriots.

Aboard ship, however, he soon had second thoughts. Instead of sailing off, he dispatched a messenger to the rebellious citizens of Norfolk, demanding that they supply his men with provisions. When they refused, a tense standoff developed, which was broken on January 1, 1776, when Dunmore ordered the ships' cannon to bombard the town. Following the barrage, he deployed landing parties with torches and instructions to burn the town down. Lacking artillery to direct against the warships, the Patriots responded by putting the homes of prominent Norfolk Loyalists to the torch. As Dunmore sailed away, both rebel and Tory Norfolk blazed.

BATTLE AT ANOTHER BRIDGE

Wealth, property, and lifestyle moved some southerners toward Loyalism. Among others, it was a matter of culture. Below Virginia, in the highlands of western North Carolina, a large number of Scottish immigrants had settled, Highlanders attracted by the similarity of the Appalachian landscape to the homeland they had left. They were by nature conservative folk, and their geographical location isolated them from the centers of political ferment. They felt no great allegiance to the English king, but they very much wanted the rebels to leave them alone, and in February 1776 a band of them organized themselves into a Loyalist militia. Fifteen hundred marched down from their homes in the hills and progressed eastward toward the coast. Their plan was to tie in with British regulars and then march together to interdict a large Patriot force reportedly on the move.

Patriot colonels Richard Caswell and John Alexander Lillington were intimately familiar with the Carolina backcountry, and they well knew the temper of the Highlanders. Certain that these men would in fact rally to the British cause, they deployed approximately one thousand Patriot militiamen with orders to quickly dig shallow trenches across the anticipated line of the Highlanders' march and prepare to ambush them near the present-day coastal city of Wilmington.

The militia put their backs into their work and made rapid progress. Only after most of the trenches had been excavated did an officer among them realize they had blundered. The trench line had been dug parallel to Moore's Creek, which meant that the creek would be at the soldiers' backs. No experienced commander would ever choose to put a body of water behind his position. To their credit, the weary militiamen immediately dug a new trench line, this time leaving themselves a route of retreat. They did not, however, bother to fill in the trenches they did not occupy.

As the old saying goes, sometimes it is better to be lucky than smart. The Scots approached the vacant trenches shortly before dawn on February 28. They assumed that the Patriot militia had dug them and then, seeing the size of the approaching Highland band, had promptly fled. The Highlanders concluded that Moore's Creek Bridge had been left undefended, and so they blithely began their march across it.

That is when the Patriots opened fire. Those Highlanders who survived the fusillade and onslaught—some 850 out of the original fifteen hundred—became prisoners of war. It was a splendid triumph, which inspirited the southern Patriots and made the local Tories think twice before again engaging against their rebel neighbors. Hoping to find a soft target, the British took a hard blow to Loyalist morale. And there was, for the Loyalists, even worse. Because the Highlanders were not an expeditionary force but were en route to join with the regulars, they anticipated a long deployment and carried with them their entire war chest. The Battle of Moore's Creek Bridge yielded a bonanza. In addition to their prisoners, the Patriot militia collected some £15,000 in gold, thirteen wagons, fifteen hundred rifles, 350 muskets, and 150 swords.

TARGET: CHARLESTON

The terrible defeat of the Highlanders at Moore's Creek Bridge shook the resolve of many backcountry Loyalists, but it did not deter British military commanders from attacking a bigger target lower down the coast. Charleston, South Carolina, was the chief port of the lower South, and the lovely city had a high concentration of Loyalist residents. How loyal? British command had no hard intelligence, but they did know that, thus far, South Carolina had not committed any overt act of rebellion. On the other hand, citizens of that colony had made no overt move toward aiding the mother country, either. But British military leaders chose to believe that the absence of hostility was an indication that an urban center like Charleston was almost certainly bound to lean toward loyalty.

On June 4, 1776, ten British warships and thirty troop transports dropped anchor off Charleston Bar. At the head of this force was none other than General Henry Clinton. Did he ponder the meaning of the absence of a Loyalist welcoming party? He did not record his thoughts on this. Nor do we know enough about him as a tactician to assume that he noted and was disturbed by the presence of newly erected forts on Sullivan's Island and James Island, positions from which the approaches to the city's inner harbor could be dominated. Another curious feature of the coastline should also have drawn his attention. The warehouses that formerly occupied the waterfront were gone, torn down. A savvy tactician would have understood that this was standard procedure for artillerists who sought to create a clear field of fire to defend against any amphibious invasion.

Unknown to Clinton, South Carolina had largely embraced the revolution. Since it was not touched by the early fighting, however, its people quietly used their interval of peace to prepare for a likely British landing. Two militia regiments—one under Charles Cotesworth Pinckney, the other under William Moultrie—had been raised, armed, and sent to garrison the new island forts. Moultrie's second-in-command was a skilled Low Country fighter named Francis Marion, soon to be known to history as "The Swamp Fox" (Chapter 24). In addition, North Carolina had sent a modest infantry detachment, and the Continental Congress dispatched Major General Charles Lee from Cambridge, Massachusetts, to supervise the erection and manning of defenses.

General Clinton planned to sail close to Sullivan's Island and commence bombardment of the fort there. While that attack was under way, his transports would begin landing troops on Long Island, a short distance from Sullivan's Island. Once disembarked, the infantry would form up and march onto Sullivan's Island, overrunning and taking the battered fort, and, after Sullivan's Island had been taken, the invasion and occupation of Charleston would be a simple matter.

On the face of it, it was not a bad plan. Its weakness, however, was poor intelligence. The truth was that most Charlestonians supported the revolution, and, proud as they were of their city, they were bound and determined to halt any invasion. In addition to misreading popular sentiment, Clinton misjudged the distance separating Long Island from Sullivan's Island. Seen from a distance, it looked like a cinch to ford. Once landed on Long Island, however, the troops found the waterway between it and Sullivan's Island unfordable. They tried, but as each man struggled in the deep water, sharpshooters on Sullivan's Island picked them off.

That left the strictly naval phase of the amphibious assault. It also fared poorly. No one had told Clinton that Sullivan's Island was surrounded by sandbars and shallows. The deep-drafted British warships, one after the other, ran aground. And that wasn't all. Their broadsides seemed to have no effect against the walls of the fort. The cannonballs did not bounce off the walls so much as they were swallowed up by them. Clinton, in fact, had no idea what he was confronting. The forts were built of timber from local palmetto trees, small palms with fan-shaped leaves whose trunks were soft but incredibly dense and therefore almost indestructible. The stout little palmetto would become the emblem of South Carolina and is today featured on the state's flag below a crescent moon.

The Carolinians did not hunker down in their forts as the British bombarded. They returned a relentlessly punishing fire against vessels that could barely maneuver in the shallows. Admiral Peter Parker abandoned one of his frigates after it ran aground, and with his other ships taking severe damage, he withdrew his flotilla. It was a humiliating defeat, especially since Parker's ships mounted more than one hundred guns between them, whereas Fort Sullivan had just twenty-one cannon. Sixty-four Royal Navy sailors were killed in action and another 131 were wounded. The defenders of Charleston lost seventeen dead and twenty wounded. Charleston remained in Patriot hands.

SAVANNAH

British political leaders were becoming increasingly discouraged by the situation in America, but the military became more determined with each defeat. They saw gaining control of the South as essential to dismantling the revolution, and they decided to try a new target, another major port town, Savannah, Georgia. Lieutenant Colonel Archibald Campbell was assigned command of thirty-five hundred regulars, who were loaded into transports, and, under naval escort, sent on their way from Sandy Hook, New Jersey, on November 27, 1778. Campbell ordered anchors dropped on December 23 off Tybee Island, at the mouth of the Savannah River.

What Campbell confronted were no more than nine hundred Continentals and perhaps 150 militiamen, both forces commanded by General Robert Howe (no relation to the British Howe brothers). The prospects for the Patriots were not promising, and they soon grew worse. British general Augustine Prevost was on the march from Florida with reinforcements intended for Campbell. That aggressive commander, however, was so confident of his position that he decided to strike while the iron was hot. Instead of awaiting the arrival of Prevost, he landed his troops at Girardeau's Plantation, about two miles south of Savannah, on December 29. His men advanced against the Continental Army's defensive earthworks, which were positioned a half-mile south of town. They were manned by seven hundred troops in addition to all 150 or so militiamen. Campbell's thirty-five hundred overwhelmed the American defenders, not so much brushing them aside as simply rolling over them. The lucky ones retreated, leaving a single unit of Georgia militia straggling behind. These men soon found themselves utterly cut off, unable to traverse the causeway across Musgrove Swamp. Faced with British bayonets or the swamp, they chose the swamp. Of the eighty-three American soldiers killed in action on December 29, almost all were victims of drowning.

Campbell and his men marched into Savannah and occupied the city without encountering any further resistance. In the early autumn of 1779, French admiral d'Estaing, having failed in the first Franco-American amphibious operation against Newport, Rhode Island (Chapter 19), and having withdrawn to the French West Indies, decided to do something to retake Savannah. General Washington pleaded with him to coordinate with operations in the North, but d'Estaing was more anxious to redeem his reputation than serve his ally. He led to the Georgia coast a fleet of thirty-three warships, mounting a spectacular total of two thousand guns, along with transports that carried over four thousand troops.

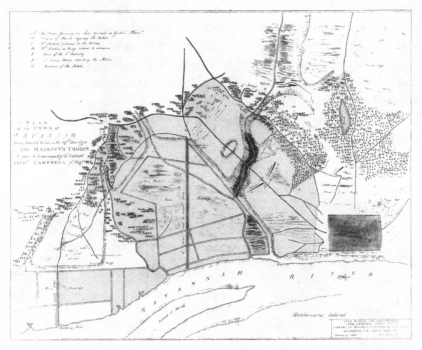

Map of the capture of Savannah (December 29, 1778). This is a hand-drawn copy made in 1891 of an original 1778 map (in the collection of the Georgia Historical Society) of British movements during the capture. UNIVERSITY OF GEORGIA LIBRARIES

The French admiral exploited the element of surprise to capture two Royal Navy warships and two Royal Navy stores (cargo) vessels, one of which carried a £30,000 payroll intended to pay the British troops now garrisoning Savannah.

With this quick success under his belt, d'Estaing immediately turned about and withdrew from Georgia. He returned on September 9 to land troops on Tybee Island, and on September 16, after American units united with the French troops, d'Estaing demanded that General Prevost surrender Savannah. The general responded by asking for a twenty-four-hour truce to ponder the demand. D'Estaing quite stupidly agreed, and Prevost used the time to prepare a defense of the city using some thirty-two hundred troops. Having done this, he sent a message to d'Estaing telling him that, after due consideration, he had decided not to surrender.

The battle did not commence until October 9, when a Franco-American force of nearly five thousand men attacked. Despite this advantage in numbers, the British fought from the cover of fortifications. Not only did Prevost hold out against the assault, he launched a vigorous counterthrust that killed or wounded eight hundred, including 650 French troops and Casimir Pulaski, the bold young Polish officer who had virtually created the Continental Army's cavalry. Prevost suffered no more than one hundred casualties.

Like Washington before him, Continental general Benjamin Lincoln, in command of the American contingent, begged d'Estaing to make another assault. It was to no avail. The Frenchman was afraid of being

Patriot general Benjamin Lincoln was forced to surrender Charleston to Sir Henry Clinton on May 12, 1780, but was tapped by General George Washington to accept Lord Cornwallis's sword in the British surrender of Yorktown on October 19, 1781. LIBRARY OF CONGRESS

caught in a storm or being ambushed by the enemy fleet. Besides, his men had been at sea so long that he now feared an outbreak of scurvy. His ships were in desperate need of refitting, he complained, and, with that, withdrew to Martinique. It was yet another Franco-American disappointment. Savannah would remain in British hands—until July 1782.

CHARLESTON, ROUND TWO

Having both conquered and held Savannah, Prevost decided to make a new attack on Charleston. In the spring of 1779, he forced Moultrie's troops to fall back on the town. But when he reached the outskirts of Charleston, he calculated that the inland defenses were truly formidable. He therefore suspended his advance and studied his options. In the meantime, South Carolina's Patriot governor, Edward Rutledge, took the astounding step of proclaiming his willingness to declare his state neutral.

Prevost was puzzled. In 1776, there was no talk of compromise. Now, there seemed a sudden collapse of will, which struck him as too good to be true. Soon, however, Prevost heard that General Lincoln was approaching at the head of a large American force. Now Prevost believed he had the explanation for Rutledge's willingness to open Charleston to

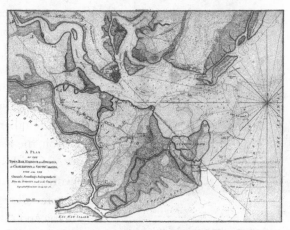

This map of Charleston, South Carolina, engraved in 1780 from cartography supplied by Sir Henry Clinton, includes the harbor and the approaches to the city.
UNIVERSITY OF ALABAMA DEPARTMENT OF GEOGRAPHY

the British. Prevost believed that Rutledge *wanted* him to enter Charleston so that he could fall under attack by Lincoln. Instead of obliging, Prevost withdrew to Savannah. Presumably to preserve morale among his soldiers—troops don't like to retreat—he encouraged them to loot liberally en route. This slowed his columns down, but that was hardly unusual for the British, who seldom hastened any march.

It was the end of 1779 before Henry Clinton cobbled together a new force to attack Charleston. He recalled to New York City three thousand soldiers who had been sent to Newport, Rhode Island, and added to these another thirty-five hundred troops: British, Hessian, and Loyalist. Royal Navy ranks furnished an additional five thousand men. With this mixed force of 11,500, Clinton boarded troopships in New York on December 26, 1779. Howling winter storms battered his fleet, scattering it, so that it was February 11, 1780, before the reassembled flotilla glided into Edisto Inlet. Clinton landed his soldiers and sailors on Johns Island, thirty miles south of Charleston.

Prevost had figured rightly that Charleston had grown militarily weak since 1776. Charlestonians essentially sat out most of the war, making plenty of money in the process by financing privateers—state-sanctioned pirates—commissioned by Congress to prey upon British shipping. Whatever privateer captains could purloin from the vessels they captured, they could keep. Privateers took a heavy toll on the British merchant marine, but they were driven more by profit than by patriotism. Soon, the elaborate defenses of Charleston, which had worked so well in the past, were allowed to fall into decay and disrepair. The palmetto forts on Sullivan's Island and James Island were abandoned. Only along the

The Siege of Charleston (June 28, 1776), engraved from an original nineteenth-century painting by Alonzo Chappel. NEW YORK PUBLIC LIBRARY

Neck, a narrow isthmus connecting Charleston with the mainland, were defensive fortifications still maintained.

Yet Clinton did not pounce. That was not in his character. Nevertheless, the tortuous deliberation with which he moved, though very much his custom, was difficult to explain in this circumstance, where his objective was so clearly vulnerable. Slowly, very slowly, he put together a siege force. His self-imposed delays were a gift to the Americans, giving them valuable time to patch up the defenses they had allowed to crumble. One is left to wonder whether Henry Clinton was purposely playing out the clock. In this war of attrition, both sides showed signs of wear. But Clinton was personally disgusted with the struggle. He had sent London his letter of resignation and was only awaiting a response authorizing him to yield command to Cornwallis.

That response reached him even as he continued, tediously, arranging his siege. London flatly refused to accept his resignation. Unable to quit, Clinton suddenly sped up his preparations. By the third week of March 1780, he was just outside of the city, awaiting some additional troops. Commodore Abraham Whipple, US Navy, realistically assessed the situation. His tiny flotilla was outrageously outgunned by the Royal Navy fleet hovering off-shore. On March 20, therefore, Whipple withdrew his ships from Charleston and sailed up the Cooper River. His timing was fortunate. British admiral Marriot Arbuthnot chose this very day to cross gingerly over the hazardous Charleston Bar. He was now within range of the city and prepared to provide massive artillery support for an overland assault.

The Cooper River flows along the east side of Charleston and the Ashley along the west. The rivers meet in Charleston Harbor at the southern tip of the city. On the night of March 28, Clinton's troops began crossing the Ashley above the city, deploying across the Neck, which thus bottled up the Patriot garrison within Charleston. There was no escape by sea or by land. On April 1, Clinton's sappers commenced digging trenches that would provide cover for a prolonged siege. Somehow, 750 Virginia Continentals slipped by the siege force on April 6 to join the garrison. It was a gallant but futile gesture. The garrison was still outnumbered on land, and nothing could be done about the massive naval firepower collected in the harbor. The reinforced garrison watched and waited.

Clinton completed his siege trenches on April 10. He dispatched a messenger to General Lincoln, demanding his surrender. Lincoln refused, and Clinton ordered the Royal Navy to commence firing on the city. He had specified that the navy gunners prepare "hotshot," loading their guns with heated ammunition called carcasses: hollowed-out cannonballs packed with combustible materials, already burning by the time they left the cannon's mouth. The hotshot assault was an incendiary attack intended to burn the town down.

The firebombing began on April 13, setting large portions of Charleston ablaze. Lincoln stood firm. He believed his situation, though desperate, was not hopeless. Continental general Isaac Huger was in the vicinity, he knew, with at least a regiment, maybe two, South Carolina militia in addition to three hundred to five hundred Continentals. Perhaps his arrival could turn the tide—or at least give Lincoln and his army a means of escape.

What Lincoln had not counted on was the presence of Colonel Banastre Tarleton, a British officer who did not fight like a regular. He was a ruthless and highly skilled commander of Loyalist forces and had a unique talent for guerrilla warfare. On April 14, with Major Patrick "Bulldog" Ferguson, he led a combined force of regulars and Tory Rangers against Huger's encampment at the village of Moncks Corner. Surprise was absolute, the assault savage, and American losses heavy. Huger made a very narrow escape, but his defeat deprived Lincoln's Charleston garrison of any hope of escaping Charleston intact. Lincoln gathered his officers in a council of war on April 19. He told them that the surrender of Charleston was now the only means of averting the complete destruction of both the garrison and the city.

Christopher Gadsden, lieutenant governor of North Carolina, who commanded a contingent of the garrison, flatly rejected surrender. He would not even hear the word, he said. He warned Lincoln that his capitulation would surely trigger civil insurrection in the Carolinas. The Continental Army would then have two enemies to fight, the British and the Carolinians.

Lincoln heard Gadsden out. The British, he ultimately decided, were the far more formidable foe. On April 21, therefore, he proposed surrender terms to General Clinton. The British commander replied with a demand for unconditional surrender. Lincoln asked for time to consider it. On the night of April 23, he sent a modest attack force in an attempt to punch a hole in the British siege line. The probe was quickly rebuffed.

Then a lull settled over the situation. It was May 8 before Clinton sent another surrender demand. Believing he might yet be able to extort some reasonable terms. Lincoln again refused. Clinton responded on the night of May 9. This time, it was not a written demand but a combined land and sea artillery bombardment the likes of which had probably never been seen in North America to that time. Reeling, Charleston's citizens themselves petitioned Lincoln to

The great British painter Sir Joshua Reynolds created this superb portrait of Banastre Tarleton, skillful and ruthless leader of Loyalist rangers, in 1782. NATIONAL ARCHIVES AND RECORDS ADMINISTRATION

surrender. On May 12, 1780, the American commander gave up, yielding in addition to the most important port in the lower South five thousand American soldiers, mostly Continentals, four hundred cannon, and six thousand muskets.

It was the worst American defeat in the American Revolution, a heavier loss than that of New York City or Philadelphia. Charleston was a portal opening into the entire lower South. Hold this place, and you could supply and reinforce and sustain armies anywhere in the region. Clinton's victory, Lincoln's defeat, instantly justified the British military decision to target the South. The fate of the revolution was now very much in doubt.

CHAPTER 22

A Trial of Souls

ON DECEMBER 23, 1776, THREE DAYS BEFORE THE BATTLE OF TRENton (Chapter 14), at an early low point of American fortunes in the revolution, Continental Army officers read aloud from a new essay by Thomas Paine. "These are the times that try men's souls," it began. "The summer soldier and the sunshine patriot will, in this crisis, shrink from the service of his country; but he that stands it now, deserves the love and thanks of man and woman." A great victory against the Hessians followed and a reversal of Washington's long retreat, but the trial of souls would continue, and combat in this revolution would often go against the Americans.

It was not just a matter of British strength, the wealth and might of a long-established empire pitted against an upstart set of colonies clinging precariously to the coastline of an American wilderness. Most revolutions fail not because of military or economic weakness but on account of human frailty. The Conway Cabal (Chapter 18) directed against Washington was an exhibition of faithlessness, selfishness, envy, and stupidity. Historians and others have often remarked on America's great good fortune in having among its colonial citizens the likes of John Adams, Benjamin Franklin, Thomas Jefferson, and George Washington, people of profound wisdom and ethical purpose. Perhaps no revolution has ever been served by such a collection of paragons come together at the right time and the right place for the right reasons. And yet, beside them, were a number of smaller men, profiteers, opportunists, and outright turncoats.

Becoming a Byword

History has produced two figures whose treachery was such that their very names became synonyms for treason. In World War II, Norway's minister president Vidkun Quisling sold out his nation to Nazi Germany. Ever since, *quisling* has been a byword for "collaborator." In the American Revolution, Benedict Arnold betrayed the Continental Army in which he served and the nation for which that army fought. Since then, a "Benedict Arnold" has been another way of saying "turncoat."

There was, however, a time when Benedict Arnold seemed an indispensable man. He was not only a talented officer but one who was bold and singularly courageous. He was instrumental in the capture of Fort Ticonderoga (Chapter 10) and performed under terrible circumstances with high valor in the misbegotten American invasion of Canada. Indeed, his brilliance and daring at the Battle of Valcour Island (Chapter 10) may have fallen short of victory, yet it saved the revolution nevertheless. And then there were the battles of Saratoga (Chapter 17), leadership of which Arnold seized from the obtuse Horatio Gates to win victories of great consequence.

With all this, Benedict Arnold was also deeply flawed, afflicted by defects in character that Sophocles or Shakespeare would have well understood. Arnold's fearlessness was fueled more by personal ambition than any other quality, and while he surely was a tactician of skill and ingenuity, he could not abide any superior who failed to acknowledge or reward these qualities. Indeed, only his capacity for contempt equaled the scope of his ambition. He judged his genius to be above everyone else's, and this made him impatient, intolerant, and, ultimately, without scruples.

Born in Norwich, Connecticut, in 1741, Benedict Arnold was the son of a middling family, whose father apprenticed him to a druggist. Young Arnold loathed the trade and, in 1758, ran away from his master to enlist in a New York militia company at the height of the French and Indian War. He did not take to soldiering, at least as a militiaman, much better than he had learning to be a druggist. Arnold deserted after just over a year and then ran to his mother to help get him out of trouble. In March 1760, he reenlisted in the militia, only to desert again—and, this time, returned to Norwich, where he managed to mend relations with the town druggist and not only resumed apprenticeship but saw it through to completion. By his twenty-first year, both of his parents had died, leaving him a respectable property by way of inheritance. He sold this, used the proceeds to move with his sister to New Haven, and there opened up his own combination pharmacy and bookstore.

To his own surprise, he proved an able shopkeeper and an even more savvy entrepreneur. As his shop prospered, he invested in the purchase of several trading vessels, which plied both the Canadian and West Indian trade routes. In 1767, now a prosperous New Haven burgher, he wed Margaret Mansfield, and subsequently became increasingly engaged in the cause of independence. In 1775, he was elected captain of a Connecticut militia company, which he led to Cambridge, Massachusetts, the epicenter of the emerging American Revolution.

What drove his newfound passion to be free of British bondage? He was by no means an ideologue. Instead, now that he was into shipping, he had learned to profit from smuggling—that is, evading the onslaught of Britain's newly enforced taxes and duties. Independence, he believed, would free him of their burden forever. Moreover, he expected great things by making a name for himself in a cause at once noble and supported so enthusiastically by the New England merchant community. He embarked on his revolutionary career with excitement and optimism. Even his disastrous wilderness march to the assault of Quebec at the end of 1775 did not dispirit him because, while the invasion failed catastrophically, it did result in his promotion to brigadier general in the Continental Army. His valor and resourcefulness at Valcour Island earned him a reputation for heroism—mostly—but there was already trouble in the air. Washington admired young Arnold, deeming him precisely the kind of enterprising officer he needed. But those closest to Washington found Arnold insufferable. To them, his chronic impetuosity and arrogance were not character flaws. They were the very foundation of his character. Most had sufficient classical education to know this epigram from Heraclitus: "Character is destiny." Accordingly, when, in February 1777, Congress created five new major generalships, Arnold was passed over. Worse, he was passed over in favor of officers junior to him.

This he could not brook. Benedict Arnold indignantly tendered his resignation, prompting Washington to plead with him to reconsider. His time, he assured Arnold, would come. Doubtless gratified that the commander-in-charge had made so personal an appeal, Arnold withdrew his letter, and, two months later, after deftly rebuffing a British assault on Danbury, Connecticut, he received his promotion to major general. Yet the vindication was not unalloyed. Congress positioned him on the roster conspicuously junior to the five who had been promoted before him. Arnold stewed, complaining that Congress had not so much promoted him as promoted others ahead of him. Once more, he submitted a letter of resignation.

What stopped him from actually leaving the Continental Army were the pressures of the war. At this time, Burgoyne began his advance into upper New York, and Arnold was summoned to join Horatio Gates's command in an operation to block the British general. The result, of course, were the battles of Saratoga (Chapter 17) and a spectacular display of Arnold's defiance of his commander.

A CONVALESCENCE IN STYLE

In his way, Horatio Gates was as deeply flawed as Benedict Arnold. He was capable of infinite pettiness, and he went out of his way to suppress reports of Arnold's tactical daring and personal courage at Saratoga. Fortunately for Arnold, few of Gates's subordinate officers had any affection for their commander. They saw to it that Congress learned the truth, and that body responded by finally conferring upon the major general the seniority he merited.

In the meantime, Arnold was convalescing from the serious leg wound he had sustained in the Bemis Heights phase of the Saratoga operation. He was assigned light duty in June 1778 as commander of the Philadelphia garrison, which had been installed in that city after General Howe withdrew his occupation forces. While the endurance and survival skills he had exhibited in the frigid wilderness of Canada were second to those of no man, he also took enthusiastically to life in the most civilized city in North America. The thing is, what passed for the "good life" there in the late 1770s took place in the high-toned social stratum of the city's Loyalists. The Tory lifestyle was elegant and amusing. Arnold and his wife were held in high esteem by this social set. At last, the irascible Arnold felt himself both admired and accepted. Arnold's Continental Army colleagues and fellow officers found their commander's fraternization with the enemy distasteful. If anything, Arnold relished their disdain and disapproval, seeing in it a golden opportunity to annoy and affront the envious subordinates nipping at his heels.

The downside to all this? Living like a Tory cost a great deal of money, a great deal more than Arnold had. The American garrison commander soon descended deeply into debt.

Arnold was being watched by Joseph Reed, president of the Pennsylvania Council. It was apparent that he was living far beyond his known income. In February 1779, Reed brought before the Continental Congress eight charges of official misconduct against Arnold. Among these were several allegations of embezzlement—the misappropriation of government funds to buy personal goods. Modern historians have no doubt that Arnold was guilty as charged, but, in 1779, the Continental Congress was not about to tarnish a hero. Four of the eight charges were dismissed out of hand, and of the four Congress investigated, Arnold was convicted of the two least serious. Washington, eager to clear the record, delivered a pro forma reprimand.

The government had done Benedict Arnold a huge favor, but, in his arrogance, he did not see it that way. Declaring that his sacred honor had been stained, he demanded to be cleared of *all* charges. While he awaited adjudication, Arnold occupied his time more pleasantly. His wife of five years, Margaret Mansfield, had died, leaving the high-living major general among the most eligible widowers in Philadelphia. Arnold was determined not to sell himself cheaply. He courted Peggy Shippen, the nineteen-year-old daughter of one of Philadelphia's wealthiest and most distinguished Tory families. Of course, courting at that level was far from a trivial investment, and Arnold dug himself deeper into debt, but he prevailed, married the young woman on April 8, 1779, and they embarked on a life together even more costly than that of his first marriage. For one thing, it took cash for a middle-aged man to keep a pretty nineteen-year old child of privilege interested. As before, Arnold was being watched. Sometimes he was questioned, and his answers became increasingly arrogant and evasive.

The Making of a Traitor

Reed and other agents of the Continental Congress were not the only eyes on Benedict Arnold. Sometime in 1779, Major John André, aide-de-camp to General Henry Clinton, began receiving letters hinting at the willingness of a certain senior American officer to render "his services to the commander-in-chief of the British forces in any way that would most effectually restore the former government and destroy the then usurped authority of Congress, whether by immediately joining the British army or cooperating on some concealed plan." He brought the letter to Clinton, who directed him to probe further by beginning a covert and coded correspondence with the officer.

André was a sophisticated officer, who knew how to read between the lines. Though the disaffected officer wrote of the "usurped authority of Congress," it was clear to Clinton's aide that he was actually little moved by loyalty to the Crown. He was desperate for cash—and that motive pointed directly to the identity of the officer in question. It could be none other than Benedict Arnold, whose spendthrift ways were common knowledge in Philadelphia, in Congress, and in both the Continental and British armies.

André shared his revelation with Clinton, who, through his aide, asked Arnold to lead an American army into an ambush. His offer for this service was coldly businesslike. The British commander-in-charge proposed a price of two guineas a head for each Continental soldier who surrendered. Arnold responded, in cipher, by demanding an additional £10,000 as an upfront retainer, nonreturnable. A hard bargainer, Clinton broke off negotiations. Alarmed, Arnold sought to reopen them in May 1780, adding, this time, a sweetener. He was in line for command of the Hudson River fortress at West Point, Arnold disclosed. Clinton's ears perked up, but no deal was offered. Weeks later, on June 15, Arnold wrote to Clinton that the West Point assignment he had mentioned was imminent. He posed the question, pointblank, would Clinton like him to arrange for the surrender of this key outpost, high above the

Hudson and commanding all traffic passing below? Arnold's price was again £10,000, regardless of outcome—doubled, "if I point out a plan of cooperation by which Sir Henry shall possess himself of West Point, the garrison, etc., etc."

Sir Henry proved as slow in his reply as he was in moving soldiers. At last, he presented his terms. Yes, Arnold could have his £20,000— but only if West Point actually surrendered. There would be nothing in advance. Nevertheless, he assured the general that, whatever the outcome, Clinton guaranteed that Arnold would not be "left a victim." Instead of pressing Clinton on what that rather oblique assurance actually meant, Arnold chose to believe that it was a promise of protection, presumably in the form of a British command position.

We do not know how difficult or easy it was for Benedict Arnold to choose treason. We do know that his creditors hounded him and that his young and pretty bride had needs. Weighing the two sets of pressures in the balance, Arnold accepted the terms. In fact, he acted instantly to show Clinton he could and would deliver. Recruiting his wife as a courier—for, he believed, no one would challenge her moving about in Tory social circles—he conveyed to the British commander-in-charge bits and pieces of the battle plan Washington and his French partner, General Comte de Rochambeau, were drawing up for their projected Yorktown campaign (Chapter 25). Apparently taking quite naturally to espionage, Arnold was careful to instruct his wife never to contact Clinton directly. Everything she had was conveyed through cutouts, most prominently among them Major André.

A mezzotint portrait of America's most infamous turncoat, Benedict Arnold, published in London on March 26, 1776, by Thomas Hart. BROWN UNIVERSITY

TREASONOUS MANEUVERING

As a thirsty man's mouth waters at the mere prospect of finding a stream at the next bend in the trail, so a bankrupt man feels relief at the mere prospect of a scheme about to bear fruit. Suddenly, however, Arnold was threatened by his own success. General Washington had plenty of well-meaning and perfectly honorable officers of indifferent military prowess. In Arnold, he saw a bold combat commander and skilled tactician. Yes, he was obnoxious, insufferable, even. So what? Arnold was the kind of man Washington wanted to lead a wing of the Continental Army in the forthcoming campaign at Yorktown, and he had every reason to believe that the glory-seeking major general would snap at the offer.

Arnold had been promised a garrison command at West Point. Imagine, then, his consternation when Washington offered him something so much grander and more glorious. Arnold declined the assignment as gracefully as he could. His wound, he said, though now three years healed, would not permit the degree of exertion such an important operation demanded. Washington was doubtless stunned. It was drastically out of character for Arnold to refuse an opportunity for heroics and, moreover, to admit a disability of any kind. Precisely because this was so shocking, Washington believed him, and when Arnold insisted that garrison duty at West Point was what his physical condition demanded at the moment, he was given that post, on August 3, 1780.

Arnold wasted no time in preparing the fort to accommodate an assault. To reduce the number of available defenders, he sent two hundred men of the garrison on a wood-cutting mission. When his subordinate officers told the new commandant that the great chain stretched across the Hudson to block passage of Royal Navy warships was in serious disrepair and required urgent attention, Arnold responded by ensuring that no one would do anything about it.

Next, Arnold colluded with Joshua Hett Smith, Loyalist brother of the former royal chief justice of New York, to weave a network of Tory spies. In this activity, Arnold was very open about his friendship with Smith. Among other Continental officers there were worries over the friendship between a high American commander, commandant of arguably the most important fort in the ongoing war, and an influential

Loyalist. But Arnold's marital situation provided effective cover. His wife was a Shippen, the Shippens were old-line Tories, and, it was only natural that her husband should have Tory friends. Doubtless emboldened by the ease with which his connection to Smith was accepted, Arnold now began to communicate directly with Henry Clinton—bombarding him with letters asking that he reconsider that retainer payment of £10,000.

Yet Arnold's recklessness in this affair did have a limit. In carrying out the espionage operation itself, he and Clinton arranged a ruse. Colonel Beverly Robinson, local leader of the Loyalist militia, would openly request a meeting with Arnold to discuss the disposition of Loyalist household property along the Hudson—an issue that was always both sensitive and pressing. Accompanying Robinson to the meeting would be Major André, out of uniform, dressed in the civilian attire of a local landowner and assuming the name John Anderson. André and Arnold agreed on a planning session together to lay out the details of the operation.

The British sloop *Vulture* was a familiar sight on the Hudson. It would draw no undue attention, and, for that reason, Major André chose it to convey him, on September 21, to a cabin Smith owned deep in the woods. There, he and Arnold schemed until after four in the morning. The hour was too late for André to go back to the *Vulture*, so he remained in Smith's cabin, intending to sail on the 23rd. War adheres to no one's calendar. Shortly before daybreak on September 23, Colonel James Livingston, commanding Patriot militia in the area, decided to attack the annoying Royal Navy sloop. He did not manage to sink it, but he damaged it so severely that it had to turn back without picking up Major André. His only option now was to make his way back to Clinton overland.

All Benedict Arnold really cared about was making £20,000. Accordingly, he talked André into remaining out of uniform and, as John Anderson, to carry back to Clinton a full packet of papers, which included a detailed description of the defenses in and around West Point. Tucking the documents between his calf and stocking, André pulled on his boot, and General Arnold wrote out official passes for André/Anderson and Smith, who agreed to guide him back to the British lines. With passes signed by no less a figure than the major general in command of West Point, Arnold guaranteed the pair that they would have no trouble with Continentals or militiamen as they made the long walk to Clinton's headquarters in Manhattan.

Unknown to Arnold, this was a most inopportune time to be walking about as a spy. The Continental Army had continued what the early revolutionary Committees of Correspondence had started: a sophisticated network of spies. Washington appointed Major General Benjamin Tallmadge as his chief of intelligence. One of his most important roles was to lead campaigns of counterintelligence against the strong network of Loyalists spies afoot. And as André and Smith were making their way to White Plains via Manhattan, Tallmadge was personally leading patrols in Fairfield and Westchester Counties in preparation for a strategy meeting between Washington and Rochambeau. Tallmadge worried that the general would be ambushed by Loyalists or even British regulars. That was the official reason for his patrol. Privately, he was deeply concerned by Benedict Arnold's conduct, even if others were not. Tallmadge had been asking questions, and one piece of information that interested him was Major General Arnold's issuance of a signed pass for one John Anderson, authorizing his safe conduct through American lines from West Point to Manhattan. To Tallmadge, this seemed a singular itinerary. Manhattan was the principal British stronghold in America. West Point was a major Continental Army outpost. Who was John Anderson? And why did Benedict Arnold want to get him from American headquarters to that of the enemy?

Tallmadge was doubtless still pondering this when he returned from patrol to find waiting for him a message saying militiamen had taken into custody in Westchester County a suspicious-looking man by the name of John Anderson. Even though he carried a pass endorsed by Major General Arnold, the militiamen thought it prudent to send him to Tallmadge's headquarters. While Tallmadge had been on patrol, his second-in-command, Lieutenant Colonel John Jameson, searched Anderson and found the plans of West Point as well as summaries of various confidential orders issued by General Washington. Jameson was not sure what the documents meant, but he knew their handwriting well enough. It was the work of Benedict Arnold. For this reason, he did not await the return of Tallmadge but sent the documents immediately to General Washington.

But, Tallmadge demanded, where was this John Anderson?

Jameson replied that he sent Anderson back to West Point, accompanied by a messenger bearing a letter addressed to Arnold, describing the papers that had been found on him. It had not occurred to Jameson that this bona fide Continental Army hero, Benedict Arnold, had given Anderson the documents. He concluded that they must have been stolen and that they were, therefore, a matter for Arnold to adjudicate with Anderson.

Tallmadge's reaction to Jameson's story is not recorded. However he responded, he wasted no time chewing out his subordinate. Instead, he issued orders to intercept Anderson and fetch him back. When Anderson found himself returned to Tallmadge's headquarters, this time face to face with the major general in charge of intelligence, he confessed to being Major John André of His Majesty's army.

Major André may have held a commission in the British army, but he was operating out of uniform and under a false name. That made him a spy. On September 29, 1780, Tallmadge convened a board of inquiry consisting of Nathanael Greene, William Alexander ("Lord Stirling"), Lafayette, Steuben, Arthur St. Clair, and Robert Howe, in addition to several junior general officers. André confessed, possibly in the hope that

British army major John André acted as turncoat Benedict Arnold's courier—and was hanged on orders of General George Washington on October 2, 1780. The artist and date of the mezzotint engraving, which is in the collection of the Tower of London, are unknown. WIKIMEDIA COMMONS

this would save him from the rope. Instead, having secured a full and free confession, the board recommended, without dissent, André's execution, forthwith. Washington reviewed the recommendation and issued the death warrant personally.

Shameless

As thoroughgoing as Tallmadge was, he had neglected to instruct the patrol he sent to apprehend "Anderson" that they should also bring back the messenger Jameson had sent to Arnold. In consequence, that man delivered Jameson's letter to the general. Thus, Benedict Arnold had it and read it even before Washington had received the documents seized from André's boot. Arnold bade a hasty farewell to his wife, boarded a barge, and was rowed down the Hudson and onto the *Vulture*. That vessel carried him to New York, where General Clinton accepted his offer to serve in His Majesty's army.

When Arnold received word of the death sentence pronounced upon André, he—now a certified turncoat in service to the king—scrawled an indignant letter to George Washington:

> *If after this just and candid representation of Major André's case the board of general officers adhere to their former opinion, I shall suppose it dictated by passion and resentment. And if that gentleman should suffer the severity of their sentence, I shall think myself bound by every tie of duty and honour to retaliate on such unhappy persons of your army as may fall within my power—that the respect due to flags and to the law of nations may be better understood and observed.*
>
> *. . . If this warning should be disregarded, and he should suffer, I call heaven and earth to witness that your Excellency will be justly answerable for the torrent of blood that may be spilt in consequence.*

The American commander-in-charge declined to dignify this remarkable missive with a response. He also declined to answer an appeal André wrote to him pleading not for clemency but for the courtesy of a soldier's death by firing squad rather than the ignominious noose: "Buoyed above the terror of death by the consciousness of a life devoted to honourable pursuits, and stained with no action that can give me remorse, I trust that the request I make to your Excellency at this serious period, and which is to soften my last moments, will not be rejected." On October 2, 1780, John André was hanged as a spy.

As for Benedict Arnold, he slipped beyond George Washington's grasp, but Washington immediately ordered that West Point and its surroundings be heavily reinforced, and then he resumed making plans for the fateful Yorktown campaign.

CONTINENTAL MUTINIES

The scheme to give up West Point to the British was foiled. That was the good news. The bad news—for the Americans—was that Arnold had not shared André's fate. The British commissioned him a brigadier general, which was a demotion from major general and carried with it a modest salary. The plot having failed, he was not, however, paid £20,000 or even £10,000 but a total lump sum of £6,315 in addition to an annual £360 pension. Moreover, he did not enjoy anything resembling a brilliant career in the British army. Sir Henry Clinton, apparently unwilling to put much trust in a traitor, tasked Arnold with leading sixteen hundred troops to raid Virginia. They captured Richmond and then destroyed a variety of warehouses, foundries, and mills. Virginia Patriot militia forced Arnold into retreat and a Continental force pursued in earnest. The force included Lafayette, whom Washington had ordered to summarily hang Arnold if he was captured. He was not captured; however, Arnold proved highly unpopular among his fellow officers, peers as well as subordinates, and on May 20, 1781, he was relieved of his Virginia command. Back in New York, he presented Sir Henry Clinton with many proposals to hit targets he believed would so cripple the American economy as to end the war. Clinton reluctantly authorized him to raid New London, Connecticut, which he and some seventeen hundred men razed on September 4, 1781. Two days later, Arnold prevailed at the Battle of Groton Heights (in New London and Groton, Connecticut) and earned renewed infamy for executing the Patriot garrison of Fort Griswold in Groton—some eighty-five men—*after* they had surrendered. From the British point of view, the high cost of Arnold's action, fifty-two British and Hessian troops killed, about 145 wounded, rendered the victory pyrrhic. Arnold fled America for Britain on December 8, 1781, when Cornwallis's surrender at Yorktown (Chapter 25) made it clear that the United States would prevail. He lived with his wife and family in London, where he was mildly admired by the Tories but thoroughly despised by the liberal Whigs—as well as by just about every professional army officer. He went into business with his sons in Canada in 1787 but was generally spurned by Canadian society and returned to London in 1791. He fought as a privateer in the French revolutionary wars, declined in health, and, in 1801, died, generally unlamented, in London.

The year of his treachery against the United States, 1780, also saw the unfolding of a mutiny in the Continental Army. It was a force long subject to abuse and neglect, its soldiers mostly unpaid and often unfed. The Second Continental Congress was roundly blamed, but it was a problem built into the Articles of Confederation. This first constitution for the United States, drawn up in 1777 but not ratified until March 1, 1781, created not so much a nation as a loose confederation of independent sovereign former colonies. Congress was without the power to levy direct taxes and had to rely on the states to fund the Continental Army voluntarily. There was never enough money, and what little there was fell into the hands of a Congress and Continental Army logistics administration that were a toxic blend of incompetence and corruption. In the end, the Continental Army was held together mainly by the character of George Washington.

That he held it together for so long was a superb achievement, but in May 1780 the first serious tremors were felt. At Morristown, New Jersey, that month, two Connecticut regiments refused to obey orders until they received their back pay. Washington responded by sending in a Pennsylvania Continental Army regiment to disarm them. A larger crisis was thereby defused, but in January 1781, those Pennsylvania troops—referred to as the "Pennsylvania Line" and famed for their implacable resolve—staged a far larger mutiny themselves. They protested having gone unpaid for months, their families left to destitution, they themselves clothed in rags no longer recognizable as uniforms. Their means of subsistence? A meager ration of bread and water. As if this were not abuse enough, they felt they had been swindled in the terms of their enlistment.

All had signed up for "three years or the duration of the war," but recruiters told them that their actual term would certainly be the shorter of the two. After three years, they demanded their release.

On the night of January 1, 1781, recruiting agents set up shop in the Pennsylvania camp with offers of $25 *in gold* for *new* recruits. This offer was made in the very presence of the half-naked, nearly starved veterans. It was enough to send twenty-four hundred of them into mutiny. They marched off to Princeton on January 3, set up camp, and sent a representative to plead their case to the Continental Congress.

Joseph Reed believed that the greatest danger of the Pennsylvania Line mutiny was the signal it sent to the British that the revolution was finally crumbling. Fearing that an attack was imminent, Reed promised to see to it that the mutineers' demands were met. In the meantime, however, Sir Henry Clinton took action. But it fell far short of a timely attack. Instead, he dispatched a pair of undercover agents to Pennsylvania to provoke additional mutinies.

They were remarkably ineffective. Their failure was in attempting to undermine the soldiers' patriotism when all the soldiers were outraged by was desperately unfair treatment. It was an appeal for redress of three pragmatic grievances: no pay, inadequate clothing, and meager provisions. Once Reed and then the Congress itself took action to right these wrongs, the mutinies ended. As for Clinton's agents, the soldiers of the Pennsylvania Line took them in hand and turned them over to their commanders, who had them hanged as spies. It was not the end of all mutinies, however. Shortly after the Pennsylvania Line was pacified, three New Jersey regiments rose up. George Washington chose not to emulate Reed. He forthwith ordered suppression of the mutiny by force. Ringleaders were identified, brought to trial, and summarily hanged.

MORE MONEY MATTERS

Treason and mutiny grab headlines, but most Americans during the revolution were more concerned with rampant and corrupt profiteering. Because Congress had no authority to tax, military funding was badly crippled, and the Continental Army looked to private sources of supply. Most of these individuals were unscrupulous, eager to exploit a market desperate for goods. Not only was Congress without fiscal authority, it lacked the power of regulation, and suppliers could extort from individual commanders almost whatever price they dared. The army was plagued not merely by a few wealthy speculators but by ordinary farmers and shop owners. It was a seller's market.

The Continental Congress did have one major fiscal authority. The Articles of Confederation authorized it to print all the paper money it wanted. At first, this proved a workable short-term solution. But paper money not backed up by "specie"—gold or silver—rapidly becomes valueless. Indeed, "Continental currency" soon became a byword for worthlessness itself. During the revolution and throughout most of the nineteenth century, a thing of no value was said to be "not worth a Continental."

As paying for supplies and provisions with Continental currency proved increasingly unacceptable even to the most corrupt suppliers, another alternative loomed. It was military seizure of supplies, food, and transportation, a practice sanitized by the phrase "impressment of goods." The Articles of Confederation did not give this power to Congress, but military commanders assumed it as being customary for armies at war. Most of them, however, were reluctant to exercise the power because they did not want to alienate the people on whose half they were supposedly fighting. Political leaders of the revolution were certainly alarmed by the prospect of the Continental Army or a Patriot militia behaving as the enemy did.

What was left? Under the Articles, Congress had the power to seek and obtain foreign loans. And this it did—relentlessly. Ultimately, it was aid from abroad that financed the American revolution, especially if by "finance," one means staving off bankruptcy. The idealism expressed in the Declaration of Independence was inspiring, and inspiration was without question necessary to creating and sustaining the American Revolution. Yet, though necessary, it was not sufficient. The revolution was decided on the field of battle as well as in the hearts, minds, and consciences of men and women—worldwide, including those individuals and governments that had deep pockets. The British army and navy had to be overcome, as did human frailty in the form of treason, mutiny, and greed.

CHAPTER 23

A Hero's Life

THE ROYAL NAVY STOOD A MUCH BETTER CHANCE OF STRANGLING THE American Revolution than the British army had of defeating it. Sea power could blockade ports, keeping imports out and exports from ever leaving. Ships could also transport troops faster than they could march overland. Amphibious operations could quickly concentrate British forces where the Patriot forces were weakest. Waterways were the highways of North America in the eighteenth century.

True, the Royal Navy was not the dazzlingly brilliant force that it had been during the French and Indian War and would again become during the Napoleonic Wars. Yet it was still sufficiently formidable to cut off North America from all trade and military aid. Crown and Parliament, however, feared blowing up the rebellion into a new international war and so largely restricted the navy's role to supporting land operations until the Franco-American alliance was concluded in 1778. At this point, the revolution had become truly international, and so the Royal Navy began to engage in earnest.

On the face of it, America did not stand much of a chance. As of 1775, the Royal Navy had 131 ships of the line and 139 warships of lesser size. The rebellious colonies had no navy at all. John Adams persuaded the Continental Congress to create one, and a tiny collection of small craft was cobbled together before Congress also resolved to build thirteen frigates. In addition to this federal effort, eleven of the thirteen states put together their own small navies. Finally, Congress commissioned civilian vessels as privateers and commerce raiders, authorizing them to commit acts of piracy against British shipping. By 1783, the end of the American Revolution, the Royal Navy fleet had grown to 468 vessels. The Continental Navy had grown as well, to a total of fifty-three ships—not all of which survived to the end of the war.

AGAINST ALL ODDS

Even with the services of the French navy from 1778 on, the odds were stacked heavily against America at sea. Traditional seaborne warfare was all about the numbers. The side with more ships and more guns on those ships pretty much always prevailed.

Still, all was not well with the Royal Navy at the time of the revolution. In 1771, the Earl of Sandwich became first sea lord, the equivalent of secretary of the navy. Extraordinarily corrupt in an era of generally corrupt British politicians, Sandwich did little to maintain the navy's ships, which fell into disrepair. As for the fleet's officer corps, Sandwich used naval rank as a means of rewarding political cronies. By the outbreak of the American Revolution, the Royal Navy was led by mediocrities and incompetents who sailed rotting ships. A measure of the decline in Royal Navy morale was the loss of sixty thousand sailors between 1774 and 1780 to a combination of desertion and in-service disease due to poor rations and the negligence of officers. The navy was critically and chronically short of sailors and relied on *impressment*—essentially abduction—to provide crews. Corruption, decay, and discouragement in the Royal Navy provided a narrow window through which the Americans might find some victories.

MAIDEN BATTLES

On June 2, 1775, the four-gun British schooner HMS *Margaretta*, along with the sloops *Polly* and *Unity*, sailed into Machias, up in Maine, to take on timber to build British barracks in Boston. Even though these were just three small vessels, the local Patriots had no ships at all. They were, however, immensely resourceful men. Hearing that the officers and crew of HMS *Margaretta* were churchgoers, the local militia stormed the chapel in Machias on Sunday, June 11. As sailors clambered out of church windows and ran for their ship, some forty militiamen set off in the few small fishing boats close at hand and forced their way aboard the schooner, capturing it after a brief fight. Two days later, HMS *Unity* surrendered—but *Polly* managed to get away. *Margaretta* was rechristened *Liberty* and put into the hands of Jeremiah O'Brien, who dueled against the Royal Navy schooner *Diligent*, which it succeeded in capturing. *Liberty* and *Diligent* thus became the first two ships of the Massachusetts navy. (The fate of *Unity* is unknown.)

On March 1776, the Continental Congress sent the newly created Continental Navy on its first major naval expedition—which turned out to be its only one. Congress commissioned a Rhode Islander farmer named Esek Hopkins, who also had some experience at sea, to command a squadron tasked with landing Continental marines in an amphibious assault against Fort Montegu on the British-held island of Nassau (at the time called Providence, or New Providence). The action took place on March 3–4, and the marines not only took the fort but bagged one hundred cannon and mortars—along with the island's royal governor, Montfort Browne, who was later exchanged for a captured American officer.

He Called Himself Jones

Hopkins led eight ships to Nassau, all converted merchant vessels mounting between twenty and twenty-four guns. Four of his subordinate officers were ranked as captains and several more as lieutenants, among whom

Esek Hopkins, the first commander-in-chief of the Continental Navy, led a successful amphibious raid on British-held Nassau (March 3, 1776) but subsequently failed to capture HMS *Glasgow* (April 6, 1776), effectively ending his naval career. The engraving, by John Chester Buttre, was published in 1881. WIKIMEDIA COMMONS

was a young Scotsman, John Paul Jones. Born John Paul in 1747, he was the son of a gardener employed by a Scots squire. The son had no desire to follow in his father's footsteps and found instead an apprenticeship to a shipowner. His master's bankruptcy released John Paul early from his apprenticeship, and he found a berth on a slaver. Next, in 1766, when he was only nineteen, he signed on as first mate on another slave ship.

His rise at sea was rapid, but John Paul could no longer stomach the cruel slave trade. He sold his financial stake in the slaver and took ship, as a passenger, bound for Scotland. That is when fate took a hand. En route, the captain *and* first mate both sickened and died of "fever." Assuming command, John Paul sailed the ship safely to its destination. Its owner rewarded him with a share of the cargo, word of his achievement spread, and he was quickly hired as captain of the *John*, out of Dumfries, Scotland. On his second voyage to the West Indies in that vessel, Paul ordered the ship's carpenter flogged for neglect of duty. Flogging was the standard mode of discipline in the eighteenth century, but the unfortunate sailor died under the punishment, and, after the *John* returned to port, the carpenter's father brought charges of murder against Paul. Captain John Paul, quickly tried and acquitted, returned to sea.

The young mariner was back in the West Indies during 1773 as captain of the *Betsy*, out of London. A mutiny erupted, during which Captain Paul killed the ringleader. In fact, witnesses subsequently testified that the mutineer rushed Paul and, in the process, impaled himself on the captain's drawn sword. Mutiny was so common in the eighteenth century that almost no jury would have convicted a captain for using deadly force to end one. But Paul feared that the earlier death of the carpenter had poisoned his reputation, and he left for America before the trial commenced. With remarkably little imagination, once he reached America, Paul disguised his identity by calling himself John Paul Jones.

Jones could not find a job and lived on the charity of friends until the outbreak of the revolution. Borrowing some money, he traveled to Philadelphia, where he found employment fitting out the *Alfred*, the first of the vessels Congress bought for the Continental Navy. He made connections with the leaders of the new service, and, on December 7, 1775, was commissioned first lieutenant serving aboard the *Alfred*.

JONES TAKES COMMAND

About midnight on April 6, 1776, Esek Hopkins led five ships back from the West Indies and was intercepted by the twenty-gun HMS *Glasgow*. Although outnumbered five to one, *Glasgow* pounced off Block Island, Rhode Island. The attack inflicted twenty-four casualties among the American sailors and badly damaged the *Alfred*. Hopkins failed to make a dent in the enemy, and this humiliation simply erased his earlier triumph at Nassau. Worst of all, the failure of the Continental Navy broke its morale, prompting officers to resign their commissions. Crews also left the service and turned to privateering. The American fleet, idled in port, was blockaded by the British in December 1776. With that, Congress cashiered Hopkins.

One of the collateral casualties of the *Glasgow* affair was the court-martial for cowardice of the captain of the USS *Providence*. He was relieved of command and replaced by John Paul Jones, who sailed *Providence* as the flagship of a small flotilla, which evaded the British blockade and embarked on a remarkable cruise, in which Jones captured or sank twenty-one Royal Navy warships, transports, and commercial vessels in addition to a Loyalist privateer. All of this was accomplished before the end of 1776.

The Continental Navy was revived—albeit very nearly as a one-man force. Moreover, Jones was far from becomingly modest. With considerable justification, he was arrogant and dismissive. Arguing from the platform of his record, he voiced objection to being classed as junior to seventeen other captains. Congress did not want to alienate those other officers, but it could not afford to lose Jones, either. The decision was therefore made to reward him *and* at the same time remove him from proximity to his fellow officers. On June 14, 1777, Jones was assigned command of the sloop *Ranger* and ordered to sail forthwith to France, where he was to take command of the frigate *Indien*, which was being built in Amsterdam for the Continental Navy. It would be the American navy's largest and best-armed ship.

Jones arrived in Brest in December, only to discover the *Indien* had been handed over to the French navy by the American commissioners, who were seeking to consummate the military alliance with the government of Louis XVI. Jones accepted the disappointment as a diplomatic necessity and left Brest in the *Ranger* on April 10, 1778 with a crew of 140. Then, on April 27-28, 1778, he raided Whitehaven on the Solway Firth in Scotland, personally leading a landing party in spiking the guns of two forts and the burning of three British warships riding at anchor. He had wanted to burn every ship in Whitehaven but ran out of time. No matter. John Paul Jones led the only American military operation on British soil during the revolution. In short, Jones had taken the American Revolution to the mother country.

John Paul Jones is depicted as a pirate in this undated British caricature. WIKIMEDIA COMMONS

Next, Jones sailed the *Ranger* across the Irish Sea to Carrickfergus, where he captured HMS *Drake* after a one-hour battle, in which Jones lost eight men killed or wounded, but inflicted forty casualties on the British. When Jones returned to Brest, on May 8, he brought with him seven captured vessels of the Royal Navy, together with their POW crews.

Captain of the *Bonhomme Richard*

In the summer of 1779, with the French alliance formalized, five French ships and two privateers were assigned to the command of John Paul Jones. He took as his flagship the East Indiaman *Duras*, a large merchant vessel built for long voyages and now fitted out with cannon. Jones rechristened it *Bonhomme Richard*—the "Good Man Richard"—in homage to Benjamin Franklin, a man wildly popular with the French and the publisher of *Poor Richard's Almanac*, which was, if anything, even more popular in that country. The ship's new name was, in fact, a brilliant stroke of diplomacy and public relations.

Jones embarked on a new campaign, aiming to hit every target of opportunity that presented itself. Off Flamborough Head in the North Sea off the coast of York, he sighted two British men o' war on September 23, 1779. They were the forty-four-gun *Serapis* and the twenty-gun *Countess of Scarborough*, which escorted a convoy of forty merchant vessels. Jones was well aware that the *Bonhomme Richard* was neither more nor less than a converted cargo vessel, built for maximum capacity, not speed and maneuverability. Its forty-two guns made it inferior in firepower to *Serapis*, especially in combination with the *Countess*. Nevertheless, the opportunity was far too important to pass up.

Jones chased *Serapis* with his flagship and deployed the three other vessels accompanying him—*Vengeance*, *Pallas*, and *Alliance*—to pursue the *Countess*. Combat commenced under a moonlit sky and did not begin auspiciously for Jones. Two of his cannon exploded, widening the firepower gap between *Bonhomme Richard* and *Serapis*. Jones, however, deftly outmaneuvered *Serapis* to avoid coming broadside to broadside with it, a position in which he would be outgunned. Instead, he rammed the enemy's stern, preventing *Serapis* from firing a broadside. The British captain, however, believed Jones had made a fatal error and called out to him: "Has your ship struck?" (meaning *Have you struck (lowered) your flag—surrendered?*) Jones shot back: "I have not yet begun to fight."

With that, the two vessels drew apart, and, this time, it was *Serapis* that collided—unintentionally—with the *Bonhomme Richard*. Jones immediately ordered his crew to lash onto the British vessel. With the enemy held captive, he pounded *Serapis* with his still-operational cannon. The British vessel returned fire, but it was too little too late, and, after two hours of bombardment, it was *Serapis* that "struck." As for the *Countess of Scarborough*, USS *Pallas* defeated it after a battle of two hours, in which four Royal Navy sailors were killed and twenty wounded, three of whom subsequently died.

Bonhomme Richard had been so severely battered that Jones abandoned it, transferring his flag to the prize ship, *Serapis*, which he sailed into Texel, Holland. He turned over that prize to the French, together with two of his own vessels, retaining only *Alliance*, in which he continued to raid British shipping before embarking, in December 1780, on his return to the United States in the French military transport, the *Ariel*. Along the way, Jones captured HMS *Triumph*, which, however, escaped before he could haul it into an American port.

JONES'S FATE

John Paul Jones was not only the most extraordinary officer in American naval history, he was the greatest seagoing raider since Sir Francis Drake. While he triumphed over the Royal Navy, however, he could not survive the envy of brother officers in the Continental Navy. The Congress proposed promoting him to rear admiral, which would have made him senior to all others in the American service. When fellow officers blocked this move, Congress promised him command of HMS *America*, under construction as the biggest vessel in the Continental fleet. Just before it was launched, however, Jones was informed it would be given to the French. As it turned out, so was Jones. He sailed with the French navy until the end of the war.

With peace, Jones left both the French and American service to accept a commission as admiral to Catherine the Great of Russia. He fought against the Turks, defeating the sultan's fleet—only to fall victim to envious Russian naval officers, who hounded him out of Catherine's service. Jones moved to Paris in 1789, where, his health and spirit broken, he died in 1793. It was only in 1905 that his remains were transferred from a Paris cemetery to the United States. In 1913, they were brought to final rest in a place of honor at the Naval Academy in Annapolis, Maryland.

FRANCE FINALLY DELIVERS

Admiral Charles Henri Hector d'Estaing proved a terrible disappointment to his American allies (Chapters 19 and 21), and every major French naval operation in American waters failed through 1781. Nevertheless, in engagements farther from American shores during this period, other French naval commanders fared much better against the Royal Navy. George Brydges Rodney, a superb Royal Navy commander, captured the island of St. Eustatius on February 3, 1781. It was a possession of the Netherlands, which had become an American ally in the revolution. Unfortunately for the British, Rodney quickly became embroiled in lawsuits over the spoils of war. He and British merchants made conflicting claims to war prizes, and Rodney, preoccupied, failed to make a scheduled rendezvous with Admiral Samuel Hood, whose assignment was to blockade Fort Royal off Martinique in order to bottle up the French fleet there. Absent Rodney, the French were able to evade Hood and add Tobago to other West Indian prizes taken earlier in the war. In the meantime, Admiral Pierre André de Suffren de Saint Tropez defeated the Royal Navy off the coast of the Portuguese-held Cape Verde Islands.

The Royal Navy began to recover when Admiral Rodney finally rejoined Admiral Hood in the West Indies on February 19, 1782. During April 9–12, 1782, in the epic Battle of Saints Passage, Rodney defeated and captured Admiral François Joseph Paul, comte de Grasse aboard his sumptuous flagship, the *Ville de Paris*. This victory, however, came after Admiral de Grasse had already successfully prevented the British fleet from evacuating Lord Cornwallis and his army from the Yorktown peninsula in the battle that ensured American independence (Chapter 25).

Another post-Yorktown British naval victory came at Gibraltar, when Admiral Richard Howe, called out of retirement, broke Spain's three-year siege of the British island fortress. Unlike the capture of Admiral de Grasse, this triumph did have some effect on the outcome of the American Revolution, giving Britain a stronger bargaining position at the Paris peace conference.

CHAPTER 24

The Backcountry War

DEFEATED AND DISCOURAGED IN NEW ENGLAND EARLY IN THE war, British strategists turned to targets in the southern colonies, where, they believed, support for the revolution was soft. Stunningly, Loyalist support proved weaker than expected, and Patriot forces gained control over most of the South during 1775 and 1776 (Chapter 21). After a lull in southern theater action during 1777, Continental major general Robert Howe launched an expedition into the South in 1778 with hopes of getting a foothold in British-controlled St. Augustine, Florida. After failing to persuade local militias to aid his campaign, Howe was replaced in September 1778 by Major General Benjamin Lincoln, who failed to eject the British from Savannah, Georgia, in September-October 1779 and the next year was among the five thousand American soldiers captured in the fall of Charleston, South Carolina, to the British on May 12, 1780 (Chapter 21).

A NEW KIND OF BRITISH COMMANDER

Both Savannah and Charleston were major port cities, both important to the supply of American forces in the South but both vulnerable to the kind of warfare for which the British were generally best prepared: combat by the regular naval and ground forces that had been created to fight and win European wars. British commanders tended to be conventional, unimaginative, rigid, and, despite the experience of the French and Indian War, unwilling to adapt to conditions farther inland, in what settlers called the backcountry.

A striking exception to this rule was Banastre Tarleton, a dashing cavalry officer who created the British Legion, a regiment of Loyalists who became infamous as the Green Dragoons—named for their forest-green uniform coats—or Tarleton's Raiders. But their official designation, as a "legion," reflected Tarleton's imaginative but ruthless approach and the nature of his unit. In the eighteenth century, a "legion" embodied a decidedly unconventional concept of combat. It combined in a single regiment and under a single commander infantry and cavalry—in the form of dragoons, infantry soldiers who maneuvered on horseback but fought dismounted—and sometimes artillery as well. The legion was designed for independent action, great mobility, and rapid movement. Tarleton made the most of these qualities.

In December 1776, he was instrumental in the capture of Continental major general Charles Lee at Basking Ridge, New Jersey (Chapter 14), which earned him rapid promotion from a mere lieutenant to lieutenant colonel. His true brilliance, however, was revealed during the siege and capture of Charleston in the spring of 1780. Sir Henry Clinton and Lord Cornwallis focused narrowly on taking the city, but Tarleton convinced them of the necessity of simultaneously suppressing resistance in the hinterland. Clinton and his like dismissed the grassroots Patriot militias as so many backcountry bumpkins, but Tarleton saw them as the core of the revolution in the South. At the Battle of Monck's Corner (April 14, 1780), northwest of Charleston, he routed Patriot militia under Isaac Huger and William Washington, killing fourteen, wounding nineteen, and capturing sixty-four of the five hundred men engaged, sending the American commanders into humiliating flight. On May 6, Tarleton fought the survivors of Monck's Corner, who had been reinforced by troops under Colonel Anthony White, at Lenud's Ferry, on the Santee River, northeast of Monck's Corner. In the initial clash, White's men captured a Legion officer and seventeen dragoons, an action to which Tarleton responded by personally leading a bold cavalry charge that liberated the POWs and killed or wounded five Patriot officers and thirty-six militiamen. Tarleton lost two men and four horses. As a result of the Patriot defeats at Monck's Corner and Lenud's Ferry, the American cavalry in the region was neutralized, and the escape routes from Charleston were cut off. In themselves, Tarleton's triumphs were tactically punishing, but, more importantly, they also proved the strategic leverage of skillful backcountry warfare. The two defeats American units suffered forced General Lincoln to surrender the city of Charleston, its garrison army of five thousand, and *himself* to General Clinton on May 12.

THE WAXHAWS MASSACRE

The line between unconventional warfare and atrocity can be extremely fine, and the daring raider of Monck's Corner and Lenud's Ferry crossed it into mass murder at Waxhaws, South Carolina. Some 420 of the 3rd Virginia Continentals were on the march to Charleston under Colonel Abraham Buford when that city fell. This suddenly left the 3rd Virginia as the only intact Patriot unit in all South Carolina. Now recognizing the effectiveness of Tarleton's backcountry operations, Cornwallis ordered him (and others) to track down Buford and destroy his force. The commander of the British Legion dispatched his scouts and quickly located the bivouac of the 3rd Virginia at Waxhaws Creek, near the present-day town of Buford, close to the northern border of South Carolina. Tarleton mustered his Legion dragoons and infantry as well as some British regulars to make the hundred-plus-mile dash to the site of the bivouac. To increase the speed of the advance, Tarleton once again acted unconventionally, ordering his infantrymen to ride with the dragoons, two men to a saddle. The first casualties of the operation were horses, a good many of which perished in the late May low-country heat under the strain of their heavy loads. Tarleton replaced the dead mounts with horses he stole along the way.

On May 29, having advanced 105 backcountry miles in just fifty-four hours, he encountered the rear of Buford's column, which had just left its bivouac. He sent to Colonel Buford a messenger bearing both a flag of truce and a demand for surrender. "If you are rash enough to reject the terms," Tarleton's note warned, "the blood be upon your head." To this, Buford scrawled his reply, "I reject your proposals and shall defend myself to the last extremity," and returned the note to the messenger.

No sooner did the British commander receive the reply than he launched a savage attack. Buford had not acted quickly enough to consolidate his column, which was strung out in a long, loose line. His officers remained astoundingly calm, ordering their men to hold their fire until the attackers were within ten paces. This would have been a perfectly good tactic if the Americans had been fighting from cover. But they were fully exposed, and thus quickly overrun and overridden in a whirlwind of slaughter.

Amid the bloodbath, Buford surrendered, asking Tarleton "for quarter"—in other words, throwing his Virginians on the victor's military honor and mercy. Tarleton accepted the surrender but then summarily ordered his men to put the disarmed Continentals to the bayonet.

Why would he do such a treacherous thing?

After the battle, Tarleton claimed that a shot had been fired at him while the surrender terms were being negotiated. Survivors' accounts strongly attest that no such thing happened. More likely, Tarleton had decided that harshly punitive terrorism would effectively demoralize the local Patriots. Of the 420 Continentals engaged, Tarleton's bayonets killed 113 and wounded 150 more. Those wounded, who were captured but soon paroled, carried with them the story of the Waxhaws Massacre, which was the bloodiest single encounter of the American Revolution. (Fifty-three others were captured unwounded and were not immediately paroled.)

Not only did Tarleton's atrocity fail to suppress Patriot fervor in the South, it revived and inflamed it. The phrase "Tarleton's quarter!" became a Patriot battle cry.

HUMILIATION AT CAMDEN

The Patriot defeats put all of South Carolina in British and Loyalist hands. General Washington selected Nathanael Greene, one of the most capable Continental generals, to be in charge of regaining the state, but Congress overruled him, installing instead Horatio Gates, the nominal victor in the Saratoga battles. With great frustration and reluctance, Washington bowed to the authority of Congress, and Gates embarked for Camden, South Carolina, a town far inland, garrisoned by twenty-two hundred troops under the personal command of Lord Cornwallis. Gates combined militia with his Continentals to build a force of forty-one hundred, giving him a two-to-one numerical superiority over Cornwallis. Simple arithmetic does not determine victory, however. Gates's paper advantage failed to reflect the reality that a good many of his men, unaccustomed to the mid-Carolina climate, were down with sicknesses associated with swamplands and marshes. Everywhere in the battlegrounds of the American Revolution, debility and disease took a heavy toll on armies, but nowhere more than in the southern interior.

It was not exceptional for an army's paper strength to be halved by illness. But Gates not only failed to account for disability in his manpower calculations, he also somehow spectacularly miscalculated his available numbers, deceiving himself into believing that he marched with nearly seven thousand effectives. But he had perhaps two thousand men fit for action, a truth that seems to have belatedly dawned on him during the night of August 15, 1780. This did not stop him from ordering a nocturnal advance against his intended objective, Camden. By happenstance, Cornwallis had that evening ordered a detachment out of the town to reconnoiter for American forces. This group blundered into Gates's column at about 2:30 on the morning of August 16. Still believing he held the advantageous position, Gates ordered an attack—though he himself chose to observe the action from the safety of the rear while subordinate officers, among them "Baron" de Kalb, led the attack.

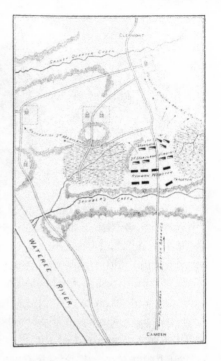

Map of the Battle of Camden (August 16, 1780) from John Fiske, *The American Revolution* (Boston: Houghton, Mifflin & Co., 1891).

While Gates was cowardly in thus relinquishing field command, he had put his forces into hands more competent and valiant than his own. Yet there was little Kalb could do with men who were sickly and inexperienced. The British did not wait meekly to be attacked but seized

General Johann de Kalb falls in the disastrous Battle of Camden (August 16, 1780).
LIBRARY OF CONGRESS

the initiative, and the left wing of the American line was shattered by the very first British assault. The right, however, performed better. Unlike the left, which consisted mostly of militia troops, the right was manned by Maryland and Delaware veterans, who held their ground until two of their commanders, Ortho Williams and Baron de Kalb, were badly wounded and taken out of action (Kalb would later succumb to his injuries). The right wing now dissolved and followed the left in a rout.

Just seven hundred of the forty-one hundred American soldiers on Gates's roster reached the safe haven of Hillsboro, South Carolina, three days after the battle. The Battle of Camden (August 16, 1780) cost nine hundred killed or wounded in Gates's command, and a thousand more were made prisoners of war. This reduced the Patriots' forces in South Carolina to two thousand, more than half of them too sick to fight. As for Gates, he had departed the field as soon as he saw the left wing collapse. Washington did not dismiss him from the Continental service but he relieved him of command for nearly the rest of the war. Gates was permitted to rejoin the army, at Newburgh, New York, only during the closing days of the American Revolution, after a 1782 congressional inquiry, which cleared him on charges of cowardice, apparently accepting his claim that his purpose in departing the field had been to ensure his survival to rebuild his army.

REVERSAL OF FORTUNE AT KING'S MOUNTAIN
Flushed with victory, Cornwallis left Camden on September 8, 1780, and headed toward North Carolina, from which he planned to sweep all

Patriot forces. He divided his command into three columns. He himself led the main force, Banastre Tarleton was put in charge of the Loyal Legion along with the British regular light infantry, and Major Patrick Ferguson led Loyalist militia forces.

Cornwallis was soon dismayed and not a little stunned by the dogged

The Battle of King's Mountain (October 7, 1780) in a nineteenth-century depiction by Alonzo Chappel. STATE ARCHIVES OF NORTH CAROLINA

resistance of North Carolina Patriots. Did they not realize that the South had been lost? Fought between an unknown number of Cornwallis's forces and some 150 Americans under William R. Davie, on September 26, 1780, the Battle of Charlotte is generally deemed a Patriot victory, since the British lost twelve killed and forty-seven wounded to just six killed on the American side. Nevertheless, Cornwallis did occupy Charlotte briefly. His heavy losses were due to a lack of intelligence about the Patriot strength in the town. Tarleton, who would normally have reconnoitered the objective before Cornwallis advanced on it, was down with dysentery, one of the hazards of life in the field.

Cornwallis did not stay long in Charlotte. With Patriot militia persistently attacking his lines of supply and communication, he gave up Charlotte. Sending Major Patrick Ferguson with elements of the 71st Regiment of Foot to screen his main column from Patriot irregulars and snipers, Cornwallis moved out. Then he decided to send Ferguson and his regiment out ahead of the main column to escort Loyalist forces along the Appalachian foothills in the borderlands between South and North Carolina. This was a serious tactical error. Separated from the main body of troops, Ferguson and his men found themselves under continual attack by Patriot militia commanded by Colonels Charles McDowell, John Sevier, Isaac Shelby, William Campbell, Benjamin Cleveland, James Wilson, and Joseph Winston.

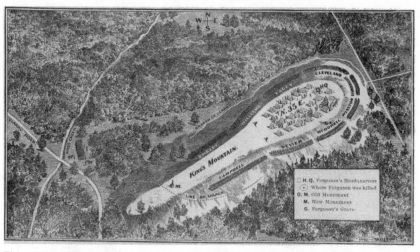

This stylized diagram depicts the American attack on the Loyalist militia led by Colonel Patrick Ferguson, a Scottish officer in the British army, at King's Mountain (October 7, 1780). Ferguson was killed in this major Patriot victory. NEW YORK PUBLIC LIBRARY

Reeling, Ferguson sought refuge by retreating to the Catawba River, from which he led his troops up King's Mountain on the border between North and South Carolina. His tactical intention was to ensconce himself and his command on the densely forested high ground. On October 7, Ferguson dug in and took a stand. To his horror, however, he soon realized he was surrounded by Patriot forces. Although the two sides were fairly closely matched in number—Ferguson holding a slim advantage with 1,105 men to the Americans' nine hundred militia troops—the envelopment was total, and the Patriots did not hesitate to fight fiercely in close combat. Just as Ferguson was pulling the trigger on an American militia officer, a sniper cut him down. The ferocity of the American assault then intensified, driven by cries of "Remember Tarleton's Quarter!" Two hundred ninety Loyalist militiamen were killed and another 163 wounded. The remainder who were engaged in the battle, 668 men, were taken prisoner. Considering the bloodthirsty nature of the engagement, Patriot losses were light, with nineteen killed and thirty-five wounded, making for a splendid victory that marked the reversal of British fortunes in the

South. Cornwallis withdrew back into South Carolina, and Loyalist influence in North Carolina had been brought to a permanent end.

THE BATTLE OF COWPENS

After going through two unsuccessful commanders in the South—Generals Lincoln and Gates—Washington finally prevailed on Congress to allow him to appoint his first choice, Nathanael Greene, to command of the entire southern region. He saw in Greene a general adept at leading and fighting conventional military forces yet also skilled in the use of irregulars, rangers, and guerrillas. Appointed to command in October, he did not take the field until December 1780. In the meantime, while waiting for him, South Carolina militia continued to harass the British. Tarleton was dispatched to deal with these guerrillas, but they had become too wily even for him. This fact impressed Greene when he finally arrived. But he also took note that Cornwallis outnumbered him three to two. Putting these two observations together, Greene adopted a strategy of avoiding major showdown battles and instead using ambush and other guerrilla tactics to slowly wear Cornwallis down.

Greene contacted the best guerrilla fighter he knew, the redoubtable Daniel Morgan of Virginia. Morgan answered Greene's call but pointed out that ill health had forced him to resign his Continental Army commission on July 18, 1779. Greene was well aware that the real reason Morgan left was because he had been passed over for command of what became Anthony Wayne's Light Infantry Brigade, and Greene now appealed to Morgan's patriotism. He pointed

Twentieth-century engraving of General Nathanael Greene, after the 1785 portrait by Charles Willson Peale. NATIONAL ARCHIVES AND RECORDS ADMINISTRATION, COLLEGE PARK

to the humiliation at Camden and told Morgan that only he was capable of redeeming that loss. Morgan had no love for Gates, of course, and he was, in fact, devoted to independence. He volunteered himself to Greene, who assigned him the mission of harrying the British in western South Carolina while he himself provided support for guerrilla operations in the north-central portion of the state. From Cornwallis's conventional military point of view, it looked as if Greene had committed the rookie error of dividing his forces in the face of the enemy, sending his army in two different directions. Acting on this impression, Cornwallis sent Tarleton to attack Morgan while he personally led a cavalry assault against Greene.

On January 16, 1781, Morgan saw Tarleton approach at the head of eleven hundred Loyalists and regulars. His own command consisted of about a thousand militiamen of widely varied ability and experience. Moreover, he was mindful of the disaster at Camden, which he attributed less to Gates's cowardly incompetence than to the inexperience of the militia. He decided, therefore, to set up the coming battle such that his militia men would not have the option of flight. He deployed his forces at a place called the Cowpens, which was little more than a backcountry cattle pasturage. Gates deliberately positioned his men with their backs to the Broad River, thereby cutting off any possibility of retreat and leaving his soldiers but two options: prevail or be killed. Next, he put his greenest soldiers in the very front line, deploying his Virginia veterans and the Continentals behind them and, farthest to the rear, his cavalry, which served as a reserve. All of this was precisely the opposite of what any military manual would have instructed. Morgan had never read such a manual.

Banastre Tarleton licked his chops as he observed the buildup of Patriot forces at the Cowpens. As he saw it, Morgan was setting up his men to receive a bayonet charge, the very tactic that had so terrified the Americans at Camden. With this, Tarleton commenced the attack.

As Tarleton's men approached, Morgan calmly instructed his riflemen: "Look for the epaulets! Pick off the epaulets!" It was brilliant advice, since epaulets identified the officers. Morgan wanted to sow chaos with decapitating blows.

Tarleton and his men advanced. Surely, it looked to him as if the Americans at the Cowpens were behaving exactly as the Americans had at Waxhaws, holding their fire, holding it until it was too late.

A contemporary print depicting cavalry commander Colonel William Augustine Washington—second cousin of George Washington—in action at the Battle of Cowpens (January 17, 1781). NATIONAL ARCHIVES AND RECORDS ADMINISTRATION

In truth, there was a vast difference. The American forces had been very thinly spread out at Waxhaws. At the Cowpens, they were closely massed to deliver deadly volleys—which they did, and at lethally close range. Moreover, they performed like well-trained Europeans rather than ill-disciplined American militiamen. After firing the first volley, the raw recruits of the front line sheared off to the left and scuttled to the rear of the American lines. This exposed the Loyalists, badly cut up by the first volley, to Morgan's second line, who were seasoned veterans. Their fire was even deadlier.

Worse yet, Tarleton's arrogant legionnaires attacked with remarkably little discipline, going after targets of opportunity. Seeing the lack of coordination, Morgan ordered his greenest troops, who had already returned to the rear, to sweep out and behind Tarleton's approaching left wing. At the same time, Morgan sent his cavalry out from their reserve positions in a great forward wheel all the way around to the rear of Tarleton's right. This caught the British commander and his men in a double envelopment. It was checkmate—straight out of the playbook of no less a figure than Hannibal, who had used the maneuver against the Romans at Cannae in 216 BC.

Morgan's stupendous victory at the Cowpens was not only a tactical masterpiece, it saved Greene's army and cost Lord Cornwallis 110 killed, two hundred wounded (and captured), and 531 captured (unwounded). The

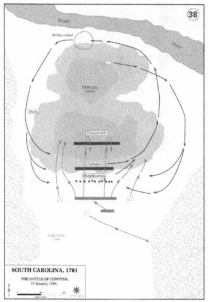

Map of the Battle of Cowpens, showing
Patriot general Daniel Morgan's masterful
double envelopment of Tarleton's British
and Loyalist troops. UNITED STATES MILITARY
ACADEMY

battle was particularly lethal for
British and Loyalist officers—the
men with the epaulets. Of sixty-
six officers engaged, thirty-nine
were killed. Morgan's losses were
a dozen killed in action and sixty
more wounded. Most important
of all, the legend of Banastre Tarleton's invincibility was shattered
and would never recover.

SWAMP FOX

Daniel Morgan was one of history's great natural military talents
and was very important in retak-
ing control of the South from
the British. He did not, however, achieve the popular culture
notoriety of another frontier guerrilla leader, Francis Marion, who
earned the nickname the "Swamp
Fox." Marion was the grandchild of a Huguenot immigrant and was raised
on his family's South Carolina plantation. He served in the French and
Indian War and was commissioned in June 1775 as a captain in the 2nd
South Carolina Regiment. After fighting in the defense of Fort Sullivan
in June 1776, he was commissioned in September of that year a lieutenant
colonel in the Continental Army. His combat experience in the Continental service included the failed siege of Savannah in 1779 and the fall of
Charleston in 1780, in which he was captured with the rest of the garrison
when the city fell to the British on May 12. At one point, after the American defeats at Camden, Monck's Corner, and Waxhaws, the small guerrilla
band he organized—its strength varying between just twenty and seventy
men—was the only Patriot force remaining in South Carolina.

Marion was a small man—"small enough at birth to be put into a
quart mug," it was said—and suffered from a frail constitution most of his

life. Nevertheless, he was an inveterate fighter and a passionate advocate of independence. It was in the aftermath of the Battle of Camden, on August 20, 1780, that he earned renown among local Patriots by leading seventeen men in an ambush of a much larger force of Loyalists and regulars, who were escorting American prisoners. He and his comrades emerged so suddenly from the swamp that the enemy was convinced they were part of some larger, as-yet unseen unit. Hastily abandoning their prisoners, who were thus liberated, they fled, carrying with them the terrifying tale of the "Swamp Fox."

From this point on, Marion's actions were for the most part similar guerrilla assaults, such as that at Tearcoat Swamp (in South Carolina, where modern US Route 301 crosses the Black River). On the night of October 25, 1780, Marion led a force of 150 handpicked men against a far superior Loyalist band. Again, the enemy was stunned by an attack miraculously materializing from out of the swamp. The Loyalists were routed, leaving behind a half-dozen dead and fourteen wounded. Marion also captured twenty-three prisoners, eighty precious muskets, and several horses. Word of this action spread through the Loyalist community and seems to have caused the local Tories to abandon a planned uprising. Tearcoat Swamp and subsequent, smaller actions also converted a significant number of backcountry Loyalists to the Patriot cause.

DISAPPOINTMENT AND DEATH AT GUILFORD COURT HOUSE

Even the unimaginative Lord Cornwallis was shaken out of his conventional tactical complacency by what Daniel Morgan had achieved at the Cowpens. He decided that he had to take steps to better adapt to backcountry warfare. Accordingly, he ordered his regulars to shed most of the heavy baggage British armies always dragged with them and, from now on, to march only with what they could carry on their backs. He then used his stripped-down, streamlined force to pursue Nathanael Greene's army, chasing it north to the Dan River, in North Carolina close to the Virginia line.

Greene was an intensely observant tactician, who duly noted the speed, so unusual for Cornwallis, with which he now moved. He correctly concluded that the British commander must be traveling very light—and that meant he was short on supplies. Greene decided to

Movements of Greene and Cornwallis in the Carolinas during January–April 1781, from John Fiske, *The American Revolution* (Boston: Houghton, Mifflin & Co., 1891).

use this to his advantage. He force-marched his troops to keep them well ahead of the pursuing British, then he crossed the Dan, taking care to appropriate every single boat in the neighborhood. The result was that when Cornwallis finally reached the river, he was not only desperately short on provisions, he found himself unable to make a crossing. The only option the frustrated commander could see was to turn back to the town of Hillsboro to resupply his force. That, of course, cost him a great deal of time, which Greene made good use of by recrossing the Dan back into North Carolina. Now *he* pursued Cornwallis, sniping at his rear while also disrupting his lines of communication. This only made the British supply problems more dire.

Yet Greene continued to avoid a showdown fight, in which, he knew, Cornwallis would have the advantage. He instead continued to wear the enemy down while recruiting backcountry folks to join his force. Now that he, Morgan, and Marion were so exuberantly frustrating the regulars and the Loyalists, the North Carolinians became increasingly enthusiastic about the Patriot cause. Greene's army grew steadily.

Patient though Nathanael Greene was, he never stopped fighting. He directed Andrew Pickens to lead ruthless raids against local Tories. In one operation, Pickens's men killed or wounded some four hundred Loyalists, which badly undercut Cornwallis's base of support in the Carolinas. At last, however, even Greene was ready to switch from guerrilla tactics and attrition. He believed the Patriot cause required some more traditional triumph, and, on March 14, 1781, he deployed his forces, now grown to about forty-five hundred men, near the town of Guilford Court House, North Carolina. His plan was to reprise Daniel Morgan's classic double envelopment of Banastre Tarleton at the Cowpens.

On the next day, March 15, in emulation of Morgan, Greene deployed his rawest troops in the front line, with the seasoned soldiers behind them. He directed the frontline militiamen to fire two volleys and then to withdraw to the rear—again as Morgan's men had done. In combat, at the commencement of the battle that day, Greene's militiamen did as they had been told, except that he had never explained to them the details of the withdrawal maneuver. Instead of shearing off in perfect order, the green troops drifted and fumbled to the rear, creating a bumbling chaos that prevented Greene from properly forming them up to create the envelopment Morgan had pulled off so brilliantly.

Still, Greene's victory might not have been spoiled. For one thing, he outnumbered Cornwallis's forces more than two to one, and, for another, just like Morgan, he still had all of his cavalry in reserve. The bold move would have been to send that cavalry in a gallop around the British position and attack Cornwallis from the rear. But while Greene did not hesitate to imitate Morgan's tactics in terms of position and movement, he was not, in the end, Daniel Morgan, and he could not quite bring himself to pour everything he had into this battle. Unwilling to risk losing too many horses and horsemen, he held back a large portion of his cavalry. As a result of Greene's half-hearted assault, Cornwallis was able to stand his ground and, though outnumbered, used his one big advantage over the Americans: artillery. He raked Greene's lines with grapeshot, the artillery equivalent of buckshot, cannon-propelled antipersonnel ammunition. Especially at close range, grapeshot was not only an effective killer, it was an instrument that induced terror. Greene was driven from the field.

Out of twenty-one hundred engaged, Cornwallis lost ninety-three killed, 408 wounded, and some twenty-five missing or captured. Of forty-five hundred, Greene suffered 126 killed, 185 wounded, and more than a thousand missing—most of them militiamen who just drifted away after the battle and could not be accounted for. Since Cornwallis remained in possession of Guilford Court House, the battle could be counted a British strategic victory. On the other hand, it had cost him a quarter of his engaged force, making for, at best, a pyrrhic victory. After winning the battle, Cornwallis not only decided to relinquish the ground so dearly won, he evacuated the North Carolina backcountry altogether, withdrawing to Wilmington, on the Carolina coast.

For his part, frustrated though he was that a great triumph had slipped from his grasp, Nathanael Greene refused to act impulsively. Reasoning that Cornwallis would now continue to march northward, into Virginia, he decided that he would leave him to be dealt with by George Washington's much larger force. Greene now led his own men farther south to continue the work of reclaiming South Carolina and Georgia.

CHAPTER 25

Upside Down

NEW ENGLAND WAS THE RADICAL EPICENTER OF THE AMERICAN REVO-
lution, but Virginia, which would come to be called the "cradle of presidents," provided many of the figures who developed and sustained the
struggle for independence, including Patrick Henry, Thomas Jefferson, and
General George Washington. Nevertheless, except for Lord Dunmore's
attack on Norfolk in 1776 and the invasion of Portsmouth on May 11,
1779, Virginia remained mostly undisturbed by significant combat. Lord
Charles Cornwallis, however, apparently alone among British commanders,
believed that Virginia was the keystone of the revolution and that taking
control of it would bring the war to a quick end. Already assigned to the
southern theater of the war, Cornwallis requested permission from General
Henry Clinton to conduct a major campaign in the state and urged him to
move all military assets out of New York and to Virginia.

Although Clinton believed that Virginia was important, he did not
share Cornwallis's strategic vision concerning the supreme importance of
the region. Even if he had, Clinton was hardly the type of commander
to go for broke by diminishing his hold on New York. By March 1781,
however, Clinton was at last persuaded to deploy more men to Virginia,
and it should be observed that numerous modern historians believe that
Cornwallis, a poor tactician but an insightful strategist, had the right idea
about the military value of Virginia, a region that straddled North and
South. But by this time, with the French fully engaged, the force Clinton
sent to Cornwallis was too little—sixteen hundred men—too late.

Arnold Raises Hell in Virginia

The commander assigned to that force was no less than the traitor Benedict Arnold, which suggests that Clinton had low expectations for the Virginia campaign. Although he appreciated Arnold's competence as a commander, he could not overlook that he was a turncoat and could not be trusted with a major command. Arnold's mission in Virginia was to do his best to augment his detachment of regulars by recruiting a body of Loyalists. Clinton advised him to troll among deserters from the Continental Army, which, often unpaid, poorly clothed, and marginally fed, was rife with discontent. Moreover, perhaps recognizing that Arnold did not respond reliably to superior command, Clinton gave him a task that did not oblige him to subordinate himself to some grand operation under Cornwallis. He was assigned instead to generally raise hell and sow chaos by means of hit-and-run raids.

Arnold and his men, which included a band of Tory Rangers under John Graves Simcoe, sailed from New York on December 20, 1780. It was a brutal voyage, which met with severe storms that sickened or injured about four hundred soldiers, half of whom remained unfit for duty by the time the expedition reached Hampton Roads on December 30. Arnold disembarked at Westover with an effective strength of just twelve hundred. He immediately set out to recruit at least eight hundred Loyalists but had to settle for 212.

If Arnold was at all discouraged, his conduct as a raider did not show it. On January 3, 1781, he captured the battery at Hood's Point, the sole artillery defense of Richmond, which was the biggest of Virginia's inland towns. Arnold invaded Richmond on January 5, encountering virtually no resistance, only two hundred militiamen having responded to Governor Thomas Jefferson's call for volunteers to defend the capital. Jefferson had been a far-left radical in the independence movement, and he was the principal author of the Declaration of Independence, but, as Virginia's wartime leader he did seem beset with a strange lethargy. General Washington had beseeched him to get his state ready to defend itself, but Jefferson did nothing.

Compounding the governor's failures was the disappointing performance of Friedrich Wilhelm von Steuben, the heroic Prussian officer who had played a central role in training the Continental army to European standards at Valley Forge (Chapter 18). As commander of Continental Army forces in Virginia, he discovered that his Prussian methods, which had worked wonders in the training of troops during the cruel winter of 1777–1778, earned him nothing but resentment in 1780–1781. What is more, his methods were not well suited to pursuing Arnold's swift-moving hit-and-run raiders. Aiming to ambush Arnold at Westover, Steuben could not get his forces to move quickly enough, and not only did he lose the element of surprise and the initiative, he found himself under a swift counterattack, which routed Steuben's Continentals.

After besting Steuben and Richmond, Arnold had no difficulty appropriating undefended American vessels and using them to transport his troops up the James, delivering destruction throughout Virginia, afterward leading his men to winter encampment at Portsmouth.

He had done considerable damage in Virginia but was frustrated by having a large command withheld from him. Worse, instead of being grateful for his performance in Virginia, Clinton was more impressed by Arnold's utter failure to rally the local Loyalists to the British cause. In spring 1781, Clinton sent Major General William Phillips to relieve Arnold, who became his second in command.

On the Patriot side Steuben, was also out—though at his own request. Exhausted and ailing, he was ready, in June 1781, to turn over his 450 Virginia Continentals to the Marquis de Lafayette and take sick leave. Lafayette was to unite those Virginians with the three light infantry regiments Washington assigned to him from New England and New Jersey. The plan was for Lafayette to coordinate operations with the arrival of a French fleet for rapid transport to assume command from Steuben. A British blockade of Newport, Rhode Island, however, delayed the departure of the French fleet long enough that they were overtaken by a British fleet under Admiral Marriot Arbuthnot. The ensuing Battle of Chesapeake Bay (March 16, 1781) resulted in a razor-thin French victory, but the brutal contest damaged the French fleet and thoroughly demoralized French admiral Charles-René-Dominique Sochet, chevalier Destouches. Destouches abandoned any idea of coordinating with Lafayette and left him to march overland from Head of Elk on the Chesapeake. In the meantime, General Clinton used this disruption in

Franco-American plans to ship two thousand reinforcements to Benedict Arnold—along with Arnold's replacement, William Phillips.

RICHMOND UNDER THREAT—AGAIN

Yet one more Franco-American amphibious operation had come to nothing. Worse, Steuben, anxiously awaiting the arrival of Lafayette, had just 450 Continental and militia troops to defend Virginia against what was now a force of three thousand British regulars and Loyalists. At Head of Elk, Lafayette was some 150 miles north of what was left of Steuben's small contingent and what was left of Richmond after Arnold's raid.

Farther north, the situation was little better. Washington had to stand by while his principal army was disbanded for lack of food and supplies. All the while, Arnold, under Phillips, continued to loot Virginia. On April 30, they were poised on the James River, with twenty-five hundred men between them, preparing to advance on Richmond, this time not merely to burn it, but to occupy it.

The theater of the American Revolution was vast, and eighteenth-century armies moved slowly, especially across a land with few roads and thick forests. For the most part, commanders adjusted to the tortuous pace of things, but, in this situation, Lafayette was acutely aware that hours, even minutes, counted. He advanced overland at forced-march speed with twelve hundred Continentals, reaching Richmond just hours before Phillips and Arnold were poised to attack the town. The journey had been difficult, and hard-pressed troops began deserting along the way. Lafayette responded with a combination of exhortation and cajolery. When this failed, he assembled his entire army to witness the hanging of one captured deserter. With this grim task complete, Lafayette addressed his men, inviting any of them who were no longer willing to make the great sacrifice to which they had agreed to present their resignation to him, in person and in writing, like professional soldiers. The young commander received not a single request—and the desertions ceased.

Lafayette was a young officer of great character. Seeing that his troops were suffering, he decided to do something about it. He borrowed sufficient funds—against his own signature and personal guarantee—to purchase cloth and pay tailors to make summer uniforms to replace the heavy winter garments with which his troops were burdened. This would give them a measure of relief as they fought under the southern summer sun. With morale revived, Lafayette's army joined Steuben's band in Richmond. Although the twenty-five hundred men under Phillips and Arnold substantially outnumbered the reinforced American garrison, neither Phillips nor Arnold was willing to accept what they knew would be the high cost of taking a well-defended—and largely ruined—town. Turning their backs on Richmond, they marched off and away from the James.

LORD CORNWALLIS AND "THE FRENCH BOY"

Phillips and Arnold might not have wanted to engage Lafayette at Richmond, but Lord Charles Cornwallis was determined to destroy him. More than ever, he was convinced that Virginia was the key to victory. He saw Lafayette as the principal obstacle to seizing control of the state and declared (according to Lafayette's own memoirs) "the boy cannot escape me." So determined was Cornwallis to conquer Virginia and crush Lafayette, he pointedly ignored a new order from General Clinton. Fearing that Washington was about to attack his garrison in New York, the British commander-in-charge ordered Cornwallis to send up to New York much of his army and to do so immediately. Instead, Cornwallis went about mustering a force of seventy-two hundred men during the late spring of 1781. This was far more than a match for the three thousand troops Lafayette finally amassed once he added local militiamen to his Continental contingent.

"Man proposes, God disposes," goes an old saying. Arnold's superior, General William Phillips, suddenly contracted typhoid fever and died. It was a fate all too common among soldiers in the field, especially in the sweltering South. Brushing aside Arnold, Cornwallis assumed direct command of Phillips's army, thereby taking control of all British and Loyalist forces in Virginia. This now gave Cornwallis about nine thousand troops, including Hessians, and the great satisfaction of knowing he now enjoyed even more overwhelming superiority of numbers over "the boy."

With high confidence, Cornwallis marched out of Petersburg and began pursuing Lafayette north. Lafayette realized that attempting a stand would be foolhardy, so he persisted in marching to elude the British.

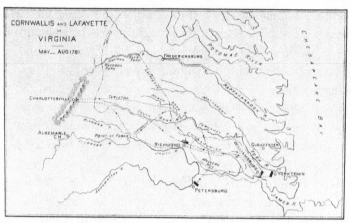

Cornwallis and Lafayette in Virginia during May–August 1781 from John Fiske, *The American Revolution* (Boston: Houghton, Mifflin & Co., 1891).

He understood that superior numbers were an indispensable advantage in combat but a burden and a liability in the chase. He took advantage of his very inferiority, and Cornwallis soon tired of the fruitless pursuit. He broke it off and dispatched Simcoe and Tarleton to resume punishing the people of Virginia. Wielding the lash in this manner may have given Cornwallis some satisfaction, but it was a fundamentally flawed strategy. Total war—war against civilian as well as soldier—could be effective when invading a foreign country, but most of revolutionary America was still under British control and would remain so to the very end of the war. This being the case, the only strategy that made sense was to focus all military resources on destroying the "rebel" army in the field. Kill the army, and the revolution would end. Now, with the pressure on his outnumbered forces relieved for the time being, Lafayette maneuvered to receive the reinforcements he so desperately needed. These came in the form of three Pennsylvania regiments commanded by one of the outstanding generals of the American Revolution, "Mad Anthony" Wayne.

The gap was closed somewhat—forty-five hundred men to oppose some nine thousand—but it was still a two-to-one fight. On the other hand, Wayne and his regiments were the best America had to offer. Lafayette decided the time had come to stop running. Cornwallis was marching

"Mad Anthony" Wayne, among the most able Patriot generals of the revolution, is portrayed in this statue at Valley Forge National Military Park, Valley Forge, Pennsylvania. PHOTO BY D. B. KING, WASHINGTON DC, VIA WIKIMEDIA COMMONS

down Virginia's York Peninsula when Lafayette abruptly turned his army about. He deployed his forces into multiple columns, using as many roads as he could. His intention was to give the impression of commanding far greater numbers than he actually had. Then, on June 26, 1781, elements of the Pennsylvania and Virginia regiments overtook Simcoe's Queen's Rangers at Spencer's Ordinary, a crossroads tavern. The fight was short, sharp, but not decisive—although it was the Queen's Rangers and not the Americans who broke it off, leaving their wounded in the tavern.

AMBUSH

Cornwallis bivouacked the principal portion of his army outside of Williamsburg as he contemplated his next move. He saw through Lafayette's ruse intended to give the impression of greater numbers, and he was thus unshaken in his confidence that the advantage in numbers belonged to him. But he also did not want to get into another futile and draining pursuit.

The pressure to decide what to do peaked when Cornwallis received a much more insistent order from Clinton demanding that he transfer a large portion of his army to defend New York. Clinton wanted three thousand troops—immediately. Coincidentally, that number was precisely the numerical advantage of Cornwallis over the combined forces of Lafayette and Wayne. Now it became even more imperative for Cornwallis to outmaneuver his own commanding officer so that he could pin down Lafayette. Cornwallis chose to march his entire army out of Williamsburg and down to the Jamestown Ford on the James River, the place at which the requested three thousand troops would have to cross to get to Portsmouth, the port from which Royal Navy ships would embark for New York. By dragging the whole of his army down there and not just the three thousand, Cornwallis reasoned that Lafayette and Wayne would assume he was evacuating Virginia by sea. That would almost surely lure "the boy" into attacking him where and when he appeared most vulnerable, crossing the James, with his army divided on either side of the river. If Lafayette took that bait, Cornwallis would be positioned to attack from ambush.

On July 6, 1781, Wayne and Lafayette proceeded to do precisely what Cornwallis predicted they would do. Wayne and his contingent marched toward what they took to be Cornwallis's rearguard. They were, however, totally unaware that most of the British force was still lying in wait on the north bank of the James. Had Cornwallis chosen this moment to attack, he would have wiped out the five hundred men of Wayne's advance force. But he held back because he did not know where Lafayette and the rest of the American army were. To attack now would be to spring the ambush prematurely, revealing the trap and scaring off "the boy." Cornwallis was determined to bag Lafayette and Wayne together.

Few moments in this long war, a war mainly of attrition, were genuinely decisive. This was one of them. Defeat Lafayette and Wayne here, and Virginia would fall. If Virginia fell to Cornwallis, the American Revolution would be dealt a blow from which it very likely would not recover.

Lafayette and his contingent were out of Cornwallis's sight but close by. The young Frenchman was silently watching the skirmish that was developing at the ford. It seemed to be going well, and he was about to commit to the fight the rest of the American forces present. But then he hesitated. Something did not look right. The numbers engaged did not add up, and he therefore began to suspect that more than Cornwallis's rearguard occupied the north bank of the James. To investigate, he sent out a single detachment to reinforce Wayne. He reasoned that the detachment would be just enough to persuade Cornwallis that he had taken the bait—if, in fact, this was a trap.

Upon the approach of Lafayette's men, Cornwallis acted. He unleashed all of his troops, who fell upon what was now a detachment of some nine hundred Americans. Had Wayne been a conventional commander, he would have ordered an immediate retreat. Instead, he did precisely the opposite of what a conventional commander would do when overwhelmingly outnumbered. He counterattacked.

Lord Cornwallis was unnerved by the sheer audacity. More importantly, so were Cornwallis's troops. They stopped, stunned, and Wayne rallied his men for a *fighting* retreat. This disengaged him from Cornwallis's attack. For the loss of twenty-eight killed, ninety-nine wounded, and twelve missing in action, Wayne forced Cornwallis to spring his trap but miss his prey.

ON TO YORKTOWN

Still, it was a minor British victory, and a minor victory was better than a defeat, Cornwallis reasoned. Perhaps he even managed to persuade himself that the bloody nose he gave Wayne was sufficient to teach both him and Lafayette a lesson. With that, he resumed the march to Portsmouth, almost certainly with the intention of obeying Clinton's orders to ship three thousand of his soldiers back to New York.

Clinton was a fatally flawed commander, overly cautious and given to repeated revision of every major decision. True to form, on July 8, he sent new orders to Cornwallis, directing him to send three thousand troops not to New York but to Philadelphia. Four days later, on July 12, he changed the orders back to New York. On July 20, he sent a radical revision, instructing Cornwallis to occupy and hold a position in Virginia at Old Point Comfort, on the north shore of Hampton Roads. Clinton believed that this would make an accessible naval base for amphibious operations.

Maybe Clinton had chosen wisely in Old Point Comfort. On the other hand, a commander capable of such waffling could not suddenly be trusted to choose the best encampment. After studying the situation, Cornwallis made his own decision. The tobacco port of Yorktown, poised on the York River, was, he concluded, a better base of operations.

It was a fatefully bad decision. What advantage Cornwallis could have seen to this position is beyond modern scholarship. On the contrary, Yorktown presented two great weaknesses. First, it was flat, offering no high ground from which to defend against a siege. Second, it was a peninsula. Perhaps Cornwallis was assuming that this made it an ideal point of embarkation onto Royal Navy ships, if evacuation became necessary, but if Gloucester Point fell to the Americans, Yorktown would be cut off by land, and there was no guarantee that the Royal Navy would be on hand to evacuate by sea.

WASHINGTON AND ROCHAMBEAU

So far, the Franco-American alliance, object of so many hopes, had been nearly heartbreaking, due primarily to poor leadership of the French fleet. On May 21, 1781, George Washington met with French general Jean Baptiste Donatien de Vimeur, comte de Rochambeau at Wethersfield, Connecticut. The two commanders were determined to create a plan that would use the combined armies of the United States and France effectively—and in close coordination with the French fleet, now under the command of an outstanding admiral, François Joseph Paul, comte de Grasse. The great potential of French aid was the possibility of bringing the long war of attrition to a victorious decision. Combined, France and America had the forces to do this.

As Henry Clinton had long feared, Washington and Rochambeau discussed striking against what was now the British center of military power in America, New York. Washington was aching to begin the operation, but Rochambeau had doubts. He deferred to Admiral de Grasse, giving him the option of attacking at New York or in Virginia.

Still, for the time being, preparations went on to target New York. In early July 1781, Rochambeau's army tied in with the Americans above New York City. Initial engagements in the neighborhood made it clear to Washington that Clinton would not relinquish control of New York lightly. Washington may have developed second thoughts about a strike here, and whatever doubts he had were crystalized by Admiral de Grasse's declaration that the Chesapeake Bay offered by far the best approach to the American mainland from the West Indies, where the French fleet was anchored. De Grasse argued that an operation against the British in Virginia would provide a much more effective opportunity for coordination of land and sea forces. Washington concurred and held a new council of war.

The plan that emerged was to use American and French troops to reinforce Lafayette and Wayne against Cornwallis while Admiral de Grasse fought the British fleet with the objective of cutting off all seaborne avenues of reinforcement and resupply. Cornwallis had put everything he had on a peninsula. It was a sack with two open ends, one that could be tied off by allied armies, the other, up against the sea, that could be knotted by the French fleet. Admiral de Grasse was given an additional assignment, to transport three French regiments from the Caribbean islands and land them to join in the Yorktown campaign.

It was a solid plan, and its objective was supremely strategic, with all the makings of a decisive battle. Everyone involved—American, French, *and* English—were aware that both public and parliamentary support for continuing the American war was waning. Score a significant, painful victory against Cornwallis, and the balance might well be tipped. But even the best of strategies is worthless without flawless tactical execution. The state of the military art in the eighteenth century, especially in the context of a raw new nation, was rich with opportunity for failure and outright disaster. Washington and Rochambeau faced a mammoth task. They had to lead their large forces south and do so very rapidly. The window of opportunity Cornwallis's tactical blunder had created would not last forever. The Royal Navy might successfully take up a position off the Yorktown peninsula or Cornwallis might realize his vulnerability and march out of Yorktown.

First and foremost, de Grasse had to position his fleet to dominate the waters off Yorktown. He was under pressure to accomplish this quickly because he had orders from his superiors to depart North American waters no later than October 15 to find safe haven before the onset of hurricane season. As for Washington, his army was facing more than the usual shortages. The sheer length of the revolution had exhausted the American treasury. Rochambeau stepped up by offering his ally half the generous war chest Louis XVI had allotted to him.

The expedition, the most ambitious operation of the American Revolution, commenced on August 21, 1781. The two generals agreed on the need to balance the imperative for speed with the absolute necessity of deceiving General Clinton into believing that New York remained their objective. Accordingly, after crossing the Hudson, the generals divided their combined commands into three columns. They sent these in a line of march that was anything but due south. For the time being, all Clinton knew is that his enemies were on the move. He assumed that they were heading toward New York. Now it was up to Admiral de Grasse to move swiftly.

It took Clinton until September 1 to realize that Washington and his French ally were bound not for New York, but Virginia. The British commander also figured out that Admiral de Grasse was looking to gain control of Virginia waters. In response, admirals Samuel Graves and Samuel Hood launched their fleets from New York on a course to intercept de Grasse's West Indian fleet as well as a supporting French fleet sailing from Newport, Rhode Island, under Admiral Jacques-Melchior Saint-Laurent, comte de Barras. In what would be the culminating operation of the American Revolution, sea power would play a critical role because the armies of Cornwallis as well as Washington and Rochambeau required seaborne supply.

The British admirals were confident that they were more than equal to the task of neutralizing the French navy, which had, so far, performed poorly in North American waters. Graves and Hood miscalculated, however, in failing to understand that de Grasse was not d'Estaing. A supremely skilled sailor, he handily beat the Royal Navy to Chesapeake Bay. De Grasse positioned French cruisers in the James River, preventing Cornwallis from escaping to the south, and other French ships took up blockading stations at the mouth of the York River. The rest of de Grasse's fleet awaited the arrival of the Royal Navy at the mouth of the Chesapeake.

THE BATTLE OF THE CAPES

On September 5, 1781, the Royal Navy and the French fought in Chesapeake Bay the most consequential sea battle of the American Revolution. It was called the Battle of the Capes or the Battle of the Virginia Capes or the Battle of Chesapeake Bay. Admiral de Grasse had the advantage of numbers, more ships and more guns, with his splendid flagship, the *Ville de Paris*, mounting 110 cannon, firepower that made it the biggest warship of its time. In a line trailing *Ville de Paris* were twenty-four more ships of the line, carrying between sixty-four and eighty-four guns each. The fleet was escorted by six very fast frigates. Graves and Hood commanded between them nineteen ships of the line and seven frigates.

Typically, the greatest factor in determining the outcome of a battle at sea during the eighteenth century was firepower. The side with more guns and ships was likely to win. The second most critical factor was the position of the opposing sides relative to one another and to the prevail-

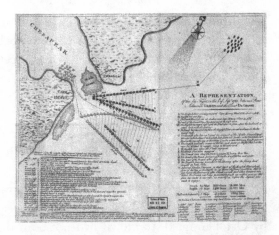

A 1781 map of the Battle of the Capes (September 5, 1781). The French ships are lightly shaded, the Royal Navy ships darkly shaded.
LIBRARY OF CONGRESS

ing winds. In this, the Royal Navy fleet had the advantage. Graves and Hood could move faster and with more range of maneuverability than the French, whose position lay entirely within the bay.

Finally, of course, there were the commanders. The Royal Navy was renowned for having some of the best, but the British sea service of the 1770s and 1780s had declined precipitously since the French and Indian War of mid-century. Admiral de Grasse proved to be a consummate ship handler, and he continually outmaneuvered his English opponents.

The firing commenced at about four o'clock in the afternoon. Two hours later, the battle was over as Graves and Hood broke off and withdrew from Chesapeake Bay, setting a return course for New York. Cornwallis was now alone with some nine thousand of his soldiers.

SIEGE

Four days after the Battle of the Capes, on September 9, 1781, Admiral de Barras linked up with de Grasse in Chesapeake Bay. The French were now unquestionably supreme in the waters off Yorktown. De Grasse landed a sufficient number of troops to raise the strength of the Washington-Rochambeau expedition to sixteen thousand men. The generals mustered their forces at Williamsburg and prepared to battle Cornwallis's army, which, though substantially outnumbered, was well dug into defensive positions.

The allied generals conferred aboard de Grasse's magnificent flagship on September 17 and meticulously planned the siege of Yorktown. Since Cornwallis occupied a peninsula, the mission was extremely straightforward, as was the plan of its execution. While de Grasse guarded against interference from the Royal Navy, Rochambeau and Washington would envelop Cornwallis as de Grasse's fleet bombarded his position. During these operations, French and American engineers would excavate siege trenches to provide cover for the army's approach to the Yorktown fortifications. There would be no great rush. Cut off from supply or reinforcement, time was Cornwallis's enemy and the allies' ally. Washington and Rochambeau would systematically invest their objective, strangling Cornwallis as if their hands were at his very throat.

Washington had good reason to be optimistic, but he was also well aware that Admiral de Grasse was under orders to leave Chesapeake Bay by October 15. If Yorktown had not been breached and won by then, there would be nothing to prevent the Royal Navy from returning with reinforcements, supplies, and a means of escape.

Indeed, at this point Charles Cornwallis had only one tactical option: hold out in the hope of rescue. On September 23, he fired off a letter to Henry Clinton: "If you cannot relieve me very soon, you must be prepared to hear the worst." On September 30, Cornwallis pushed to consolidate his defensive position, ordering the abandonment of his outermost ring of entrenchments. He calculated that he could hold out longer by contracting his perimeter, which would provide denser defensive fire. A closely defended "wall" would be harder to breach than a more distant one, in which troops were more widely dispersed. What was unnerving, however, was that no sooner had Cornwallis withdrawn his men from his outer works than the Franco-American forces rushed in to occupy them and to use them as cover for their close-range artillery. On October 1, American ground artillery added its bombardment to that coming from de Grasse's fleet.

Washington's close-up artillery pounded away for just one day shy of a full week. On October 6, General Washington personally broke ground for the initial "approach trench"—a trench dug at an angle to Cornwallis's fortifications to provide cover for the final advance of assault troops and their artillery. On October 9, additional artillery was hauled farther forward through the approach trench. Again, Washington stepped up to fire the first shot himself. The siege and approach trenches allowed Franco-American artillerists to place their guns precisely where they wanted them. They rained down fire both on Yorktown, Cornwallis's main position, and Gloucester Point, which Banastre Tarleton had been tasked with holding. Indeed, the forward guns had sufficient coverage to drive off the last two British frigates remaining on the Chesapeake River.

COUP DE GRACE

Alexander Hamilton, General Washington's aide-de-camp and the future secretary of the treasury in the future first president's Cabinet, volunteered to serve with a gallant French officer in leading a daring nighttime bayonet attack against the defenders of two "redoubts" (forward defensive positions) near the York River on October 14. The stealthy nocturnal assault—all bayonet, no noisy firing—surprised the defenders and routed them out of their positions. Hamilton sent back a report to Washington: The way was clear to extend the approach trenches all the way to the river. Washington set his engineers to work, and thus Lord Cornwallis and his army were isolated from the rest of the world.

Cornwallis sortied 350 of his troops against one of the lines of allied trenches on October 16. An act of desperation, the attack was a surprise and prompted the Americans to pull back. But it *was* an act of desperation without the possibility of follow-up, and Rochambeau sent a unit of French grenadiers to crush the British sortie.

Cornwallis realized he was out of reasonable moves. Perhaps, therefore, something more or less unreasonable would avail. He contemplated a breakout across the York River to Gloucester Point under cover of darkness. From the Point, he would have to accomplish a forced march—all the way to New York. Faced with the prospect of ignominiously surrendering his entire army, Cornwallis decided to try. He launched his elite Guards and units of light

Alexander Hamilton, as painted by the great American portraitist John Trumbull in 1792. NATIONAL PORTRAIT GALLERY, WASHINGTON D.C.

infantry in boats to quietly row out to Gloucester Point. Having reached it, they were to send the boats back to pick up more troops. Before daybreak, Cornwallis hoped, his army might silently ooze out of the bag into which he himself had put them.

Although the first contingent made it across the river, a sudden squall stranded the boats at Gloucester. Cornwallis abandoned all hope of escape, and, on October 17, 1781, he sent out from his last-ditch entrenchments an officer bearing a white handkerchief. A Lieutenant Denny of the Pennsylvania Line was the first to catch sight of a drummer mounting the British parapet. Soon, he heard the sound of a drum beating the "parley," a signal requesting a truce. Now, the officer, his handkerchief unfurled and raised above his head, "made his appearance outside [the British] works. The drummer accompanied him, beating."

General Washington silenced the Franco-American artillery and dispatched one of his officers to meet the British representative. The American officer tied a handkerchief over the emissary's eyes, sent the drummer back to Yorktown, and guided the man, as Denny recounted, "to a house in the rear of our lines. Firing ceased totally."

The offer carried by the officer was this: a two-hour armistice, during which Lord Cornwallis would compose and deliver, in writing, his proposed terms of surrender. Washington agreed, and, true to the emissary's words, the American commander had the British surrender proposal in his hands before the time was up. Cornwallis asked for the parole of his troops and their safe conduct to England.

George Washington felt no need to bargain. He sent back a reply that surrender must be unconditional. Cornwallis returned his agreement before the day ended.

It was, as it turned out, the very day, October 17, 1781, that Henry Clinton dispatched from New York a column to rescue his commander in Virginia. Word of the surrender reached the column en route, and they turned back to New York on October 19, the same day that the surrender of Lord Charles Cornwallis and his army was formalized with a solemn ceremony.

Cornwallis himself, pleading illness, did not attend the ceremony but sent in his stead General Charles O'Hara, bearing his lordship's sword.

The Franco-American army that had won Yorktown was arranged in a double column one mile in length. On the right were the Americans, on the left the Frenchmen. Heading up the double line was Washington astride his mount. A mile away, at the foot of the line, Rochambeau sat on his horse. At a time appointed and agreed to, the army of Lord Cornwallis began a slow march out of their fort, their colors held tightly cased, furled in token of surrender. Before reaching the head of the line, each soldier threw down his weapon, and marched between the American and French lines, every British eye turned toward the French and scornfully away from the Americans.

General O'Hara approached Washington, who dismounted to meet him. O'Hara held out his sword to the American, who stepped aside, nodding to General Benjamin Lincoln, who had been made prisoner after the surrender of Charleston. Lincoln accepted the weapon. And so, the surrender was made, and eight thousand British soldiers—of the nine thousand, all those who were still fit for duty—marched off not to parole but to prison camps. Only Cornwallis, along with his principal subordinates, was granted a parole to New York, on terms pledging him never again to raise his sword against the United States.

THE WORLD TURNED UPSIDE DOWN

Even the most momentous news moved at a glacial pace in the world of the eighteenth century. Word of the fall of Yorktown did not reach London until late in November. Lord Germain later reported that Prime Minister North took the news "as he would have taken a ball in the breast," gasping out, "Oh God! It is all over."

At the surrender itself, British regimental pipers reportedly played a popular tune called "The World Turned Upside Down," a kind of extended version of the popular expression "when pigs fly":

> If buttercups buzz'd after the bee,
> If boats were on land, churches on sea,
> If ponies rode men and if grass ate the cows,
> And cats should be chased into holes by the mouse,
> If the mamas sold their babies

To the gypsies for half a crown;
If summer were spring and the other way round,
Then all the world would be upside down.

And so it must have seemed—the old order inverted—whether or not this tune was actually played. It was not that the United States had won its independence, for it had not yet done that. But that this mere *rebel* army, even with French help, should defeat a *British* lord and a large force of *British* soldiers seemed utterly topsy-turvy. The surrender was supposed to have been the other way around.

And what of Lord North's gasp of despair? The truth is that, as of October 19, 1781, thousands of British troops remained in North America, and the British remained in possession of every major American port except for Boston. They hardly seemed a defeated force. No matter. After six years of war—increasingly unpopular in Britain—the will to fight was about spent. On December 20, 1781, Parliament voiced its consensus that continuing a war to hold the American colonies was no longer worth fighting.

CHAPTER 26

Never a Good War or a Bad Peace

CORNWALLIS SURRENDERED YORKTOWN ON OCTOBER 19, 1781. JUST two months later, on December 21, Parliament voted to make peace in America. George III greeted that House of Commons resolution with rage. He wailed that letting go the American colonies would surrender the Empire's position as a world power. In turn, Lord Germain, 1st Viscount Sackville, who served in Lord North's Cabinet as secretary of state for America, responded to the king's rejection of Parliament's resolution by resigning from the North government in February 1782. George was outwardly unimpressed. He told Lord Germain that he would find another with sufficient stomach to continue the fight.

But his search never really got under way. George ultimately, grudgingly, realized he was a constitutional, not an absolute, monarch. That meant, among other things, that he did not hold the purse strings of government. Parliament did. Unless that body agreed to fund the war, the war would have to end. Americans saw their struggle as a fight against tyranny, but, as it turned out, King George III did not have the cash to be a tyrant.

THE LONG CODA

Some great symphonies end with a few firm chords. Others end only after a coda. A word derived from the Latin *cauda*, meaning tail, a coda is a continuation of the piece, sometimes for many more measures. Although Yorktown sounded the final chords of the American Revolution, they were nevertheless followed by a very long coda.

In the South, as the Yorktown campaign was being conducted in Virginia, Patriot general Nathanael Greene fought British forces led by Francis Rawdon-Hastings. When Rawdon-Hastings fell ill, the very able Alexander Stewart took over. He refused to relinquish the key port cities of Savannah and Charleston, and since Greene lacked the manpower to force a siege of either of the two towns, he campaigned against Loyalist militias in the Carolina backcountry. By September 1781, he had built a force of some two thousand men, and decided he now had sufficient strength to seize more of the initiative. On September 8, he came upon Stewart's camp of some two thousand men at Eutaw Springs, South Carolina, on the Santee River. A foraging party had been sent out to gather sweet potatoes. Upon these unfortunate troops, Greene descended, also ambushing a party of Loyalist cavalry scouts under a Major John Coffin, who managed to elude Greene and warn Stewart of the approach of a Patriot force.

Stewart quickly formed a line of battle in front of his encampment. Against this defensive formation, however, Greene's militia performed magnificently. They got off seventeen consecutive volleys, one after the other, until Stewart's men finally broke through their line. But the battle was hardly over. Stewart's troops broke through the militia only to find themselves confronting Continental soldiers from Maryland and Virginia. These troops stood their ground and then counterattacked, driving the British back at bayonet point.

A little victory can be a dangerous thing. Flushed with martial adrenaline, the Americans threw discipline to the wind and stormed Stewart's camp, falling upon the soldiers' tents, which they plundered while ignoring the fact that most of Stewart's army was in flight. British major John Majoribanks, who commanded Stewart's reserves, counterattacked from the concealment of thicket. Many of the stunned Continental dragoons were simply paralyzed with bewilderment and massacred. Taking advantage of the chaos, Majoribanks withdrew his men into a nearby brick house, which became a makeshift fort, from which they poured out musket fire as well as shots from a small cannon called a swivel gun.

It was an especially brutal exchange. As they hastily withdrew, many American soldiers grabbed those British stragglers who had failed to reach the safety of the house before the door was slammed shut. The

American troops used these men as human shields as they backed away from the gunfire. Seeing this, Majoribanks led a sortie out of the house in an attempt to rush the withdrawing Patriots. In the resulting skirmish, Majoribanks was killed. Greene retreated, having suffered five hundred killed or wounded out of two thousand men engaged. The British held onto their camp, but suffered a tactical defeat, with 693 killed, wounded, or missing. Thanks to the very heavy losses on both sides, Eutaw Springs, an obscure battle in an obscure Carolina swamp, is generally counted as the last major fight of the American Revolution.

Eutaw Springs was a battle Greene should have won handily. Instead, he suffered either a defeat or a pyrrhic victory, depending on how one looks at it. The bitter exchange made a heavy impact on the morale of Greene's southern army. What combat did not claim, sickness, the expiration of enlistments, and desertion did. One way or another, half of Greene's force quickly melted away. And when the American general smelled mutiny brewing, he singled out a Private Timothy Griffin, found guilty by court-martial of nothing more than mocking an officer. Greene stood him up before a firing squad.

Despite the dark cloud over Greene's little army, by December 9, 1781, the British military presence in the entire South was confined to the garrisons occupying Savannah and Charleston. The Savannah occupiers withdrew on July 11, 1782, and those in Charleston left on December 14. Greene then moved into Charleston, established a headquarters, and worked mightily to keep what was left of his army together. The

Fought on September 8, 1781, near present-day Eutawville, South Carolina, Eutaw Springs was the last major battle of the American Revolution. NEW YORK PUBLIC LIBRARY

Continental Congress officially declared the war over in April 1783, but Greene struggled to keep his command intact until August 1783, when word of that declaration finally reached him.

TRANS-APPALACHIA

Elsewhere, in the frontier west of the Appalachian Mountains, the defeat of Cornwallis had virtually no effect. Here, the American Revolution was a war as much between white settlers and Native Americans as it was between Patriots and Loyalists. In both Kentucky and the Ohio country, the wilderness remained aflame.

The Gnadenhutten Massacre in Ohio (Chapter 20) drove the Delaware Indians to mount a series of bloody vengeance raids, which, in turn, touched off the so-called Second Moravian Campaign. Led by Patriot militia colonel William Crawford, the operation was aimed at destroying all "hostile" Native American settlements. Terrible and indiscriminate as the campaign was, Crawford's command, a rabble 450, was hardly up to it. On the night of June 4-5, 1782, they were surprised by Shawnee and Delaware near Sandusky (in present-day Ohio). The Native Americans killed, wounded, or captured forty to fifty of Crawford's men, a triumph that inspired the Mohawk war leader Joseph Brant to conduct yet more raids. Indeed, well after the Treaty of Paris ended the American Revolution on September 3, 1783, the vast territory encompassed between the Appalachian Mountains and the Mississippi River remained very much at war, a war that would endure for more than a decade, until August 20, 1794, when "Mad Anthony" Wayne defeated the Shawnee and other "hostiles" at the Battle of Fallen Timbers in the Northwest Indian War, which spanned 1785–1795.

DISCORDANT DISCUSSIONS IN PARIS

Cornwallis surrendered on October 19, 1781. King George III held out longer. He accepted Lord Germain's resignation on February 11, 1782, and he was powerless to countermand the resolution passed in the House of Commons on March 4, which said, in so many words, that anyone continuing the war in America was an enemy of king and country. On March 20, the prime minister, Lord North, resigned to avoid facing a no-confidence vote in Parliament. George had no choice but to call for the formation of a new government and ended up with a parliamentary majority opposed to the war. Charles Watson-Wentworth, the Marquis of Rockingham, became prime minister and demanded that the Crown recognize the independence of the United States.

Rockingham chose Richard Oswald of Auchincruive, a Scots merchant and advisor to the British government, to serve as head negotiator with the American representatives in Paris. When Oswald arrived on April 12, 1782, he found only Benjamin Franklin awaiting him. Franklin's fellow treaty commissioner John Adams was in Holland, negotiating a loan for the infant republic. John Jay, the third American commissioner, was in Madrid, as ambassador, wrestling with America's supremely difficult Spanish allies. And Henry Laurens, the fourth commissioner, had been held as a British prisoner of war since 1780. Oswald dipped into his own considerable fortune to personally pledge the staggering bail of £50,000 that secured Laurens's release from the Tower of London and his presence at the negotiating table.

Congress had assigned the American commissioners two objectives: secure British recognition of American independence and negotiate in strict adherence to French guidance. But Congress was far from Paris and did not see what the canny Franklin, who was on the scene, immediately recognized. French negotiators were far less interested in fostering the well-being of the infant United States than in securing the New World claims of its European ally, Spain. Indeed, in Madrid, Commissioner Jay was rapidly discovering that Spain was in no rush to acknowledge American independence. It demanded from Jay that America sharply limit its territorial claims. The Spanish negotiators insisted on retaining their kingdom's dominion over Florida and the entire Mississippi Valley, including navigation of the Mississippi River. When Jay finally arrived in Paris from Madrid on June 23, he bitterly denounced Spain as an enemy to American liberty nearly as adamant as Britain had been. Negotiating peace was one thing, it became apparent, but the commissioners had to negotiate that peace without surrendering to France and Spain—or alienating them.

Although mindful of the duties Congress had assigned him, Franklin laid out for his fellow commissioners three of his own objectives. First, the commissioners must obtain from the British sovereign and government unconditional recognition of independence. Second, they were to negotiate the acquisition of as much North American territory as possible. Finally, they were to secure a guarantee of access to international waterways and to the abundant fisheries of Newfoundland. But, as the negotiations proceeded, the French representatives proved increasingly unwilling to lend their cooperation in attaining the second two objectives.

On September 9, 1782, John Jay discovered that Charles Gravier de Vergennes, the French foreign minister who acted as chief treaty negotiator for the French, had covertly sent his private secretary to England to conduct separate peace talks with the British. Jay learned that Vergennes proposed peace with Britain on the basis of how America looked at the moment. That is, Britain would retain Maine, New York City, a vast tract in the Ohio country, and both Charleston and Savannah. Franklin was aghast. With Jay, he proposed that the British Crown authorize Oswald to treat not with the thirteen colonies but with the "United States." Doing so would be a de facto recognition of American independence, which would instantly sever the new nation from diplomatic dependence on France. No friend of France, Britain agreed, and the treaty talks now proceeded apace. By October 5, the agreement had been drafted, including favorable US-British boundaries, an outline of a procedure for the evacuation of British troops, a guarantee of free access to the Newfoundland fisheries, and a pledge of free trade and navigation of the Mississippi.

On October 26, shortly after this breakthrough, John Adams, who had concluded a treaty of "commerce and amity" with the Netherlands on October 8, arrived in Paris. He agreed with Jay and Franklin that the treaty with the British should be finalized without consulting the French. By November 5, all the commissioners—Laurens having just arrived—approved a final draft, and, on November 30, signed a provisional treaty, which was submitted for ratification by the governments of Britain and the United States.

There remained one detail. In December, Franklin broke the news of the provisional treaty to Vergennes. Predictably, Vergennes was flabbergasted. Franklin countered his objections by assuring him that "nothing has been agreed in the preliminaries contrary to the interest of France."

Between 1783 and 1784, the great Benjamin West painted this group portrait of the American treaty commissioners in Paris. He left it unfinished because the British commissioners declined to sit for their inclusion in the painting. From left to right: John Jay, John Adams, Benjamin Franklin, Henry Laurens, and William Temple Franklin. WINTERTHUR MUSEUM AND COUNTRY ESTATE

So esteemed was Franklin in French courtly and governmental circles that the Franco-American alliance was pulled back from the precipice, and France even made a new loan to the United States for six million livres.

Having now been ratified by all the governments involved, the Treaty of Paris was signed on September 3, 1783. The document recognized the independence of the United States. It set boundaries that excluded Canada but extended westward more or less along the forty-fifth parallel to the Mississippi, southward to the thirty-first parallel, and east to the Atlantic Ocean. It gave the United States access to the fisheries off the banks of Newfoundland and Nova Scotia and pledged both Britain and the United States to honor all legal debts while renouncing any penalties against citizens of any nation that had been involved in the hostilities. The treaty also laid out the details of the evacuation of British troops and guaranteed to open the Mississippi River to navigation by both the United States and Britain.

The most difficult issue the negotiators had to deal with was the so-called Loyalist question. The British government wanted the rights of Loyalists protected and their confiscated property restored to them. The American commissioners regarded the Loyalists as traitors and balked at the British demands. In the end, the British negotiators agreed that the treaty would stipulate that Congress would merely "recommend" to the states that they "correct, if necessary," any acts of confiscation of the estates of British subjects. With that, the treaty was signed and greeted joyously and proudly by most Americans. Of the treaty, Franklin remarked drily: "There never was a good war or a bad peace."

"Signing the Preliminary Treaty of Peace at Paris, November 30, 1782" is a 1905 print after a nineteenth-century painting by the German artist Carl Wilhelm Anton Seiler. LIBRARY OF CONGRESS

ENDS AND LOOSE ENDS

General George Washington resigned his commission as commander-in-chief of the Continental Army on December 23, 1783, declaring that, "Having now finished the work assigned me, I retire from the great theater of action, and bidding an affectionate farewell to this august body [Congress] under whose orders I have so long acted, I here offer my commission, and take my leave of all the employments of public life." He set off for Mount Vernon, his beloved Virginia plantation on the Potomac. He had no idea that, six years later, in 1789, he would begin his first term as the first president of the United States.

The resignation of Washington was bittersweet, yet it was also proof of the triumph of an infant democracy, in which no warrior would rule. Emotions in the new country were mostly of joy and hope, but problems were aplenty, too. The Continental Army, underfed, undersupplied, and largely unpaid, verged on mutiny again on March 10, 1783 and during June 17–24. The veterans' problems were symptoms of a wider and deeper economic crisis. Under the Articles of Confederation, drawn up late in 1777 and ratified early in 1781, the new "nation" was really a loose association of thirteen independent states. Congress was without authority to levy direct taxes and was thus left with no way to finance the debt incurred in fighting the revolution. The Continental currency Congress had authorized and issued amounted to a pile of IOUs, backed neither by gold nor silver. Individual states also issued their own currency, almost all of it similarly based on nothing of agreed-upon value. The result was financial panic and runaway inflation.

Having led the Continental Army to victory and the nation to independence, General George Washington resigned his commission to Congress on December 23, 1783, in its temporary meeting place at what is today the Maryland State House in Annapolis. With this act, he helped to ensure that the United States would be a republic rather than a military dictatorship. The painting, commissioned in 1817, is by John Trumbull and was placed in the Capitol rotunda in 1824. ARCHITECT OF THE CAPITOL

A significant portion of the war's $170 million debt had been paid down during the revolution itself. But about $27 million remained—and creditors demanded gold, not more promissory notes masquerading as "currency." In 1786, the United States defaulted on interest payments to Spain, France, and the Netherlands.

TOWARD A CONSTITUTION
The financial crisis was a terrible threat to the new nation but carried one great benefit. It moved Congress to hold a constitutional convention. The meeting was supposed to address the weaknesses of the Articles but ended up scrapping them for an entirely new concept of government, transforming the United States from a loose confederation to a genuine nation.

The convention met against the backdrop of other monumental problems. First, there was the issue of how to incorporate the Loyalists into the new nation. The struggle between Patriots and Loyalists turned an aspect of the American Revolution into something more like a civil war. To prevent that civil war from reigniting, action had to be taken. Most states had confiscated Loyalist property during the fighting. As part of the Treaty of Paris, the British established a commission to examine the claims of 4,118 Loyalists, and the commission disbursed some £3,300,000 to compensate these people for their losses.

This was a start toward healing, but only a start. Although the Treaty of Paris guaranteed that no one would suffer further penalties for actions during the war, Loyalists continued to suffer persecution for some years after 1783. This sent between sixty thousand and one hundred eighty thousand of them fleeing to Canada or the West Indies. Others moved into the western frontier and sometimes even made alliances with Native Americans to fight the "Americans." In this was planted the seeds of the War of 1812.

While the Loyalist question continued to simmer, there was another class of American who suffered even worse oppression. The revolution had liberated white America from British "tyranny." Most of black America, however, remained enslaved to white tyranny. In 1790, the first US census counted 697,897 slaves, a number that would grow to 1,191,354 by the third census, in 1810.

Loyalists and slaves were not the only groups left behind by independence. The economic hardships wrought by the war created new poverty and hit very hard those already struggling. In western Massachusetts, the government, dominated by coastal-based mercantile interests, levied heavy taxes to pay down state debts yet rejected state-issued paper money as payment and generally suppressed passage of all legislation intended to provide debtor relief. Throughout the region, foreclosures and imprisonment for debt became epidemic. In August 1786, this situation incited armed mobs to attack western Massachusetts courts, forcing the delay of legal action against delinquent debtors. Daniel Shays, a veteran of the Continental Army, emerged as the leader of the mob action, which became known as Shays's Rebellion. Under the Articles of Confederation, the federal government was powerless to send forces to stand against the uprising. This left the state militia and a private army funded by wealthy merchants to beat down the protestors during January–February 1787. It was yet another nail in the coffin of the feckless Articles.

THE CONVENTION MEETS

The financial crisis, which spawned Shays's Rebellion, moved Congress to convene at Annapolis, Maryland, in 1786 a convention to discuss problems of interstate commerce and perhaps modify the Articles of Confederation. Realizing that the issue of commerce was part of something much bigger, the Annapolis delegates called for an outright constitutional convention, which met in Philadelphia in May 1787.

The fifty-five delegates elected George Washington president of the convention. Edmund Randolph, leader of the Virginia delegation, proposed the so-called Virginia Plan, by which a central federal government would be created, consisting of a two-chambered legislature, an executive branch, and a judicial branch. This sounds familiar, but the Virginians wanted an extremely strong central government, in which the chief executive was elected not by the people but by the members of the legislature (who were popularly elected), and he would hold office not for a defined terms of years but, like a king, for life. Representation in both chambers of the legislature would be proportionate to state population.

Many delegates objected to both the authority and tenure of the chief executive and to a system of representation strictly proportional to population. William Paterson of New Jersey proposed "The New Jersey Plan" as an alternative. It would retain most of the Articles of Confederation—including equal representation for each state—but added a separate, independent Supreme Court.

Daniel Shays (left) and fellow "rebel" Job Shattuck, leaders of the Massachusetts "Regulators" who conducted Shays's Rebellion, are pictured in a woodcut published in *Bickerstaff's Boston Almanack* (1787). NATIONAL PORTRAIT GALLERY, WASHINGTON

Debate became acrimonious between these two proposals until Roger Sherman of Connecticut offered what historians later called the Connecticut Compromise, or the Great Compromise. He proposed a bicameral legislature, in which the "upper house," the Senate, would provide each state with equal representation, and the "lower house," the House of Representatives, would provide representation proportional to each state's population. There would be a strong chief executive, but he would be elected not by the representatives in the legislature, but by an Electoral College whose members ("electors") were voted into office by the popularly elected legislatures of each state, with each state entitled to as many electors as it had senators and representatives combined.

The Great Compromise set William Johnson (secretary of the convention), Alexander Hamilton, James Madison, Rufus King, and Gouverneur Morris to work drafting a document. After thirty-five of the fifty-five convention delegates approved the text, Congress submitted it to the states for ratification. This ignited a new controversy between those who supported the proposed Constitution (a faction called the "Federalists") and those who opposed it (the Anti-Federalists). Delaware, Pennsylvania, and New Jersey ratified the Constitution right away, but a total of nine states were needed for final ratification. To sway the nation toward ratification, Hamilton, Madison, and John Jay collaborated on a series of essays collectively titled *The Federalist Papers* and published during 1787 and 1788 in various New York newspapers under the collective pseudonym of "Publius."

The Federalist Papers put on display three of the most brilliant political and legal minds this planet has ever known. The essays laid out the case for the Constitution, analyzing the weaknesses of the Articles of Confederation and explaining how a strong central government was best suited to governing a large and diverse nation because it would prevent any single special interest from taking control. *The Federalist Papers* drove ratification of the Constitution, with Virginia holding out until the Anti-Federalist objection that the Constitution failed to guarantee individual rights was overcome by a promise that a "Bill of Rights" would be added to the document immediately after ratification. Madison drafted these first ten amendments to the Constitution, which were based largely on the Virginia Declaration of Rights, adopted back in 1776. The Constitution was ratified on June 21, 1788, and the Bill of Rights on December 15, 1791.

FATHER OF HIS COUNTRY

The Constitution went into effect on March 4, 1789, and the next month the US Senate met to tally ballots cast by members of the Electoral College for the first president of the United States. George Washington won election without a single dissenting vote. John Adams was elected his vice president. The result was no surprise. It had been with the informal but firm understanding that Washington would be the nation's first president that the framers of the Constitution entrusted so much power to the chief executive. The revolution did not prove him to be a military genius, but it did show America and the world that he was a great leader—yet no tyrant. As the commander who won the revolution, Washington could have proclaimed himself king or the equivalent. But he did no such thing. His mission accomplished, he withdrew from command and into private life until his country called on him again.

Then, inaugurated in New York City on April 30, 1789, Washington invented the presidency, an office briefly described in Article II of the Constitution but awaiting someone to actually design and build it. Washington built it brilliantly, creating a Cabinet in which Thomas Jefferson was secretary of state, Henry Knox secretary of war, Alexander Hamilton secretary of the treasury, Samuel Osgood postmaster general, and Edmund Randolph attorney general. As president, Washington was firm and straightforward, yet rigorously restrained. He believed in avoiding conflict with Congress and leaving all legislation to that body, taking as his role seeing to the faithful execution of the laws Congress passed.

Washington vehemently declared himself opposed to the formation of political parties. From the start, it was a losing fight. By the time he was elected to a second term, two bitterly opposing parties had come into being, the conservative Federalists, headed by John Adams and Alexander Hamilton, and the more liberal Democratic-Republicans (a name bestowed on them by a later generation of historians; at the time, it was called the Republican Party), headed by Thomas Jefferson and James Madison. To the joyous relief of the nation, Washington accepted election to a second term of office, but subsequently refused a third, establishing a two-term precedent that was unbroken until the twin crises of the Great Depression and World War II moved Americans to elect Franklin Delano Roosevelt four times. (The Twenty-Second Amendment, ratified on February 27, 1951, limited the number of times an individual is eligible for election to the presidency at two.)

Six years after the Treaty of Paris and the birth of independence, the United States finally emerged as something very like the nation we know today, with a Constitution, a bill of individual rights, a Congress, a president, and an independent judiciary. Slavery, the final issue left unresolved by the Constitution, would ultimately bring the horrific civil war the revolution itself narrowly avoided. Perhaps we should call the conflict of 1861–1865 the Second American Revolution. Like the first, it was a product of its time, the culture of its time, and the special genius of its time. Both wars were wars fought to claim the course of American civilization.

George Washington declined to serve a third term as president, instead returning to private life on his plantation, Mount Vernon. His slaves—whose emancipation was a provision in his will—are seen at work, as is, in the background, the great plantation house. The lithograph was made about 1853 in Paris. LIBRARY OF CONGRESS

Index

A

Abercromby, Maj. Gen James, 18

Abraham, Chief, 233, 234

Acts of Trade, 57

Adams, Abigail, 9, 131

Adams, John, 30, 93, 123, 127, 129, 236, 311
  and American Enlightenment, 51, 52
  on Americans, 36
  and Boston Massacre, 67
  and Continental Army, 109
  creation of navy, 264
  and Declaration of Independence, 128, 131
  and deism, 48
  elected vice-president, 319
  meeting with Howes, 143
  on Otis, 9
  on Paine, 43
  in Second Continental Congress, 98, 123
  on Stamp Act, 58
  on treaty with Britain, 312

Adams, Samuel, 58, 69, 80, 236
  attempted arrest of, 79, 82, 83, 84
  and Boston Massacre, 66, 67
  on French alliance, 201–2
  "Massachusetts Circular Letter," 61

African-Americans
  after the revolution, 316
  in American Revolution, 37–38
  in the Battle of Rhode Island, 214–15
  Loyal Ethiopians, 236

Ahnyero (Oneida warrior), 167

Alden, Lt. Col. Ichabod, 226, 227

Alexander, Gen. Adam Stephen, 178

Alexander, Gen. William, 137, 140, 152, 178, 202
  on board of inquiry, 258

Allen, Ethan, 52, 94–96

attack on Canada, 99, 100, 101

capture of Fort Ticonderoga, 96–98, 109, 118, 163

America

alliance with France, 212–13

attitudes on revolution in, 35–44

concept of pursuit of happiness in, 33–34

Constitution of, v, 230

creation of Continental Congress, 71

Dickinson's *Letters* in, 61–62

early colonies in, 25

early occupations in, 31–32

Enlightenment in, 52–53

frontier of, late 1800s, 229

impact of Grenville Acts, Proclamation Line, 6–7, 56–57

Quebec Act in, 72–73

Regulators in, 63–64

religion in, 45–50

social classes in, 27–31

Stamp Act in, 58–60

Tidewater and Piedmont regions in, 6

and Townshend Acts, 60–61, 62

See also American Revolution; United States; *specific places, individuals*

American Crisis, The (Paine), viii, 155

American Revolution

beginning of, 3–4, 121–22

causes of, vi, vii–x, 2, 8–10

Declaration of Independence, 122, 124

and French and Indian War, 5–6

impact of geography on, 4

impact of Proclamation of 1763, 6

length of, 222

Native Americans in, 223–27

Patriots and Loyalists in, 38–44

science, philosophy and religion's impact on, 49–53

slaves and black soldiers in, 37–38, 316

southern theater in, 235–47

See also America; *specific individuals, specific battles*

American Revolution, The (Fiske), 181, 189, 191, 212, 277, 294

Amherst, Brig. Gen. Jeffrey, 20, 22, 23

Anderson, Enoch, 179

André, Maj. John, 260

and Arnold, 253, 254, 256, 257, 258–59

Anton, Carl Wilhelm, painting by, 314

Arbuckle, Capt. Matthew, 230

Arbuthnot, Adm. Marriot, 245, 291

Armytage, James, Charles, 141

Arnold, Benedict, 94, 96, 170, 201, 249–61
  attack on Canada, 99, 100, 102–5, 107–8, 109
  Battle of Bemis Heights, 193
  Battle of Groton Heights, 260–61
  capture of Fort Ticonderoga, 96, 98, 118
  at Freeman's Farm, 187, 188, 190
  in Virginia campaign, 290, 291, 292
Articles of Confederation, v, 317
Attucks, Crispus, 66, 67
Augusta, HMS, 199–200
Augusta, Princess, 54

B
Bach, Johann Sebastian, 48
Barras, Adm. Jacques-Melchior Saint-Laurent, comte de, 300
Barré, Isaac, 58
Barrett, James, 87, 88, 89
Battle of Alamance, 64
Battle of Bemis Heights, 191, 192–94, 222
Battle of Bennington, 170–72, 185
Battle of Brandywine, 178–79, 197, 222
Battle of Brooklyn Heights, 136, 137, 140–41
  See also New York City (NY)
Battle of Bunker Hill, 112–13, 115, 117–18, 222

Battle of Camden, 277–78, 282, 285
Battle of Charlotte, 279
Battle of Chesapeake Bay, 291
Battle of Concord (MA), 3, 42, 87–89, 90, 92, 121
  impact of, 94, 222
Battle of Cowpens, 281–84
Battle of Fallen Timbers, 232, 310
Battle of Fort Mercer, 198–99, 200
Battle of Fort Washington, 148, 149
Battle of Freeman's Farm, 185–90
Battle of Groton Heights, 260–61
Battle of King's Mountain, 279–81
Battle of Lake George, 17
Battle of Lexington, 3, 42, 84–87, 90, 91–92, 121
  impact of, 94, 222
Battle of Long Island, 142, 177
Battle of Monck's Corner, 274
Battle of Monmouth, 210–12, 213, 222
Battle of Moore's Creek Bridge, 237–38
Battle of Oriskany, 167–70, 222
Battle of Paulus Hook, 218
Battle of Princeton, 160, 222
Battle of Rhode Island, 215
Battle of Saints Passage, 272
Battle of Saratoga, 190, 222, 251
Battle of Savannah, 208
Battle of Stony Point, 215–17

Battle of the Capes, 300–301

Battle of the Wilderness, 17, 134
Washington in, 109–10

Battle of Trenton, 157–59, 248

Battle of Valcour Island, 106–8, 222

Battle of Yorktown, 299, 302–6, 307–8

Baum, Lt. Col. Frederick, 171, 172

Beaujeu, Capt. Liénard de, 16

Beaumarchais, Pierre Augustin Caron de, 196

Beccaria, Cesare, 33

Bennington (VT). See Battle of Bennington

Bentham, Jeremy, 33–34

Bickerstaff's Boston Almanack (1787), 317

Black Fish, Chief. See Shawnees

Black Watch Highlanders, 145–46

Blue Jacket, Chief, 230, 232

Bonhomme Richard. See Jones, John Paul

Bonvouloir, Achard de, 195–96

Boone, Daniel, 229, 230–31

Boston (MA)
Boston Massacre, 1770, 2, 64–67
Boston Tea Party, 69–71, 72
importance of, 132, 133
map of, 90

Bouquet, Col. Henry, 20, 23

Braddock, Maj. Gen. Edward, 14, 15–17, 110
and Mohawks, 134

Bradstreet, Lt. Col. John, 18

Brant, Joseph, 168, 169, 224, 228, 310
attacks by, 225–27, 232–33
and Butler, 170
meeting with Chief Abraham, 233

Brant, Molly, 224

Brant, Nichus, 224

Breed's Hill, 113, 114–17
See also Battle of Bunker Hill

Breymann, Heinrich von, 172

Britain. See Great Britain

British East India Co., 67

British Legion. See Tarleton, Col. Banastre

Brodhead, Col. Daniel, 227–28, 233

Brown, Capt. Christian, 226

Brown, John, 100–101

Browne, Montfort, 266

Buford, Col. Abraham, 275, 276

Burgoyne, Maj. Gen. John, 95, 105, 112, 184, 201
attack on Fort Ticonderoga, 162, 163, 164, 165–66
Battle of Bemis Heights, 192–94
Battle of Bennington, 170–72
and Clinton, 190–92
at Freeman's Farm, 185–90
Native Americans with, 166–67, 185
in New York, 251

offers to Indians and
Loyalists, 166–67
and Saratoga Convention,
194, 195
strategy of, 174
Burke, Edmund, 124
Burns, James MacGregor, 52
Bushnell, David, 142, 200
Butler, John, 168, 169, 170, 225,
226
Butler, Maj. Walter, 170, 233
Butler, Zebulon, 226
Buttre, John Chester, engraving
by, 266

C
Cadwalader, Col. John, 157
Caldwell, Rev. James, 219
Calhoon, Robert M., 121
Campbell, Col. William, 279
Campbell, Lt. Col. Archibald, 240,
241
Campbell, Samuel, 226
Canada
Arnold's attack on, 99–108
and Second Continental
Congress, 98–99
Carleton, Gen. Guy, 134, 162, 163
in Quebec, 104, 105, 106,
108
Carlisle, Earl of, 220, 221
Caswell, Col. Richard, 237
Cayugas, 224
Chappel, Alonzo, paintings by, 97,
244, 279

Charles III, King, 3
Charleston (SC)
attacks on, 239–40, 243–47
capture of, 273, 274–75
Chase, Samuel, 131
Chatham, Lord, 225
Chauncy, Charles, 46
Chew, Benjamin, 182
Civil War, vi, 320
number of battles in, 222
Clap, Thomas, 52
Clark, George Rogers, 229, 230,
231–32, 234
Clark, Jonas, 83
Cleveland, Col. Benjamin, 279
Clinton, Gen. Henry, 112, 114,
117, 139, 219, 297, 299–300
and Arnold, 259
Battle of Monmouth and
aftermath, 210–12, 213, 214
Battle of Stony Point,
215–16
control of New York, 298,
299–300, 304
orders for Cornwallis, 293,
295, 302
replaces Howe, 210
in Rhode Island, 153
in South Carolina, 219, 238,
239, 243, 244–46
Virginia campaign, 289, 290,
291–92
Clinton, George, 137
Clinton, Maj. Gen. James, 227,
228

Clinton, Sir Henry, 262
　and Arnold, 253, 254, 256,
　　260
　and Burgoyne, 190–92
　capture of Charleston, 243,
　　274
　Philipsburg Proclamation, 38
Coercive Acts, 71
Coffin, Maj. John, 308
College of William & Mary, 50
Common Sense (Paine), viii, 42–43,
　125–26, 206
Congress (galley), 107, 108
Constitutional Convention,
　317–19
Continental Army, 98, 109, 110,
　209
　in 1783, 314
　effectiveness of, 175
　1780 mutiny in, 261–62
　profiteering in, 262–63
　Pulaski's cavalry unit in, 208
　spies for, 257
　Steuben's training of, 205–6
　See also specific battles,
　　individuals
Continental Congress, 71, 73–76
　on African-American
　　recruitments, 215
　alliance with France, 195–97,
　　209
　Carlisle Convention in, 221
　constitutional convention of,
　　315, 317–20
　creates Continental Army, 92

　creation of navy, 264–65
　financial authorizations of,
　　263
　Gen. Sullivan at, 143
　importance of New York
　　City to, 138, 143–44
　Indian Dept. in, 223
　investigation of Arnold, 252
　See also Second Continental
　　Congress
Continental Navy, 264–65, 266,
　268
　See also Jones, John Paul
Contrecoeur, Capt. Claude-Pierre
　Pécaudy de, 12–13, 16
Conway, Thomas, 202–3
Conway Cabal, 248
Cooper, James Fenimore, 19
Copley, John Singleton, 80
Cornplanter (Seneca chief), 233
Cornstalk, Chief, 229, 230
Cornwallis, Lord Charles, 177,
　181, 182
　battle at Princeton, 159–60
　battle for New York City, 139
　at Camden (SC), 276,
　　277–78
　in the Carolinas, 278–79,
　　281, 282, 283–84
　and de Grasse, 272
　at Guilford Court House,
　　287–88
　in New Jersey, 153–54
　pursuit of Greene, 285–86
　surrender of, 310

and Tarleton, 274, 275
Virginia campaign, 289,
290–97
at Yorktown, 297–98, 298–
99, 302, 303–4, 307
Court, Joseph-Désiré, painting by,
162
Crawford, Col. William, 310
Currency Act, 57
Currier & Ives lithographs, 81

D
Dance-Holland, Nathaniel,
painting by, 56
Davie, William R., 279
Davis, Isaac, 88
Dawe, Philip, 68
Dawes, William, 83, 84
Dean, James, 224
Deane, Silas, 126, 161
alliance with France, 196,
202, 209
Dearborn, Henry, 187, 188
"Death of General Warren"
(Trumbull), 117
Declaration of Independence, v, 1,
4, 47, 122, 124
See also Jefferson, Thomas
"Declaration of the Rights of
Man and of the Citizen"
(Jefferson), 47
Degonwadonti. See Brant, Molly
de Grasse, Adm. François Joseph
Paul, comte, 272

at Yorktown, 298, 299,
300–302
Delaplace, Capt., 97
Delaware, 318
Delaware Indians, 11, 233, 310
Democratic-Republicans, 319
Denison, Nathan, 226
Denny, Lt., 304
d'Estaing, Adm. Charles Henri
Hector, 213, 214, 271
in Georgia, 241–43
Destouches, Charles-René-
Dominiqui Sochet, chevalier,
291
Dewey, John, 47
Dickinson, Emily, 47
Dickinson, John, 122–23, 127
Letters of, 61–62
Diligent, HMS, 266
Dinwiddie, Lt. Gov. Robert, 12,
13, 18
Donop, Col. Carl Emil Kurt von,
198–99
Drake, Sir Francis, 271
Dumas, Jean-Daniel, 16
Dunmore, Lord, 80, 236
proclamation of, 38
Duquesne, Marquis, 12
Durrell, Rear Adm. Philip, 21

E
Eagle, HMS, 142
Earle, Ralph, painting by, 205
Ecuyer, Simon, 23
Edwards, Jonathan, 46, 52

Emerson, Ralph Waldo, 47
England. *See* Great Britain
*Essay on the First Principles of
Government* (Priestly), 33
European Enlightenment, 52
Eutaw Springs (SC), battle at,
308–9
Evans, Joshua, 180
Ewing, Gen. James, 157

F
Falcon (ship), 113
Fanning, Edmund, 63, 64
Federalist Papers, The, 318
Federalists, 319
Feltham, Lt., 97
Ferguson, Col. Patrick, 246,
279–80
Fiske, John. *See American
Revolution, The* (Fiske)
Forbes, Brig. Gen. John, 19, 20–21
Fort Clinton, 191
Fort Constitution, 181
Fort Detroit, 23, 230
Fort Duquesne, 13, 15, 20–21
Fort Lee, 147, 148, 149
Fort Mifflin, fall of, 200
Fort Montgomery, 191
Fort Niagara, 17, 20, 21, 22
Fort Oswego, 18, 21
Fort Rouillé, 11
Fort Saint Frédéric, 15, 17
Fort Stanwix, attack on, 167–68,
185
See also Battle of Oriskany

Fort Ticonderoga, 20, 94, 109
attack on, 163–65
capture of, 96–98, 118, 249
Fort Washington, 147, 148, 149
Fort William and Mary, 77
Fort William Henry, 17, 19
Forty Fort, 226
France
alliance with America, 195–
97, 201–2, 209, 311, 312–13
causes of revolution in, vi,
1–2
French and Indian War,
14–23
Seven Years War, 18, 22–23
Franklin, Benjamin, 30, 51, 52
alliance with France, 161,
196, 209, 269, 311–13
and Braddock, 15
and Dickinson, 123
draft of declaration of
independence, 128, 129
and Galloway, 49
meeting with Howes, 143
opposition to, 202
and Pulaski, 207–8
and Stamp Act, 60
and Steuben, 205
Fraser, Gen. Simon, 106, 164, 193
at Freeman's Farm, 186, 188,
189
Frederick, Prince of Wales, 54
Frederick II, Landgrave, 136
Frederick the Great, 205

French and Indian War, viii, 5–6, 12–24, 37, 46, 56
  British army in, 111
  Native Americans in, 223
  Washington in, 13–14, 16–17, 24, 109–10

G
Gadsden, Lt. Gov. Christopher, 246
Gage, Gen. Thomas, 71, 111, 174
  and Adams and Hancock, 76–78, 79, 82
  at Bunker Hill, 112, 113, 114, 117
  raid on Concord, 82, 83, 84
Galloway, Joseph, 49, 75
  "Plan of Union" of, 122
Gansevoort, Col. Peter, 167, 168, 169
Garrick, Edward, 65
Gates, Gen. Horatio, 175, 201, 203, 207, 249
  and Arnold, 251
  Battle of Bemis Heights, 192–94
  at Camden (SC), 276–78, 282
  in Continental Army, 110
  Conway on, 202
  at Freeman's Farm, 187, 188, 189–90
  letter to Burgoyne, 166
  and Saratoga Convention, 194, 195

George II, King, 8, 11, 24
George III, King, v, vii, viii, 54–56, 123, 307
  Coercive Acts, 70–71
  end of the war, 234, 310–11
  and Grenville, 56–57, 58
  and Howe's plan, 162
  and Lord North, 55–56
  and Navigation Acts, 54–55
  peace commission by, 220
  policy towards America, 2–3
  Proclamation Line of, 6–7, 8
  Proclamation of 1763, 6
  Quebec Act, 72–73
  recapture of Fort Ticonderoga, 165
  signs New England Restraining Act, 79
  tea tax, 62
Georgia, settlement of. See Oglethorpe, James Edward
Germain, Lord, 1st Viscount Sackville, 162–63, 210, 307, 310
  on Yorktown, 305
Germantown, Battle of, 181, 182, 183–84, 197
Glasgow, HMS, 113, 268
Glover, Col. John, 157
Gnadenhutten Massacre, 310
Graves, Adm. Samuel, 300
Gray, Samuel, 66
Great Awakening, 46–48
  See also Edwards, Jonathan
Great Britain

1765 acts by, 59
Dickinson's *Letters* in, 61
feelings about American independence in, 111
French and Indian War, 11–23
and Magna Carta, viii, 3, 7, 9, 40, 75
quality of troops in, 111
Quartering Act, 8, 59, 71
resources for war in, 173
Royal Navy in, 110, 264–66
Royal Navy of, 264, 265
Seven Years War, 18, 22–23
Stamp Act, 39, 58, 59
taxation by, 8–10
treaty talks with US, 312
treaty with Native Americans and Virginia, 11–12
See also American Revolution; *specific battles, individuals*
Great Compromise. *See* Sherman, Roger
Greene, Col. Christopher, 198, 199, 215
Greene, Gen. Nathanael, 143, 148, 178, 183, 207, 213, 276
and Andrés trial, 258
Cornwallis's pursuit of, 285–86
at Guilford Court House, 287–88
Knyphausen's attack on, 220
and Lafayette, 197

and Morgan, 281–82
in So. Carolina, 308, 309–10
Green Mountain Boys, 95, 96, 100
See also Allen, Ethan
Grenville, Lord George, 56–57
acts of, 57–60
Grey, Maj. Gen. Charles, 180, 216
Griffin, Pvt. Timothy, 309
Gu-cinge (Seneca chief), 225

H
Hale, Nathan, 146–47
Halifax, Lord, 12
Hamilton, Alexander, 51, 52, 303, 319
on battle in Philadelphia, 179
Gates accusations against, 203
Great Compromise and *Federalist Papers*, 318
Hamilton, Henry, 231, 232
Hancock, John, 31, 39, 83, 84
attempted arrest of, 79, 82
leads Committee of Safety, 77, 94
and Second Continental Congress, 98–99
Hand, Maj. Gen. Edward, 230
Hannibal, 283
Hart, Thomas, painting by, 254
Harvard, founding of, 50
Hat Act, 57
Hawthorne, Nathaniel, 47
Heath, Gen. William, 149, 152
Hemingway, Ernest, 47

Henry, Patrick, 59, 236, 289
    speech by, 80–81
Herkimer, Gen. Nicholas, 168–69,
    170
Hessians, 136, 144, 157
    attacks in Pennsylvania, 178,
    179
    in Battle of Bennington, 171,
    172
    at Fort Mercer, 198–99
    at Fort Ticonderoga, 164–65
    See also Riedesel, Baron
    Friedrich
Historical & Political Reflection
    on the American Revolution
    (Galloway), 122
Hitchcock, Daniel, 160
Hood, Adm. Samuel, 272, 300
Hopkins, Esek, 266, 268
Hopkinson, Francis, 200, 201
Hortalez & Cie, Roderigue, 196
Hosmer, Pvt. Abner, 88
Howard, Frederick. See Carlisle,
    Earl of
Howe, Gen. Robert, 240, 258, 273
Howe, Gen. William, 108, 111–
    12, 160, 187
    after New York victory,
    152–53
    attacks on Forts Washington
    & Lee, 148, 149
    at Breeds Hill, 114–15, 116,
    119
    at Bunker Hill, 113, 114
    and Clinton, 190, 192
    at Fort Mercer and Fort
    Mifflin, 198, 200, 201
    on French-American alliance,
    210
    on Hale, 146
    New York City attack, 132,
    133–34, 135, 136–40, 145–46
    Pennsylvania attacks, 173,
    174–75, 176–79, 180, 183
    plan to attack Philadelphia,
    162–63, 165
    and Sullivan, 142–43
    White Plains attack, 147–48
Howe, Lord Richard, 119, 120,
    176, 272
    at Gibraltar, 272
    goes to West Indies, 214
    New York City attack,
    136–37, 138, 139, 140, 144,
    145
Howe, Maj. Gen. Robert, 258, 273
Huger, Gen. Isaac, 246, 274
Hull, William, 146
Husbands, Herman, 63
    See also Regulators
Hutcheson, Francis, 33
Hutchinson, Gov. Thomas, 69

I

Indien (frigate). See Jones, John
    Paul
Inflexible, HMS, 107
Inquiry into the Original of Our
    Ideas of Beauty and Virtue
    (Hutcheson), 33

Intolerable Acts, 70–71, 73, 74, 75
  Port Act, 73
Iroquois Confederacy, 224, 225,
  227–28
Iroquois Six Nations, 11
Irvine, William, 106

J
James, William, 47
Jameson, Lt. Col. John, 257, 258
Jay, John, 123, 318
  negotiations with Spain, 311,
  312
Jefferson, Gov. Thomas, 9, 43, 51,
  129, 208, 289
  and Abbé Sieyès, 47
  and American
  Enlightenment, 52
  Declaration of Independence
  by, 1, 2, 32–33, 34, 128–31,
  206
  defense of Virginia, 290
  and deism, 48
  on human rights, 9
  secretary of state, 319
Jefferson Bible, 48
Jenkins' Fort, 226
John, King. See Magna Carta
Johnson, Guy, 224
Johnson, Sir John, 168, 232, 233
Johnson, Thomas, 123
Johnson, William, 15, 17, 19, 21,
  224, 318
Jones, John Paul, 267–71
Jonquière, Marquis de La, 11

K
Kalb, Gen. Johann de, 162, 206,
  208
  at Battle of Camden, 277,
  278
  and LaFayette, 197
  at Valley Forge, 204
Kerouac, Jack, 47
Killroy, Pvt. Matthew, 66
King, Rufus, 318
King George's War, 5, 11
King William's War, 5
Kirkland, Samuel, 224
Knowlton, Lt. Col. Thomas, 145
Knox, Henry, 118, 144, 160, 183
  secretary of war, 319
Knyphausen, Baron Wilhelm von,
  160, 177, 178
  in New Jersey, 219–20
Kosciuszko, Tadeusz, 163, 206–7,
  208
Kuhn, Thomas, v

L
Labaree, Leonard Woods, 39
Lafayette, Marquis de, 47, 161–62,
  197, 213
  and André, 258
  Battle of Monmouth, 211,
  212
  and Carlisle, 221
  at Valley Forge, 204, 208
  in Virginia campaign, 291,
  292, 293–94, 295–96, 297
Langdon, Capt. John, 77

Langford, Edward, 66
Last of the Mohicans (Cooper), 19
Laurens, Henry, 311, 312
Laurens, Lt. Col. John, 155
Learned, Gen. Ebenezer, 170, 193
Lee, Arthur, 196
Lee, Gen. Charles Henry, 110,
  152, 153
  Battle of Monmouth, 211,
  212
  capture of, 154–55
Lee, Henry, IV, 32, 129
Lee, Maj. Gen. Charles, 134–35,
  138
  in South Carolina, 239
  Tarleton's capture of, 274
Lee, Maj. Henry, 129, 217–18
Lee, Richard Henry, 129
  and French alliance, 201–2
  resolution by, 127–28
Lee, Robert E., 129, 217
Lee, Sgt. Ezra, 142
Legardeur de Saint-Pierre, Capt.
  Jacques, 12
Lenud's Ferry, 274
Leslie, Col. Alexander, 78–79
*Letters from a Farmer to
  Inhabitants of the British
  Colonies* (Dickinson), 123
Lexington Green, "battle" at, 84,
  85–87, 90
Lignery, François-Marie Le
  Marchand de, 20–21

Lillington, Col. John Alexander,
  237
Lincoln, Gen. Benjamin, 192,
  246–47, 273, 275
  and Prevost, 242, 243, 244
Lincoln, Pres. Abraham, 176
Little Turtle's War, 232
Lively (ship), 113
Livingston, Col. James, 256
Livingston, Robert R., 128, 129
Locke, John, 33, 51, 130
Louis XVI, King, vii, 2, 3
  and Great Britain, 208
  support for America, 161,
  184, 194, 195–96, 197
Loyalists, 39–44, 132
  in the South, 235–47, 280–81
  and Treaty of Paris, 313, 316

M
Madison, James, 51, 52
  Great Compromise and
  Federalist Papers, 318–19
Magna Carta, viii, 3, 7, 9, 40
  and Quebec Act, 73
Mahicans, 37, 224
Mahwood, Lt. Col. Charles,
  159–60
Mailer, Norman, 47
Main, Jackson Turner, 31
Majoribanks, Maj. John, 308–9
Mansfield, Margaret, 250, 252
Margaretta, HMS, 265–66
Marion, Francis, 239, 284–85

Mason, George, 52
Massachusetts
    Shays' rebellion in, 316–17
    support for independence in,
        80, 124
Massachusetts Bay Colony, 25
Mauduit du Plessis, Chevalier de,
    198, 199
Maxwell, William, 106
McClellan, Gen. George B., 176
McCrea, Jane, 166, 171
McDougall, Alexander, 147
McDowell, Col. Charles, 279
McLane, Allen, 216, 217
McNeil, Mrs., 166
Melville, Herman, 47
Mercer, Hugh, 148, 160
Merlin (ship), 199–200
Miami Indian village, raid on, 12
Mifflin, Thomas, 137
    opposition to Washington,
        201–2, 203
Mitchell, Major, 84
Mohawks, 37, 224
Molasses Act, 57
Monckton, Brig. Gen. Robert, 15
Monongahela. See Battle of the
    Wilderness
Monro, Lt. Col. George, 19
Montcalm, Marquis de (Louis
    Joseph), 18, 19, 20, 21, 22
Montgomery, Hugh, 65–66
Montgomery, Richard, 99–100,
    101, 102–4
Montresor, John, 146–47

Moran, Percy, painting by, 159
Moravians. See Abraham, Chief;
    Delaware Indians
Morgan, Col. Daniel, 104, 195,
    201
    Battle of Bemis Heights, 193
    Battle of Cowpens, 281–82,
        283, 284, 285, 287
    at Freeman's Farm, 187–88
Morris, Gouverneur, 318
Motier, Marie Joseph Paul de. See
    Lafayette, Marquis de
Moultrie, William, 238, 239
Munroe, William, 83
Murray, James, 65
Murray, John. See Dunmore, Lord
Mutiny Act, 59

N
Native Americans
    in American revolution,
        36–37, 38, 223–27, 310
    with Burgoyne, 185
    and Christianity, 45
    1776 council of, 229
    in French and Indian War,
        12, 14, 17
    Pontiac's Rebellion, 23–24
    raids by, 230, 233, 234
    and Treaty of Greenville, 232
    See also specific tribes;
        individuals
Naval Stores Acts, 57
Navigation Acts, 54–55, 56–57
New England Restraining Act, 79

New Hampshire, constitution of, 124

New Hampshire Grants, 95

New Jersey, 59, 124, 127, 136, 318
    See also Battle of Monmouth

Newton, Sir Isaac, 50, 51, 52

New York City (NY)
    attack on, 144–46
    Battle of Brooklyn Heights, 135, 136, 137–42
    neutrality of, 133

Nicholas II, Czar, vii

Nietzche, Friedrich, 150, 151

Nine Years' War, 5

North, Lord Frederick, 55–56, 123, 305
    and British East India Co., 67–68
    reconciliation proposal of, 123
    resignation of, 310–11
    tax plan of, 93

North Carolina, Highlanders in, 236–38

Northwest Indian War, 310

O

O'Brien, Jeremiah, 266

Oertel, Johannes Adam Simon, painting by, 3

Oglethorpe, James Edward, 25–26, 27

O'Hara, Gen. Charles, 304, 305

Ohio Company, 11, 12

"Olive Branch Petition." *See* Dickinson, John

On Crimes and Punishments (Beccaria), 33

Oneidas, 37, 228

Onondagas, 224, 228

Osgood, Samuel, 319

OSS (Office of Strategic Services), 82

Oswald, Richard, 311, 312

Otis, James, 9, 42, 57, 59
    "Massachusetts Circular Letter," 61

Owandah, 224

P

Paine, Thomas, viii, 42, 43, 44, 155, 208, 248
    and American Enlightenment, 52
    Common Sense, 125–26, 206

Palmes, Richard, 66

Paoli, Pasquale, 180

Paoli Massacre, 180–81

Parker, Adm. Peter, 240

Parker, Capt. Jonas, 85–86

Paterson, William, 317

Patriots, 35, 36, 38–40
    and Hessians, 157
    and Regulators, 63
    See also specific individuals

Patton, George S., Jr., 150

Peale, Charles Willson, paintings by, 53, 110, 281

Pedrick, John, 78
Penn, Richard, 123, 124
Penn, William, 123
Pennsylvania
    Continental Army in, 261–62
    ratifies Constitution, 318
    Society for Promoting the
    Abolition of Slavery in, 27
Percy, Lord Hugh, 90–92, 139
Philadelphia (PA)
    Battle of Brandywine,
    178–79
    Continental Congress in,
    73–76
    importance of, 132–33,
    173–74
Philipsburg Proclamation. *See*
    Clinton, Sir Henry
Phillips, Gen. William, 164, 195
    death of, 293
    in Virginia campaign, 291,
    292, 293
Pickens, Andrew, 286
Pickering, Timothy, 78–79
Pigot, Maj. Gen. Robert, 114, 115,
    116, 214
Pinckney, Charles Cotesworth,
    238
Pitcairn, Maj. John, 83, 85–86, 90,
    91
Pitt, William, 60
Pitt, William (Elder), 18–19, 21,
    55
Pittston Fort, 226
Pluck-kemeh-notee, 229

Plumb, J. H., 54
Plymouth Plantation, 25
Polly, HMS, 265, 266
Pontiac's Rebellion, 6, 23–24, 56
Poor, Gen. Enoch, 193
Prescott, Col. William, 113, 116
Prescott, Dr. Samuel, 83, 84
Preston, Capt. Thomas, 65, 67
Prevost, Gen. Augustine, 240, 242,
    243
Priestley, Joseph, 33
Providence, USS. *See* Jones, John
    Paul
Pulaski, Casimir, 179, 207–8, 242
Pulling, John, 82, 83
Puritanism, 45, 46–47
Putnam, Gen. Israel, 113, 137,
    144, 148
    at Bunker Hill, 114, 115, 116
    in Continental Army, 110

Q
Quakers, theology of, 49
Quartering Act, 8, 59, 71
Quebec Act, 72–73, 99
Queen Anne's War, 5
Quincy, Josiah, 67
Quisling, Vidkun, 249

R
Rall, Col. Johann Gottlieb, 158
Randolph, Edmund, 317, 319
Rawdon-Hastings, Francis, 308
Reed, Col. Joseph, 156, 157
Reed, James, 114

Reed, Joseph, 152, 262
and Arnold, 252
Regulators, 63–64
Republic of Vermont, 95
Revere, Paul, 30, 74
engraving of Boston
Massacre, 66
midnight ride of, 82, 83–84
ride to Sullivan, 77
Reynolds, Sir Joshua, paintings by,
105, 247
Richmond (VA), Arnold's capture
of, 260, 290, 292, 293
See also Virginia
Riedesel, Baron Friedrich von,
163, 164
at Freeman's Farm, 186, 188,
189
See also Hessians
Rittenhouse, David, 53
Robinson, Col. Beverly, 256
Rochambeau, Gen. Comte de,
254, 257
at Yorktown, 298, 299, 302, 303
Rodney, Adm. George Brydges,
271–72
Rodney, Caesar, 127
Rodney, George Brydges, 271–72
Roebuck, HMS, 199–200
Rogers, Robert, 146
Romans, Bernard, 113
Romney, George, paintings by, 44,
169
Roosevelt, Franklin Delano, 320
Royal Navy, 110, 264, 265

battles of, 265–66
and Rodney, 271–72
Rush, Dr. Benjamin, 53, 125
and French alliance, 201–2
Russian Revolutions, causes of,
vii, 2
Rutledge, Gov. Edward, 143, 243,
244
Rutledge, John, 123

S
Saint-Pierre, Capt. Jacques
Legardeur de, 12
Sandwich, Earl of, 265
Saratoga Convention, 194, 195
Saunders, Vice Adm. Charles, 21
Savannah (GA), 273
attack on, 240–43
Scammel, Col, 195
Schuyler, Gen. Philip, 170
attack on Canada, 99
in Continental Army, 110
Schuyler, Hon Yost, 170
Second Continental Congress, 42,
98–99, 126–27, 261
Dickinson's petition, 122–23,
124
on French alliance, 209–10
and North's plan, 93
See also Continental Congress
Second Moravian Campaign. See
Crawford, Col. William
Senecas, 12, 224
Serapis. See Jones, John Paul
71st Highlanders, 139

71st Regiment of Foot, 279
Seven Years' War, 5, 13, 18, 22–23
Sevier, Col. John, 279
Seymour, Capt., 195
Shattuck, Job, 317
Shawnees, 11, 229, 230–32
Shays, Daniel, 316, 317
Shelby, Col. Isaac, 279
Shelley, Percy Bysshe, 54
Sherman, Roger, 128, 129, 318
Shippen, Peggy, 252, 254, 256
Shirley, Gov. William, 14, 15,
    17–18
Sieyès, Abbé, 47
Simcoe, John Graves, 290, 294,
    295
"Sinners in the Hands of an
    Angry God" (sermon), 46
Skene, Philip, 166
Smith, Joshua Hett, 255, 256, 257
Smith, Lt. Col. Francis, 83, 85, 87,
    90, 91
Smith, William, 52
Somerset, HMS, 113
Sons of Liberty, 39, 58
    See also Adams, Sam
Sosnowski, Józef, 206
South Carolina, 127
    constitution of, 124
    militia in, 238–40
    Waxhaws Massacre, 275–76
Spain, 311
    in Seven Years' War, 22–23
St. Clair, Maj. Gen. Arthur, 106

attack on Forth Ticonderoga,
    163, 164, 165
attack on Fort Ticonderoga,
    168
on board of inquiry, 258
St. John's College, 50, 52–53
St. Leger, Gen. Barry, 184
    attack on Fort Stanwix,
    167–70
Stamp Act, 39, 58, 59
Stark, Gen. John, 114, 171, 172
Stephen, Gen. Adam, 183
Steuben, Baron Friedrich
    Wilhelm Augustus von,
    204–5, 206, 208
on board of inquiry, 258
and Lee, 155
in Virginia campaign,
    290–91, 292, 293
Stewart, Alexander, 308
Stiles, Ezra, 52
Stirling, Lord. See Alexander, Gen.
    William
Structure of Scientific Revolutions,
    The (Kuhn), v
Stuart, Charles Edward, 41
Stuart, James Francis Edward, 41
Suffolk Resolves. See Warren, Dr.
    Joseph
Suffren, Adm. Pierre André de,
    272
Sugar Act, 57
Sullivan, Gen. John, 77, 137,
    142–43, 178, 182, 232

attack on Canada, 105–6
attack on Iroquois
Confederacy, 227, 228
battle at Newport, 215
battle for New York City, 139
and d'Estaing, 213, 214
"Swamp Fox." *See* Marion, Francis
Symmetry (ship), 113

T
Tallmadge, Maj. Gen. Benjamin,
257, 258, 259
Tarleton, Col. Banastre, 246, 247,
274–75, 279
attack on Buford, 275–76
in battle of Yorktown, 303
in So. Carolina, 281, 282,
283, 287
in Virginia campaign, 294
and Waxhaws Massacre,
275–76
Tarrant, Sarah, 79
Taylor, Daniel, 191–92
Tea Act, 1773. *See* North, Lord
Frederick
Tecumseh, 232
Thatcher, Dr. James, 191–92
Thayendanegea. *See* Brant, Joseph
Thomas, Maj. Gen. John, 105
Thompson, Brig. Gen. William,
105–6
Thoreau, Henry David, 47
Thunderer, HMS, 107
Tomlins, Christopher, 29

Townshend, Charles, 60–61, 62,
67
Townshend Acts. *See* Townshend,
Charles
Treaty of Alliance, 197
Treaty of Amity and Commerce,
197
Treaty of Easton, 20
Treaty of Greenville, 232
Treaty of Paris, 23, 95, 313, 316,
320
Treaty of San Ildefonso, 23
Trent, Capt. William, 12
Trumbull, John, paintings by, 98,
104, 117, 129, 195, 303, 315
Tryon, Gov. William, 64
Turtle (submarine), 142, 200
Tuscarora tribe, 37
Twilight of the Idols (Nietzsche),
150
Twiss, Lt., 163–64
Two Treatises of Government
(Locke), 33
Tyron, William, 225

U
United States
Constitution of, 261, 320
founding of, v–x
independence of, 313
war's debt in, 314–15
See also America; American
Revolution
Unity, HMS, 265, 266

University of Virginia. *See*
Jefferson, Gov. Thomas

V

Valcour Island, Battle of, 108
Vaudreuil, Marquis de, 17
Vergennes, Charles Gravier de,
195, 196, 197, 312
Vermont. *See* Republic of Vermont
Ville de Paris (ship), 300
Villiers, Maj. Coulon de, 13
Virginia
    and Bill of Rights, 318–19
    Cornwallis's campaign in,
    289, 290–97
    Council of Safety in, 236
    treaty with Native
    Americans, 11–12
Virginia Plan. *See* Randolph,
Edmund

W

Wageman, Michael Angelo, 141
Walpole, Horace, 13
Ward, Artemas, 110, 114, 118
Warner, Col. Seth, 100, 164–65
    in Battle of Bennington,
    171–72
War of 1812, 316
War of the Austrian Succession, 5,
11, 187
War of the League of Augsburg, 5
War of the Spanish Succession, 5
Warren, Dr. Joseph, 74, 75, 79, 82

Washington, Col. William
Augustine, 283
Washington, Gen. George, 31, 98,
109–10, 222, 236, 289
    and Arnold, 100, 250, 251,
    252, 254, 255, 257, 259
    attack on Boston, 118–19,
    120
    attack on Canada, 105
    attack on Trenton, 158–59
    battle at Princeton, 159–60
    Battle of Monmouth, 210–
    12, 213, 214
    Battle of Stony Point, 216,
    217
    battles for New York City,
    137–41, 143, 144–46, 150–
    52, 153–54
    battles in Pennsylvania,
    178–79, 180–84
    commands Continental
    Army, 98, 215
    at constitutional convention,
    317
    and Conway Cabal, 201–3,
    248
    crosses the Delaware, 155–58
    defense of Philadelphia, 175,
    176, 177
    elected president, 319–20
    in French and Indian War, 5,
    12–14, 16–17, 24, 109
    and French support, 209
    and Gates, 278

and Greene, 276, 281

on Iroquois Confederacy, 227, 228

and Lafayette, 197

and Lee, 135, 136, 152, 153

and mutiny in army, 261, 262

resignation of, 314, 315

and Rochambeau, 298, 302

and smallpox outbreak, 161

at Valley Forge, 203–4

in Virginia campaign, 292

in White Plains, 147–48, 149

at Yorktown, 299, 302, 304, 305

Washington, William, 274

Washington (galley), 107, 108

Watson-Wentworth, Charles, 311

Waxhaws Massacre. *See* Tarleton, Col. Banastre

Wayne, Gen. "Mad Anthony," 106, 155, 232, 281, 294

Battle of Fallen Timbers, 310

Battle of Germantown, 183

Battle of Monmouth, 212

Battle of Stony Point, 216, 217

and Cornwallis, 295, 296–97

and Hessians, 179–80

Webb, Maj. Gen. Daniel, 18, 19

West, Benjamin, painting by, 313

Whipple, Comm. Abraham, 245

White, Col. Anthony, 274

White, Hugh, 65

Whitefield, George, 46

Whitman, Walt, 47

Wilkes-Barre Fort, 226

Wilkinson, James, 203

Willett, Col. Marinus, 168, 169–70, 233

Williams, Ortho, 278

Williams, William Carlos, 47

Williamson, Col. David, 233–34

Wilson, Col. James, 279

Winslow, John, 15

Winston, Col. Joseph, 279

Wintermoot's Fort, 226

Wolfe, Maj. Gen. James, 20, 21, 22

Wood, Grant, painting by, 84

Wool Act, 57

Wooster, Maj. Gen. David, 105

Wyandot, 11

Wyoming Valley (PA), forts in, 226

Y

Yale, 50

Young, Edward, 32

Printed in the USA
CPSIA information can be obtained
at www.ICGtesting.com
LVHW090259100923
757639LV00002B/67